WALTER LIPPMANN

WALTER LIPPMANN

Public Economist

Craufurd D. Goodwin

Harvard University Press

Cambridge, Massachusetts
London, England
2014

Library of Congress Cataloging-in-Publication Data

Goodwin, Craufurd D. W.

  Walter Lippmann : public economist / Craufurd D. Goodwin.

      pages cm

  Includes bibliographical references and index.

  ISBN 978-0-674-36813-2 (alk. paper)

  1. Lippmann, Walter, 1889–1974. 2. Economists—United States—Biography.

3. Journalists—United States—Biography. 4. Keynesian economics—United States.

I. Title.

  HB119.L56G66 2014

  330.15'6092—dc23

  [B]

                              2014011214

Contents

Preface

I first became aware of Walter Lippmann's writings on economic subjects in the 1980s while conducting research on one of the many topics that interested him, and I was struck by the similarity of his approach to that of scholars in the new schools of public policy that had sprouted up at American universities in the 1960s and 1970s either newborn or converted from schools of public administration. They both used whatever disciplines seemed appropriate, and they took their priorities from current public policy debates rather than the dictates of the disciplines. This led to an article in the journal *Policy Sciences* (Goodwin 1995). More recently I was encouraged to return to Lippmann for a paper to be given at a conference entitled "The Economist as Public Intellectual" (C. Goodwin 2013). There I discovered Lippmann to be even more compelling as a subject for study than I had remembered and that parts of his enormous archive at Yale University Library were now available on microfilm. This book is the result of three subsequent years of delightful reading in, and thinking about, his many published works and his abundant correspondence, especially the columns entitled Today and Tomorrow, which spanned thirty-six years of his career.

It is hardly an exaggeration to say that Lippmann could write faster than many people can read. This has made research on him challenging.

There are several thousand columns alone. I am grateful to my colleagues in the Center for the History of Political Economy at Duke University for putting up with repeated presentations of early drafts of this work and for responding politely to many Lippmann anecdotes. Bruce Caldwell, Director of the Center, was especially kind to read the entire manuscript and suggest many improvements. I am grateful to the Perkins Library of Duke University for purchasing the microfilms of the Walter Lippmann Papers MS 326 held at Yale University Library and for obtaining a state of the art machine with which to read them. The libraries of the following institutions have kindly agreed to the publication of manuscript material in their possession: Columbia University; Kings College, Cambridge; New York Public Library; and Yale University. I am grateful also to librarians at Harvard, Yale, and Columbia universities and to the New York Public Library for various kindnesses. Two anonymous readers of the manuscript, and Angus Burgin, have provided exceptionally helpful comments and suggestions.

Note on Citations and Abbreviations

This study is based substantially on three bodies of material: Walter Lippmann's books; his Today and Tomorrow columns over the years 1931–1967; and the Walter Lippmann Papers, MS 326, contained in the Yale University Library. The Papers are filed into several series, designated here by roman numerals, and then into folders with Arabic numerals. Two series are of special interest: Series I, Correspondence up to and including 1930; and Series III, Correspondence 1931 and thereafter. Citations in the text include sender, recipient, date, location in the Walter Lippmann Papers, series, and folder, as in "WL to Joe Smith, December 25, 1935, WLPIII F123."

Abbreviations Used in Text

HT   *New York Herald Tribune*
NR   *New Republic*
R   The Reminiscences of Walter Lippmann (1950), Columbia University Center for Oral History
WL   Walter Lippmann
WLP Walter Lippmann Papers, MS 326, Manuscripts and Archives, Yale University Library
WP   *Washington Post*

Introduction

FROM THE ONSET of the Great Depression to the years after World War II Americans were faced with a long and agonizing series of economic policy questions. What had caused the economic collapse and what could be done about it? How should the domestic economy be reformed to make it resistant to future crises? How might the distribution of income and wealth be reshaped so as to become more equitable and humane? Should large concentrations of power in capital and labor be broken up or constrained in some way? How might the dramatic soil erosion in the South and Southwest, symbolized by the Dust Bowl, be reduced? Could human liberty be preserved if the economy were reconstructed to meet these problems? With the decline of the European empires after World War II how might the global economic system be reshaped to achieve both efficiency and justice? As more and more countries during the 1930s abandoned the gold standard and free trade, what new institutions could be envisaged to resist this drive toward autarky? As the war clouds gathered toward the end of the 1930s and Pearl Harbor was attacked in 1941 new and urgent questions were raised about how to mobilize a free market economy for war, and then how to return to peace, a peace in which by default the United States found itself the leader of the free world.

When Walter Lippmann began his career as a journalist there were no professional economists like Milton Friedman, John Kenneth Galbraith, or Paul Krugman who, years later, would become skilled at, and enthusiastic about, addressing a lay audience and guiding the American public. Nor were there many spokesmen in government, the private sector, or the media who had the skills to enlighten citizens about economic affairs. The public could not turn to friends and neighbors for informed advice because few had been to college or taken a course in economics. But there *was* Lippmann. From 1931 until 1967 he wrote columns for the *New York Herald Tribune* and then the *Washington Post,* initially four days per week, then three, and then two, with time off for vacations and trips overseas. Ultimately the column was syndicated in more than two hundred papers across the country and abroad. At his peak Lippmann wrote for an audience that may have reached eight million in a standard format of approximately a thousand words. He primarily addressed three areas of concern, with a focus on whichever seemed most urgent at the moment: domestic politics, foreign affairs, and economic policy. Over the fifteen years from 1931 to 1946 he wrote approximately fifteen hundred columns in the *Herald Tribune,* of which about a thousand were concerned to some extent with economic issues. Toward the end of World War II he became so exercised by what he perceived to be ignorance of, and mistakes in, American foreign policy that he left economic policy as a primary focus to a new generation of commentators, spokesmen who came on the scene after war service and the Employment Act of 1946, such as Leonard Silk, Paul Samuelson, and Walter Heller. Foreign policy from then onward became his dominant concern. But he returned from time to time to economic policy with interesting things to say about topics such as postwar inflation, the Marshall Plan, the New Frontier, and the Great Society. In the postwar years he was more reticent than in the 1930s; he observed that "speaking economics" was like speaking a foreign language. You quickly lost your fluency if you did not practice regularly (WL to Seymour Harris, October 4, 1946, WLPIII F998).

Lippmann's style was distinctive and very effective with his audience. He did not patronize and was resolutely nonpartisan. He supported candidates for public office whose positions pleased him regardless of party affiliation. He could and often did change his mind about people and policies. He read widely but made every effort not to be identified with any group or ideology. For example, although he drew from both traditions he was careful not to present himself either as a Keynesian or an Austrian. He was often impatient and he tended to become disillusioned quickly with politicians after they had been elected, especially presidents of the United States. His approach in most cases was to explain the salience of a problem and then set out the relevant considerations. Often he experienced and reflected upon a problem well in advance of bringing it to his readers. He preferred to make use of theory only after he had gathered a lot of empirical evidence. Theory was less a guide to him than it was a confirmation of his conclusions. He used the literature of the social sciences frequently but seldom gave citations. He consulted scholars widely about the matters he had under review, but their names did not often appear in the columns. Whether this neglect of attribution was because he wished to persuade without the use of authority, hoped to protect the privacy of his sources, presumed his audience did not care about bibliography, or believed all good ideas should be in the public domain, he did not say. His style was to lay out his arguments simply and without jargon, often repeating them in a series of regular columns and implying at the end that now his readers knew as much about the subject as he did. It is impossible to gauge precisely Lippmann's influence upon his readers, but it must have been substantial. Indeed, it seems he could help to make or break a political career, and he could speed or retard the passage of a bill through Congress. Certainly politicians from city councilors to presidents recognized his influence and regularly paid court. Even when he was just beginning his columns his access was remarkable. As an example, in the first year of his column President Herbert Hoover invited him to a private lunch and named a date. Lippmann replied that he was tied up that day but suggested another. The president readily accepted (WLPIII F1070). His welcome in high places seemed not to limit Lippmann's independence as a public economist. No politician or policy advocate could count on his endorsement if his own analysis did not support the case.

There is a large literature about Lippmann's life and achievements, including an excellent biography (Steel 1980), an intellectual biography

(Riccio 1996), an edition of his letters (Blum 1985), an extensive oral history (The Reminiscences of Walter Lippmann [1950], in the Oral History Collection of Columbia University, hereafter R), several collections of his articles and columns, and a number of biographical essays (e.g., Rovere 2001 and Latour 2010), some of which are quite critical (e.g., Eulau 1951, 1952, 1954, 1956). He even appears as a character in a novel (Auchincloss 1991). A helpful bibliography is contained in "Guide to the Walter Lippmann Papers MS 326" (Yale University Library 2012, 16–17). Usually he is portrayed as a pioneer journalist, social theorist, and political philosopher. Some of his most vigorous critics have been political scientists who have characterized him variously as liberal, progressive, conservative, realist, and pragmatist, and sometimes as an enemy of democracy (Williams 2007). For much of his career he was also a public intellectual concerned with economic issues—a "public economist," and one of the best of that kind ever. This is a study in the diffusion of economic ideas by Lippmann, with a sharp focus on what he did and how he did it, what positions he took on economic issues, what arguments he made in their defense, and how he prepared for his role. What were the secrets that enabled him to hold so many readers spellbound over decades on arcane subjects in economics? He was neither a professional economist nor a conventional journalist. But he had innate brilliance, a wide range of contacts, and a commitment to self-education. Much of his secret was in his style, and for this reason he is quoted extensively in this book. He wrote primarily in three places: in books, in magazine and journal articles, and in his regular column Today and Tomorrow. The last of these was what his regular readers followed faithfully, and it forms the foundation of this study.

1

The Making of a Public Economist

WHO CAN SAY with confidence what prepares someone for a career, in this case one as a public economist? We can only speculate. In this chapter those aspects of Walter Lippmann's family background, education, and early experience in journalism, public service, and scholarly endeavors are described that seem relevant to his later career.

Education

The only child born to an upper-middle-class German-Jewish family in New York City in 1889, Lippmann led a privileged, even pampered early life. His father worked in the clothing business, and his mother inherited wealth from her family in real estate (Steel 1980, 8). His parents while still quite young decided to devote themselves mainly to pleasure, and he became accustomed to summers in Europe and regular visits to luxurious spas, starting when he was seven. He quickly demonstrated his attraction to celebrities; he met President William McKinley and the war hero Admiral George Dewey (Steel 1980, xiii). He haunted the art galleries of Europe in cities where his parents visited, and one summer Isabella Stewart Gardner, the great Boston patroness of the arts, befriended him in a museum in Paris

and became his guide (Steel 1980, 10). He explained in his reminiscences
that as a child his inclinations were all toward the arts and literature with no
sign yet of interest in public policy: "I was interested in the classics—Latin
and Greek—in Italian art, and in architecture—Gothic architecture. While
I was in Paris, I spent a lot of time at the Louvre. I used to go when it opened
and stay till it closed for three or four weeks at a time—rather ignorantly, I
think. I read Ruskin. Ruskin had made a great impression on me" (R 24). It
seemed to Lippmann then that he might become an art historian, and in
1928, well into his career as a political journalist, the editor of the magazine
Creative Arts could ask him still to write an article on painters of the Middle
Ages (Lee Simonson to WL, May 14, 1928, WLPI F1133). He declined.

Lippmann's early and continuing attachment to the humanities and the
arts is relevant to his later work as a public economist. It helps to explain his
close and continuing friendships with artists and humanists who often influenced his views on public policy. They included Bernard Berenson and
Kenneth Clark the art historians, Laurence Stallings the novelist and
screenwriter, Eugene O'Neill and Edna Ferber the playwrights, Lee Simonson the set designer, Deems Taylor the composer, Marsden Hartley the
painter, and various members of Mabel Dodge's salon in Greenwich Village. It was typical that he intervened with the U.S. Immigration Service to
facilitate the return of D. H. Lawrence to his New Mexico ranch after the
scandalous publication of *Lady Chatterley's Lover* (WL to Joseph Cotton,
January 16, 1930, WLPI F287). It was ironic that Lippmann had been highly
critical of Lawrence's "Reflections on America" in the *New Republic* a decade before (NR, December 15, 1920, 70). Through his connections in literature and the arts Lippmann was open to opinions, insights, and values
often at odds with those of the politicians, social scientists, and journalists
with whom he spent much of his life. His training, especially in the classics
and creative literature, led him later to use metaphors, analogies, and short
narratives to illustrate his findings and thereby to reach his readers more
effectively than many of his journalistic contemporaries. For example, to
explain the position of FDR after Pearl Harbor he told the story of Lincoln
after the battle of Bull Run. He was accustomed to begin a review of the
prospects for the new year in a column with a title that was a quotation from

Macbeth: "Watchman. What of the night?" Throughout his career he avoided much of the technical terminology of the social sciences that might put off his audience, and to make his points he told stories with which they were likely to be familiar. He began his scholarly book *Public Opinion* with a long quotation from Plato about humans living in a cave.

From his own experience Lippmann came increasingly to conclude that a liberal education, rather than simply intense specialization in a technical subject, was essential for the development of effective leadership in all walks of life. Especially in the social sciences, he found that too strong a focus on a few simple variables rather than on a larger, more complex context led to absurd conclusions. He became a good friend of Robert Maynard Hutchins, president of the University of Chicago, and he admired the University of Chicago's "Great Books" approach to undergraduate education. He praised the St. John's College experiment with great books in his columns (HT 12/27/38), and in July 1942, when he found that poor leadership had set back the American forces in Libya, he told of an American professor of geography (unnamed), lacking a liberal education, who had proposed that Switzerland be carved up into its linguistic components and delivered to the relevant European powers so as to "meet democratic specifications" (HT 7/4/42). This professor "had become so immersed in the abstractions of the science that he had lost all sense of the realities of the world, that Switzerland for him was not actually Switzerland, but a patch of color on a map and some statistics about the languages of the Swiss nation. . . . This is what happens when specialized sciences which are concerned with human affairs are studied without knowledge of the tradition of wisdom and without the discipline of a moral education. All the great educators, beginning with Plato and Aristotle, have insisted that training in the art of distinguishing good and evil must precede the making of practical judgments in human affairs. Milton himself, a sharp critic of the scholastic education of his day, designed a plan of education in which he took special care to postpone the study of politics until the pupil had learned with some judgment to 'contemplate upon moral good and evil.' " Lippmann remarked that John Milton had noted specifically that a liberal education should precede the study of "economics" as well as of other social sciences. Lippmann wrote during World War II: "If Western civilization is to survive and renew its vitality, we shall have, therefore, to revive and renew our schools. So when the war is over, we have a rendezvous with ourselves to consider as a matter of high priority, the restoration and reconstruction of American education." Drawing on his own experience Lippmann was convinced that the study of history was the essential foundation of a liberal education. At a memorial service in 1932 for one of his first history teachers, he said: "From him I learned for the first time that the world is round and that the history of man is a long one. By him I was taught to realize the great truth that beyond the mountains there are people also, that the history of the world is not a collection of events, but the chief source book of all wisdom" (WLPIII F79).

Lippmann attended a good private school in Manhattan, the Sachs Collegiate Institute, founded by a partner in the Goldman Sachs firm, and there his academic prowess quickly showed; he became editor of the school paper, a leading debater, a successful athlete, and a class prize winner. He entered Harvard in 1906, described by William Leuchtenburg in 1985 as "by all accounts one of the most gifted undergraduates to attend Harvard in this century" (introduction to WL 1914a). He was determined while in college to explore disciplinary specialties and settle upon an occupation for life. His class included such later luminaries as T. S. Eliot, Stuart Chase, and Heywood Broun (Chase 1930, contained in WLPI F241), and he maintained contact with many of them afterward. At first he was determined to continue with study of the arts and humanities and took mainly courses in literature, history, and philosophy. "I took almost no courses in government or economics." However, "I very soon converged on the philosophy department and took all of [George] Santayana's courses at Harvard, I think without exception." The impact of Santayana was very great. "I felt a good deal of personal inspiration from Santayana. He had a profound influence on my life. I read all his books again and again, particularly *The Life of Reason*" (R 25 and 26). This five-volume work has been described as the first extended treatment of pragmatism, a subject of continuing interest to Lippmann. Santayana returned the admiration and made Lippmann his teaching assistant. Elsewhere in philosophy Lippmann did not take to Josiah Royce but admired William James, who sought him out after reading a piece Lippmann had contributed to the student newspaper. He turned to psychology where he took courses from Edwin B. Holt (R 28) and developed a lifelong dislike of the work of William McDougall, noted for his theory that social behavior was determined by inherited instincts. Lippmann found that despite a full course load in which he did well enough to win a college scholarship each year, he had time to read "everything that I could lay my hands on. I just read at random" (R 30). He read "very extensively in what was then modern literature—Ibsen, Shaw, Meredith, Wells, Hardy." He also read Rudyard Kipling, Henry James, and "the Irish—Yeats and Dunsany" (R 31). Throughout his undergraduate years Lippmann showed little desire to focus and specialize.

A critical transformation occurred in Lippmann's attitude to scholarly endeavor as a result of a fire in 1908 in the working-class community of Chelsea near Boston that made him for the first time intensely aware of poverty and destitution. For guidance on how to help change these distressing conditions he found the humanities lacking. He could not find answers in the works he was reading, "Goethe, Dante, Lucretius, and fine arts." So he turned to "political writers such as Veblen, Ward, and Beard" and then on to the social sciences (R 31). He took sufficient courses that in his fourth year he qualified for a master's degree in philosophy. In economics he seems to have taken three courses but was not impressed by them, especially because of their abstract behavioral assumptions and perhaps too because of the rare "B" he received in one. He took Econ. 1, the introductory class taught by Frank W. Taussig. The texts were John Stuart Mill's *Principles of Political Economy* and Henry R. Seager's *Introduction to Economics* (1904) (syllabus and notes in WLPI F1335). The latter remained an object of ridicule with him for years to come. In his first book, *A Preface to Politics,* he wrote: "I have in my hands a text-book of six hundred pages which is used by the largest universities as a groundwork of political economy. This remarkable sentence strikes the eye. 'The motives to business activity are too familiar to require analysis.' . . . I myself was supposed to read that book pretty nearly every week for a year. With hundreds of others I was supposed to found my economic understanding upon it. We were actually punished for not reading that book. It was given to us as wisdom, as modern political

economy" (WL 1913, 60–61). From the lecture notes made by Lippmann it
appears that Taussig's course was substantially descriptive and definitional
and not likely to intrigue a brilliant mind. All the same he made a strong
impression on Taussig, who wrote a formal letter of appreciation at the end
of the course of a kind received by few students in introductory economics
from a leader of the discipline. It said: "I congratulate you upon your work
in Economics 1, which has been of the first order and not less so because
your point of view is in some ways different from mine. I judge that, from
your being a candidate for a degree, you are to leave the university this year.
I should have been glad to have the opportunity to see you in a course like
Economics 2" (Taussig to WL, June 23, 1909, WLPI F1192). The low point
in Lippmann's career in economics at Harvard was a course given by
Thomas Nixon Carver, one of the most doctrinaire American economists of
the time. Lippmann took it, he said, so as to see how the other side thought.
"I regarded him as the opponent of all I believed in. I took his course to
understand what I regarded as the opposition" (R 34). One suggestion from
Carver's class, which Lippmann confirmed later through a letter to the professor (WL to Carver, December 4, 1914, WLPI F227), was that poverty
could be reduced by denying the poor marriage licenses. Carver replied to
the letter as follows: "Dear Sir . . . I have often suggested some restriction
on marriage as one item in a comprehensive program for the elimination of
poverty. When it comes to a real issue of this kind, however, the socialists
are always laissez faire stand-patters, as they are on every real issue." Carver
reported that as a trustee of the Massachusetts State School for the Feeble-
Minded he favored some restriction to prevent students at the school from
"reproducing themselves." The situation with the poor was quite similar:
"Economically incompetent people tend to multiply almost at the same
rate. That tends to increase the supply of the unemployable as well as those
with a low grade of skill. The presence of large numbers of such people,
however, is a constant menace to the laborers who are just above that level."
Carver attached to this letter his full "Programme of Reform," which included, in addition to the expected constraints on monopoly and advocacy
of land value taxation, "The discouraging of vicious and demoralizing developments of public opinion, such as: 1. The cult of incompetence and self

pity. 2. The gospel of covetousness, or the jealousy of success. 3. The emphasizing of rights rather than obligations. 4. The worship of the almighty ballot and the almighty dollar." Then, perhaps with an eye to his former student's tastes and current journalistic career with the *New Republic*, Carver added two items, handwritten and with italics: "5. The idea that a college education should give one a 'gentlemanly appreciation' of the ornamental things of life. 6. *The idea that capitalizing verbosity is productive business*" (Carver to WL, December 5, 1914, WLPI F227).

Lippmann was one of the founders at Harvard of a socialist club (the Harvard chapter of the Intercollegiate Socialist Society), and thereby was confronted with the other extreme from Carver's positions. The club members were very earnest and called each other "comrade." Yet this was socialism of the heart rather than of the head. It was neither "scientific" nor "revolutionary" and it dealt hardly at all with socialist economic theory. The doctrine was eclectic and today might be called "communitarianism." One member even called for sympathetic study of Henry George, though George was highly critical of socialism (Rene W. E. Hoguet to WL, September 16, 1908, WLPI F552). The approach of the British Fabians to socialism appealed a good deal to Lippmann, but Marx figured not at all. "I had been reading people like Shaw and Wells, and therefore I began to pick up that side of them. Then I went on to the Webbs. The book which made me at that time a socialist was a book of Fabian essays. I never read Karl Marx. In fact, I took it for granted from reading essays which despised Karl Marx as an obsolete economic thinker. I never read Karl Marx until twenty years later" (R 32). There was a practical quality about the Fabians that appealed to Lippmann; he found some of the American reformers too utopian. "I thought Bellamy's *Looking Backward* was a fascinating book, but I wouldn't say it had any great influence, because I was too non-Utopian in my own feeling about things to believe that that was to be taken seriously as a project of society" (R 33). He joined the British Fabian Society in 1909, and he attended the Fabian Summer School in 1914, where he met G. D. H. Cole, John R. Hobson, and other luminaries.

Lippmann demonstrated early on his willingness to tweak the conservative establishment. In 1911 he nominated W. E. B. Du Bois, the great

American sociologist and civil rights pioneer, for membership in the Liberal Club of New York. The nomination was rejected (Caroline M. [indecipherable] to WL, October 19, 1911, WLPI F715). But he crossed swords as well with the more radical members of the Harvard socialist club who wanted more action, notably with his classmate John Reed, future friend of Lenin who chronicled the Russian Revolution in *Ten Days That Shook the World* (1919) and was buried in the Kremlin wall. While working in New York, Lippmann presented a paper to a socialist club on Staten Island and a member told him of her "awful shock" at his doctrinal apostasy when he "disclosed the fact that you believed that under socialism there would be both rent and interest. I am not aware of any other socialist holding the same view, no matter how reformist or 'opportunist' he might be, and I am at a loss to know how you ever determined in your own mind—as I suppose you have done—that you are a Socialist at all" (Bertha W. Howe to WL, April 15, 1913, WLPI F569).

Lippmann offered his own definition of socialism at that time, which was more closely allied with feminism and egalitarianism than with the public ownership of property.

> In short, the making of a better society is the training ground for feminism. I call that better society socialism. I don't identify it with the Socialist Party. I don't identify it with government ownership, or the general strike. I think of it as a society in which social opportunity has been equalized, in which property has lost its political power, a society in which everyone has a genuine vote, not only a ballot, but a real share in economic development, and free access to the resources of civilization. Such a society cannot be realized without feminism. It will, I believe, in large measure be made by feminism. (WL to Marie Howe, February 16, 1915, WLPI F570)

Lippmann's departure from Harvard in 1910, in his fourth year, without even waiting for his master's degree, signaled his rejection both of the mainstream social sciences as disciplines to which he could devote his life and of the academic world as a place in which to dwell. Over the next two decades he went through what amounted to a series of internships in other fields and other places from which he could make his career choices: he spent time in socialist endeavors, investigative journalism, government service at several levels, and the editorship of a magazine and a newspaper.

Searching for a Career

For a short time after graduation Lippmann worked at a socialist paper, the *Boston Common,* but his first real job gave him deeper insight into one career choice that lay before him, investigative journalism. The prominent "muckraker" Lincoln Steffens was planning an exposé of Wall Street similar to those he had conducted of municipal governments, and he came to Harvard looking for an assistant. He asked who had "the ablest mind that could express itself in writing" (Hartshorn 2011, 184) and was told Walter Lippmann. The investigation for Steffens in which Lippmann did most of the legwork yielded an eight-part series called "It" in the popular periodical *Everybody's Magazine* in 1910–1911 (the first part is Steffens 1910); this documented monopoly in the banking industry and the overwhelming power of J. P. Morgan (Steffens 1910). The furor it created was fuel for a congressional inquiry (the Pujo Committee) that led to the Federal Reserve Act of 1913. Lippmann appreciated that muckrakers drew attention to issues of public concern that otherwise might be neglected by government and the scholarly community. But he worried that their methods were not sufficiently thorough and careful to provide a basis for sound policy formation. Throughout his life he looked for the right balance between rigor and relevance, and here he thought the weight was much too heavily on relevance. There was no real research by Steffens. His approach was the antithesis of science. "I was also rather startled to find that he never read anything. He was only interested in seeing people. He never wanted to read anything. He never read any books on the subject he was writing about, and that rather put me off. He was a journalist, and he liked a sensation for its own sake" (R 43). Lippmann retained an affectionate regard for his old boss but did not follow in his footsteps.

After the Chelsea fire Lippmann did volunteer work in the community. He gave lectures to a working-class audience on the fine arts, including one on embroidery. An opportunity to really experience socialism in action, however, opened with the election of the first socialist mayor in America, George Lunn, in Schenectady, New York, in 1912. After the brief interlude with Steffens and *Everybody's Magazine* he gladly took a position as Lunn's executive secretary. He reflected very candidly on the frustrations of this experience in a long letter to the National Office of the Socialist Party in 1913 (reproduced in Stave 1975). The essential problem for socialists in power, he wrote, was that their doctrine was mainly about the simple redistribution of income and wealth. Take from the rich and give to the poor. That was all very well, but it implied many losers as well as winners. In a democracy this led to a constant struggle to stay in office. Socialists proposed more services for citizens (parks, schools, medical attention, and so forth), but these services required higher taxes, which alienated property holders, who were a key voting block. Lippmann distinguished socialists from progressives and other "reformers" who promised institutional change and improvements in efficiency so that their reforms, in theory at least, could lead to tax reductions as well as more equitable distribution. "The distinction is roughly this: that reformers propose to use the profits to reduce taxes; that Socialists propose to spend the profits socially." If socialist municipal governments hoped to remain in power they had little choice but to become reformers in fact while retaining the socialist label if they so wished. Politically "the Socialists are in the grip of the progressives."

From this conclusion it was natural for Lippmann to shift his allegiance from the socialists to other reformers, and this he did in his first book, *A Preface to Politics* (1913), published soon after formation of the Progressive Party by Theodore Roosevelt in 1912. Lippmann went through life attempting to avoid labels, but "progressive" is one that has stayed with him. It is anachronistic to call Lippmann an Institutionalist because the term and the body of thought that the term connotes were still in the future. But in his early writings he was responding to the questions and problems that were inspiring Wesley Mitchell, Walton Hamilton, and other Institutionalists of the time, men who would be at the core of the movement and would become his friends in just a few years. Moreover, Lippmann was at this time more scholarly than directly political, and if a label must be applied Institutional seems as appropriate as progressive. Lippmann's argument in this book was that conventional social scientists concerned with reform were, like Thomas Nixon Carver, merely drawing up lists of rules that were based on simple assumptions of human behavior. These reformers were what he called "routineers" when they should be "inventors." They approached social policy by proposing some modest "tinkering" with practices and institutions; they thought the basic structures were eternal. They had missed entirely the Darwinian and Freudian revolutions. "And no matter how much we talk about the infusion of the 'evolutionary' point of view into all modern thought, when the test is made political practice shows itself almost virgin to the idea" (WL 1913, 16). Eighteenth-century thinking from which the modern social sciences drew inspiration too often embodied a static perspective. "Our own Federal Constitution is a striking example of this machine conception of government. It is probably the most important instance we have of the deliberate application of a mechanical philosophy to human affairs" (WL 1913, 16). Lippmann called for a turn away from the knee-jerk public policy positions of classical economists, like the punishment of monopolies and imposition of land value taxation, because the full consequences of such proposals were not well understood. He called for imaginative and flexible openness to governmental intervention. "For the object of democracy is not to imitate the rhythm of the stars but to harness political power to the nation's need. If corporations and governments have indeed gone on a joy ride the business of reform is not to set up fences, Sherman Acts and injunctions into which they can bump, but to take the wheel and to steer" (WL 1913, 22). Frequent resort to unsubstantiated taboos was clear evidence of failures of public policy. "Social systems like ours, which do not even feed and house men and women, which deny pleasure, cramp play, ban adventure, propose celibacy and grind out monotony, are a clear confession of sterility in statesmanship. . . . It is impossible to abolish either with a law or an axe the desires of men. . . . Only by supplying our passions with civilized interests can we escape their destructive force" (WL 1913, 34, 37, and 44). Even though politicians and old-fashioned social scientists preferred to think of society as static, it was above all dynamic and therefore required a creative and flexible policy structure. "For while statesmen are pottering along doing the same thing year in, year out, putting up the tariff one year and down the next, passing appropriations bills and recodifying laws, the real forces of the country do not stand still. Vast changes, economic and psychological, take place and these changes demand new guidance. But the routineers are always unprepared" (WL 1913, 25). The impact of Lippmann's work with Lincoln Steffens is evident in this book. For example, he writes of "the whole economic life of this country. It is controlled by groups of men whose influence extends like a web to smaller, tributary groups, cutting across all official boundaries and designations, making short work of all legal formulae, and exercising sovereignty regardless of the little fences we erect to keep it in bounds" (WL 1913, 21). The influence of Thorstein Veblen was also obvious on Lippmann's thinking; for example in his assertion that "[o]ur primary care must be to keep the habits of the mind flexible and adapted to the movement of real life" (WL 1913, 29).

During his last semester at Harvard in 1910 Lippmann joined a seminar given by Graham Wallas, one of the early leaders of the Fabian movement in Britain (Qualter 1980) visiting from the London School of Economics, and the experience was memorable for both. Wallas dedicated his next book, *The Great Society,* which contained the substance of the seminar, to his student Lippmann, and Lippmann claimed that he read the book repeatedly for inspiration. Wallas's message was that progress in the social sciences called for much more study and application of the evolving discipline of social psychology. This message was repeated prominently by Lippmann in *A Preface to Politics*, and indeed throughout much of his writings thereafter. About economics, Lippmann wrote, "The Economic Man—that lazy abstraction—is still paraded in the lecture room; the study of human nature has not advanced beyond the gossip of old wives tales" (WL 1913, 62). And more generally, "we deny truth, falsify facts, and prefer the coddling of our theory to any deeper understanding of the real problem before us" (WL 1913, 124). Self-interest should not simply be assumed; it must be examined thoughtfully and critically. He agreed with Graham Wallas that "some economist ought therefore to give us a treatise in which this property instinct is carefully and quantitatively examined" (WL 1913, 66). Anything less would perpetuate the reputation of economics as the handmaiden of predatory capitalism. "The orthodox economists are in the unenviable po-

sition of having taken their morals from the exploiter and of having translated them into the grandiloquent language of high public policy. They
gave capitalism the sanction of the intellect" (WL 1913, 70). Yet there was
reason for hope. "The world has recently begun to see through this kind of
intellectual fraud" (WL 1913, 123).

Despite these reservations about the current state of economic science,
the message of *Preface* was optimistic. If only economists and other social
scientists would attend to Darwin and Freud they could produce a modern
body of thought that would willingly be accepted and used by statesmen
facing the daunting task of reconciling the eighteenth-century emphasis on
human freedom with the twentieth-century reality that government was
needed for social improvement. "The provision of schools, streets, plumb-
ing, highways, libraries, parks, universities, medical attention, post-offices,
a Panama Canal, agricultural information, fire protection—is a use totally
different from the ideal of Jefferson" (WL 1913, 202). He saw a bright future
ahead for the modern politician. "In that kind of statesmanship there will
be a premium on inventiveness, on the ingenuity to devise and plan. There
will be much less use for lawyers and a great deal more for scientists. The
work requires industrial organizers, engineers, architects, educators, sanit-
ists [*sic*] to achieve what leadership brings into the program of politics"
(WL 1913, 225). What society needed most were those who could help to
implement the change that was needed: "the task of reform consists not in
presenting a state with progressive laws, but in getting the people to want
them" (WL 1913, 223).

The reception of this short book by a little-known recent college graduate was remarkable. Sigmund Freud arranged for it to be reviewed favorably in the journal *Image* (WL to Frederick J. Hoffman, November 18,
1942, WLPIII F1059). It was a stroke of good luck that Teddy Roosevelt
took the book with him on vacation in Brazil and was charmed, in part no
doubt by the positive references to his own wisdom and accomplishments
(WL 1913, 186, 214, 226). This led to a meeting with Lippmann in May
1914 and a warm friendship thereafter (Steel 1980, 64–65). President
Woodrow Wilson read the book in 1914 (Cooper 2009, 256). At a very
young age, therefore, Lippmann was seen as one of the coming bright stars

of the progressive movement with a career in politics or journalism ahead. Undoubtedly the warm reception of his book gave Lippmann confidence to write the second book that came soon after.

An Institutional Fabian

Lippmann's second book, *Drift and Mastery* (1914), was infused with new thinking and evidence of new personal contacts, but the essential message was unchanged. Serious research on social questions was needed before political action was undertaken. *A Preface to Politics* was written in Maine with a roommate who was translating Freud; this next book was written in England where he saw much of Wallas, H. G. Wells, George Bernard Shaw, Hobson, Leonard Woolf, Sidney and Beatrice Webb, and other Fabians. He absorbed much from this environment. When the book was published complimentary copies went to Hobson, Wells, Leonard Hobhouse, S. K. Ratcliffe, and Charles Booth (WL to Fisher Unwin, October 22, 1914, WLPI F1226). It seems as if, all of a sudden, Lippmann discovered the richness of the wide range of reformist thinking then in the air and was stimulated by what it might provide. This book, like *Preface*, reflects a deep reading of Thorstein Veblen but also anticipates the discussion of the separation of ownership from control in *The Modern Corporation and Public Property* (1932) by Adolph Berle and Gardiner Means. Indeed the latter book would become the "scaffolding" for some of his later thinking (WL to Felix Frankfurter, September 10, 1932, WLPIII F816). The subtitle of Malcolm Rutherford's recent study of the Institutionalists, *Science and Social Control* (2011), suggests the approach Lippmann was taking. He had come to conclude that "drift" in public policy, meaning mainly acceptance of the status quo, should be overcome and "mastered" by the application of science, meaning social science and psychology in particular, to current problems. He wrote: "This is what mastery means: the substitution of conscious intention for unconscious striving. Civilization, it seems to me, is just this constant effort to introduce plan where there has been clash, and purpose into the jungles of disordered growth. But to shape the world nearer to the heart's desire requires a knowledge of the heart's desire and the world. You cannot throw yourself blindly against unknown facts and trust to luck that the result will be satisfactory" (WL 1914a, 148). And again: "What men need in their specialties in order to enable them to cooperate is not alone a binding passion, but a common discipline. Science, I believe, implies such a discipline" (WL 1914a, 154). Lippmann offered a capsule history of economics, in which he claimed that Adam Smith and Karl Marx had the deepest insights into the economies of the two centuries in which they lived but with the enormous economic, political, and social changes that had occurred they had become largely irrelevant in the contemporary world. "One can say without fear of contradiction that they are the two most fertile minds that have dealt with the modern problem. But the orthodox economists and the orthodox Marxians are out of touch with the latent forces of this age; both have proved themselves largely sterile" (WL 1914a, 167). In his reminiscences years later Lippmann characterized his two early books modestly as "sophomoric books, just careless" (R 88). This seems too harsh; at a minimum they point ahead to how he would direct his career.

In the consideration of public policy Lippmann proposed at this time leaving aside all inherited verities including "the sanctity of property, the patriarchal family, hereditary caste, the dogma of sin, obedience to authority" (WL 1914a, 16) and starting from scratch. He conceded that muckraking journalists like Steffens and Ida Tarbell had revealed many of the real problems of the modern economy. "Muckraking is full of the voices of the beaten, of the bewildered, and then again it is shot through with some fine anticipation. It has pointed to a revolution in business motives; it has hinted at the emerging power of labor and the consumer—we can take those suggestions, perhaps, and by analyzing them, and following them through, gather for ourselves some sense of what moves beneath the troubled surface of events" (WL 1914a, 34). But in searching for solutions for these troubles neither the muckrakers nor the orthodox economists had been successful. It was necessary first of all to go beyond the conventional notion of the economic man. "For in science, art, politics, religion, the home, love, education, the pure economic motive, profiteering, the incentive of business enterprise is treated as a public peril. Wherever civilization is seen to be in question, the Economic Man of commercial theorists is in disrepute . . . the old economists were bad psychologists and superficial observers when they described man as a slot machine set in motion by inserting a coin" (WL 1914a, 36–37). It must be understood, Lippmann wrote, that the business managers no longer truly represented the interests of the owners (later the "principal agent problem"), and their behavior must be examined afresh. "The managers are on salary, divorced from ownership and from bargaining. They represent the revolution in business incentives at its very heart" (WL 1914a, 43). Similarly the fiction of consumer sovereignty had to be replaced by a sophisticated theory of consumer behavior: "few consumers feel any of that sense of power which economists say is theirs" (WL 1914a, 52). It had to be recognized that consumption was not the result so much of innate tastes as of education. "Advertising is in fact the weed that has grown up because the art of consumption is uncultivated" (WL 1914a, 53). He was especially impressed by the psychologist Ordway Tead's book *Instincts in Industry* (WL to Alfred Harcourt, January 12, 1918, WLPI F1195) and the work of Z. Clark Dickinson of the University of Minnesota entitled "The Analysis of Economic Motives" (WL to Dickinson, July 14, 1919, WLPI F340; Dickinson 1922). Attempts to enrich economics from psychology were not yet widely accepted in economics, and Lippmann was on the frontier.

He was a frequent advocate for Freud, urging his own publisher Mitchell Kennerley to publish Freud in English (WL to Mitchell Kennerley, July 1, 1913, WLPI F826). He set forth the reasons for his enthusiasm in an article for the *New Republic* in 1915. He saw a close parallel between the impact of Freud and that of Darwin. They both stimulated attention to new lines of thought, and no one claimed they were the last word. They both made humans wince, and so much the better: "These researches of Freud challenge the very essence of what we call ourselves. They involve the sources of our character, they carry analysis deeper into the soul of man than analysis has ever been carried before" (NR, April 17, 1915, 9). Perhaps the best thing the layman could do in addressing Freud was to take the measure of the scientist himself: "What we can do is to get the sense of his method and the quality of his mind. We can say that we recognize in him the type of imagination, the sense of reality, the honesty before fact, the logical penetration, and the background of experience which are likely to yield fruitful results"

(NR, April 17, 1915, 9). Lippmann was confident that the influence of Freud would be wide and deep. "From anthropology through education to social organization, from literary criticism to the studies of religions and philosophies, the effect of Freud is already felt" (WL 1914a, 10).

In 1914–1915 Lippmann argued with Wesley Mitchell, the Institutionalist economist at Columbia University, who could not see the potential contribution to economics from Freud. He wrote in appreciation of a mention Mitchell had made of him in a publication, and then launched into Freud. "Thank you very much for sending me your 'Human Behavior and Economics.' I feel like a man in a blue flannel suit at Mrs. Astor's dinner party. My mere presence in such company is so extremely embarrassing that I want to go and hide my impertinence. . . . I'd like to talk Freud with you, and try to convince you of my faith that he is not a sensational and inaccurate thinker, as you imply, but a profoundly careful inheritor of the best scientific traditions. I'd like to try to show you that he differs radically from the James-McDougall-Tichnor-Wundt psychologies to which Mr. Wallas adheres, principally in the meaning he has given to the word 'unconscious.' Freud has worked on the mechanism of conduct from the practical point of view of the educator and physician; the theoretical psychology which he has created is the product of direct application; its origin is thoroughly pragmatic and its elaboration is in the hands of applied psychologists" (WL to Mitchell, December 3 [1914], Wesley C. Mitchell Papers, Box 11, Columbia University Library). Mitchell replied: "I still feel much as I did after reading 'A Preface to Politics,' viz., that the service rendered by Freud's ideas is quite capable of being gotten from psychological analysis of people like Thorndike, for example" (Mitchell to WL, February 6, 1915, WLPI F827). They agreed to continue the argument face to face. In 1915 Lippmann tried also to persuade Judith Bernays, Freud's niece, to prepare an article on Professor Freud for the *New Republic*. "The more personal it is the better, and I should prefer that you talk about his scientific theory only as much as you have to in order to illuminate the man" (WL to Bernays, February 10, 1915, WLPI F194). He kept in close touch with Carleton Parker, UC Berkeley economist and fellow disciple of Graham Wallas, who was taking the lead in efforts to incorporate psychology into economics. He helped to organize Parker's tour through eastern universities, and he mourned Parker's untimely death in the flu epidemic of 1918 (Cornelia Parker 1919, 104–115, and WL to Cornelia S. Parker, May 27, 1918, WLPI F852). Clearly Lippmann was coming to be recognized as a player in the efforts to integrate psychology into economics, and Richard T. Ely tried to persuade him to write a book for his Citizen's Library, to be called "The New Progressivism," which would deal with "psychical problems among others" (Ely to WL, March 1, 1916, WLPI F366).

Lippmann picked up the idea, presumably from Henry George, that there was a large surplus of production, or unearned income, which could be captured for legitimate public purposes: "A fund of wealth exists which to-day is being diverted into the pockets of those who do no adequate service—we may call that fund the Social Surplus. It is made up of all the leaks, the useless payments, the idle demands, the inefficiency, the extortion and parasitism of industrial life. This surplus is the legitimate fund of progress." The emphasis of Alfred Marshall on the importance of pecuniary incentives for performance, and productivity as the explanation for reward, had, he thought, misled those who tried to understand economic growth. "Power, position, pull, custom, weakness, oversupply, the class monopoly of higher education, inheritance, accident, the strategy of industrial war—these are the things which determine income—not the incentive which is necessary" (WL 1914a, 72–74).

Concentration of industry intrigued Lippmann, and he regretted that the Sherman Act had been based simply on emotion rather than on serious analysis. Concentration, he observed, could yield economies of scale, in which case it should be encouraged, or collusion in restraint of trade, in which case it should be proscribed. The challenge was to tell the difference between the two results: "Big business is a business that has survived competition. But when competition is done away with, who is the Solomon wise enough to know whether the result was accomplished by superior efficiency or by agreement among the competitors or by both?" (WL 1914a, 84–85). Simple prohibition of concentration grew out of the traditions of an earlier era of small-scale production and could lead to the loss of the benefits of technological progress. "Those who cling to the village view of life may deflect the drift, may batter the trusts about a bit, but they will never dominate business, never humanize its machinery, and they will continue to be the playthings of industrial change" (WL 1914a, 87).

Drift and Mastery, like *A Preface to Politics,* was light on prescription both for further research and for action, except of the most general kind. Overall Lippmann insists on institutional renovation to respond to change. "Institutions have developed a thousand inconsistencies. Our schools, churches, courts, governments were not built for the kind of civilization they are expected to serve." In most cases enlightened education of the leaders seemed the most promising reform: "To prepare them for the unexpected means to train them in method instead of filling them with facts and rules" (WL 1914a, 93). At this early date he toyed with the idea of national planning. "You have to make a survey of the natural resources of the country. On the basis of that survey you must draw up a national plan for their development" (WL 1914a, 98). The state must intervene whenever the case was overwhelming to do so. "You have to see to it that technical schools produce men trained for such work; you have to establish institutes of research that shall stimulate the economic world not only with physical inventions, but with administrative proposals" (WL 1914a, 98). He was sympathetic even to something like a regulated economy. "You have to find ways of making the worker an integral part of his industry. That means allowing him to develop his unions, and supplying the unions with every incentive by which they can increase their responsibility." Consumers too should expect some constraints. "You have to devise and try out a great variety of consumers' controls. For some industries you may have to use public ownership, for others the cooperative society may be more effective, for others the regulating commission" (WL 1914a, 99).

Public Service

After Lippmann left his job with the socialist mayor he joined Herbert Croly in 1913 as a member of the editorial board of the *New Republic,* which was then getting under way as a weekly medium of progressive thought. But this too did not last long. As the nation got ready for war, he was pressed into government service in a job he had somewhat disingenuously suggested for himself. In a letter of May 5, 1916, he proposed to

recently appointed secretary of war Newton Baker that he needed more
staff, perhaps organized in something like an in-house think tank. "I was
wondering whether it might not be a good plan to do what I understand the
British Treasury Department did at the outbreak of the war. They went to
Oxford and Cambridge and got a number of specialists in economics and
said to them: 'Now you have no administrative work whatsoever—your job
is to think out and report on certain large theoretical problems.' Mightn't it
be a good scheme for you to have a voluntary, inconspicuous number of
people whose business it would be to analyze and make suggestions about
the kind of thing we talked of and digested—reports about conditions of
public opinion in this country and elsewhere. To formulate methods not
only of censorship but of positive press agenting and to deal in general with
all those matters of morale d.c. [District of Columbia?] army men are not so
likely to understand, and for which people like you tied to a devastating
task cannot have time to think about at length" (WL to Baker, May 5, 1916,
WLPI F97). Baker replied that he had read Lippmann's letter "several
times" and needed to reflect on whether he might not get such advice as
Lippmann offered from the War College, but he was cautiously positive
about the proposal. "Now and then I have wanted things in a hurry and
have them surprisingly quickly by calling upon the War College for them.
But this, of course, has to do with military things and nothing whatever to
do with the far subtler sort of work which has to be done to keep myself in
touch with what the sound heart and head of the country think and expect
and want from the War Department" (Baker to WL, May 10, 1916, WLPI
F97). Lippmann made a similar suggestion to President Wilson a few weeks
later through his secretary Joseph Tumulty. He cited British precedent
once again for establishing "reconstruction committees to study the economic and political problems arising from the settlement of the war and
from conditions after the war in order to formulate expert advice for the use
of the administrators" (WL to Tumulty, August 8, 1916, WLPI F1210).

The upshot was that Lippmann was appointed assistant to Secretary
Baker in 1917 with duties that were far less cerebral than he had hoped. For
example, he was engaged with interservice committees "to consider the adjustment of wage schedules at armories and naval yards" (Baker to WL,
August 15, 1917, WLPI F97). "My job really was to hold Sam Gompers'

hand all through that summer, carry messages back and forth, and try to persuade him to agree to things that would prevent strikes in war industries" (R 9). In this job he came to know Franklin Roosevelt, who often represented the Navy Department in meetings.

Lippmann's original plan was more nearly followed when he was seconded by Colonel E. M. House to become secretary of what became known as "The Inquiry," a secret research group set up in New York City to prepare advisory material for the president in a manner very much like that proposed by Lippmann in his letter to Baker and in concept somewhere between a Council of Economic Advisers and a RAND Corporation. Initially Lippmann was deeply impressed by the application of the social sciences that went on at the Inquiry. The approximately 125 researchers at the peak (Hodgson 2006, 160), led by the geographer Isaiah Bowman, many from Columbia University just down the road, were largely given free rein, and Lippmann even engaged Thorstein Veblen, with whom he maintained contact, as consultant (WL to Harold Laski, October 3, 1917, WLPI F688). He recalled later that Veblen's memo of advice arrived the week when they were charged to provide explanatory background material for Woodrow Wilson's Fourteen Points (Dorfman 1934, 374).

As the war came to an end Lippmann made a list of a dozen postwar "issues" that should now be addressed by the Inquiry, including demobilization, industrial transformation to peace, war debts, tariffs, educational reform, and governmental reorganization. "What appears to be needed is a disinterested analysis and forecast of these issues, together with the preparation of a number of alternative programs which can be put at the disposal of the President" ("Memorandum on Reconstruction," December 19, 1917, WLPI F1221). He had a brave vision for how this project could be carried out. "The procedure would be about as follows: To plot out the main issues tentatively. To select scholars of an administrative type and divide the field among them. . . . The results could then be laid before the heads of departments at Washington for criticizing and for preparation in the form of legislation." In 1918, back at the *New Republic*, Lippmann repeated this suggestion for "a confidential commission for the scientific planning of reconstruction questions." Now the list of issues to be addressed was down to nine and the reemployment of veterans was at the top of the list. This plan for a new advisory structure close to the president was remarkably like the Council of Economic Advisers that would be created after the next war. "None of these problems can be dealt with quickly, unless there has been a preliminary period of calm and disinterested study, and above all, study which is carried on without publicity. I should strongly urge against intrusting the work to what is called a representative committee of prominent people, that is to say, a commission in which the various interests affected are supposed to be represented. . . . I should recommend an organization quite similar to that of the Inquiry, that is, an organization with one man at the head who has the complete confidence of the President: under him two or three assistants guided by the same sympathies who actually administer the detail of the research; and with about fifteen or twenty men of the right kind, clerical assistance, and with proper access to Washington bureaus the trick could, I imagine, be done" (WL to House, May 11, 1918, WLPI F564). He made a similar recommendation to a commission of inquiry in New York State for a "permanent organ of research and consultation for the guidance and assistance of the legislature and the executive" (April 11, 1919, WLPI F1026).

But Lippmann did not stay around in 1918 to implement his plan. He was on the road again, this time with a commission in military intelligence and attached to the general staff in Europe, one of six officers in a "psychological warfare unit." His orders from the War Department, dated July 3, 1918, which he may have drafted himself, were quite breathtaking in their generality: "You are authorized and directed to proceed to England, France, and Italy for the purpose of making special studies in economic and political matters for the use of this Department in connection with the work being done at the direction of Colonel E. M. House in conjunction with the Department of State. . . . It is felt that it is best to leave entirely to your discretion, the methods to be pursued by you in prosecuting your studies" (Robert Lansing to WL, July 3, 1918, WLPI F1221). Secretary Baker was more specific in a letter to General John Pershing: "Captain Walter Lippmann has been commissioned to assist the War Department in the dissemination of propaganda. . . . the vigorous prosecution of his work on behalf of the Inquiry and the State Department will aid us in the preparation of the material to be used as propaganda" (Baker to Pershing, July 2, 1918, WLPI F1221). Lippmann's studies were well received. Baker wrote him on August 29, 1918, "Your letters of August 9th and 15th have just reached me. They are so full of interest that I am sending them to the President for his information" (WLPI F1221). Woodrow Wilson, who had come to know Lippmann during the presidential campaign of 1916 in which he was endorsed by the *New Republic*, wrote to Baker on August 22. "I am warmly obliged to you for having let me see the enclosed. Lippmann is always not only thoughtful but just and suggestive" (Wilson to Baker, August 22, 1917, WLPI F97, and Cooper 2009, 355).

Lippmann's final experience in government was as an aide to President Wilson at the Peace Conference in Versailles, and there again he felt acutely the need for a mechanism to provide effective intelligence and policy advice. He was compelled to write a summary memo of interpretation for the president on the Fourteen Points without any files or background materials. It appears that in some respects Lippmann's gloss was more influential than the original text (Cooper 2009, 450; Hodgson 2006, 188). By this time he was becoming uneasy about the way the Inquiry was moving, and he wrote to Colonel House: "The greatest weakness of the Inquiry is its divorce from responsibility and from intimate knowledge of current affairs. That a certain objectivity has been gained from this is undeniable, but the time has come to ask ourselves whether the Inquiry is not now in danger of becoming too academic and out of touch with European ways of thinking" ("Preliminary Memorandum on Great Powers," October 26, 1918, WLPI F1221). In contrast to the muckrakers who, he concluded, had moved too far toward relevance, these academics seemed committed too much to rigor. Like John Maynard Keynes in the British delegation Lippmann grew increasingly frustrated with the peace negotiations and was glad to return home and, despite his heady experience in government and the military, move back into the private sector.

Intellectual Foundation

By the end of World War I Lippmann was known as a brilliant young intellectual in the progressive movement who had scaled the heights of government in an amazingly short time and had attracted the attention of powerful patrons. But he did not yet have much of a presence either in the media or in the academic world. That changed in the 1920s. He returned to the *New Republic* in 1919 but left in 1922 to join the editorial staff of the *New York World,* the most prominent progressive newspaper in the country, edited by his wartime colleague Frank Cobb. In the middle of the decade he succeeded Cobb, who died suddenly, as chief editorial writer, and in 1929 he was named editor. In this role he sustained the interest of the *World* in economic affairs, working with two economist colleagues, Charles Merz and William Scroggs. He developed sources that gave him insight into issues of the moment. One was Adolf Berle Jr., a well-connected young lawyer, soon to be a founding member of Franklin Roosevelt's Brain Trust, with the inside story on such matters as the forces behind protective tariffs and efforts to weaken restraints over corporate misbehavior (Berle to WL, April 25, 1925, and May 6, 1929, WLPI F141). During the 1920s Lippmann's correspondents among an expanding acquaintance of eminent persons included Winston Churchill (WLPI F248), John Galsworthy (WLPI F440), Sinclair Lewis, Frederick Jackson Turner, Charles S. Merriam, H. G. Wells, Sidney Webb, Rebecca West, Harold Laski, Lewis Mumford, Alexander Woollcott, and Gilbert Murray. He also provided economic commentary for Franklin Roosevelt, by then governor of New York.

It is too much to suggest that Lippmann in the 1920s set out consciously to prepare himself for his later role of columnist, but looking back it seems he made wise choices. In particular the reputation he gained among intellectuals, and the economics discipline in particular, served him well. Leaders in academe came to see him not merely as an interpreter of their work but as a contributor in his own right. He wrote four books that attracted wide scholarly attention, and he took on various roles that were typically reserved for insiders, such as gatekeeper to publication and reviewer of academic programs, as well as close friendships with prominent leaders of the profession, most notably John Maynard Keynes.

The four significant monographs that Lippmann produced during the 1920s while helping to edit a magazine and then a major daily newspaper were *Liberty and the News* (1920), *Public Opinion* (1922), *The Phantom Public* (1925), and *A Preface to Morals* (1929).

Whereas his two prewar books were intellectual calls to arms, these four included attempts to construct new arms. The first two arose from Lippmann's brief but intense experience during World War I with propaganda and censorship, where he had to face the reality that the "public" could be manipulated and was not inclined necessarily to support well-reasoned public policy. Often, he found, the public did not have firm views based on thoughtful consideration. Voters were malleable and could be manipulated even to accept policies that were contrary to their own best interests. Lippmann left the army with these concerns clearly in mind. He wrote Ellery Sedgwick, editor of the *Atlantic Monthly,* in April 1919: "I have started to write a longish article around the general idea that freedom of thought and speech present themselves in a new light and raise new problems because of the discovery that opinion can be manufactured. The idea has come to me gradually as a result of certain experiences with the official propaganda machines, and my hope is to attempt a restatement of the problem of freedom of thought as it presents itself in modern society under modern conditions of government and also with a modern knowledge of how to manipulate the human mind" (WL to Sedgwick, April 7, 1919, WLPI F80).

Lippmann left military service, where he had been a propagandist, with a vivid sense of the heavy responsibilities of journalists to make certain that misrepresentation of the kind he had observed could not happen in peacetime. He addressed the subject in a slim volume entitled *Liberty and the News* (1920c). This book gave him a prominence in the media that he did not have before. He insisted that the development of a corps of competent journalists was critical to a democracy because "the public, when it is dependent on testimony and protected by no rules of evidence, can act only on the excitement of its pugnacities and its hopes" (WL 1920c, 24). The most important public need was for "the facts" because ignorance was a constant danger to democracy: "Men who have lost their grip upon the relevant facts of their environment are the inevitable victims of agitation and propaganda. The quack, the charlatan, the jingo, and the terrorist, can flourish only where the audience is deprived of independent access to information" (WL 1920c, 32). True facts were needed as much in government as among the public. "Decisions in the modern state tend to be made by the interaction, not of Congress and the executive, but of public opinion and the executive" (WL 1920c, 36). It was impossible to exaggerate the importance of accurate information. "There can be no liberty for a community which lacks the information to detect lies" (WL 1920c, 38). Lippmann had faith that the responsible application of the social sciences by the media was the surest way to build consensus and a collaborative spirit among the people. "There is but one kind of unity possible in a world as diverse as ours. It is unity of method, rather than of aim; the unity of the disciplined experiment. There is but one bond of peace that is both permanent and enriching: the increasing knowledge of the world in which experiment occurs. With a common intellectual method and a common area of valid fact, differences may become a form of co-operation and cease to be an irreconcilable antagonism" (WL 1920c, 40). The responsibility of the journalist in defending liberty fell roughly "under three heads, protection of the sources of news, organization of the news so as to make it comprehensible, and education of human response" (WL 1920c, 42–43). This required "not the slick persons who scoop the news, but the patient and fearless men of science who have labored to see what the world really is. It does not matter that the news is not susceptible of mathematical statement. In fact, just because the news is complex and slippery, good reporting requires the exercise of the highest of the scientific virtues. They are the habits of ascribing no more credibility to a statement than it warrants, a sense of the probabilities, and a keen understanding of the quantitative importance of particular facts" (WL 1920c, 49). He called for establishment of some kind of endowed "political observatories" to generate reliable facts and interpretations of them: "Liberty is not so much permission as it is the construction of a system of information increasingly independent of opinion. . . . For the real enemy is ignorance, from which all of us, conservative, liberal, revolutionary, suffer" (WL 1920c, 57 and 58). Lippmann did more than attack ignorance and misrepresentation in the news; he set out to focus light upon them. In a pioneering study with his friend and colleague at the *New Republic*, Charles Merz, he published in 1920 a damning content analysis of the coverage by the *New York Times* of the Russian Revolution entitled "A Test of the News" (supplement to the *New Republic*, August 4, 1920).

The second short book that emerged from the proposed long article for the *Atlantic Monthly* was entitled *Public Opinion* and looks more like Lippmann's reading notes on the subject than a finished product. But it did the most to raise his visibility in the academic world. He cites writers from a wide range of disciplines to form his ideas: classics, history, political theory, economics, modern novels, and above all psychology. He debunked the idea that public opinion could be accessed as the settled collective views of a community. He emphasized that the "pictures in our head" may be very different from "the world outside," as Plato had observed from the cave. This made predictions about human responses hard to construct and therefore policy formation difficult in a democracy. He rejected the use of a simple utilitarian calculus to understand human behavior. "Try to explain social life as the pursuit of pleasure and the avoidance of pain. You will soon be saying that the hedonist begs the question, for even supposing that man does pursue these ends, the crucial problem of why he takes one course rather than another likely to produce pleasure, is untouched. Does the guidance of man's conscience explain? How then does he happen to have the particular conscience which he has? The theory of economic self-interest? But how do men come to conceive their self-interest in one way rather than another?" (WL 1922, 14). In his discussions of the relatively new discipline of psychology Lippmann was responding to current enthusiasms without as well as within academe. For example, in 1922, the year in which *Public Opinion* was published, Dorothy Straight, the wealthy patron of the *New Republic,* set out to address "certain psychological questions" through a discussion group in New York City that included, in addition to Lippmann, such luminaries as William Ogburn, Judge Learned Hand, Herbert Croly, Thomas Lamont, Leo Wolman, Alvin Johnson, Eugene O'Neill, Heywood Broun, and Sherwood Anderson. The group examined how the "new" psychology might enlighten humans about themselves, the economy, education, conflict, religion, creativity, and old age (Straight to WL, November 21, 1922, WLPI F1166).

In *Public Opinion* Lippmann complained of unnecessary secrecy in government and poor performance by the newspapers in bringing facts to light. He was concerned also by the increasing use of models in the social sciences. He worried that "stereotypes" based on ignorance, including those that went into social scientific models as assumptions, obscured reality. Regrettably, stereotypes had become a widely accepted part of modern thinking: "the stereotype not only saves time in a busy life and is a defense of our position in society, but tends to preserve us from all the bewildering effects of trying to see the world steadily and see it whole" (WL 1922, 41). However, the stereotype had many unfortunate consequences. "With modification and embroidery, this pure fiction, used by economists to simplify their thinking, was retailed and popularized until for large sections of the population it prevailed as the economic mythology of the day" (WL 1922, 42). This myth caused people to misunderstand reality: "Our attention is called to those facts which support it, and diverted from those which contradict. So perhaps it is because they are attuned to find it, that kindly people discover so much reason for kindness, malicious people so much malice" (WL 1922, 43). Classical economists as well as socialists used stereotypes, and they were both misled. "Both assume that the unlearned dispositions fatally but intelligently produce a certain type of behavior. The socialist believes that the dispositions pursue the economic interest of a class; the hedonist believes that they pursue pleasure and avoid pain. Both theories rest on a naïve view of instinct" (WL 1922, 63).

In most cases, Lippmann argued, the notion that there was a meaningful "public opinion" to be discovered and taken into account was mistaken. Individuals did not think as part of a community. "Leaders often pretend that they have merely uncovered a program which existed in the minds of their public. When they believe it, they are usually deceiving themselves. People do not invent themselves synchronously in a multitude of minds. That is not because a multitude of minds is necessarily inferior to that of the leaders, but because thought is the function of an organism, and a mass is not an organism" (WL 1922, 79). The idea of a public consensus rested on a false presumption of "a pre-established harmony, inspired, imposed, or innate, by which the self-opinionated person, class, or community is orchestrated with the rest of mankind" (WL 1922, 85).

One way to interpret the implications of Lippmann's findings about mass psychology is that stable public opinion is a fiction and a successful

government must necessarily be ruled by a select group of expert philosopher kings, who can discover what is best for the public and then, without
attending to their own self-interest, implement it. But this is not the way
Lippmann saw it. Indeed, quite the contrary. His plea is for reasoned study
by specialists of all the issues that face a society and for effective distribution of the results of their studies to all parts of society through government,
the mass media, the educational system, and by well-informed public intellectuals like the British Fabians. To a critic of *Public Opinion* who complained that the book was "an argument for the omnicompetence of the
scientific spirit," he replied, "That's just what it isn't. It is the most convincing demonstration I could make of the inadequacy of the scientific spirit. . . .
In fact, the chief emphasis of the book is directed against the dry, thin ratio-
nalist" (WL to Gerald Johnson, May 18, 1928, WLPI F618).

Supplementing his early works, which described the difficulty citizens
had in understanding the complex problems of a modern democracy, *Public Opinion* went further to suggest that these citizens could easily be manipulated in the formation of their conclusions and were dependent on
journalists and experts to show them the way. John Dewey in *The Public
and Its Problems* (1927) disputed the Lippmann argument that guidance
from experts would necessarily improve citizen understanding; he felt
confident that citizens could solve the problem of interpreting the world
on their own. Thereafter there were references in the literature to the
"Lippmann-Dewey debate," but it has been suggested that this "debate" is
mainly a fabrication (Schudson 2008). Lippmann's old *New Republic* colleague Herbert Croly went so far as to suggest that Lippmann's position was
an indictment of democracy. Another foray into the discipline of psychology that added to Lippmann's reputation as a serious scholar in the early
1920s, beyond his study of public opinion, was a critique of the use by the
military of intelligence testing during World War I (Pastore 1978).

The last two major books by Lippmann in the 1920s, *The Phantom
Public* (1927) and *A Preface to Morals* (1929), were not as closely tied to his
future role as public economist as were his first four. In the first of these he
restated the message of *Public Opinion* more bluntly and for a less sophisticated audience. He emphasized the importance of public education not

only because some members of the public were expert and others not, but because some were insiders and others not. Rather than seeking to discover the public's views on a complex subject so as to act upon them, leaders should explain a problem as clearly and simply as possible to the various segments of the public who were outsiders with the pros and cons of the possible policy options laid out for choice. Then with this information the voters could choose. There are parallels to this rejection of the myth of simple citizen sovereignty by Lippmann in 1925 to the rejection of the myth of consumer sovereignty by John Kenneth Galbraith in *The Affluent Society* three decades later. In both cases the questioning of these accepted verities caused some dismay among readers who saw rejection of democracy in the first case and of the market economy in the second. But this is not a fair interpretation of these claims. Lippmann and Galbraith both called for improvement in democratic government and in the free market to make the world a better place, not for their replacement.

A Preface to Morals (1929), Lippmann's last big book before starting his life as a columnist, is as much a contribution to theology and cultural history as to social science. The theologian Reinhold Niebuhr found that "[n]o one has made a better analysis of the moral confusion of our day than does Mr. Lippmann," but a serious defect of the book was "his confidence in rational self-discipline as a solution of our social problem" (Niebuhr 1930). Lippmann began with a discussion of "the dissolution of the ancestral order," the structure that had provided moral guidance and values to a society in its early stages. Now the successors to these sources of authority, secular humanism and formal religion, were both in crisis. The modern state was challenged to discover a new basis for distinguishing good from evil, and for regulating institutions and social practices within itself. This was by far the most popular book by Lippmann to date and was a Book of the Month Club selection. It seems to have struck a chord with many prominent people. For example, Francis Biddle, the former attorney general, told Lippmann in 1964 of finding strong evidence to this effect. He reported that "[Harold] Laski wrote to [Supreme Court Justice Oliver Wendell] Holmes in 1929: 'Walter Lippmann sent me his *Preface to Morals* last week. I thought it a superb definition of an attitude wholly sympathetic to me and written with a severe beauty beyond praise.' Holmes's wife had just died, and he did not answer immediately, as was his custom. Then he wrote [to Laski]: 'after interruptions I have finished W. Lippmann's book. I was as much impressed as you were—and think it will hit a great many people where they live'" (Francis Biddle to WL, February 2, 1964, WLPIII F222). Lippmann's old mentor Newton Baker sent him comments about *Preface to Morals* that must have given him great pleasure. Baker wrote: "I have not read a book in a dozen years which has satisfied and stirred me as this one has. Indeed, you have held out a hand of hope when, I confess, I was beginning to get into a good deal of an intellectual quagmire" (Baker to WL, May 14, 1929, WLPI F99). Ronald Steel suggests that this book was so successful because it was "perfectly attuned to its times, codifying the anxieties of a generation that had grown tired of its binge and was ready for a little renunciation. . . . The very act of reading the book seemed to give one access to the sanctum of the elect. Lippmann had put his finger on the problem of the moment, laid it out in terms simple to grasp, phrased it in a vocabulary that flattered the reader's intelligence, and proposed a self-sacrificing but noble way out of the maze" (Steel 1980, 263).

During the decade of the 1920s, in which Lippmann was extraordinarily productive, his instincts seemed at least as much those of the tenacious academic scholar as of the journalist. Together with his *World* colleague W. O. Scroggs, he prepared for the Council on Foreign Relations two volumes in the series *The United States in World Affairs,* and, not satisfied with telling the story from the outside, he went after archives. As the Hoover administration wound down in 1931 he set out to get the whole story by asking cabinet secretaries Henry Stimson and Ogden Mills "to open up their files to us" (WL to Edwin Gay, July 31, 1931, WLPIII F874). By the start of the 1930s Lippmann could have continued with conventional journalism, or he could have moved into academia. His six books qualified him as a leading public intellectual. But for reasons described in Chapter 2 he became a public economist.

2

Building Intellectual Community

MOST INTELLECTUALS ARE EMBEDDED in some kind of supportive group from which they draw creative nourishment. Sometimes this group is clearly defined within a profession, such as college and university teaching and research. In such cases there are regularized meetings, lectures, publications, close colleagues where the intellectuals are employed, and networks of relationships that grow up and sustain intellectual activity over a lifetime. In other instances a single major institution is large enough in itself to create the supportive group. Sometimes the intellectual community is very informal and made up of people from similar occupations like business or farming or government, or professions like law or medicine, or ideological communities of socialists or libertarians. Lippmann was involved closely with none of these; he read and wrote alone in his study on the Upper East Side of Manhattan, later in his home on Woodley Road in Washington, D.C., or at Wading River on Long Island, Sanibel Island, Florida, or Mount Desert Island, Maine. Sometimes he used assistants and secretaries but always in a clerical capacity and never as joint authors. His acquaintance with a very wide literature puzzled his friends, who wondered how one person could read so much. Lewis Gannett suggested that newspapers publish Lippmann's reading list, and Lippmann replied with embarrassment that this would not be possible because he was "a persistent reader of a few chapters in a great many books" (WL to Gannett, November 2, 1932, WLPIII F861). He insisted on silence while writing, and he turned his desk away from the window to avoid distractions. He took advantage of various gathering places like the Council on Foreign Relations, but he seldom became identified closely with them. He did not regret this situation. Quite the contrary: he was by nature a loner, and he preferred not to be associated very closely with any discipline, institution, or dominant mentor. Indeed, these tastes may help to explain why he was never tempted to accept, or explore in depth, offers of senior positions in government that were offered him, and professorships at Columbia, Harvard, the University of Chicago, and elsewhere.

The Professional Life of a Public Intellectual

Lippmann was an enthusiastic joiner of social and dining clubs where he could reach out to interesting people, but he was a reluctant joiner of professional groups. An amazing number of professional bodies tried to adopt him, offering awards, honorary memberships, appointments to boards, and other perks: these included associations of economists, political scientists, sociologists, historians, lawyers, humanists, and even classicists and poets. He usually declined on the ground that the views of any one group seldom matched his own, and more important because at some future time he might be required to take issue with their views publicly. One example of this reticence about group membership illustrates his stance. In 1933 he was approached by the American Committee on Economic Policy, a group headed by his two close friends, Alvin Johnson and Wesley C. Mitchell, with stated objectives remarkably close to his own. They described themselves as "an alliance of economists and civic leaders to make the fundamentals of our economic problem as clear as possible to the ten million men and women who are the backbone of the churches, the clubs, the farm and labor groups, of business, schools and colleges. We believe this to be the educational opportunity of the hour. Democracy is succumbing before the march of Fascism in many nations. We may forestall Fascism in America by the spread of economic literacy, by the educational revitalizing of Democracy as our nation strives to meet the economic challenge of this paradoxical period of plenty and starvation" (Johnson to WL, October 6, 1933, WLPIII F1156). Clearly, with his large audience of readers, membership in the committee by Lippmann would have been a major coup. Nevertheless, he replied: "I am in great sympathy with the object of it and delighted with the quality of men who are handling it. But I don't feel I ought to join because I have found it a sound rule not to join any committee which expresses opinions on things on which I may have to write. So I must send my regrets" (WL to Johnson, October 11, 1933, WLPIII F1156). Given this condition of professional aloofness it was necessary for Lippmann to arrange alternatives to the conventional forms of intellectual community. He did this mainly one on one.

While much of Lippmann's life was devoted to solitary reading and writing, this is not to say that he was unknown in the scholarly world. Lippmann's serious works during the 1920s certainly helped to establish his reputation as more than a conventional journalist. But more prosaic roles he played with respect to the economics profession during that decade also contributed to his reputation. First, he became an influential gate-keeper to publication. Economists who wished to publish the results of their research in the 1920s had at least six directions in which they could go: scholarly journals, other publications of professional organizations, university presses, commercial book publishers, weekly and monthly magazines, and daily newspapers. In the last three of these, at least, there was some likelihood they would meet Walter Lippmann. His reputation for native brilliance, eclectic interests, wide contacts, shrewd judgment, and speed reading made him the ideal acquisitions editor or referee for publishers. He was drawn into these functions many times, sometimes in connection with his regular employment and sometimes on a freelance basis for extra remuneration. It began with the *New Republic*, where he helped to build a stable of distinguished contributors. His most famous acquisitions coup was Keynes's *Economic Consequences of the Peace* in 1919, first as a series of articles for the *New Republic* and then as a book for Harcourt Brace, where he had taken a supplementary editorial position. Evidently on this occasion his friend Felix Frankfurter was the intermediary with Keynes (WLPI F420). At Harcourt he was imaginative in identifying and soliciting books from promising authors, for example John Dewey and Wesley Mitchell in 1921 and R. H. Tawney in 1922 (WLPI F827 and F1193). Harcourt used Lippmann regularly as a referee for serious scholarly books in several fields; for example, Harcourt insisted that he read Gustav Cassel's *Theory of Social Economy* before they published it in the United States (Alfred Harcourt to WL, October 28, 1922, WLPI F506). Harcourt used Lippmann also as idea man for large-scale book projects. In 1919 the firm gave approval for a "political classics" series, the brainchild of Lippmann, to be edited by Harold Laski (WL to Laski, August 19, 1919, WLPI F688). In 1920 Lippmann suggested that Alexander Meiklejohn, president of Amherst College, be invited to prepare "a sober and informed statement analyzing carefully the position of the teacher and the scholar under present economic conditions and the consequences for society" (WL to Alfred Harcourt, January 8, 1920, WLPI F506). In 1919 Harcourt explained the firm's plans, in which Lippmann had an important place. "What we are striving for is the most distinguished list possible in the realms of history, economics and the social sciences generally. A list that will be free from the inhibitions of many of the older houses and also free from the sentimental radicalism of most of the newer ones" (Harcourt to A. E. Zimmern, December 5, 1919, WLPI F1323).

Those who submitted to the *New Republic* and to Harcourt, and those whom Lippmann solicited, could expect from him much more than a perfunctory set of suggestions or response to material received. He usually read the works himself and gave detailed comments. One example may suffice. In 1920 the young Carter Goodrich, at the start of a long and distinguished career as economic historian that ended at Columbia University, submitted to Lippmann a manuscript on "the British labour situation" entitled "The Frontier of Control," which grew out of a project begun under Walton Hamilton at Amherst and a scholarship to study in Britain (Goodrich to WL, January 26, 1920, WLPI F465). Lippmann proceeded to give Goodrich the kind of thoughtful commentary received normally from a graduate school mentor. He began by listing "the defects of the book" and then gave detailed suggestions for how a good book might be created from what he had read thus far (WL to Goodrich, January 28, 1920, WLPI F465). There followed a correspondence about sources, readers for the final manuscript, and even solicitation of an introduction from the dreaded Seager, the author of Lippmann's undergraduate textbook. Understandably, Goodrich was extremely grateful and wrote Lippmann a long, enthusiastic letter about *Public Opinion* when it appeared two years later, saying he planned to use it as a text in his Amherst classes (Goodrich to WL, July 10, 1922, WLPI F465). By the end of the 1920s leaders of the profession had come to see Lippmann at the very least as a public spokesman for sound policy views, and he received many letters of thanks and congratulation. Frank Fetter from Princeton suggested that Lippmann publish a collection of his editorials supporting free trade.

Professional Acquaintance

Lippmann's friendships and relationships with economists and policy makers were so numerous and important to his own development that it may be useful to suggest categories by which they may be understood. First, there were those to whom he went designedly for occasional advice and comment on his thinking as it evolved. Examples include the statistician and banker Leonard Ayres, whom he met while working in the War Department and with whom he maintained a lifelong friendship; Bernard Baruch, the economic czar of World War I; Thomas Lamont, partner in J. P. Morgan; and Senator Carter Glass. Sometimes while beginning to think about a topic he would stimulate an authority to open up his heart and send a torrent of commentary. This was true especially of some senior figures in government who seemed anxious for this kind of exchange: for example, Ogden Mills, secretary of the treasury under President Hoover, and Eugene Meyer and Marriner Eccles, successive chairmen of the Federal Reserve Board. One may suspect that these interventions were simply attempts to manipulate public opinion by those in power. The tone of the correspondence, however, usually suggests two other factors at play. First, Lippmann was an excellent listener and respondent, and it must have been thrilling to connect with such a fine mind, journalist or not, on a problem on which one was engaged. Second, for scholars or bureaucrats it could be startling and exhilarating to find that their ideas, interpreted by a skilled journalist like

Lippmann, could have extraordinary impact. A mention in a Lippmann column could have dramatic results. Authors and publishers testified to how a notice by Lippmann elicited thousands of book orders and could even drive a title out of print overnight.

Carl Snyder, economist and statistician at the New York Federal Reserve Bank, who wrote Lippmann dozens of letters over the years, thanked him profusely in 1937 for the impact on his work from a single reference in a column: "I have not written to tell you how deeply I appreciated your article and the very handsome bouquet it contained. I have had from it the most surprising reaction, showing how great is the influence of gifted expositors. People, who so far as I could discover had never read four pages of anything I have written or said, have said they cannot understand the graphs et cetera, have written, wired or telephoned for copies of the paper you referred to. . . . I assure you nothing like this has happened before in more or less of the last eighteen years. So you see that you are a true wonder-worker" (Snyder to WL, November 30, 1937, WLPIII F103). Curtice Hitchcock of the Century Publishing Company wrote to tell the publisher of the *Herald Tribune* in 1939 that a single mention of an Arthur Salter book in Lippmann's column had led to sales of twelve hundred copies in New York City in one day and a sellout across the country. He said, "I don't know of any instance in publishing history where a single commendation of a book has resulted in as immediate and overwhelming a response" (Hitchcock to Ogden Reid, April 6, 1939, WLPIII F1054).

Sometimes Lippmann's approaches to potential informants were quite cunning. In 1936, while attempting to understand the contributions of the Austrian economists to the analysis of business cycles, Lippmann contacted B. M. Anderson of Chase National Bank, said to be the most prominent American Austrian at that time, with an innocent inquiry that led to an extended and mainly one-sided correspondence with Anderson. His method on this occasion was reminiscent of the one he employed with Thomas Nixon Carver almost twenty years before when writing for the *New Republic*. Since Anderson was one of the most well-known and vociferous critics of the New Deal, Lippmann's inquiry sounded delightfully innocent. He wrote: "I have been working for some years on a book on collectivism. From time to time I have seen things you have written on planning which have helped me a lot. I wonder if you could send me the whole collection on that subject? And would you also be so good as to tell me what you regard as a classic statement of the view that prices arrived at in the open market are the best regulator of production? The doctrine can be found, as I know, in Ricardo. I cannot find it explicitly in Adam Smith, though of course it is implicit in Smith" (WL to Anderson, December 24, 1936, WLPIII F85). This brought forth from Anderson just what Lippmann hoped for, a long and detailed letter of reply, with many more to follow.

Naturally, Lippmann's closest professional contacts were among the economists and others in New York City, where he lived until 1938. Professional economists who were members of the Century Club in New York, led by Carl Snyder of the Federal Reserve Bank, began to meet informally after war broke out. Even though by then he had moved to Washington, it was natural for Lippmann to be included on the list (Snyder to WL, May 4, 1942, WLPIII F683). He was ideologically and methodologically eclectic in his relationships, and among economists to whom he went for advice from time to time in New York and elsewhere were the American Institutionalists Wesley Mitchell, Alvin Johnson, Richard T. Ely, Frank Tannenbaum, and Adolf Berle. His acquaintance on the right was as strong as on the left: Henry Simons, Lionel Robbins, and Friedrich Hayek, among others. He knew the British economists Frederic Benham, William Beveridge, and Thomas Balogh; and the mainstream American economists Edwin Nourse, Harry Gideonse, E. R. A. Seligman, Herbert Feis, Jacob Hollander, Harold Moulton, F. W. Taussig, Mordecai Ezekiel, Seymour Harris, Leon Henderson, Fritz Machlup, and A. G. Hart. Those in government included Chester Bowles, Gardiner Means, and Randolph Burgess. Usually there was a reciprocal relationship in place. The case of Seligman, the distinguished Columbia economist, is a case in point. In 1916 Lippmann published an article by Seligman in the *New Republic* entitled "A National Inheritance Tax" (March 15), one of Seligman's favorite topics. Then in the 1920s, when Lippmann was at the *World*, Seligman wrote to him about public opinion (1922), then Lippmann's favorite topic; the inheritance tax again (1925); the proper role for the state in the economy (1926); and the case for a United

States of Europe (1929). Economists with bees in their bonnet or quick fixes to complex problems usually irritated Lippmann or bored him. He was adept at turning them off with a polite acknowledgment and little more. These included William Trufant Foster, Waddill Catchings, Henry S. Dennison, and Irving Fisher when arguing for 100 percent money; advocates of a commodity-backed money supply, such as Samuel Elder; and the followers of Frederick Soddy and Henry George. Lippmann was especially close to Alvin Johnson at the New School, and was comfortable with most of the growing community of Institutionalist economists in and around New York. There was a slightly sycophantic tone to some of the letters he received from some economists. For example, Richard T. Ely wrote him in 1932: "Reading your articles carefully, I feel that we are working along similar lines and reaching similar conclusions; you from your point of view and me from my point of view which is somewhat different" (Ely to WL, November 23, 1932, WLPIII F704). It is symbolic perhaps that when the Institutionalists Wesley Mitchell and Walton Hamilton wished to gain membership for a colleague in the Cosmos Club they turned to Lippmann as the third nominator.

Lippmann attended professional meetings of economists both as an occasional participant and as a reflective, and usually complimentary, journalistic observer. He remarked from the American Economic Association annual meeting in 1914: "These latter-day professors looked more like highly trained business men, and if we had been told that this was a convention of steel manufacturers or of general insurance agents, we might easily have believed. The faces were for the most part clean-shaven, and there was a plentiful representation of clear-eyed, square-chinned, decisive young men, who seemed anything but absorbed in unrealities. The time has passed when the economist was a harmless devotee of white magic and the professor a lay monk." They were unlike their nineteenth-century predecessors "somnambulistically trudging the roads hewn out of the rock by Adam Smith and Ricardo" (WL 1915a, 9). These younger economist "experts" were finding that they were useful in business and government, but still they tended to be narrow and technical, with limited vision. "The specialized economist, the capable, alert man whom we see at this convention, has not perhaps the firm grip of the early economists, and he is prone to brush aside theoretical discussions with perhaps too intolerant an indifference. His very qualities carry defects" (NR, January 2, 1915, 10). He came away from the American Economic Association meeting with nagging doubts about the usefulness to society of these modern economists when faced with the big picture. "Where in our American universities or in the American Economic Association is the scholar who will endow this class with a philosophy and an understanding?" (NR, January 2, 1915, 10).

It was not only economists who saw Lippmann as an effective spokesman for their ideas and their discipline. He was in great demand more widely, with political scientists often in the lead. Harold Laski and Graham Wallas of the London School of Economics and Charles Merriam of the University of Chicago were political scientists who came often to his door. Prominent sociologists with whom he interacted included Howard Odum and Lewis Mumford. He carried on a complex discussion of the supply-side effects of tax reductions with the influential congressman and former treasury secretary Ogden Mills, and he debated the merits of hydroelectric dams with Senator George Norris, a founder of the Tennessee Valley Authority. In history he maintained close connections with Allen Nevins, Samuel Eliot Morrison, Henry Steele Commager, and other giants of the field. Alfred Zimmern, a young historian trained in Britain but with broad interests and many connections in Europe, was introduced to Lippmann by Graham Wallas in 1911 and remained a close friend and adviser for many years. Among other things, Zimmern introduced Lippmann to Austrian economics in 1916 through an article by Ludwig von Mises, which he translated for Lippmann's use.

Prominent businessmen and lawyers contacted Lippmann with comments and usually with expressions of admiration. These read like a pantheon of leadership in the American economy of his time: Alfred P. Sloan (General Motors), Robert Brookings, F. R. Coudert, Thurman Arnold, Robert Wood (Sears Roebuck), Owen Young (General Electric), Frank Gannett (Gannett publications), Averill Harriman, David Lilienthal (Tennessee Valley Authority), and Andrew W. Mellon. Thomas Lamont, senior partner of the J. P. Morgan firm, offered commentary and information throughout the 1930s. There is the sense in this correspondence that

Lippmann was using the businessmen for information and argument while they were using him as potentially a spokesman for their ideas to the world.

An Invisible Seminar

In addition to the many professional social scientists, businessmen, and political figures to whom Lippmann went for advice and comment on specific policy issues there were a number of close friends and confidants with whom he sustained a continuing conversation on more general economic subjects extending sometimes over many years. (The group of friends with whom he felt a commitment to liberal values is dealt with in Chapter 8.) Several other members of what may be thought of as his personal seminar deserve some mention here. The most remarkable may be Russell Leffingwell, who kept up a running correspondence with Lippmann. He was a distinguished lawyer, editor of the law review when a student at Columbia, one of the founders of the Council on Foreign Relations, holder of several high positions in the Treasury Department during World War I, and partner in J. P. Morgan, rising to chairman. It was his practice very often to deconstruct one of Lippmann's columns and send the result to him. He was not destructive or carping but he made his points forcefully and effectively. He gave the Wall Street position on many subjects, but he was not always predictable. He admired Keynes but disliked many of Keynes's policy proposals. He wished to retain the gold standard until shortly before it was abandoned and he worried about inflation. When Lippmann heard from a Keynesian enthusiast, or from Keynes himself, with a position on some controversial policy issue, he knew that he could reliably hear the other side from Leffingwell.

A second member of the invisible seminar was Felix Frankfurter, friend since college days and the *New Republic,* professor at Harvard Law School, a founder of the American Civil Liberties Union, and appointed to the Supreme Court by President Roosevelt in 1939. Frankfurter reminded Lippmann often and at length of their joint roots in and responsibilities to the progressive movement, and he was especially critical of what he took to be Lippmann's loss of faith in the inherent goodness of the working class.

Perhaps with an eye to Lippmann's increasing number of friends among business leaders, Frankfurter wrote in 1933, "Of course I do not believe that vice inheres in the rich and virtue in the poor. But for too long we have been operating on the assumption that the converse is the truth, and more particularly that the rich are the guardians of wisdom and should control affairs" (Frankfurter to WL, March 11, 1933, WLPIII F817). Frankfurter's continued hectoring became too much for Lippmann, and their correspondence broke off in 1933, only to be revived in much reduced form some years later.

A third member of the small group of correspondents with whom Lippmann felt especially comfortable conversing about foundational economic and social issues was William Allen White, the beloved editor of the *Emporia* [Kansas] *Gazette,* friend of Teddy Roosevelt (D. Goodwin 2013, 13), and a founder of the Book-of-the-Month Club. Lippmann called him "a beautiful combination of John the Baptist and the Pope of our profession" (WL to Mrs. William Allen White, October 20, 1932, WLPIII F2226). White shared many of Frankfurter's values, and he too worried that Lippmann might be abandoning his progressive and liberal origins. But since he was farther away from Washington politics and in middle America, he claimed that he could take a more detached view. He was shaken by the depression and applauded Lippmann's efforts to find a solution consistent with personal freedom. He wrote in 1932: "My heart-break at liberalism is that it has sounded no note of hope, made no plans for the future, offered no program" (White to WL, April 19, 1932, WLPIII F2226). He urged Lippmann to keep his gaze above all on the working class, and one can see in his letters some of the language used later in Lippmann's columns. White wrote: "Chiefly it seems to me our job in these next few decades is to establish some sort of peace and security for those in the stratum lower than the comfortable middle class. . . . That means a redistribution of wealth, but not a greater redistribution of wealth than I have seen in my generation which has been somewhat encouraged by politics but largely has come out of the accumulation of an economic surplus" (White to WL, April 26, 1932, WLPIII F2226). He shared Lippmann's growing fear that the competitive market system was in mortal danger because of the instinct in government to restrict it. "I see absolutely no evidence that Congress has learned its lesson of the dangers in attempting to tinker with the price structure through tariffs, artificial wage scales, and subsidy loans to producers of unwanted commodities" (White to WL, undated, WLPIII F2226). White often was the voice of the farmers to Lippmann. He saw farm debts during deflation as a major obstacle to recovery. "America is being held back by her debts. Unless something is done to adjust these debts to the basis on which they were contracted, she will be crippled for a decade" (White to WL, May 7, 1932, WLPIII F2226).

A potential fourth member of Lippmann's invisible seminar was Abraham Flexner, a close friend of Lippmann and his wife over a long period. He was a senior executive of the Rockefeller Foundation, author of the Flexner Report, which modernized medical education, and founder of the Institute for Advanced Study in Princeton. Like the others in the seminar Flexner felt sufficiently comfortable with Lippmann that he could tell him exactly what he felt and be confident there would be no resentment or ill feeling. He also brought the perspective of a distinguished natural scientist to Lippmann's work. Where Leffingwell scrutinized the newspaper columns, Flexner read the books with great care. Here is how he began his review for Lippmann of *The Phantom Public*:

> I think you have completely proved two things: (1) that the atomic theory of democracy, that is, that every individual man is competent to bear the load that theoretically democracy imposes on him, is absurd; and (2) that the public as an intelligent organism does not exist. That is a good deal to have accomplished within so short a compass.
>
> I am not, however, entirely clear that you have explained just how it is that things do come to pass in a democratic country. I dare say there is no one way. Sometimes practically the entire public may get warmed up and with enormous momentum achieve a definite end—for example, when it comes to going in to war. But there are other ends, lots of them good, some of them questionable, which, it seems to me, are accomplished in other ways and in ways which, except incidentally, you do not seem to me to take into account sufficiently.
>
> Suppose, dropping all general considerations, you were to study what might be called the genesis and physiology of specific movements in this country in the last seventy-five years—slavery, hard and soft money,

humanitarian legislation, health legislation, educational legislation in the
Southern States, antivivisection, prohibition. I suspect that you would
find that democracy is that form of social and political organization which
most readily devises intensive and well directed organs, aiming at specific
ends, and that somehow what the prophets call the "remnant" thus organized acquires the energy and weight out of all proportion to its mass.
Certain it is that conservative, aristocratic societies do not produce these
organs in anything like the abundance with which they are produced in
America. Aristocracies have a way of leaving things to families or to bureaucratic experts, who are in governmental posts, though, as democracy
has invaded foreign aristocracies, specific organizations have become
more numerous and more effective. I think you would find a study of public education in the south since 1890 enormously instructive, as showing
how democracy can achieve ends which abroad are mainly left to officials.
(Flexner to WL, October 29, 1925, WLPI F399)

Flexner was chiding Lippmann about his tendency to pessimism. Every author should have such a thoughtful, candid, and responsive friend.

John Maynard Keynes: "Renaissance Man"

Lippmann's warm friendship with Maynard Keynes was the most important of his close relationships with professional economists. It began when
they served together in 1919 at Versailles and lasted until Keynes's death in
1946. To understand the closeness and longevity of this relationship it helps
to reflect on the close parallels in their careers and characters. They were
born only six years apart into family privilege and moved effortlessly
through excellent schools and universities. They both struck everyone,
even in their earliest years, as child prodigies. Despite their later engagement with economics neither was attracted to the subject at first. Their initial interests were in philosophy, literature, and the arts. They took little
economics as undergraduates and found the prospect of postgraduate study
and a full-time career in academe unappealing. They both wanted to act on
a wider stage and to speak to a larger audience with a longer list of topics
than they could envisage at even one of the best universities. They both

went through periods when they edited magazines and newspapers. By their twenties they were recognized by the political leaders of the countries in which they lived as talented and valuable, but they themselves stayed on the edge of political parties. They were shrewd businessmen, amassed substantial wealth, and lived in comfort and style. They were prolific writers and followed similar strategies of mixing serious academic works (*Treatise on Money, General Theory, Public Opinion, The Good Society*) with publications aimed at a larger audience and a richer market (*Economic Consequences of the Peace, A Preface to Morals*). By middle age both gained celebrity status enjoyed by few public intellectuals in their time. Much of the thinking of Lippmann and Keynes is remarkably congruent. They were both concerned to save democracy and free market capitalism rather than to threaten, profoundly change, or destroy them. Their evolving positions on macroeconomic questions, developed with a good deal of interaction, are very similar. Their positions on domestic market issues differ more, in part because of the different circumstances in which they lived. They were both shrewd and manipulative, and despite the warmth of their friendship it is clear that each used the other. For example, Lippmann was used by Keynes for his connections and political influence in America. Lippmann contributed to and advised Keynes about the *Manchester Guardian* supplement on Europe's Reconstruction put together by Keynes in 1922 (Keynes to WL, April 6, 1922, WLPI F656). Lippmann used Keynes for his ideas and contacts in Britain. One of Keynes's distinct contributions was to link up Lippmann and his publishers with members of the Bloomsbury Group and other artists and intellectuals: Lytton Strachey, Virginia Woolf, Leonard Woolf, E. M. Forster, Sibyl Colefax, Kenneth Clark, and Clive Bell were all part of the exchange. Keynes invited Lippmann to dine in 1921 at his Gordon Square home specifically to meet the art critic Clive Bell (Keynes to WL, December 12, 1921, WLPI F656). Here are some of Lippmann's reminiscences in 1950 of his friendship overall with Keynes:

> I have a very profound admiration for Keynes. I really believe that he's one of the most influential men of our century and that Keynes will be remembered as Adam Smith is remembered—on the same level of

eminence. I think he's changed the thinking and the policies. What he really did from my point of view, and the thing I'll always remember, is that he, to my mind, really knocked out the Marxian analysis of what capitalism had to do—the theory of the inevitability of cycles and the helplessness of man in dealing with the business cycle, which would have resulted in the overthrow of the whole free society of the world and which did result in the overthrow of the German society and the Weimar Republic. Keynes has broken that, and we know now that with all the faults of these broken states, they have a remedy against unemployment that did not exist before Keynes. Unemployment was an act of God that you couldn't do anything about. Keynes' ideas have now filtered through to the governments, and they've filtered through to the people. (R 152–153)

On a more personal level, Lippmann said:

I had general discussions with Keynes over a period of twenty years. He always visited me when he came here, and I always visited him when I went to England. We corresponded. He was sort of like a man of the renaissance. His interests were general.

I once said to him, "You know, I've only learned what economics I know since I left college. I never studied economics in college."

He said, "Neither did I. I never took an economics course the whole time I was in college." (R 153–154)

Lippmann and Keynes often exchanged ideas and manuscripts before they were published. In his introduction to the first extract from *Economic Consequences of the Peace* published in the *New Republic* Lippmann described this work eloquently and with foresight. "His book is in part a forecast of the disasters which acts of so great immorality and foolishness may possibly bring on us and in part an attempt to indicate some means of amelioration and of safety for a kind of civilization, which, in spite of its mean imperfections and recent tragical consequences is still the best starting point from which may grow humane improvements and a new social evolution for Western Europe" (NR, December 24, 1919, 103). Lippmann suggested that he first became aware of Keynes's evolving and revolutionary macroeconomic thinking when he read the *Tract on Monetary Reform* in 1923 (WL to

Joseph Davis, March 24, 1966, WLPIII F585). Lippmann was alert to defend Keynes from critics in America (e.g., WL to W. M. Reedy, May 4, 1920, WLPI F1029, concerning an article critical of Keynes in *Reedy's Mirror*, St. Louis, Missouri), and he seems to have kept up to date on the flow of Keynes's publications. He received *A Treatise on Money* as soon as it appeared, and he wrote to Alfred Harcourt: "if any human can make the theory of money clear to me it will be Keynes" (WL to Harcourt, December 10, 1930, WLPI F506). Lippmann tended to ignore attacks on Keynes from professional economists that began to appear soon after publication of the *General Theory,* but he did not conceal his enthusiasm from friends, even those he knew to be critical. He recommended Keynes to journalists and others. In 1937 he advised Arthur Krock, the *New York Times* columnist, to read the three articles recently published by Keynes in the London *Times* (WL to Krock, April 7, 1937, WLPIII F1256). He never agreed that there was a fundamental inconsistency between Keynesian doctrine and free markets. Henry Simons made this claim to him in 1938 from the University of Chicago after reading *The Good Society.*

> I was a bit annoyed, both by your tribute to Keynes and by those few pages in the text which reflect his influence. These pages reveal, to me, some of the confusion which is Mr. Keynes' main contribution to monetary discussion. Elsewhere you remark that Keynes has shown how urgent problems may be solved within the framework of the liberal system. Reviewing his last book, I remarked, casually but seriously, upon its possibilities as the economic bible of a fascist movement. There is point in both observations; but mine, I believe, is more deserving of emphasis. From the standpoint of the liberal cause, Mr. Keynes is irresponsible and untrustworthy—I say this with regard to his writing about money, disregarding his more glaring sins in the *Yale Review* article—and his followers are simply a menace, politically and intellectually. (Simons to WL, October 5, 1938, WLPIII F1949)

Lippmann apparently failed to take the bait, and there is no evidence of a response to Simons. While Lippmann may have been reluctant to praise Keynes publicly because of the controversy surrounding Keynes's "New Economics," and not wishing to be labeled a "Keynesian" or follower of any particular

doctrine, he was often working behind the scenes to advance Keynes's ideas
and reputation. In 1936 he was asked by the Harvard administration for his
views on an honorary degree for Walt Disney. Here is his reply:

> I do not know Walter Disney and have no idea what he is like personally,
> but I should not much care to see him get an honorary degree. Mickey
> Mouse is charming, but my impression is that he has commercialized his
> success to such a degree that the thing is more a factory production now
> than an artistic production. I think the idea behind the suggestion is a
> good one, however, but the particular example selected is unfortunate.
>
>   Since you give me the chance to make suggestions for honorary de-
> grees in general, I wish you would consider John Maynard Keynes. In my
> opinion he has proved himself to be, since 1919, not only the best prophet
> but it might almost be said that his views are today more influential in the
> policies of governments and central banks throughout the English speak-
> ing world than those of any other man. He is not in high favor among aca-
> demic economists in America, and of course much of his work is highly
> controversial, but he is an extraordinarily original thinker, exercises
> great influence both in practical life and in the academic world, and alto-
> gether would seem to me the living economist who is likely to be remem-
> bered the longest. I thought, for example, it was a pity he was not in-
> cluded in the Tercentenary degrees since he is a man of far greater
> reputation than the British economist to whom we gave a degree [evi-
> dently the Australian Douglas Berry Copland]. (WL to C. A. Coolidge,
> November 25, 1936, WLPIII F1004)

Keynes seems to have been fully as enthusiastic about Lippmann's contributions as Lippmann was about his. He wrote to Lord Macmillan, minister
of information, in 1939, wondering if something might be done "quite privately" to see that Lippmann's columns were "widely and promptly available" in the "neutral press, including South America, and also throughout
the Empire press." He explained: "The point of these articles is that they
are extraordinarily interesting, well-informed and serious. Rather different
in this way from almost anything. A genuine discussion, and yet readable
by a wide public, as American experience has shown" (Keynes to Macmil-

lan, December 14, 1939, Keynes Papers, Archive Center, King's College Cambridge). When Macmillan demurred on grounds of cost Keynes replied testily, "[Y]our letter confirms the prevailing opinion that money is only available for what is useless" (Macmillan to Keynes, December 18, 1939, and Keynes to Macmillan, December 19, 1939, Keynes Papers). Keynes took the idea up again with Macmillan's successor, Lord Reith, suggesting this time that the recipient newspapers of the Lippmann columns rather than the ministry pay the cable charges: "some of them have seemed to me far more effective than anything which could be written by an Englishman, particularly as they have the objectivity of a friendly neutral and are all the more convincing because they are far from free of criticisms" (Keynes to Reith, March 14, 1940, Keynes Papers).

Perhaps the second most important friendship after Keynes in the community of those with whom Lippmann shared values and perspectives over an extended period was Lewis Douglas, one of the most prominent anti-Keynesians of the time and the lone congressman from Arizona. Seeing how he balanced the conflicting views of these two close friends tells a good deal about how he was in the final analysis his own man. Douglas wrote to Lippmann in December 1931 in appreciation of a morning column he had just read that reflected "such a wise philosophy of sufficient but not too much humility." He inquired, "If it is not asking you to sink too low in the scale of human beings, may I have the pleasure of calling on you" (Douglas to WL, December 21, 1931, WLPIII F640). They met and called on each other often thereafter for more than two decades. Above all they shared with each other their views on a long succession of issues: the veterans' bonus, the gold clause in contracts, how to combat isolationism in America, the dangers of uncontrolled speculation, and fixed versus flexible exchange rates. Lippmann did with Douglas what he did with other good friends—he used him to help gauge the validity of what others with different views said. In May 1934 he asked Douglas from London if the Budget Bureau, which Douglas then directed, could provide him with data on current government expenditures that were not part of "the ordinary expenditure of the government" or "the substitution of government obligations for old private obligations." He wrote in explanation: "I have been seeing something of Keynes in the last week and he lays great stress upon the volume of excess expenditures which does not fall under either of the two categories above. His estimate is that the amount of this directly inflationary expenditure has been somewhere around 400 millions a month since January, but that it has fallen off in the month of May. Have you any figures that bear upon this point? I think the point is of sufficient importance to justify trying to put the figures together in order to see whether and to what extent there is a relationship between this type of expenditure and the increase of production throughout the country" (WL to Douglas, May 25, 1934, WLPIII F640). Clearly Lippmann was groping to understand the income multiplier. He must have known that his inquiry would elicit a strong critique of Keynes from Douglas, and he was not disappointed. This was the way in which he could check what he was hearing from one close friend against the testimony of another. Douglas wrote:

> Frankly, I have no sympathy with Keynes' point of view. What he really is saying is that you can spend your way back to recovery by confining your expenditures to objects which produce nothing. Possibly one can obtain a clearer picture of what such policy entails and where it leads in a relatively simple economy—an economy which is not as complicated as is the economy of such states as New York, Pennsylvania, New Jersey or Massachusetts. It might, therefore, be illuminating to him and to others to examine the economy of the State of Arizona, which is simple. The largest single industry and the one upon which the state depends for about 75 per cent of its activity is the copper industry. With very few exceptions the copper mines are closed down. The State is therefore producing nothing, or substantially nothing, and yet up to a month ago there was an atmosphere of hectic prosperity within the state. The question, it seems to me, for Mr. Keynes and for others who believe as he believes to answer is "How long can that prosperity last when it is producing nothing or substantially nothing?"
>
> If Mr. Keynes believes in government spending as the way out and if he believes that in the final analysis expenditures, to be effective, must be for the purpose of producing, then Mr. Keynes and others who believe apparently as he believes must go the "whole hog" and advocate govern-

ment ownership of all means of production, for it is only in industry that there can be found productive objects of expenditure.

Mr. Keynes and others are intent upon depreciation of currency as another way out, that is, depreciation in terms of foreign exchanges. It has often occurred to me that if their position be sound it might be wiser to advocate a strengthening of other currencies in relation to ours, thus avoiding the bad internal and external effects of deliberate depreciation. The appreciation can be accomplished by frankly giving away a large part of our surplus gold, by cancelling inter-governmental debts, and by reducing tariffs.

I recommend to Mr. Keynes a study of what the Constitutional Assembly in France in 1789 did. There has been very little work done on the subject. Much has been done about the Assignat period, but very little has been written on the budgetary position which led to the Assignats. As nearly as I have been able to determine, the Assembly did substantially what we have done. It balanced its ordinary budget through economies and immediately proceeded to make huge expenditures for public works and relief. The issue of Assignats paralleled the deficits thus created. I suppose that now, just as then, the argument will be made that conditions are different, that the climate is different, that the temperament of our people is different, that we have great natural resources which France did not have (remember, always, the Assignats were issued against the finest and most productive lands in France). (Douglas to WL, May 28, 1934, WLPIII F640)

Lippmann welcomed this denunciation of one friend by another, reached his own conclusions on the substance, and remained close to both. He also remained a lifelong Keynesian.

The wide panoply of sources and contacts discussed in this chapter might seem like a recipe for confusion, but Walter Lippmann made of it his own distinct community. In assembling and deploying such a distinguished group of interlocutors, he demonstrated that it was not necessary for a prolific public intellectual of the first rank to be lodged in a university or some other comparable establishment. A journalist could lead the life of a public economist in comparative isolation.

3

"You Can Always Tell a Harvard Man"

It remains a puzzle how Lippmann, with all his responsibilities as author, editor, and political journalist, kept up so well with the fast-moving social sciences and academic affairs in general during the turbulent depression years. Part of the explanation lies undoubtedly in his voracious reading, his extended friendships, and his development of a complex set of intellectual relationships discussed in Chapter 2. But unlike conventional academics he did not have daily exchanges with colleagues, the stimulus of classroom teaching, time specifically designated for serious research, or participation in professional societies to sustain his intellectual engagement and keep him on the frontier. He made up for a good deal of this lack through his remarkably close association with Harvard University from his days as an undergraduate to the end of his life.

The University in the Good Society

Two dominant questions in Lippmann's mind from *A Preface to Politics* onward were, first, how the social sciences broadly defined could be applied effectively to society's emerging problems, and second, how citizens might be educated through the social sciences about the policy choices before them. The elite universities, he concluded, must play a key role in answering these questions. He expressed this view eloquently in a column celebrating Harvard's three hundredth anniversary in 1936. He began by reaffirming the claim made by his friend Keynes in the same year about the ultimate power of ideas; surely, he said, universities had special responsibilities as the unique custodians of these ideas. "Through centuries of war, revolution, and catastrophe, with nothing but men's faith to protect them, they have persisted as witnesses to the fact that a great idea is the most enduring of all foundations" (HT 5/26/36). Lippmann appreciated that the role of university faculty as policy advisers was a delicate one; they must be well informed and relevant, but they must not be too close to their policy clients. The right relationship must be carefully established. "This is the appropriate moment in the history of the world to celebrate the idea of a university and to take the occasion to define and to reaffirm most especially the basic relation between teaching and scholarship on the one hand, and the power and the policies of government on the other. . . . There are many not only in the European despotisms but here as well, that do not hold that view, who think, to put it bluntly, that the politicians should run the professors or that the professors should run the politicians. Thus there are those who would reduce the universities to the position of bureaus in the ministry of propaganda and there are those who would invite them to become the advisers of politicians, the directors and planners of national policy." But the worst response universities could make to these two alternative strategies would be to say a pox on both your houses and withdraw from their contacts with society. "Against these two views, the one crudely destructive, the other subtly destructive, of the advancement of learning, the celebrations this year will affirm the principle that if the universities are to do their work they must be independent and they must be disinterested. The meaning of this principle can perhaps be grasped most readily by saying that while popular government cannot be operated without parties, it cannot be worked by parties alone. Outside the party system there must be independent authorities in whom the people have confidence. Where popular governments have been successful these independent non-partisan authorities are invariably strong and greatly respected" (HT 5/26/36). Universities must tread the fine line between independence and direct influence and fearlessly offer advice while eschewing party politics.

> The choice has to be made. If there are to be universities which are not controlled by the government, if there are to be universities free of the government because they are privately endowed, if in accepting these endowments the universities are to be able to insist on their freedom from the promptings of private interest, then the universities themselves must also renounce the ambition to play a part in partisan political controversy. This does not mean that professors must not be consulted in matters where they are professionally competent. But it does mean that professors must not be office holders and political advisors to office holders. For once they engage themselves that way, they cease to be disinterested men, being committed by their ambitions and their sympathies. They cease to be scholars because they are no longer disinterested, and having lost their own independence, they impair the independence of the university to which they belong. (HT 5/26/36)

At the Harvard birthday party in which he took part Lippmann turned again to the role of universities in guarding the truth, this time with a more optimistic tone. "They have a more ancient title than any government to define the human destiny: they draw upon the deepest allegiances of civilized men, and the conscience which they inform will in the end judge—it will not be judged by—the policies of states. In the final recording the question will not be whether the universities have served the contemporary purposes of states and of the partisans within them. It will be whether states have been loyal to that great tradition of order actuated by the love of truth of which the universities are the appointed guardians" (HT 9/17/36).

All this being said Lippmann did not approach his alma mater solely with adulation and applause. Indeed, quite the contrary. He reacted to it as he did to other social institutions and asked how it could be made better and specifically in what ways it might be improved. After leaving Harvard he maintained close and continuing links, always with his early experiences in the background, some satisfying ones and others less so. He was naturally involved with any program at Harvard related to journalism, and he was instrumental in the establishment of the Nieman Fellows in 1937, supported with a bequest from the widow of the publisher of the *Milwaukee Journal*. The program describes itself now as "the oldest and best known study program for journalists in the world." Lippmann was brought in at the start. He set forth his suggestions for the "controlling principles" of such a program in a letter to President James Bryant Conant in 1936. He urged that the program be for advanced postgraduates who already had some experience in journalism. "The opportunity, then, should be offered to them not as a chance to learn anything more about journalism, but as an opportunity to improve their general education and to specialize in the fields where they are already working" (WL to Conant, May 13, 1936, WL-PIII F1004). He rejected the notion of a curriculum constructed especially for journalists; fellows should be guided in their choices of graduate courses but should not be directed. "Thus their own demonstrated interest and competence would become the guiding principle of the work they undertook at Harvard, and no special organization would be required. It seems to me that all that would be needed would be the money for the scholarships plus two or three men willing to spend a good deal of time advising them on courses." Rather than a program to expose scholars to the possibility of a career in journalism Lippmann wanted a program in the liberal arts that would provide some training to the best young journalists, especially in the social sciences. The biggest challenge might be to persuade publishers that it was in their interest to allow their best staff upon whom they depended to take up a fellowship. Conant replied that Lippmann's ideas were "just what I had in mind" (Conant to WL, May 20, 1936, WLPIII F1004). Lippmann was quite critical of the first class of Nieman fellows (WL to Conant, November 25, 1938, WLPIII F1004), but he remained close to the program as it evolved, and he left a generous bequest in his will for its support. The building housing the program was named after him in 1979. At the dedication fellow columnist James Reston remarked, "[H]e had trouble reconciling the perversity of human character with his own quest for The Good Society, the folly of man's indifference with his own search for truth" (WLPIII F2339).

President Conant asked Lippmann regularly for advice about the relationship between Harvard and the media, especially how to obtain good coverage in the major newspapers (e.g., Conant to WL, January 9, 1934, and WL to Conant, May 21, 1937, WLPIII F1004). Lippmann even kept track of the student newspaper, the Harvard *Crimson*. In 1934 he complained to Conant of unsubstantiated rumors published in the paper about Rexford Tugwell. "Now obviously if unfounded and irresponsible rumors are to be published on the front page of the Harvard *Crimson* it's going to be extremely difficult for the university to complain when commercial newspapers publish unfounded and irresponsible stories. . . . when you work out your publicity policy the question of how to get the Crimson into responsible hands and to hold it to decent standards will be quite as important as how to deal with Boston newspapers" (WL to Conant, January 9, 1934, WLPIII F1004).

A Better Economics Department

From the time he left Harvard in 1909 Lippmann returned often to maintain contacts and check his thinking with Frank Taussig, Allyn Young, and others in the Economics Department whom he respected. Typically the faculty were pleased with the way in which he interpreted economics at the *New Republic,* the *World,* and the *Herald Tribune.* The high regard for Lippmann at Harvard seldom flagged. Typically, Taussig wrote him in 1924: "Let me say just a word in appreciation of the way in which you are handling the editorial columns of '*The World.*' You are doing all that we expected of you, and that is saying a great deal. I do not always agree with you, but what you say always makes me sit up and think; and it always makes me respect the intellectual quality and moral spirit which pervade it" (Taussig to WL, June 20, 1924, WLPI F1192). Later, Taussig wrote more succinctly: "Everything you write is good" (Taussig to WL, March 8, 1928, WLPI F1192). Apart from the economists on the faculty he had a number of other close friends at Harvard and in the environs with whom he visited and with whom he often stayed, including his old mentor Santayana in philosophy, Felix Frankfurter in the Law School, Arthur Holcomb in the Government Department, and Ellery Sedgwick, editor of the *Atlantic Monthly,* in which he published the first version of *The Good Society.*

Lippmann's opportunity to explore serious reform at Harvard began in 1929 when he was appointed to the Committee to Visit the Department of Government, and then the committees for Harvard College in 1931 and the Department of Economics in 1933. In 1933 he was elected to the Harvard Board of Overseers for a six-year term and he became chair of the economics visiting committee. He was told informally that this last position was largely honorific and that his main functions would be to hold an annual dinner and raise a little money for the department. But such instructions would not do for Walter Lippmann. He began by rejecting the fund-raising responsibility, explaining how as far as he was concerned a journalist should never seek funds for any purpose from those he might be required to criticize in the future. Then, he announced in a letter to the committee that their true function, as their charge implied, was seriously to appraise the Economics Department and make recommendations to the university administration for improvement. The committee membership he inherited was made up mainly of Wall Street lawyers and bankers, and to these he added some remarkable movers and shakers and good friends: Alvin Johnson, director of the New School for Social Research; Roger Baldwin, founding director of the American Civil Liberties Union; and Christian Herter, a promising young politician making his first run for Congress who would later serve as governor of Massachusetts and secretary of state. Lippmann made it clear to his committee that he wanted them to learn a lot about the department by meeting the faculty, reading their books and articles, and checking them out with economists elsewhere. Baldwin in particular devoted considerable time to his new responsibilities and conducted a serious review. He reported to Lippmann with a detailed document attached: "I not only spent some time at Harvard attending classes and consulting members of the faculty and students, but I have talked with the presidents of a number of universities and with the heads of Economics Departments" (Baldwin to WL, May 2, 1939, WLPIII F2348). In due time Baldwin suggested for appointment by Harvard "Gardiner Means, Walton Hamilton, Jacob Viner, Mordecai Ezekiel, Clarence Ayres (now at the University of Texas) and Broadus Mitchell (at Johns Hopkins). These are not men of the age indicated in your visiting committee's last report, 25 to 35, but they are men of national reputation of a stamp considerably different from any of those now on the Harvard faculty" (Baldwin to WL, February 1, 1938, WLPIII F2348). There is no evidence that these suggestions were welcome or were followed up.

In a rare and remarkable example of an external noneconomist proposing to reform a prominent economics department Lippmann set himself three goals for the six years that he would have as chair of the visiting committee: to improve the faculty, to reconstruct the curriculum, and to reconsider the appropriate role for an economics professor in society. These seem like obtrusive goals for an outsider, but Lippmann did not see himself as outside the Harvard community. As an alumnus he remained a part of it. He had only a narrow window, from 1933 until 1939, in which to achieve these ambitious objectives. In 1933 most of the department members from Lippmann's days as a student were either gone or nearing retirement, and the main challenge he saw was to reload the faculty. The first obstacle was the chair, Harold Burbank, who was apparently not very interested in making changes. Lippmann's strategy was to enter into a quiet conspiracy with President Conant and Dean Kenneth Murdock to bypass the chair and proceed from on high. Lippmann agreed to conduct an evaluation of the existing faculty and pass along the impressions of his committee and their external contacts to these administrators.

Following a meeting with the senior faculty in 1935 he wrote about some of them to Conant. Although the department considered Edward Mason and Edward Chamberlin to be their most promising members, Lippmann was unenthusiastic. He told Conant: "I came away with a strong impression that Mason was probably the type of very useful teacher who fits well into the routine of a job and might make a very excellent chairman of the department, but that he is not likely to make important contributions to economic science. . . . As to Chamberlin, I gather that he is regarded as the most original thinker that the department has produced. And that he is the man looked upon as most likely to do really important work. I ventured to raise the point that his book was unnecessarily obscure and that this might be a sign of a certain lack of intellectual mastery. Nobody agreed with me, but I have a distinct reservation nevertheless. No doubt there are branches of mathematical economics that I could never hope to understand, but the kind of book that Chamberlin has written deals with a subject on which I have read a great deal, and I have found that really good men on the subject manage to make themselves pretty clear to an attentive reader" (WL to Conant, February 28, 1935, WLPIII F2345).

Lippmann found the younger faculty even less promising than the older ones. Seymour Harris "appears to be a respectable, plodding, uninspired fellow. And this impression which I got from the talk fits in with the impression I got from his book, which is a mountain of unorganized root facts. I suppose there would always be a subordinate place in a department for a man of that sort." By contrast Overton Taylor, the historian of economics, "appears to be something of a genius with the eccentricities of a genius. And everything I heard about him made me feel that he was well worth watching carefully and very sympathetically. He cultivates a philosophical treatment of economics, which I think of extreme importance as a balance to the tremendous concentration in the department on statistical and mathematical economics" (WL to Conant, February 28, 1935, WLPIII F2345).

The best hope for improvement in the Harvard faculty, Lippmann concluded, would be to bring in new faculty from outside the university. In particular he wanted more economists who were engaged with the exciting economic issues of the time. But here he found major obstacles: the department seemed unfamiliar with good outsiders and was not inclined to look for them. He told Conant: "I had a long private talk with Burbank about outside men, and came away with the impression that the department was not as well acquainted as it might be with men in their thirties who have not made an academic reputation, but who might be just the men we're looking for. Here is an example of what I mean: I asked Burbank whether the department had considered Winfield Riefler, who was associated with the Federal Reserve Board in Washington. Burbank had heard of Riefler, but he had clearly never considered him. By coincidence, a few hours later, I learned that Flexner had got Riefler for his Institute of Advanced Studies in Princeton. Now Flexner is a very good judge of originality in scholarship, and if Riefler was good enough for him he was good enough to have been carefully considered by Harvard. Then I mentioned Leon Henderson, who is chief economist of the N.R.A., and incidentally its most effective critic. Burbank had never heard of him. These two incidents make me feel that the search for first rate men is not being carried out as effectively as you would probably wish it to be and that it probably will not be carried out until there is younger and more vigorous leadership in the department itself. I am writing this, of course, in the spirit of your own request to me some weeks ago for very frank and entirely confidential comment, and what I say is absolutely personal and doesn't represent my committee" (WL to Conant, February 28, 1935, WLPIII F2345).

Perhaps because of his own interest in the mid-1930s in industrial relations and the causes of the Great Depression, Lippmann complained that the Harvard Economics Department lacked both a good labor economist and a competent macro theorist. To fill the first gap he proposed Leo Wolman, then at Columbia and formerly at the University of Michigan and the New School for Social Research in New York, and much involved with the labor conflict of the time. This suggestion caused some controversy among the members of his visiting committee and others in the university. One committee member from the business community wrote to him: "The opposition to Mr. Wolman of which I have heard seems to center around his race [presumably that he was Jewish] and the fact that he is considered by some a radical and a member of the so-called Brain Trust. As to the question of race or religion, that in no way has any influence on me, and I personally would never think of making a decision for or against a man on these lines. I should dislike very much, however, to add to the university staff at the present time anyone who might be considered a radical in the extreme sense of that word, as I believe the university has suffered in the minds of many people from the activities of at least one of the staff during the last year" (Orrin G. Wood to WL, June 8, 1934, WLPIII F2344). The president of the New York Stock Exchange, another member of his committee, wrote: "I have a very distinct reservation in advocating his [Wolman's] appointment to this position in view of the fact that he is now, and probably will be for some time, so busily engaged in Washington and elsewhere. It would seem to me that the University should have its Professors working full time at their jobs, and giving their entire endeavor and interest in the same direction. In the case of Wolman this would seem highly impossible for some time to come" (Richard Whitney to WL, June 14, 1934, WLPIII F2344). By contrast Thomas Lamont, another financier, thought Wolman's appointment would be "an admirable one" (Lamont to WL, June 20, 1934, WLPIII F2344). After all parties had finally given their approval of Wolman's appointment he declined the offer and remained at Columbia for the rest of his career. He also remained a lifelong friend of Lippmann.

For the macroeconomic position Lippmann urged the university to bring back Lauchlin Currie, who had left Harvard for government service on the advice of Dean Kenneth Murdock when it seemed "the situation in his Department was such that he could not hope for completely just consideration of his merits" (Murdock to WL, June 4, 1934, WLPIII F2344). Lippmann informed the dean: "Unless I am greatly mistaken, and judging only by reading the book [*The Supply and Control of Money in the United States,* 1935], he is much more the sort of person we seem to be looking for than, let us say, Professor Seymour Harris who has just been recommended for appointment as Associate Professor in the same field that Currie works in" (WL to Murdock, May 22, 1935, WLPIII F2345). Lippmann invited Currie to lunch in New York in June 1935 to discuss the matter and reported to Murdock that Currie wished to spend one more year in Washington and then return to "academic work." "However he was already in conversation with the University of Chicago about an appointment" (WL to Murdock, June 6, 1935, WLPIII F2345). Murdock wrote to Burbank about the possibility of reappointing Currie but predicted to Lippmann that "it will do no good and will simply provoke from him a statement that Currie is a dangerous person who believes in inflation or some equivalent remark" (Murdock to WL, June 10, 1935, WLPIII F2345). Apparently Murdock predicted correctly. The department was said to be too scattered to hold a meeting on the subject, and Lippmann's suggestion was not raised again.

Lippmann's first report as chair of the Economics Department visiting committee was in 1936 and when printed and published attracted attention in the national press (HT 7/1/36 and Holcomb to WL, July 7, 1936, WLPIII

F1064). It is the sort of thoughtful, balanced, and carefully constructed document that is today prepared regularly by external visitors for units of a university. He touched delicately on many of the large questions facing the department: relations with the burgeoning Graduate School of Business; pressures from undergraduates; criteria for appointment, promotion, and tenure of faculty; and research priorities. He concluded by addressing two of the most sensitive issues before the department. First, should a job candidate's or a faculty member's views on public policy be taken into account in employment decisions? This issue was especially salient because one of the instructors in the department had recently disputed public statements by former president Abbott Lawrence Lowell. Lippmann insisted that a conflict arose "only where the governing authorities do not respect the principle of free inquiry or where teachers do not respect the criteria of scholarship." He voiced what amounted to a ringing defense of academic freedom for all university faculty members: "The question is whether or not he arrived at his views by thorough scholarship and by intellectual processes which command the respect of his peers. . . . He is judged by whether his intellectual and emotional processes conform with the traditions of scholarship. If they do, he is eligible for appointment on the principle that a university must put its final trust in the beneficent working of honest, self-disciplined and scholarly inquiry" (report contained in WLPIII F1004).

The second issue was related to the first and was whether a faculty member could legitimately spend time away from the university on activities that were not clearly either teaching or research. This question had been raised by some of the businessmen on the visiting committee who had difficulty seeing why the familiar employer-employee relationship should not hold at the university. Lippmann responded again with an eloquent defense of activities by academics in civil society that were not directly related to their regular university employment. "The question is whether the outside activity is incidental to the man's teaching and research or vice versa. Where is his primary field of interest? If he regards his position on the faculty as a base for a public career, we believe he should be invited to devote all his time to the public service. If, on the other hand, and, in the concrete instances we have observed this is predominantly the case, he treats his public activity as clinical experience and an opportunity for study, we see no reason for any criticism. The distinction, while it may appear to be a subtle one when stated in the abstract, is real and usually obvious enough in practice. It is a distinction which scholars will have no great difficulty in making" (report contained in WLPIII F1004).

The Economist in Civil Society

Lippmann's impassioned defense of academic freedom in the 1936 report was in timely anticipation of the promotion cases of two instructors in economics, J. Raymond Walsh and Alan R. Sweezy, that came to a head in 1937 when they were not granted second-term reappointments before the decision was made about the desirability of their permanent tenure. Perhaps without sufficient reason the cases became a landmark in the struggle for academic freedom in American universities. Both men were on the political left and members of the teachers union, and so it was suspected that they were terminated ("ousted" was the term used in the *Boston Beacon*) for political reasons. The facts are difficult to determine with confidence, but it appears that the Economics Department was informed that with the financial constraints of the depression they could not promote additional junior faculty for at least two years. They took this to mean that they could recommend candidates for promotion but could not expect action until after the two years had passed, and so positive recommendations on Walsh and Sweezy were put forward. The president and the dean of Arts and Sciences, on the other hand, took this action by the Economics Department to mean that they understood that all recommendations during these two years, no matter how meritorious, would be turned down. There was widespread suspicion throughout the university and in the public that both the department and the administration wished to be rid of these candidates, who were perceived as troublesome, and that each was attempting to blame the other party. A petition was signed by 131 members of the Harvard faculty asking for a full inquiry by a committee of nine senior professors that were named.

Lippmann was brought into this controversy from the beginning, indeed even before the beginning. In 1932, probably because of his recent appointment to the Harvard College visiting committee and the tenor of his columns at the time, he received a plaintive cry for help and "direction" from one of the candidates, J. Raymond Walsh, whom he did not know at that time. Walsh wrote in part:

> The situation will be familiar to you. A few of us here at Harvard, instructors and graduate students in the Department of Economics, have become increasingly burdened with the seeming remoteness of the College from the difficulties that beset the world. We have had, or are having, reasonably good training in a field of academic work that should possess unusual practical importance at the moment. We have a good bit of disinterestedness, I think, that kind of eagerness to sink individually into something larger than ourselves that a College experience can engender. With such a disposition, and such a moderate amount of professional equipment, and with the world needing disinterested men on a thousand fronts, the personal question strikes us most forcefully: Is there not something that we can do, deliberately not accidentally? Can we not be used in some minor way, as obscure cogs in a far-reaching organization of the reconstructive forces of the world? To fail to have some contact with such events as these, other than that which comes from a discussion of them, appeals to us as a deep failure indeed, one that would seem to leave our lives without a center.
>
> But we can't seem to get an answer to the question. Heavy despair and inertia rest on so many to whom we might turn. Others, in positions of national leadership, do not speak with confidence nor with insight— nor often times with honesty. Or so it seems.
>
> This is the reason I write to you. (Walsh to WL, April 26, 1932, WLPIII F2323)

While reading this lament Lippmann must have felt some pangs of memory of his own frustration while studying the social sciences at Harvard almost a quarter century before. He too had been seized by urgent contemporary problems and had been disturbed by the apparent unconcern of the economists. Lippmann agreed to meet with Walsh and his colleagues, but there is no record of whether this happened. As far as we know Lippmann's next contact with Walsh was after he had learned the instructor would not receive tenure.

President Conant spelled out the circumstances of the Walsh-Sweezy case to Lippmann as clearly as he could in April 1937 and asked for advice (Conant to WL, April 13, 1937, WLPIII F1004). Lippmann consulted with Judge Learned Hand and Alvin Johnson, two of his most trusted friends, and they all agreed that an impartial committee should be appointed immediately to investigate and clear the air. After first agreeing to this strategy Conant then changed his mind. He wrote Lippmann: "The situation seems to be quieting down and after careful consideration and sampling of opinion here and there, I have decided to reverse my opinion in regard to the question of an outside committee's making an investigation at this time . . . even an investigation by you, as Chairman of the Committee to Visit the Department, might be misunderstood at this time and stir up certain aspects of the controversy which we hope will tend to quiet down. I should be particularly fearful of the consequences if you were to interview the younger members of the staff" (Conant to WL, April 22, 1937, WLPIII F1004). Lippmann doubted that the matter would indeed quiet down, and he was right. After consulting with Taussig and others he became convinced that much of the fault lay with Chairman Burbank and some action should be taken quickly in that direction. He replied to Conant:

> Now if we are to apply the general principles contained in the Report to the Overseers, it is of the utmost importance that the department itself should make the recommendations without bias, with a broad sense of intellectual responsibility, and with imagination about the development of economic science. I am afraid that under the present chairman the quality of the department does not meet these requirements, and I am inclined to think that that may be the basic cause of this whole trouble; that the trouble will be repeated until there is a new chairman and a change in the center of authority within the department itself. After all, while there is little doubt that the principles of the report are the right principles for maintaining academic freedom, you do have the

responsibility of seeing to it that there is a healthy intellectual atmosphere in these autonomous departments. Three years' contact with it
has convinced me that the atmosphere is not healthy. (WL to Conant,
May 5, 1937, WLPIII F1004)

Lippmann also assured Dean Murdock that "I am satisfied that a grave personal injustice has been done to Walsh and Sweezy personally, and I also
am satisfied in my own mind that there has been a serious error of judgment
which should be repaired" (WL to Murdock, May 5, 1937, WLPIII F1004).
Working closely with his friend and fellow overseer, the lawyer Grenville
Clark, Lippmann concluded that the only thing for Conant to do was to welcome an inquiry by the committee of nine and manage the news as much as
possible, a practice with which he had some experience. The letter from
Conant to the overseers announcing this policy on May 26, 1937 looks like it
was written by Lippmann, and probably it was (see WL to Conant, May 21,
1937, WLPIII F1004). Conant wrote to Lippmann on May 29, "May I express
again my deep gratitude to you for your assistance in that matter . . . your
help was invaluable" (Conant to Lippmann, May 29, 1937, WLPIII F1007).
The nine committee members submitted their report on May 2, 1938, and
found that there had been lack of communication between the dean, the president, and the department, as well as "defective administrative procedure connected with the President's ruling." They recommended that "the injustice
be remedied, so far as possible," even though by this date both Walsh and
Sweezy had resigned from the university. After this slap on the wrist from the
committee, President Conant accepted the report and the matter died down.

Lippmann's second and final report from the Economics Visiting Committee was oral, not printed, perhaps because of the attention attracted to
its published predecessor. Here he dwelt especially on what he considered
to have been the unfortunate separation of the study of economics from
studies of government and history, and he wondered whether it was too late
to achieve some recombination of these disciplines in the first two undergraduate years at least, bringing together "in these courses a progressive
education in economics, government, sociology and history, confining the
specialized courses to the junior and senior years and the graduate school.
I am wondering whether undergraduate instruction could not best be orga-

nized around a study of the classical texts in political science, with the appropriate history accompanying them, so that at the end of his undergraduate course the student would have a systematic and connected acquaintance with what the most influential thinkers have had to say, from antiquity to recent times" (WLPIII F2348). In other places Lippmann called for internationalization of the undergraduate social sciences curriculum so that students could reach conclusions about policy alternatives from examining the experience of other countries. He wrote to Ellery Sedgwick in 1939: "My own conviction, after six years on the Overseers dealing with the Departments of Economics and Government, is growing to be that the academic problem arising out of the elective system, graduate specialization, and stabilized or shrinking university income are insoluble without a drastic change in the curriculum and that the clue to the kind of change needed can be found at St John's [College, Maryland]" (WL to Sedgwick, January 11, 1939, WLPIII F1916). When in 1936 Lippmann was named chair of the Visiting Committee to the Philosophy Department, as well as of the Economics Committee, he responded that he would be "delighted because I spent more time in that department than in any other when I was at college, did a little teaching there, and care very much about it. Also it is a nice calm place compared with Economics in this troubled world. Now if we can succeed in marrying the Department of Philosophy with the Department of Economics we shall really accomplish something!" (WL to Allison Burr, November 5, 1936, WLPIII F340).

The start of the war and the end of his term as overseer in 1939 took Lippmann away from his close involvement with Harvard's internal affairs. He was somewhat disappointed, no doubt, by what seemed to have been a limited impact over the decade. He could not resist a parting shot. In 1933 he had advised his close friend Thomas Lamont to provide an endowment to Harvard for "university professors" who would be genuinely engaged in interdisciplinary activities of all kinds. Now President Conant asked Lamont whether in light of financial exigency these funds could be used instead to relieve the current budget crisis in the social sciences, perhaps naming some current faculty members such as Sumner Slichter "university professors." Lippmann urged Lamont to hold firm to the original intent, and he restated his views about the need for reforms.

I feel that the plan he suggests is tantamount to abandoning the policy he announced when he was inaugurated. To devote your gift to supplementing the budgets of three departments, is, it seems to me, to confess publicly the failure of his original plan to surmount the departmentalization of knowledge. It merely perpetuates the evil that his policy and your gift were designed to remedy. Professor Slichter will not be a university professor; I do not see that he will be doing anything which he is not now doing. The use of the money for this purpose will relieve but only temporarily, I think, the budgetary difficulty in three departments but it will not relieve the vice of departmentalization.

Moreover, my own observations have convinced me that the budgetary problem and, its corollary, the personnel problem, arise out of departmentalization and specialization, and that they are not curable in the long run except by a drastic reorganization of the curriculum. Therefore, I hate to see this endowment used as a palliative for the budget instead of its being reserved as fresh capital for the support of a revised curriculum.

I feel that in essence Mr. Conant is proposing to invest new capital to cover old deficits, and I do not think this is sound or wise. I think it will hardly encourage others to give new money to Harvard if they see that after all the promises of six years ago, this anti-climax is the result.

So I hope this money will be reserved for the original purpose, and I should much prefer to see it kept in cold storage until the University really has a man and a policy and a plan which will realize the original idea. For that idea was more than a good idea. It indicates the direction the University will have to take if it is to solve the budgetary problem, the personnel problem, and above all the intellectual problem in the field of the social sciences. (WL to Lamont, December 13, 1939, WLPIII F1279)

This seems to have been the last intervention by Lippmann in Harvard affairs before World War II took all of his attention. His recommendation about the Lamont gift was not accepted, and Sumner Slichter became Lamont Professor of Economics.

LIPPMANN'S INTENSE INVOLVEMENT with Harvard University during the 1930s, and especially with the Economics Department, demonstrates the depths of his engagement with the academic world at the time that he was addressing critical issues of public policy. It also shows the high regard for him in the university world as an academic player, not as a conventional scholar but as a serious intellectual with a complex role deserving of respect. Lippmann revealed remarkable self-confidence, even hubris, in setting out as an outsider with few academic credentials to reform one of the major departments in one of the great universities of the world. It should be no surprise that in this he accomplished relatively little.

4

Recovery

WHERE THEN DID Walter Lippmann stand when he began his extraordinarily successful newspaper column in 1931? He had sampled many of the main intellectual disciplines in the humanities, the arts, and the social sciences, with emphasis on philosophy, political science, law, economics, and psychology. He had concluded that he would never be comfortable specializing in just one, but he was excited at the challenge of making combinations among them. Within economics he had been exposed to classical economics, socialist doctrine, evolving Institutionalist ideas, and the new Keynesian macroeconomics. He felt most comfortable with the last two. His contacts and friendships were remarkably wide and rich. In addition to prominent economists he could call for advice from partners in J. P. Morgan, distinguished scientists, labor leaders, or even an occasional president or prime minister. His main concentration on economics began at the start of the 1930s and ended after the Second World War. When he tried to understand the prospects for postwar inflation in 1946 he wrote to Seymour Harris: "I feel like a man who learned to speak a little French, but hasn't spoken it for so long is afraid he can't say what he means" (WL to Harris, October 4, 1946, WLPIII F998).

Possible careers Lippmann had considered, or sampled briefly, were in the academic world, investigative journalism, public service at the municipal, state, and high federal levels, and the editing of a major magazine and an influential daily newspaper. None of these had continuing fascination for him, and some caused deep unease. Life as a university professor was perhaps the only one that had some attraction, and perhaps his problematic experience with Harvard tipped the balance away from that. He settled more and more on a permanent career as an independent columnist. He was importuned with job offers for other careers from all over before and after the *New York World* folded in 1931, and his response to one is revealing. After he delivered a commencement address at the University of North Carolina in 1930 he was approached by a well-connected North Carolina journalist who said he believed there were enough enthusiastic board members to support his election as university president. There was nothing wrong with the university, this man wrote, "except there has been no education done there for many years" and now it was challenged by "an enormous pile of stones, arranged somewhat gothically, by Mr. Duke's money" only twelve miles away (Ben Dixon MacNeill to WL, May 27, 1930, WLPI F774). Lippmann expressed gratitude for the inquiry but explained: "It is more fun to write than it is to be an executive of any kind, however noble, however useful, however honorific. I could not endure being a public character. I have had just enough direct experience of being a public official never to want to have anything remotely resembling it again. That's about all there is to it" (WL to MacNeill, May 29, 1930, WLPI F774).

The life that appealed most to Lippmann was that of his British Fabian friends, to whom he had been introduced by Graham Wallas, a life that combined serious scholarly endeavor with civic engagement, public education, politics at a distance, and to some degree with creative literature and the arts. The best way to achieve this life in America, he concluded, was as a newspaper columnist. In this role he took on enormous challenges, since the beginning of his new career coincided with the onset of the Great Depression. His good friend Felix Frankfurter helped him to spell out what his objectives should be at this time. "The very title of your column, 'Today and Tomorrow,' has made me assume that your purpose is very different from that of the daily editorial writer, and that your central aim is more towards a wider, perhaps even remoter, education of public opinion than the promoter of this or that *ad hoc* piece of public business" (Frankfurter to WL, April 7, 1932, WLPIII F816). At the naming of Lippmann House at Harvard in 1979 James Reston suggested that "it should be dedicated to the ideal Walter had in mind—of bringing the thought of the university into the daily press—and also the personal ideal of living the private life of a professor at the salary of a columnist" (WLPIII F2339).

Finding the Problem

When World War II ultimately wound down and Lippmann faced a postwar world, looking back he wondered what had caused the economic disasters of the previous two decades. He concluded that they were the result mainly of mistaken thinking that, sadly, was "from twenty-five to fifty years behind the times . . . we have been trying to conduct American affairs in the twentieth century with minds formed in the nineteenth century" (HT 8/17/43). The principles used to confront the depression in the early 1930s, he claimed at that time, were part of "the dogmatic debris of the post-war muddle" (HT 11/25/32). Three aspects of economic thinking had been at fault. First, after World War I the United States had refused to take part in multinational institutions that would restructure the world economy. American leaders held to the mistaken belief that the global economic system, if left alone, would organize itself spontaneously and optimally in the face of the decline of empires and the dislocation of war. There was no need for intervention of any kind. The United States could remain in splendid isolation, benefiting from flows of trade and investment but not getting more deeply involved in what they considered were the corrupt peccadilloes of the old world. The United States was exceptional, the city on the hill, and should maintain her purity and her safety through isolation from all that her immigrant population had left behind. The previous century of the Pax Britannica leading up to World War I, interpreted through classical economic theory, seemed to demonstrate conclusively that, for the United

States at least, laissez faire was always the best policy internationally as well as at home. This interpretation gave America a false sense of security and led to the comforting conviction that there was no obligation to exert leadership on the global stage then or in the future. In this respect "our failure to adjust our thinking and our diplomacy to the realities made the 20s and the 30s a period not of reconstruction after the other war, but the prelude to the next war" (HT 8/18/43).

The second kind of mistaken thinking of the interwar years grew not only from isolationism but also from undeveloped macroeconomics, both in theory and application: "We did not understand why in this century a condition of reasonably stable full employment must be a paramount purpose of national policy . . . that the involuntary unemployment of able-bodied workers has in the modern world become intolerable. It is intolerable because they have votes and political power and enough education to use them. It is intolerable because, owing to the progress of economic science, involuntary unemployment has become a preventable disease" (HT 8/17/43). Failures in macroeconomic thinking occurred within the economics profession and the market economy as well as among policy makers in government.

The third failure of economic thinking grew out of the circumstance that for over two centuries America had enjoyed the status of international debtor and had not learned how to behave as a major creditor. In particular, despite the large war debts that the Allies incurred during World War I, the United States took steps to limit imports, the main means whereby debtors could obtain foreign exchange to service and repay the debts. The result was that international obligations to the United States, if repaid at all, tended to be paid in gold, resulting in dislocations of various kinds, including deflation in the paying countries and a crisis for the gold standard system. Despite this new reality of creditor status the United States rejected all responsibility to help construct an international exchange system to replace the gold standard and to rethink the consequences of international debt: "For the twenty years between the two wars we had the mentality, and we clung to the policies, of a debtor nation. The boy had become a man. But the man behaved like a boy. As a result our commercial and financial policies brought disaster upon ourselves and upon the world" (HT 8/17/43). With this perspective in 1943 it is no surprise that we find Lippmann devoting so many of his columns in the previous thirteen years to the search for solutions to these policy puzzles through economic thinking appropriate for the time.

From his student days at Harvard, Lippmann was attracted more to what we now call macroeconomic issues—employment, growth, poverty, and so forth—than to the microeconomic aspects of markets. There were two dimensions to his curiosity. He was intrigued by seemingly inexplicable fluctuations in overall economic activity, and some of his earliest reading was in the Fabian underconsumptionist literature of John R. Hobson. There he could see links to his favorite subject of social psychology. He read anything he could get his hands on about economic fluctuations in the 1920s, including Wesley Mitchell's *Business Cycles,* the writings of William Trufant Foster and Wadill Catchings, Austrian business cycle theory, statistical studies by F. C. Mills, and of course Keynes. In 1914 he attempted to put together for the *New Republic* a special supplement entitled "Unemployment," which characterized economic fluctuations, and he explained to a potential contributor, "The scheme as it stands now is to devote the first five or six thousand words to a general survey of the problem, which is to act as an introduction. It is to be followed by three articles dealing with immediate constructive measures: one on Unemployment Insurance, which is to be written by Dr. [Walter] Weyl; one on the Problem of Public Enterprise, as a method of off-setting depression in private industry; and one on a National System of Labor Exchanges. Each of the three articles is to have about four thousand words" (WL to John Andrew, October 22, 1914, WLPI F63). He searched widely for solid data about unemployment in academe and elsewhere (e.g., WL to Frances Kellor, September 28, 1914, WLPI F645).

The second dimension of his concern with unemployment was with the actual suffering of the working classes during downturns in economic activity, and he sought to get a sense of the dimensions of this problem from the prolific descriptive writings of Charles Booth (1840–1916), the English social researcher, with whom he corresponded (WLPI F170). He appreciated that the human costs of unemployment went beyond the economic; they were psychological and emotional as well. He could see during the

1920s that totalitarian movements in Europe were growing out of the soil of macroeconomic failure.

As a public economist writing about current policy questions Lippmann recognized that he should not get ahead of his audience, and during the 1920s his readers were concerned mainly to make hay while the sun shone. He had to keep his worries about recession to himself until the Great Depression struck and pressure for understanding and for political action appeared among his readers. As he wrote in 1927: "When you remove economic discontent you remove what is certainly the greatest cause, if it is not the mainspring, of political activity. Politics carried on for justice, for liberty, for prestige, is never more than the affair of a minority. For the great majority of men political ideals are almost always based upon and inspired by some kind of economic necessity and ambition" (WL 1927, 25). He did succeed in publishing an occasional article on macroeconomic issues in the *New Republic* before the depression began, for example a thoughtful review essay by Alvin Johnson in 1915, "Causes of Crises," on the relevant literature, from W. Stanley Jevons to H. L. Moore. Johnson regretted that so much of this literature was "vitiated by a propagandist purpose," and he called for a "corps of experts to make visible to us the actual contours of the foundation on which we suppose we are resting." Only with reliable macroeconomic foresight could compensatory fiscal policy be implemented with confidence. "If restriction of private industry were known to be inevitable four years in advance, we should find it hard to excuse a government that failed to concentrate its own undertakings in such a way as to increase public employment when private employment diminishes" (NR, February 6, 1915, 19). Lippmann tried once again to organize a symposium on unemployment after he returned to the *New Republic* at the end of the war, but this seems not to have happened before he departed for the *World* in 1922. He found to his dismay that when the crisis hit in 1929 there was still little grasp among economists of the enormity of the problem or its causes. "It may be that at the present stage of human knowledge we are not equipped to understand a crisis which is so great and so novel, and that this is the explanation of the failure of our political, financial and industrial leaders to justify themselves. Is there any one who foresaw the whole crisis and predicted its course? I do not know of anyone" (HT 4/29/32).

By the time Lippmann began his columns in the *Herald Tribune* in September 1931 the Great Depression was firmly in place and was unquestionably the issue of the moment. It seemed clear to most people that this was not a short-term crisis but something more serious. At last he had his readers' attention. In the opening paragraph of his first column in the *Herald Tribune,* entitled "Magical Prosperity," he wrote that "it is no longer open to serious question that we are in the midst, not of an ordinary trade depression, but of one of the great upheavals and readjustments of modern history." The costs of the depression in terms of lost production and employment were not what worried Lippmann the most; rather, he pointed to the dislocation of human lives and the collapse of democratic governments. By the end of 1931 "[a] dozen governments have been brought down by it. In all the five continents it has upset the normal expectations of men by which they had been planting and making, buying and selling, borrowing and lending." Yet thinking in America seemed paralyzed fully two years into the depression: "As a people, in our corporate capacity, we have not yet begun to acknowledge the reality of the change and to formulate our national purposes for dealing with it. As a nation we continue to stand just where we stood two years ago, refusing in any responsible fashion to consider whether the increasing political insecurity in the world (which is reflected in mounting armaments), the increasing obstructions to trade, the separate complications of debt and reparations, are a probable foundation for the restoration of prosperity. Thus far our national response has been to stand pat in all such matters, and to believe that in sixty days, ninety days, or six months, the dove would return with the olive branch, the flood would recede, and business would go on as usual" (HT 9/8/31). After two years, he insisted, economic thinking about the origin of the crisis and what to do about it remained unpersuasive. "Whereas up to the autumn of 1929 we had dreamed that depressions were abolished, we have since clung with passionate faith, worthy of some better object, to the idea that a boom and a crash and a recovery follow each other, like winter and summer, in a fixed cycle."

Skeptical as he was of monopoly in all its forms (see Chapter 7), he rejected the suggestion that governmental price supports worldwide, such as those for coffee in Brazil, had interfered with "orderly deflation" and thereby caused the depression (WL to Leonard Ayres, December 19, 1933,

WLPIII F137). He was scornful of business cycle theory in general since it seemed to promise an inevitable return to prosperity after a recession. He thought of the Great Depression as a serious crisis with no clear end in view rather than as a phase in a cycle. He hoped wistfully for a "prophet of whom it can be said that his teachings were comprehensive and prompt and sufficient. It has been said that this is a crisis of over-abundance. It is also a crisis of the human understanding, and our deepest failures have not been failures arising from malevolence but from miscalculation. Our need is to determine where we are and where we can go, and then on this fog-bound sea to steer not by the winds and not by the whims of the passengers but by the compass. To attempt this we must take to heart the recent admonitions of Mr. Justice Brandeis that 'if we would guide by the light of reason we must let our minds be bold'" (HT 4/29/32).

The depression seemed especially poignant and politically explosive to Lippmann because he, and others, could see that the suffering was really not necessary. He told a gathering of social workers in 1932: "There is a profound difference between this crisis and all its predecessors. This is the first time when it is altogether evident that man's powers to produce wealth had reached a point when it is clearly unnecessary that millions in a country like the United States should be in want. In all previous crises there was some doubt as to whether the wealth of the nation was sufficient. That doubt no longer exists" (HT 5/21/32). By 1933 Lippmann found the situation to be even more urgent and dire than he had thought in 1931. "The dangers of war and of political disintegration must be averted primarily by a resumption of employment. There is no other way. The political tension in the world today reflects the economic tension and it cannot be relaxed effectively by proposals to disarm, by security pacts, by diplomatic combinations and by protestations of good intentions. The world must go back to work or it will go to war" (HT 4/14/33).

The Task of the Public Economist

As he struggled to understand the causes of depression and what to do about them Lippmann mused about how to bring the people along on his search. A lesson he drew from the experience of the Hoover administration was that it had failed to mold and to "align public opinion behind it" so that its acceptable policy options became very limited. Instead of seeking to rally support for the actions that it thought desirable the administration was always "waiting with its ear to the ground trying to find out what policy an untutored and unled public opinion favors" (HT 12/3/31). Government treated public opinion as "fixed and final" whereas, in fact, the public was "breathless and bewildered" (HT 12/3/31) and open to persuasion, as Lippmann had explained in *Public Opinion* in 1922. He continued to believe throughout his career that public opinion polls designed to discern the public's views on complex public policy issues were iniquitous in that they were likely to mislead government. He chided Elmo Roper in 1942 for a poll that asked "what kind of a post-war world Americans want." He called the questionnaire "a distinct disservice" (Roper to WL, March 24, 1942, and WL to Roper, March 6, 1942, WLPIII F1836).

Certainly President Hoover had supplied little intellectual leadership at a time when ideas were at a premium. "There is a belief abroad in the land that Mr. Hoover and his colleagues have not, could not, will not, adjust their mind to the fact that the world is passing through one of the great historical changes of modern history. There is lacking, therefore, in the Administration's contact with the public, the basis of sympathy and understanding" (HT 12/3/31). Without guidance from the middle the "mind of the nation" was confused by two competing approaches at the extremes, from conservatives and from progressives. "The conservative feeling is that the country must work with and through the existing powers to set the economic machine running again; the progressive feeling is that the existing powers have forfeited the right to the confidence of the country by failing to avert the breakdown of the economic machine" (HT 4/12/32). Lippmann's own preliminary view was that it would be better to stick with the conservative view in the short run and move to the progressive view later on. "In a realistic view of the situation it is plain, I think, that the time is too short and the crisis is too urgent to make serious reforms in the economic system and then set it going again. It must be set going again long before the desirable reforms can be invented, debated, enacted and introduced, or else there will be a breakdown on such a scale as no sincere progressive would care to face." At the same time, "[t]he lessons of history are worth remembering at a time like this and no lesson is so clear as that a social order is almost never imperiled until conservatism has become insensitive, inflexible and sterile" (HT 4/12/32). One of the greatest dangers for both the short and the long run was that government under the pressure of impending elections would take action to address the depression before it understood the problem. "No amount of propaganda for a recovery will serve as a substitute for the solution of the problems that impede recovery" (HT 9/8/32). Lippmann told an "educational convocation" at New York University that the main problem ahead was not a technical one, as some were saying, but was the discovery of appropriate economic policies that could be persuasive to the American democracy and to partner nations throughout the world. According to the report of his talk in the *Herald Tribune*:

> Mr. Lippmann, in discussing the advisability of a planned economy program, said that the major problem today "is to resolve the paradox of poverty and insecurity amidst plenty, to resolve it in a world of separate but interdependent nations and by democratic processes. The problem of our times has not been properly stated when we have said that invention and technical skill have reached a point where a high and secure standard of life is possible for the whole people. It is true that our physical resources are adequate, our technological progress is sufficient to justify the belief that the era of scarcity it ending. It is true in terms of engineering alone that the abolition of poverty is in sight. But the engineer, like the philosopher, is not king. The democracy is king. In our social order the power is widely distributed among the people and it is their opinion, their prejudices, their notions of their needs and their interests which command us at all the important moments of decision. But the democracy, though it is king, is itself a limited monarch. Its power is confined within the boundaries of the nation. Beyond those boundaries it exercises influence but not sovereignty. Yet the affairs with which we have to deal, the plans we have to formulate, the policies we adopt, are inextricably involved in a world-wide economy." (HT 11/18/32)

Modern man had conquered much of the natural world but still had not mastered the society in which he lived. Looking forward to the presidential election just ahead, Lippmann mused on Thanksgiving Day 1932 that

modern man "has not yet learned how to enjoy that conquest, to manage
those tools and to distribute that plenty. And so, with incalculable power
and inexhaustible resources at his command, multitudes are in want, and
all the nations are anxious. . . . And if they ask for anything today, it must
be for the imagination to conceive, the patience to understand, the courage
to deal with the hidden and complex causes of all this vast confusion and
waste. . . . We live in a world which is suffering not from the scarcity of nature, but from our own lack of the knowledge and discipline necessary to
manage it" (HT 11/24/32). At this time his close friend Felix Frankfurter
was one who urged upon him the task of public education. "What does
need and need cryingly your help, is the education of the public and public
men, in a hardy critical and detached judgment upon the proposals and
lack of proposals that are chargeable to our present political and financial
guides" (Frankfurter to WL, April 12, 1932, WLPIII F816).

After the election of President Roosevelt Lippmann mused again about
public opinion and economic policy in a democracy, and he concluded that
trust must be developed gradually for a program overall rather than for the
components of a program piecemeal. Here he drew heavily on the conclusions he had reached in his little book on public opinion in 1922.

> Can there be an informed and responsible public opinion aroused and
> organized and convinced on the multitude of questions which press for
> solution, on the details of economy and of taxes and government financ-
> ing, on debts, currencies, tariffs, armaments and foreign policy, on farm
> relief and banking reform and railroad reorganization, and all the other
> items on the agenda? There can be no national opinions on all these sub-
> jects and every one knows it. What there can be is a national opinion de-
> termined to support the program of the new Administration, a national
> decision that that program is better than no program, a national decision
> to take one line and hold it, a national decision that unity on any reason-
> able policy is better than disunity and confusion. That is the only way, as
> I see it, in which complex issues can be dealt with promptly. It is the only
> way public opinion can be mobilized, by fastening attention upon the
> simple but paramount task of providing the necessary authority for a na-
> tional program. (HT 2/24/33)

He saw the problems to be addressed as relevant to other countries of the world as well as to the United States, and he used the language of the American Institutionalists to make his point. "The central problem of bringing the industrial system under social control and of regulating it in a world economy is certainly as pressing in the stable democracies as it is in the unstable ones" (HT 3/2/33). Throughout, Lippmann remained mindful of the different ways by which leaders in society approached public policy. At one extreme some leaders used "theory" as a guide, at the other extreme some used "experience." He called for an amalgam of these two approaches, or what others might have called common sense and he called "wisdom." "Thus it comes about that in decisions which have to be reached when there is great disturbance men cannot rely upon a 'theory' or upon 'experience' but must look for that mixture of reason and experience, charity, sympathy and wit which is called wisdom" (HT 5/11/33). The study of history had a crucial role in sustaining humility in policy makers and in equipping analysts for the task of persuasion. "One can learn from history. And no man should pretend to govern men who has not steeped his mind in the human tradition. But what history teaches is above all humility, that pride of opinion and easy certainty are folly, and then that he who would search for the lessons of experience will never reach the end. Daily he must put to the test of his clearest insight into the immediate what he thinks he has gathered from the books he has read and the stories he has read" (HT 5/11/33).

Since even presidential administrations had not been successful in informing the public about the nature of the economic problems and their solutions, what could be done to make the situation better? One possibility was for leading journalists to take their responsibilities as public educators very seriously. They should not become irrevocably committed to any political party, candidate, or officeholder. They should decline to testify before Congress lest they become positioned in the debate and even intimidated by the process. "I think it is not a wholly unfounded fear" (WL to William Hard, March 24, 1937, WLPIII F988). He thought also that respected journalists could lead their readers to appreciate the breadth of human wisdom and avoid monocausal explanations. Whenever he found an opportunity he urged that more humanities be introduced into programs

from which distinguished journalists were likely to emerge, such as the
School of Public and International Affairs at Princeton (WL to Frank W.
Rounds, February 1, 1939, WLPIII F1849). He advised a young man contemplating a career in journalism: "The thing to go to college for is not
journalism but a general education—that is to say, for history, economics,
science, language—so that when you go to a newspaper you will have more
background" (WL to Richard M. Halsey, March 20, 1945, WLPIII F962).

Finding the Cause of Depression

The usual practice for Lippmann in confronting any new economic question was to examine the supposed answers in the professional literature and
then consider whether they made sense. In this case he determined that the
consensus among economists, as far as he could see, was that a "bubble"
had been created somewhere in the economy that led to market conditions
that subsequently could not be sustained. The bubble this time was in the
stock market and was encouraged by banks that became willing partners in
speculation. Even respected public figures like Mayor Jimmy Walker of
New York succumbed to the "greed and acquisitiveness of the speculative
spirit" (HT 5/31/32). When the bubble burst markets were dislocated and
commerce was reduced, including commerce in labor, and unemployment
increased. There was excess supply of goods and services in most markets.
The normal expectation in such a situation was that signals would go out to
reduce prices, and it was necessary only to wait until prices had fallen in all
relevant markets for new equilibria to be established with full employment
and maximum production once again. "In fact, the essence of the theory is
that the prelude to any recovery is to liquidate and cancel the accumulated
miscalculations of the preceding boom. Therefore the one sure way to prolong a depression is to resist it by trying to stand pat, rather than to carry
through the ultimately inevitable adjustments in as cool and orderly a way
as possible" (HT 9/8/31). This was as true in labor markets as elsewhere;
the only sensible approach for the businessman was to cut wages carefully
and wait for employment to revive. It was claimed in the literature, he reported, that "the maintenance of the rate of wages keeps up the cost of labor

in his product but does not help the workers. Their income is cut when they have less work to do" (HT 9/25/31).

This conventional approach argued for the futility of any active governmental policy. "There can be only the existing stagnation of trade until the long agony of deflating wages and prices down to lower levels is carried through to the bitter end" (HT 12/22/31). A medical analogy was sometimes used to extend this argument for inaction during a depression, and Lippmann tried this out. Depression, it was said, was like a purgative, and to limit this medicine would only prolong the malady. Lippmann tried to work out the implication of this notion. "In this large sense depression and crisis are not the collapse of our system, but a furious purge. Conceivably a system can be devised which would be stable without accumulating an insupportable burden of vested interests. But until such a system comes into being there is in every society as we know it a fatal tendency to accumulate too many obligations, to let arrangements become rigid, to let those who have retired from active life acquire too large claims, to let the grip of the place holders become too strong, to let seniority and privilege block the advance of youth and enterprise. So there must come inevitably a time of liquidation" (HT 7/22/32).

Lippmann's first move to test hypotheses about the main cause of the depression was to explore the origin and nature of the bubble that supposedly had burst and caused the catastrophe. In this he was informed by experience with Lincoln Steffens on Wall Street before World War I and friendships with several Wall Street bankers. He found that he agreed with the story of a Wall Street bubble but not with all of the details. He worried that many commentators on the political left were prepared to blame the bubble on sinister operators called "bear raiders," financiers who manipulated the markets up and down to make profits. They claimed the raiders were doing very well from the collapse. He found these dubious assertions, partly because they were being denied in bountiful correspondence he was receiving from Wall Street. "Our ancestors thought that many of their troubles were caused by the evil eye. This disposition to believe in malignant powers is always aggravated in times of strain and confusion. For in the absence of clear and compelling explanations and of a general conviction

about what needs to be done, men sink back into their more primitive habits of mind, and superstition flourishes among them. The notion that bear
raiders could produce such a market as this is nothing but superstition"
(HT 4/13/32). Some critics on the political right thought there were "Democratic bears" determined through their actions to embarrass President
Hoover. He found this charge equally improbable. Some Republican leaders of finance, such as Richard Whitney, president of the New York Stock
Exchange who testified before Congress, claimed unpersuasively that Wall
Street in general had absolutely nothing to do with the crash: "It is [just] a
market place." This interpretation he found to be preposterous. Lippmann's
friends among the partners of J. P. Morgan were so deeply "upset" with
his explanation of the financial bubble that they prepared for his use
an eighteen-page refutation (Thomas Lamont to WL, January 16, 1934,
WLPIII F1277).

Lippmann found neither the shrill critique of Wall Street from the left
nor the vigorous defense by the bankers on the right to be persuasive or useful in the emergency, and he called for more humility all around: "the Stock
Exchange bases its claim to immunity from public regulation upon the thesis that its own capacity for self-government and self-discipline are a better
protection to the public than any laws which could be enacted. That thesis
is true when the self-discipline is courageously applied. Has it been? That
is the question. . . . For the Stock Market has become the greatest popular
market in the world, and its members have the duty to regard themselves
collectively as trustees of an immense public interest" (HT 4/13/32). Accordingly Lippmann set out to construct his own middle-of-the road interpretation of events. Since World War I, he wrote, the securities markets had
grown very quickly in response to a large volume of savings looking for at-
tractive investments. Neither demanders nor suppliers in these expanded
capital markets were well informed of the facts and both were prepared to
hold unreasonable expectations of profitability. "It has become impossible
for the public who own securities to arrive at sound judgments about the
position of their property. They are entirely dependent, therefore, upon advice, and in the nature of things they are dependent to a very great degree
upon the advice of their brokers" (HT 4/13/32). The public was encouraged

by these "brokers and bankers to indulge in bull speculation during the boom. They believe, and I think rightly, that those who were presumably in a position to know did not adequately protect them. It is true that the American people ignorantly and greedily indulged in bull speculation. But what sticks in their minds is that they were encouraged, often by methods of high-powered statesmanship [salesmanship?], to give themselves up to this folly" (HT 4/13/32).

When the bull market became unsustainable in 1929 and turned downward, most believed this could not be possible. "There was a general benevolent conspiracy, under the aegis of the President [Hoover], to regard the old state of affairs as 'normal' and to keep everything where it was. Producers kept up prices, wages and wage costs were maintained, big governmental and corporate expenditures were encouraged, and the Farm Board proceeded in a big way to pour money into the commodity markets. The general belief was, and there were few who did not share it, that the 'depression' was a kind of squall which would pass quickly and would, if every one ignored it, put no one to any inconvenience" (HT 1/28/32). Lippmann worried that against this naïve interpretation of the situation, ill-considered legislation to constrain the stock market might do more harm than good, since the root of the problem was in human nature, which could not be changed simply by a new set of rules. "The popular feeling against the stock market will be a good thing for this country if, instead of producing silly laws to protect fools, it engenders a general revulsion against gambling for easy money. The mischief is not curable by laws. The mischief is in the realm of the spirit" (HT 5/31/32).

By 1931 it had been two years since the bubble had burst, and still the winds of depression were blowing hard; this was no squall. The stock market bubble, in fact, had not really burst so much as gradually deflated. So why had the price adjustment supposedly required for the cure taken so long? Lippmann speculated first that there was widespread money illusion throughout the economy and that prices were really more than equilibrating mechanisms. Both firms and trade unions were fearful to make price reductions that would send discouraging signals to their constituencies of stockholders and union members. They preferred to conceal the truth through quantity adjustments and wait for the day when their rigid prices would once again be the equilibrium ones. In the meantime essential adjustments were put off. "The notion that there would be a quick recovery to the 1929 level was wrong. The notion that business would soon be proceeding as usual was wrong. Production fell off and with it the earnings of labor. But the administration in Washington and the spokesmen of the trade unions have gone right on talking as if they had maintained the purchasing power of labor. What they have actually succeeded in doing is to divert attention from the real problem and to establish a passionate interest in an unreal problem" (HT 9/25/31).

In order to test the hypothesis that price movements downward were likely to restore full employment and establish a new equilibrium Lippmann examined the case of the railroads, one of the largest regulated sectors of the economy, using recent research by Sumner Slichter. He found that even if the railroads were given authority quickly to reduce rates they probably could not do so. Their costs were mainly fixed through long-term contracts with workers and suppliers, bond interest, and taxes. Swift rate reduction would probably mean bankruptcy. "Looked at in a larger perspective, the railroads present the most important example of the economic, social and political perils which result from making an industrial fabric rigid with fixed charges and then subjecting it to a violent deflation of prices" (HT 10/22/31).

Still another reason for the slow price adjustment, Lippmann suggested, was that President Hoover believed that the reasons for the collapse lay overseas, and if only isolation could be increased from misbehaving foreigners, prosperity would return at the old price levels. Hoover urged price makers to stand pat, for if the old price levels were reduced before protection could be increased sufficiently it might be hard for sellers to raise them again. "The guiding principle of the present administration has been that the post war structure of debts and prices was essentially normal and sound, that the depression was a temporary interruption, and that recovery consisted in maintaining by artificial means as large a part of the debt structure as possible in the hope that the level of prices would rise again to support it. The principle is no longer credible" (HT 12/6/32). Hoover had spoken of "the critical dangers and assaults swept upon us from foreign countries" and of how "our major difficulties find their origins in the economic weakness of foreign nations." The implication of this Hoover doctrine was that to reduce prices in the face of this external onslaught would be tantamount to accepting defeat (HT 10/6/32). "Mr. Hoover has not yet become willing to admit that the post-war policies and their consequences in the inflated debt-structure of the 'new era' need to be revised" (HT 12/7/32). More specifically, "The assumption was that the 1929 level of prices, wages, profits was normal and that a resolute concerted effort should be made to maintain it" (HT 11/24/31). At best Hoover's policy would take a long time to bring relief and would generate many imperfections. Despite Hoover's objections to deflation a good deal had occurred anyway. "There has been a relentless movement down to a new price level. But the movement has not been uniform. For some prices and some wages are protected by a kind of monopoly. They have come down more slowly than unprotected prices and unprotected wages. The result is that today the whole economic system is out of adjustment because the relationships between all kinds of buyers and sellers, employers and workers, borrowers and lenders, are radically different from what they were two years ago" (HT 9/25/31). The helter-skelter deflation that had occurred had not led, as was hoped, to new stable equilibria. "The prices received by farmers have fallen 50 per cent. The prices paid by farmers have fallen only by about 20 per cent. Farm wages have fallen 35 per cent, wages in factories perhaps ten per cent, wages on railroads not at all" (HT 9/25/31). The administration should admit that its attempts to sustain the price level did not work, and to restore confidence they should look for a new policy: "Its moral and political resistance to the deflation is no longer justified. The policy has failed. It should be abandoned, and the Administration should return to a position of neutrality" (HT 9/25/31).

The most prominent example of a nation that had tried just the reverse of the Hoover policy to restore prosperity by restoring the predepression price level was Britain, where an aggressive policy of active deflation had been adopted to restore prosperity at lower price levels. There had been much suffering and turmoil in Britain as a result and thus far not much evidence of a return to prosperity. Instead, there had been merely an increase in the "dole." When attempting to understand the reasons for the

slow recovery from the depression Lippmann was especially impressed by
the work of Gardiner Means, then at the Department of Agriculture, on the
relationship between industrial concentration and price inflexibility. Means
had suggested some kind of governmental intervention in price determination as an alternative to the breakup of large corporations: "a non-dictatorial
technique of economic coordination within which the market can be employed as a useful tool . . . an additional framework which supplements the
contractual and property framework so as to produce the results the contractual and property framework alone fails to accomplish" (Means to WL,
February 7, 1935, WLPIII F1480). Lippmann found that Means's analysis
"throws more light on the immediate situation than anything else that I
know of" (WL to Means, December 27, 1934, WLPIII F1480).

Lippmann agreed with one aspect of Hoover's explanation for the depression, that part of the cause lay overseas, but not for the reasons Hoover
suggested. Moreover, Lippmann concluded that the worst policy was the
one Hoover endorsed to increase isolation through tariffs and other restrictive devices. The foreign problem seen by Lippmann grew out of the "political debts" (HT 1/12/32) that had been incurred during and after World
War I, before and after the United States entered the war. The United States
had insisted on providing assistance to Britain and France through loans
rather than grants, with substantial interest and repayment obligations.
Then at Versailles all the Allies demanded additionally that the vanquished
Germans make reparations payments that were beyond their means to fulfill. In the decade since the treaty the following scenario had evolved. Germany, unable to meet its reparations commitments, which required an un-
attainable surplus in its balance of trade, had borrowed abroad at high
interest rates, mainly from American banks and financial institutions,
thereby increasing substantially its sovereign debt. The borrowed funds
went to Britain and France for reparations, and finally back to the United
States to repay the war debts of these two countries. When the American
banks eventually faced a liquidity crisis after the stock market crash of 1929
and declined to make more loans to Germany, the Germans could not make
reparations payments, British and French loans could not be repaid to the
United States, and the whole multinational circular flow came to a halt.
Thus the United States has been operating a kind of revolving fund in

which private American money flowed to Germany, was paid to the European creditors as reparations and by them returned to the United States as debt payments.

This fantastic system broke down in the spring of 1931 when no more private money was forthcoming to make the reparation and debt machine work (HT 1/12/32). The sclerosis that was introduced into the international payments system by the resulting moratoria, suspensions, revisions, and so forth, reduced the value of the outstanding loans made by the American banks and increased these banks' liquidity problems even more. Domestic lending did not recover, and the depression continued (HT 9/17/31 and 11/24/31). Throughout the 1920s, at least, there was nearly universal unwillingness to recognize the dangerous situation that was developing. "The outstanding facts are that at the culmination of the Coolidge era [1928] we were selling nearly a billion dollars more than we bought, lending a billion abroad, and drawing heavily on the depleted gold supplies of the outer world. These three facts go a long way to explain the illusions of prosperity. We were selling prodigiously and acquiring paper evidences of debt, and on this paper we were pyramiding values and enjoying that appearance of extreme prosperity which is characteristic of inflation" (HT 9/13/32). Lippmann claimed that the financier Paul Warburg was one of the few to recognize the problem that faced the country and its cause; he was "a true, a timely, and courageous prophet" (HT 12/17/31).

It is worth noting how similar Lippmann's description and analysis of the Great Depression of the twentieth century are to views of later economists about the Great Recession of the twenty-first century. Both found that part of the cause lay with bubbles blown up and burst at home; another part originated with structural imbalances with Europe. In the 1930s the bubble was in the stock market; eighty years later it was in securitized subprime mortgages. In the 1930s the imbalances were mainly with Germany, France, and Britain; in the twenty-first century they were with southern Europe.

Finding the Cure

After discovering that the two approaches to counteracting the depression tried thus far—sustain prices artificially while waiting for recovery to

materialize (Hoover), and force prices down to a new equilibrium
(Britain)—had not worked well where they had been tried and had caused
much suffering, Lippmann called for a fresh approach. He responded with
annoyance to those in government or outside that claimed that any search
for an answer to the depression would lead inevitably to Soviet-type planning. He wrote to Louis Domeratzky in the Commerce Department: "It
seems to me that there is something confusing about the notion that the
Russian economy is all planned, and that ours is unplanned. In both countries those who control capital have to judge the future, and that's the science of planning. It seems that our bankers misjudged our future badly in
the four or five years preceding the depression. But I do not know of any
reason why we should be certain that the men who control Russian capital
will judge their future so much more wisely than we have judged ours" (WL
to Domeratzky, October 22, 1931, WLPIII F625). As the Hoover administration ended he rejected the idea that with sufficient carefully constructed
rules in place there would be little need for a strong and imaginative governmental authority, a doctrine that would be enunciated in the scholarly community by Henry Simons a few years later. "There is at stake a controlling
element in the whole process of economic recovery, and the President of the
United States proclaims to the world that no American authority now exists
which can investigate the facts and can recommend action" (HT 11/29/32).
This doctrine he thought was a disgrace. The 1920s had been a decade in
which leadership in government, such as was called for by the progressives,
had been dismissed as unnecessary and even counterproductive. For this
false doctrine of negativity the nation was now paying a high price. "For if
you teach a people for ten years that the character of its government is not
greatly important, that political success is for those who equivocate and
evade, and if you tell them that acquisitiveness is the ideal, that things are
what matter, that Mammon is God, then you must not be astonished at the
confusion in Washington. . . . It is not only against the material consequences of this decade of drift and hallucination, but against the essence of
its spirit that the best and bravest among us are today in revolt" (HT
5/20/32). It was not enough to fall back on obsolete ideas developed long
ago; the result of doing so thus far had been anarchy and corruption.

In December 1932, Lippmann was invited by President Nicholas Murray Butler of Columbia University to join a distinguished group of professional economists and others to conduct a "very intensive and intimate" study of "the outstanding economic and social problem of our time," the challenge of economic reconstruction (Butler to WL, December 28, 1932, WLPIII F349). He accepted with alacrity, but apparently because of other commitments was unable to take part in the discussions. Despite the preparation of special studies for the group by Benjamin Anderson, Jacob Viner, Alvin Hansen, Mordecai Ezekiel, and others, Lippmann was disappointed with the outcome, concluding presumably that it did not reflect the kind of brave new thinking that he thought was essential in the current crisis. Concerning the final report he wrote: "My feeling, however, is that the report is not good enough either in substance or in style to be published and that it would be a mistake to issue it. However, this is a purely personal opinion which I express frankly but diffidently, and I should maintain the opinion only up to the point of saying I cannot sign the report" (WL to Arthur D. Gayer, April 6, 1933, WLPIII F483). Lippmann was looking for something that would do more to rock the boat and question the status quo.

Lippmann was moved by the promises made to the American people by Franklin Roosevelt in his acceptance speech after his nomination in 1932. Lippmann wrote a few months later that the Republicans had lost credibility. "A policy of declared impotence, followed by actions based on prejudice and favoritism and contradictions is no way to protect the vital interests of a great people. The thing is a mess and there is the utmost need for a new deal" (HT 11/29/32). At the same time the Democrats did not get off without criticism. Lippmann complained that despite the inspiring rhetoric FDR was light on specifics. "A lot is said by the Roosevelt faction about 'economic issues' being 'paramount.' But what these paramount issues are they are careful not to say. . . . Where, for example, does he stand on the tariff, on reparations and debts, on farm relief, on taxation, on banking reform, on the railroad problem? I do not know" (HT 11/26/31). Lippmann thought that 1932 was the year when the Democrats should have emerged with a creative plan for a worldwide attack on the global depression. Instead, they had nothing to propose and seemed frightened to challenge the

isolationism of the Republicans. "The unresolved issue which confronts
the Democrats is whether they will accept or whether they will oppose the
Republican post-war doctrine that America is a closed economic system. . . .
The Democrats do not know as yet whether they should take the path of
perfect isolation or of consistent and far-reaching co-operation" (HT
2/9/32). The result of the Democratic waffling was an impression that candidate Roosevelt was "a man of only moderate capacity" (HT 2/12/32). Perhaps he did "not have a sufficiently able mind nor a sufficiently strong character to be entrusted with national leadership at this time" (HT 4/15/32). He
certainly gave no indication of becoming the dynamic and charismatic
leader the people longed for. "The trouble with Franklin D. Roosevelt is
that his mind is not very clear, his purposes are not simple, and his methods
are not direct" (HT 6/7/32).

Lippmann was always casting about among contemporary writers for a
vision of a new economic order that would relieve current suffering, and to
some extent he found one in the work of the British economist Sir Arthur
Salter (later Lord Salter) who put forth in a book entitled *Recovery: The
Second Effort* (1932) a "general program of debt adjustment, tariff reduction,
monetary arrangement, economic reform, and political stabilization." Sadly,
"the world is just as likely to resist his remedies and liquidate the crisis by
the processes of default, bankruptcy, and a general lowering of the standard
of life" (HT 4/7/32). The world needed dynamic leadership like that of
Salter with respect to the economy and could not wait: "bold and generous
actions have to be taken simultaneously and in co-ordination on several
fronts: by the bankers in the realm of credit, by business men in the realm of
enterprise, by Congress in the realm of commercial and fiscal policy, by the
State Department in the realm of political security, and by the President as
the field marshal of the whole campaign" (HT 4/8/32). Lippmann wrote
despairingly to Salter in 1932 that there seemed little likelihood that such
leadership would come from America any time soon (WL to Salter, April 28,
1932, WLPIII F1877).

Strong leadership was needed especially for two tasks: first, to assem-
ble the best minds and deduce from their findings just what should be done
in this desperate emergency. This was needed because the "pathology of

the depression" tended to generate prophesies of doom and salvation that were not helpful. For example, he devoted four columns to a detailed study of "technocracy," a body of doctrines propounded especially by engineers that he found to be without merit. "They may be honestly intended. But they are none the less a collection of booby-traps" (HT 2/3/33). The second task for leaders in the United States was to counter resistance in the American public to essential, but counterintuitive, elements of policy reform. One was the need to work cooperatively with other countries to find a mutually agreeable solution to the depression rather than respond positively to the instinctive call for isolation from, and barriers against, foreigners. Another grew out of a fallacy of composition that suggested that because a sensible approach for a family was to reduce spending in a time of crisis this rule could automatically be translated to the whole economy. The truth was quite the contrary. This was a time for the country to increase spending. But in 1932, with the Congress and the presidency about to turn over, Lippmann was not optimistic. He wrote: "Our danger is neither from 'radicalism' or 'conservatism' but from incoherence and paralysis. What we have to fear is the inability of the government to determine policies and to execute them. . . . For we are suffering not from tyranny but from weakness, not from evil purposes but from confused purposes, not from stupidity but from impotence" (HT 7/19/32).

A New International Economic Order

If the two public policies to combat depression by sustaining prices at old levels and by wrenching prices painfully downward did not work, the next most promising alternative would seem to be to operate from the demand side and affect those demand-side forces determining prices. To accomplish this successfully would require global economic cooperation. To build a more efficient and stable international economic system would require serious attention to all aspects of trade, factor movements, and exchange rates. For all this to be done there might have to be substantial reforms on both the domestic and international fronts. Internationally, it would be necessary for all the parties involved with war debts and reparations to get together and settle the issues once and for all, perhaps with an immediate and reduced cash settlement. The commitments and obligations of debtor nations would have to be cut back substantially, as they should have been at Versailles in the first place, so that international economic relations could return to their main function of facilitating trade and investment:

> There can be no ordering of government budgets, no stabilization of currencies, and no real beginning of a restoration of confidence, while the future course of these great payments is undermined and at the mercy of domestic politics in all the countries. The bases of a definite policy have to be laid very soon. . . . The revival of long term investment, which is indispensable to a recovery from present conditions, cannot take place if war debts and reparations, with all they involve in the way of international confusion and bitterness are left hanging unsettled over the financial markets. (HT 12/17/31)

An obstacle to achieving this solution to the debt problem was the widely accepted doctrine that those who incur debts must be required to pay them back. Anything else would be immoral. "Dishonest debtors," the doctrine made clear, were out to "frisk the pockets" of honest lenders and must be resisted (HT 7/14/32). Some critics were prepared to argue that in refusing to pay their debts the Germans were simply demonstrating again the duplicity they had shown in World War I (HT 10/6/31). But everyone ("the governments and the voters," HT 1/12/32) must come to recognize, Lippmann insisted, that without a settlement all would suffer, the British, the French, and the Americans as much as the Germans. "It would be going too far to say that the world cannot hope to recover under the policies imposed upon it by Congress and the [French] Chamber [of Deputies]. The world can recover if and when it has paid the price. The price is continuing deflation, for with German credit unrestored, all the financial markets will remain frightened, and credit everywhere must tend to contract. There can be little confident enterprise while this situation continues" (HT 12/22/31). Lippmann was persuaded "by virtually all the British economists" that "the whole system of political payments" "has wrecked the international exchanges, has made the gold standard unworkable, and has brought about the great deflation of world prices" (HT 3/18/32). He was always looking for homely metaphors to explain his arguments to readers. Here he compared prices in world trade to the air we breathe; the level had to be just right for things to proceed smoothly. "They are like the supply of oxygen in a room. The people in the room are for the most part unconscious of the quality of the air they breathe. But let some one increase the supply, as during the recent inflation, and the people in the room will become preternaturally lively. Let some one shut off the supply, as in the deflation, the strongest and the brightest will grow listless and faint" (HT 12/1/32). The solution of the European stalemate should be settled quickly lest the stimulus of world trade disappear: "the proposal to postpone is, it seems to me, based upon a dangerous illusion" (HT 1/19/32). The result would be a long period of stagnation. The stark alternatives in debt policy were "Cancellation, Repudiation and Revision." Since the first two were deeply unpalatable, "there remains Revision, the well established policy of the wise creditor who finds that circumstances have changed radically for his debtor" (HT 11/16/32).

Essential as revision of debt policy was to resumption of world trade, it was not clear to Lippmann that this was possible in the American democracy. Politically it might be necessary to relieve the distress at home before achieving a solution of problems abroad. Americans were so enraged with their own unsustainable personal debts that they were unwilling to relieve others abroad even if this would improve their own circumstances in the medium term. "There is little doubt, I think, that the determining factor in public opinion is the present plight of American private debtors. The position is incomprehensible without an understanding of the relationship between popular feeling about war debts and popular distress caused by farm and urban mortgages" (HT 12/5/32). Lippmann found that members of Congress did not seem to connect the interests of their constituents with the health of the world economy. Senator Kenneth McKellar of Tennessee was a case in point. His state was primarily agricultural, and "of the total American production of tobacco 40 per cent was exported, of cotton nearly 45 per cent was exported, of lard about 29 per cent." Yet "Senator McKellar's notion of how to serve the people of Tennessee is to treat their customers as if they were brigands" (HT 7/14/32). Somehow the American people must be made to understand that recovery of domestic output and employment, not recovery of debts alone, should be the objective of government policy. "It is upon a recovery of business rather than upon the collection of the whole debt that we need to fix our attention. It is only by a rise in world prices, a resumption of investments, and the revival of trade that production can again provide employment to the unemployed, incomes to the taxpayers and relief to the budget. There is no other way to help the taxpayer or any one else. For what will it profit the taxpayer if we collect the whole debt this year and by doing it knock down world prices another ten or twenty per cent?" (HT 11/23/32).

Despite his optimism in 1931 that if only people of goodwill, aware of their genuine self-interests, would get together they would achieve compromise on important international economic issues, from his increasing understanding of human psychology he became less sanguine. He wrote in 1933: "It follows that the governments of Great Britain, France and the United States—since they represent the predominant financial power of the world—need to be armed by their people with authority to take simultaneous action on a multitude of separate questions. The problem is not how to settle the debts. Or how to reduce tariffs. Or how to stabilize currencies. Or how to expand credit and promote capital investment. The problem is how to get all of these things, and many more besides, done together and promptly and in an atmosphere of confidence and good will" (HT 4/7/33). With the debt, as with other international economic issues, the challenge to politicians was to bring onboard their constituencies to accept policies and practices that might seem to be not in their immediate, narrow self-interest. "For statesmanship of this high order it is necessary that there should exist in all the countries concerned a dominant public opinion which appreciates the problem as a whole. It is a complicated problem and it is not easy to think about more than one aspect of it at a time. Yet the welfare of mankind depends upon the number of people who will make the effort to consider its many aspects before they plump finally for a particular solution" (HT 11/30/32).

When the decks were ultimately cleared of unsustainable debts and reparations, Lippmann wrote, a structure must be put in place to defend and increase free trade, to make "the volume of trade be greater and the world richer because of a more efficient division of labor" (HT 3/16/32). Free trade was a principle from which Lippmann never varied. In 1924 he wrote the redoubtable Nicholas Murray Butler, president of Columbia University, asking how such a "convinced liberal" could press for higher tariffs. Butler sent a long and defensive response (Butler to WL, October 23, 1924, WLPI F215). In 1929, at the request of the *Christian Science Monitor*, Lippmann had prepared an official editorial position for the *New York World* on the Hawley-Smoot tariff bill. "The framers of the Hawley Smoot Tariff Bill are interested only in those who produce goods inside the United States for sale in the American market. They are not interested in the consumer. They are not interested in the cost of living. They are not interested in the importer. They are not interested in the position of the United States as creditor or as world power. Their sole objective has been to make prices high and business profitable for domestic producers. No doubt they honestly believe, insofar as they consider the matter at all, that if they can monopolize the American market for American producers all classes of Americans will somehow share the benefits. Nobody engaged in writing this bill has tried to think out, or was capable of thinking out, the effects of these increases upon the prosperity of the Nation or the general standard of living. The reason why the domestic seller alone was considered is that the domestic seller alone is sufficiently organized to bring political pressure upon individual Congressmen" (July 1929, WLPI F909).

Protective tariffs like Hawley-Smoot were unquestionably inefficient and corrupting, yet quotas, embargoes, and other periodic interruptions handled administratively by irresponsible officials, such as those that were being proposed to combat the depression, could be more deeply and continually destructive. "Since the quotas can be changed almost without notice, or turned into embargoes mitigated by licenses of exemption, the international market for goods is decisively controlled by the arbitrary action of officials. The mere existence of such power is in itself destructive of all systematic economic foresight; a power of this kind cannot be exercised intelligently since there is no intelligent principle which can guide the officials in exercising it. The system must develop into gross favoritism and

almost certainly into corruption. Tariff legislation is a scandalous process
in every country; but quota fixing by administrative decree can hardly fail
to be more scandalous still" (HT 3/16/32). In 1932 Lippmann remained un-
equivocally in support of free trade, and he felt beleaguered by spokesmen
from both parties who seemed to have succumbed to the seductive illogic of
protection. Democrats had joined the Republicans in Congress to argue
that "anything that can be produced, no matter how expensively, would be
entitled to have a duty high enough to destroy any advantage possessed by
the foreign producer. The protectionist theory can not be carried further. . . .
Thus, by the will of Congress, supported let us admit by the prevailing
public opinion, a shattering blow has been struck at those very American
producers who, because of superior efficiency and other advantages, are
most fitted to be in business. It is they who pay for the absurdity of protecting the uneconomic producers, and their losses are felt by the whole nation
in increased unemployment and reduced profits" (HT 4/5/32). Lippmann
gave clear, textbook-like examples of how comparative advantage could increase the welfare of both trading partners, using Cuban sugar exchanged
for American automobiles as an example. By contrast, under protection
"Cuban and American labor engaged in sugar are both impoverished and
there are less well paid jobs in the automobile plants" (HT 4/5/32). Under
the Hawley-Smoot protective tariff American foreign trade had fallen by
more than half in just two years. The principle that had been adopted was
that "the American producer ought to have a monopoly in the home market.
It is a plausible theory and almost the whole world is adopting it. It is plausible but it is absurd" (HT 4/5/32).

    In 1931 Lippmann's old boss Newton Baker asked him to suggest a
"tariff plank" for the upcoming campaign in which he was contemplating a
run for the presidency. Lippmann suggested "a world-wide reduction of all
tariffs by some small amount, say 10 per cent" (WL to Baker, July 10, 1931,
WLPIII F150), but he confided to Baker a little later that he was discouraged by how little had been done to deal with a critical situation. The Reconstruction Finance Corporation, created under Hoover at the beginning
of 1932, was "at best a kind of financial Red Cross operation which cannot
and will not touch the deeper causes of the troubles. . . . My own view is

that while a certain amount of improvement is probably in prospect we must count on three things at least. The first is that in any event the really serious consequences of the depression still lie ahead of us. The second is that a false and temporary recovery is a distinct possibility. The third is that no satisfactory recovery is conceivable unless there are far-reaching changes in international economic policies. I think we have greatly to fear the restoration not of confidence but of complacency" (WL to Baker, July 29, 1932, WLPIII F150).

Lippmann was pleased by FDR's acknowledgment in his campaign for the presidency that bilateral treaty negotiations were needed to drive down the tariffs that had risen so rapidly worldwide. Roosevelt had recognized that "a wholly new conception of the tariff is now needed and that existing conditions in the world will make it necessary henceforth to deal with the tariff not simply by Congressional log rolling or even by supposedly scientific inquiries, but by the negotiation of tariff agreements" (HT 4/20/32). Yet he reminded Roosevelt that mechanisms were required to make sure that tariffs when once reduced did not spring up again. First of all he wanted a tariff "truce" that would keep rates at current levels, and then he wanted restraints on "flexibility" that permitted a nation to raise rates in cases of supposed "hardship." "The first necessity in tariff policy is to get rid of this exaggerated flexibility so that the terms on which producers can compete in markets will not be subject to the caprice of governments acting under the pressure of special interests. There is need, in short, of a world wide tariff truce which will guarantee that for some decent length of time tariffs and other obstructions will not be raised. There are few measures more urgently needed to promote recovery. But such a truce cannot be made except by international agreement" (HT 9/22/32). He suggested to FDR that once tariffs had been stabilized worldwide, efforts should be made then to achieve a set of global and uniform cuts in tariffs of 10 to 20 percent, very much as they would later be reduced under the successive General Agreement on Tariffs and Trade (GATT) rounds after World War II. "Cuts of this kind applied horizontally involve no such bartering as the Governor [Roosevelt] appeared to have in mind in his Seattle speech. The horizontal cut would apply generally; it would involve no logrolling over schedules in Congress or in the field of diplomacy. It would be as 'scientific' as any tariff can be, and as just, for it would increase the volume of international commerce generally and the benefits would distribute themselves widely. Once a cut has been made the rates should be allowed to stand for an agreed period of years" (HT 9/22/32). When Roosevelt entered the White House Lippmann made the case for accelerated bilateral trade negotiations as the best way to achieve continuing tariff reductions, and he cited the authority of his old teacher Frank Taussig in support of this strategy. "Mr. Taussig's views are always of importance owing to his great knowledge of the tariff. They are of special importance at the present time because it is plain that the Roosevelt Administration must soon make far-reaching decisions in regard to the tariff" (HT 3/22/33).

Lippmann grew increasingly cynical about public opinion as a guide to the formation of international trade policy, and later in the decade he applauded Secretary of State Cordell Hull's courageous efforts to reduce tariffs bilaterally in the face of opposition. "Speaking of the compromises of statesmen, Mr. Keynes once remarked that maybe 'this is the best of which a democracy is capable of, to be jockeyed, humbugged, cajoled, along the right road.' The remark may well be applied to the series of treaties which Secretary Hull is negotiating so painstakingly and so painfully" (HT 5/14/36). Lippmann wrote to his friend and fellow journalist William Allen White in April 1932 that the future of world prosperity depended on whether a new international economic order could be discerned and implemented. "The great difficulty in seeing into the future, to my mind, lies in trying to decide whether or not the die is cast for a world of more or less self-sufficient, or at least isolated economic empires, or for a truly international world with international markets. All our conclusions depend upon which premise we adopt and I don't know that any of us is yet able to decide that fundamental question" (WL to White, April 22, 1932, WLPIII F2226).

As Lippmann contemplated the ill-fated World Economic Conference set for London in 1933, a gathering planned under Hoover to explore a return to stability but undermined by Roosevelt, he claimed that a consensus had emerged among right-thinking people about the way to restore world trade. The target must be to restore high prices to the precrash level through all means possible. "The experts desire, as does everyone else, a rise in the level of world prices and the maintenance of that level. To this end they advocate a readjustment of international debts and tariffs, the abolition of exchange restrictions, the stabilization of currencies on the gold standard, a policy of cheap money and credit expansion in countries possessing ample gold, and the balancing of public budgets" (HT 2/15/33). At the same time he warned that the defenders of free trade now faced a conjoined two-flank attack from nationalist protectionists on the right and socialist planners on the left. Free traders must remain ever vigilant. "This new philosophy has a strange parentage. It is the offspring of a marriage between social interests which have usually been regarded as irreconcilable, between the super-protectionists, who have been held to be highly 'reactionary' and the planners and collectivists who have been held to be extremely 'progressive.' The student of history will recognize, I think, that this union of ideas has been foreshadowed as a possibility for more than a hundred years. It is one of the conceivable developments of the philosophy of Alexander Hamilton. It is very clearly indicated in the conservatism of Disraeli. It becomes even more definite in the nationalism of Bismarck. In the field of the social sciences the basic conception of a national economy, as distinguished from the cosmopolitan economic philosophy of Adam Smith, was worked out by Friedrich List as long ago as 1841" (HT 6/13/33). Lippmann's concern about the London conference, where many representatives from many nations would discuss complex economic questions, was that they would fail to agree, and with its collapse the conference would do more harm than good to the cause of free trade: "it seems to me clear that a general conference is the wrong way to go about doing things which urgently need to be done, that the chances of success are too small and the costs of a failure too great, and that in fact such a general conference would confuse, distract, and delay the effort to settle these questions" (HT 6/3/32 and 7/4/33).

Your Money or Your Life

The two reforms that Lippmann first proposed to relieve the depression, international debt reduction and free trade, were easy for him to comprehend and explain. He learned about the first from Maynard Keynes at

Versailles and about the second in class with Frank Taussig at Harvard. But these were both long-run solutions to what had become an urgent short-run problem. Lippmann's uncertainty about how to combat the depression in the short run was shared by most economists in government and by many in academe. Some believed that standing pat and waiting for a new full-employment equilibrium to materialize was the only way to go. But the country was already very tired of waiting, and other policies were proposed. At one extreme "structuralists" argued that fundamental flaws in the free market system had been revealed by the depression; planning and controls would be required to restore prosperity. At the other extreme some found that the problems were mainly monetary in nature. Reform of the banking system and manipulation of the money supply could bring back the old price levels and the good old days. Still others claimed the fault lay with the foreign exchange rate of the dollar, embedded in the price of gold under the gold standard. If the gold price of the dollar were reduced, exports would increase and imports would decrease, thereby raising prices and employment in both sectors. A third approach to the problem was to increase total demand for goods and services through public expenditures and transfer payments of various kinds. William Barber describes how the Roosevelt administration explored all of these approaches to the depression under the New Deal and by 1938 had come to a conclusion about which to select among them. "Roosevelt's decision to embark unapologetically on a 'spend-lend' program in April 1938 appeared to signal that the administration had come to terms with an Americanized version of Keynesian aggregate demand management" (Barber 1996, 116). What we shall see in what follows is that Lippmann followed the same path as Roosevelt but reached the Keynesian conclusion four years earlier in 1934. Moreover, by expressing his Keynesian views so often and so effectively in his columns he may have had a part in the administration's own evolution over time.

    Monetary and fiscal policies were a challenge for Lippmann to deal with confidently. For a start he thought that the American federal government was so weak he wondered if it could ever conduct a complicated and coordinated macroeconomic policy successfully. "In no other highly industrialized country is the democracy so strong and the government so weak"

(HT 7/20/32). As early as September 1931 he struggled with the question of whether in this situation an aggressive open market policy by the central bank might be the answer to the depression. Would readily available credit at moderate interest rates stimulate the economy and restore prosperity, as some suggested, or just cause inflation, as the critics claimed? Recognizing the reputation his columns were gaining among the sophisticated elite, various government officials offered to help him understand the issue. Eugene Mayer, chairman of the Federal Reserve Board and an advocate of a more robust monetary intervention, even invited him to spend a weekend at his home in Mount Kisco "when we could have a quiet talk" (Meyer to WL, September 22, 1931, WLPIII F1496).

Commenting on the Democratic Party Convention of 1932 Lippmann remained conservative; he was pleased that the Democrats were hesitant to propose radical departures. "In so far as the keynote address represents the views of the dominant elements of the Democratic party, it is a matter of extraordinary interest that they have chosen to stand not upon some policy of monetary manipulation or artificial stimulation of business, but upon the thesis that the way to recovery is through the restoration of trade by the lowering of domestic tariffs and by international co-operation" (HT 6/28/32). By the end of that year, however, he was willing to concede that there was a need to deal with "monetary disorders," but it was unclear just what he meant by this and he still looked for ways "the Federal budget is to be reduced" (HT 9/8/32). Lippmann had not had serious exposure to monetary and fiscal theory and policy before this time, and he had been told repeatedly by friends in the business community that meddling in this area could cause inflation, shake confidence, and generate instability. Yet he could see that lack of confidence and instability already characterized the worsening depression.

It was not until Roosevelt announced a bank holiday in 1933 that Lippmann was prepared to challenge monetary orthodoxy. He had been willing earlier to suggest that to facilitate a national monetary policy "a new banking system is imperatively needed" that would depart from "the old states' rights philosophy" (HT 7/1/32). Now he was convinced that there was too much monopoly power by the large banks and too much weakness among the small ones. He speculated that the whole fractional reserve system, with redemption in gold, was a house of cards and might explain the worsening deflation that was at the root of the depression. "Now this panic to convert deposits into currency and currency into gold was the final stage of the deflation during which the people have been converting property into bank deposits. The stages of the downward movement have been, first, a flight from property into bank deposits, then a flight from bank deposits into currency, and finally a flight from currency into gold" (HT 3/9/33). The task ahead was to make the downward spiral change course and move back upward. "It follows that a restoration requires that the process should be reversed, that gold should be converted into currency, currency into bank deposits, and that bank deposits should be used to buy goods. It follows from this that three fundamental things have to be done: 1. it must be made expensive and dangerous to hoard gold. 2. there must be the assurance that there will, in the President's language, be 'an adequate but sound currency,' adequate in the sense that anyone can obtain currency if he desires it, sound in the sense that the currency will be controlled to prevent any exorbitant rise in prices. 3. there must be established an adequate and sound banking system, adequate in the sense that it can serve the business of the country, sound in the sense that the sound banks will be sound beyond question and the unsound banks won't open" (HT 3/9/33). Lippmann looked abroad for models of "a sound banking system." "Steps will have to be taken to centralize the banks to a much greater degree than ever before. By branch banking and by mergers of various kinds under national control we seem to be headed toward the establishment of a system like the British and Canadian, in which there are fewer banks of very much greater size. It is plain that the managers of these fewer and greater banks will have vastly increased responsibilities. They will have to protect many more depositors and they will have to serve the needs of much larger commercial areas" (HT 3/10/33). He wondered even whether recession might be like a purgative that would periodically cleanse the system of unsound institutions and lead to a stable economic system in the long run. Under this evolutionary interpretation the ending of a depression too quickly could be counterproductive by preserving weak institutions.

Lippmann declared candidly in April 1932 that the proper role for the Federal Reserve System remained a mystery to him. He was excited when the Fed announced experimental purchases of government securities on the open market as a way of stimulating recovery, but he was not clear why. In the crisis he seemed ready to forget the fears of inflation from an active monetary policy, which had been repeated to him so many times. He admitted that "the theory behind it is a relatively new one in the practice of central banking and there is no entirely adequate past experience upon which to rely." Nevertheless, "the risks of not succeeding in it are far less than the risks of not trying it" (HT 4/19/32).

As he struggled with the question of whether such a radical policy as a vigorously managed money supply was appropriate he received what amounted to an extended tutorial, with data and charts, from the Cornell economist F. A. Pearson who, with his colleague George F. Warren, was also making his views known at the time to the White House. Pearson argued forcefully to Lippmann that a contracting money supply amounted to a "blind policy of deflation," leading to liquidations and much suffering throughout the economy (Pearson to WL, December 17, 1932, March 23, 1933, and April 11, 1933, WLPIII F1678). Pearson believed in the great power of price level changes, and he questioned the promise of exchange rate adjustments to stimulate the economy: "It is only for a short interim that revaluation permits one country to buy or sell at an advantage over the other. The importance of this factor is temporary and transitory, but has been magnified until it has become the foremost problem in the minds of many persons" (Pearson to WL, April 29, 1933, WLPIII F1678). He was doubtful also that interest rate reductions discussed later by Keynes in *The General Theory* (1936) could make much of a difference. "The price of credit and the amount used are largely a result of business activity (especially construction), and only to a limited extent, the cause of it. Building activity does not begin until there is a distinct shortage of buildings and buildings sell for enough so that it is profitable to build them. No ordinary change in interest rates would be sufficient to check building. Low interest rates would tend to stimulate it, but are not sufficient to start building. The same principles hold true of textile, automobile, and other industries"

(Pearson to WL, October 7, 1936, and February 8, 1937, WLPIII F1678). Pearson indicated in December 1933 why he spent so much time persuading Lippmann of the correctness of his price-level theory of business fluctuations. "A brilliant individual, the vice-president of one of the five largest corporations in the United States, made the following comment yesterday in my presence: 'I like to think that I can do my own thinking, but when I cannot, I let Walter Lippmann do it'" (Pearson to WL, December 1, 1933, WLPIII F1678).

Lippmann seems to have been persuaded by Pearson and Warren that at least they should be given a hearing (HT 11/24/33). He told the businessman Henry Dennison, who worried about inflation, that if aggressive open market operations made prices rise too rapidly they could always be made to move in the opposite direction. "There would be no excuse, it seems to me, for our having a runaway inflation except through sheer incompetence and cowardice" (WL to Dennison, May 4, 1933, WLPIII F605). At the same time he wrote to Senator Carter Glass that he was uneasy about giving the Federal Reserve too much leeway. "The question that arises in my mind is whether it is not desirable at this session of Congress to take measures which would make the credit-creating power of the Federal Reserve less elastic. I am not sufficiently expert in these matters to suggest how that might be done, but I feel that this is the proper way to deal with what may come to be a very serious problem in the future" (WL to Glass, December 10, 1933, WLPIII F896). He worried in particular that "gold profit in case of devaluation" could cause an inflationary spurt resulting from increased bank liquidity, and he suggested to Senator Glass that this might justify some action by government (WL to Glass, December 29, 1933, WLPIII F896). Lippmann vowed to get up to speed on monetary theory and policy so as to guide his readers. "Difficult as the subject is, it is of such great importance to every one that an effort to understand it is in order. I am by no means certain that I understand it, for the monetary experts have not yet made their mysteries very intelligible" (HT 4/19/32). At that point all that he could say with confidence was that banks were contracting loans and contributing to deflation and this must be stopped. "Now as long as this vicious spiral is in progress a readjustment is impossible. For while employers are cutting costs to adjust themselves to one level, the level itself sinks and their costs are again out of line. If the level of prices could be stabilized almost anywhere, industry could adjust itself to that level by reducing fixed charges, salaries, wages, and retail prices. But with the level falling faster than the readjustments can be made, the depression appears to have no end and confidence is demoralized" (HT 4/19/32).

He thought that easy money from the Fed would drive down interest rates and increase bank liquidity. "The expectation is that if the policy is boldly pursued two things must happen: first, the member banks, having become highly liquid, will cease to be afraid of not being able to pay off their depositors; second, they will become very tired of earning one or two per cent or even nothing on their liquid funds and will be tempted to begin buying other bonds and extending credit to borrowers" (HT 4/19/32). To those who cried "inflation, beware," he replied, "If this reading of events is correct the present policy of forcing up prices of bonds in order to diminish their yield may be looked upon, not as an inflation at all, but as an attempt to bring the cost of money down to a point where there can again be a profitable equilibrium among the factors of production. It may well be that the true significance of the Federal Reserve policy, therefore, is not merely to make the banks liquid and then to tempt them to extend credit, but also to make the cost of credit so reasonable that at these lower levels enterprise can again become profitable" (HT 4/19/32). Federal Reserve open market operations had become for Lippmann by September 1932 the only public intervention that he felt confident would stimulate recovery without causing inflation or loss of confidence. "What is certain is that in the past the accumulation of a surplus of idle money has been followed by economic recovery" (HT 9/29/32). Lippmann clearly was becoming an enthusiast for aggressive open-market operations targeting bank liquidity and the domestic price level. Pearson did his part by insisting to Lippmann throughout the 1930s that deflation, not inflation, remained the problem to be addressed (e.g., Pearson to WL, March 16, 1937, and November 6, 1937, WLPIII F1678).

In the months that followed his first appreciation of an active open-
market policy Lippmann undertook a self-directed crash course in monetary economics. He was assisted by Treasury and Fed officials as well as
experts on monetary issues outside government who kept the letters and
messages coming. Carl Snyder of the New York Federal Reserve Bank, in
particular, claimed that both excessive credit creation in the 1920s and then
declining credit in the 1930s explained the depression. After the crash in
1929 the only way to get investment moving again was to keep interest rates
low and credit readily available. He wrote in 1931 that "the industrial machine" was "actually running at about 80 or 85 per cent of its normal speed.
All it needs is a little oil" (Snyder to WL, November 20, 1931, WLPIII
F1971). Sadly, "the economists can't be convinced" (Snyder to WL, October 14, 1932). But he was delighted that Lippmann was. By early in 1933
Lippmann had become comfortable with a managed money supply that
would raise price levels to precrash levels. "The measure of desirable 'reflation' if that is the word for it—is a rise in prices to a point where, at the existing level of wage rates, re-employment can become general without excessive profits. This does not mean, I hasten to add, that wage rates must not
rise after employment has recovered and been stabilized. It means that
during the process of recovery and re-employment, prices, particularly
wholesale prices which are more deflated than wage rates, must be allowed
to catch up" (HT 3/11/33). When Lippmann was away from the column
later in 1933, preparing the Godkin lectures for the following year, Snyder
suggested why he still kept the letters and memos coming in a steady stream.
"R[oosevelt] has been strongly advised, I am told, of a program that, as I
take it, is not very far from your own general outlook, and that reasonable-
minded men might get behind. I wish you were back on the job, to give it
a shove. That might be decisive" (Snyder to WL, September 22, 1933,
WLPIII F1971).

Lippmann discovered quickly that his own innocence in the monetary
field was exceeded by that of most of his readers and people of prominence,
and he determined to learn as much as possible himself, set others straight,
and point out their errors. He began with proposals that he thought made

no sense. For example, he explained that a bill before Congress to "elevate the average price of wholesale commodities by about 50 percent" was "inherently absurd and impossible." Actual Fed policy was, and could only be, to "raise the *general* price level and not the wholesale ievel alone." The new program of monetary intervention overall, he claimed, was "one of the most interesting, and potentially one of the most important, ever undertaken in the conscious control of human affairs" (HT 5/5/32). Moreover, "if the present experiment succeeds—a power over human affairs will have been demonstrated to exist which calls for the utmost wisdom and disinterestedness by those who exercise it" (HT 5/5/32). Lippmann reminded those who would give credit to President Hoover for the Fed's "very promising open-market policy" that the Fed was a "non-partisan organization which is not in theory, or, it may be assumed, in practice, a part of the Administration" (HT 9/15/32). He found it necessary to explain to Senator William Borah, an influential inflationist for whom he nevertheless had high regard, that the Fed's open market operations mainly increased bank deposits and not currency in circulation. "The only difference between what Senator Borah desires and what the System is trying to do is that the Senator wants to expand a tiny part of our total money supply [currency], whereas the System is trying to expand the main part of our money supply" (HT 10/14/32). Lippmann worried that a sudden increase in currency in circulation, as Borah proposed, if implemented by those who did not know any better, could actually cause a bank panic and ultimately deflation, thanks presumably to a sudden drop in velocity (the rate of turnover of money) (HT 1/25/33). During the turbulent early months of 1933 Lippmann expressed impatience with the slow pace of open market operations: "There ought to be no further delay about making it clear, through large purchases of government securities, that the Administration's monetary policy is seriously and resolutely to be carried out" (HT 5/23/33). Thereafter he seldom wavered in his advocacy of an active monetary policy, and he was in firm support of the Eccles bill in 1935, which centralized authority in an open market committee in Washington. He brushed aside those who complained of too much concentration of power. "Economic science is at present a long way from having achieved a reliable and settled theory of monetary policy. There are profound questions about which the very ablest men differ. It would be a mistake therefore to claim for the bill that it is a remedy for the curse of inflation and deflation. But it can be said, surely, that it is better to proceed into the obscure region of monetary control with our eyes open because we know who is responsible than to drift in the dark with responsibility divided" (7/30/35).

Lippmann was quick to approve open-market operations, but he was more hesitant to support departure from gold. He praised Hoover's decision in 1931 to resist Britain's lead in leaving the gold standard. Like it or not, he wrote, gold was here to stay. "It may be that the desire for the convertibility of currency into gold is merely a superstition of the Western capitalist world. It is none the less one of the real facts which control the financial behavior of the multitude of owners, large and small, throughout the world system of which the United States is so important a part" (HT 9/6/32). He applauded the unified response of the two American political parties to the recent gold crisis by attempting to bring "the budget into approximate balance and . . . limiting the works program to projects which did not theoretically increase the government deficit." The symbolism was important. "The net effect of these actions was to prove to the world that the United States Government not only did not mean to depreciate the currency, but did affirmatively mean to maintain its gold value" (HT 9/6/32).

By the time FDR decided to leave the gold standard in 1933 Lippmann was on board. Another sacred cow had fallen. He thought that this act allowed the United States to complete the full takeover of its monetary policy, and he urged that the dollar be allowed to depreciate to some sort of full-employment equilibrium exchange rate. "For the evidence is now, I believe, conclusive that a decision to maintain the gold parity of currency condemns the nation which makes that decision to the intolerable strain of falling prices" (HT 4/18/33). France, the only major country that remained on the gold standard, discovered this to her pain. When the domestic currency was overvalued the consequences were severe. "The attempt to balance the budgets of government and of private enterprises calls for continual reductions of wages, salaries and expenditures. These in turn destroy purchasing power. This in turn reduces revenue. At the same time the effort to pay out gold on demand forces the banks to be liquid. In order to be liquid they must contract credit. The contraction of credit stifles business. The contraction of business again reduces revenue. There is, in short, the vicious spiral of deflation" (HT 2/8/34). Ultimately the United States would have to return to some sort of stabilized exchange rate system to prevent a competitive downward spiral of rates among its trading partners. But now, with this departure from gold, the exchange rate, like other macroeconomic variables, could be established at a level that brought it in line with overall American objectives. "The time is at hand, therefore, when the United States should assume control of its own monetary policy so that when the moment comes to stabilize currencies internationally we shall not make the mistake that Great Britain made in 1925 of stabilizing the dollar at a point so high that we are doomed to a long period of deflation and depression" (HT 4/11/33). He explained to his skeptical friend Leonard Ayres: "My view is that we cannot possibly develop a sound policy for the future until we come to some understanding as to why the monetary reconstruction of the 1920s broke down. If we can agree on the diagnosis, we have some hope of finding a cure. For then we'll know what we are trying to do. It's precisely because the so-called money people have no intelligible explanation of the monetary phenomena of the last ten years that I distrust intensely their demands that we return immediately to the gold standard. There was something radically wrong the last time the world returned to the gold standard. Within a year of the time the process was completed, the world price level collapsed. I cannot believe that there is no connection between the two things. For that reason I think we have got to make up our minds first of all why our bed collapsed, and when we have done that we're in some position to argue about the practical value of the remedies" (WL to Ayres, December 29, 1933, WLPIII F137).

In 1933 Lippmann applauded Roosevelt for following the lead of the British in establishing an "equalization fund" through the Reconstruction Finance Corporation to manage the exchange rate (HT 10/24/33 and 10/27/33), but he warned that the president must never use this fund for political purposes (HT 10/31/33). With characteristic caution and after hearing from a number of "monetary enthusiasts" with conflicting advice, he suggested that confidence would be strengthened by limiting this intervention. "The relationships of gold and currency and credit and price are obscure. They are so obscure that one is entitled to suspect any one who pretends that money is the subject of an exact science and that he knows that science. Mathematical equations and so-called economic laws do throw light on aspects of monetary situations, but in the framing of a particular policy there are no exact rules" (HT 11/2/33). Perhaps following a suggestion from Lewis Douglas (Douglas to WL, June 27, 1933, WLPIII F640), Lippmann recommended that limits be placed on exchange rate management so that fears of inflation could be minimized: "the Administration will obtain all the benefits that can be had from a change in the value of money by proceeding now to fix an upper and lower limit of devaluation" (HT 11/2/33). He was delighted when Roosevelt adopted this approach (HT 1/16/34 and 1/17/34).

Lippmann himself retained some fear that inflation might be the result of monetary management, and he reminded the authorities that they could move in both directions, that they could restrain prices as well as stimulate "reflation," as Lippmann now was calling it (HT 11/10/33). Moreover, as government became an active money manager it must be transparent and issue a statement of principle as to what was intended. He contemplated even some sort of "High Court of Finance" to guide the process. The Fed board, he thought, was too close to the banks to do this and maintain concern for the public good (HT 1/18/34 and 1/19/34). He supported Federal Reserve chair Marriner Eccles's proposals for reform of the board. He worried that money management, if not kept under tight control, might favor the export sector. He read the literature in economics concerned with monetary policy, and he recommended to his readers especially a study by Frederick Mills for the National Bureau of Economic Research. He admitted that the writings of G. F. Warren and F. A. Pearson of Cornell University, from which he himself had benefited, were rather opaque (HT 11/10/33, 11/14/33, and 11/23/33). At the same time, citing the work of the French economist Charles Rist, he defended them from the charge by the vice-chairman of the Fed that they were "crack pots." He reminded the critics of Warren and Pearson that in contrast with the "collectivist branch" of the Brain Trust they were in favor of "managed currency" and not a "managed economy" (HT 11/24/33). By 1935 Lippmann concluded that the need for flexible exchange rates had passed and he had become again "a stout defender of the gold standard, after what I think was a necessary moral holiday during the year 1933" (WL to Leonard Ayres, March 26, 1935, WLPIII F137).

5

Keynesian Conversion

THE FINAL MACROECONOMIC SACRED COW to appear before Lippmann
in his search for the cause of the depression, after free trade and the gold
standard, was the balanced fiscal budget. He began his columns in 1931
devoutly orthodox on this matter. On fiscal policy, he wrote that "maintaining an absolute confidence throughout the world in the credit of the United
States" was of paramount importance and therefore "the balancing of the
Federal budget by reducing expenditures and by increasing revenues is the
fundamental and indispensable problem before Congress" (HT 1/5/32). He
admitted that maintaining a balanced budget during a depression by reducing expenditures and increasing taxation was one of the most painful obligations facing modern democracies. But it had to be done. Sadly, "in no
great country has an ordinary political assembly had the courage or the discipline to tax and to economize effectively" (HT 3/29/32). The United
States must show the way. The issue of budget balancing was presented by
Lippmann mainly as a test of moral courage among politicians who were
understandably uncomfortable delivering bad news to their constituents.
"For the task of balancing the budget is an inherently painful one: it consists
in distributing not favors and privileges but burdens and sacrifices" (HT

4/22/32). Yet failure to bite the fiscal bullet would undoubtedly worsen that dreaded lack of confidence that so many said was at the root of the depression: "It would be disastrous to confess by our actions that we do not much care whether we pay our bills or not and that we do not have the character to tax ourselves and make sacrifices. We could afford a deficit. We could not afford to show ourselves flabby, timid and flustered" (HT 4/22/32). Apparently his conviction that "responsible" fiscal policy was a necessity was strengthened by conversations with foreign business and political leaders. He wrote to Senator Cordell Hull in January 1932 that the decline of liberal governments in Germany and Britain was because of their failure "to understand government finance." The Democratic Party must stick firmly to "a policy of drastic economy and widespread taxation" (WL to Hull, January 4, 1932, WLPIII F1104). He wrote Felix Frankfurter in 1932 that "my observations in Europe convinced me profoundly that the balancing of the budget was an extremely urgent necessity" (WL to Frankfurter, April 8, 1932, WLPIII F816).

At home as well as overseas Lippmann received regular encouragement in his insistence on a balanced budget from authorities such as Arthur Ballantine, assistant secretary of the treasury (Ballantine to WL, December 17, 1931, WLPIII F157); the financial guru Bernard Baruch (Baruch to WL, September 23, 1931, WLPIII F178); and the National Economy League (Harvey Chase to WL, December 1, 1932, WLPIII F1582). His friend Thomas Lamont, partner in J. P. Morgan, warned that deficit financing to pay for public works would have just the opposite effect to that hoped for : "the cost of paying for these emergency works in the way of increased taxation, whether or not part of such cost is funded by bond issues, would represent an additional burden on business which would seriously retard business recovery and the natural increase in employment resulting therefrom" (Lamont to WL, January 5, 1932, WLPIII F1276). Ogden Mills, secretary of the treasury under Hoover, assured him that "[o]nce we abandon the principle of a balanced budget, our defenses are down. . . . If the Administration ever attempts to compromise this principle, my best judgment is that the dam will go out and the flood will follow" (Mills to WL, May 27, 1932,

WLPIII F1512). Becoming a little irritated by these repeated dire warnings, Lippmann reminded Mills that in reality "[a]n actually balanced budget is not in sight" (WL to Mills, June 3, 1932, WLPIII F1512).

As the Hoover administration drew to a close Lippmann was reasonably confident that no politician then on the horizon had the courage to do what was needed fiscally. One political party was as irresponsible as the other: "both parties are in the grip of deep-rooted popular prejudices" (HT 7/13/32; also 10/18/32 and 10/26/32). The only force that could make politicians move was the voice of the people, and he urged that this be mobilized in every way. "Our problem can be solved only by the awakening of an informed and powerful public opinion. It is necessary, therefore, to seek clear ideas on the real meaning of this confused struggle to balance the budget" (HT 5/3/32). Lippmann had hoped that perhaps in Hoover's last year in office public opinion in favor of a balanced budget would influence him, but it seemed that the forces on the other side were too strong: "If there existed the morale in Washington and the public spirit in the country to deal with lobbyists and organized minorities, the best way to make the cuts would be by careful examination of all the expenditures. But such a procedure is not possible under existing conditions" (HT 5/11/32). The only way forward seemed to be an across-the-board cut in all public expenditures.

To those who called for budget deficits to finance public works and as a way of reducing unemployment, Lippmann responded in 1931 and 1932 that, regrettably, such irresponsible behavior would so reduce confidence in the stewardship of government that the public expenditure from deficits would likely do more harm than good and crowd out private projects in greater amount. Moreover, he feared that public expenditures financed by bonds rather than taxes would sop up the new funds made available through the open market operations of the Federal Reserve; lenders, instead of going to the private sector, would pick the safer option and buy government bonds. Pay as you go had to be the watchword for government. "If such a fiscal program as this could be carried out in the next year, if it could be begun in the next few months with the promise of final success, it is as certain as anything can be that the beneficial effects would be wide and immediate. The Administration which carries it out would command confidence throughout the nation and throughout the world" (HT 12/20/32). He continued to accept the argument that to tough it out while the economy adjusted might be the best way to proceed. It seemed to have worked in other places. "Within this country and in others there has been taking place a stupendous readjustment through failures and bankruptcies, through the curtailment of production, the cutting of wages and salaries, through economies and reorganizations. The result is that a large number of producers are now in a position to make money at lower prices, and on smaller volume than they needed before they went through the deflation" (HT 9/7/32).

Iconoclasm

By 1932 he did, however, admit that there was an unorthodox view of the matter. "The heretic school believes that the lack of confidence is really a subjective condition among business men, bankers and investors, and that, therefore, the government, which can afford to take risks that private individuals are afraid of, should temporarily fill the vacuum left by the absence of private initiative" (HT 5/12/32). But for the moment he remained not persuaded by this heterodoxy, and in the election of 1932 he urged "orthodoxy" and "sound fiscal policy" on both candidates (HT 10/28/32). After the election the crisis worsened, yet he still called for draconian tax increases and expenditure cuts. "There is no escape from the fact that the budget cannot be brought into balance even next year without colossal new taxes, taxes greater than any now under consideration, unless Congress will retrench on public works and amend the veterans' laws" (HT 12/8/32). He was uneasy that Roosevelt as a candidate seemed to waver on the cuts that were needed (HT 1/10/33). Even in the darkest days of early 1933 Lippmann insisted that deficit finance was the certain route to "immediate and uncontrolled inflation, which would be disastrous" (HT 3/8/33). He was pleased with the principle behind the "Economy Bill" in Congress that all appropriations should be recommended by the executive and approved by the Congress (HT 3/14/33). This supposedly would increase the president's power to restrain the legislature and reduce "pork." Lippmann was also relieved by the restraints on public expenditure imposed by his friend

Lewis Douglas as director of the Bureau of the Budget in the Roosevelt cabinet. With Douglas in command orthodoxy would prevail. "Now a government which has asserted its control over its expenditures and its access to revenue has accomplished what 'balancing the budget' means. It is master in its own house, and having become the master, it is entitled again to borrow for any social purpose which can be made intelligible to the people. . . . For the government is now freeing itself of the outside forces that were paralyzing it, and as long as it remains free, as long as it continues to be clearly stronger than any vested interest, the fight to 'balance the budget' is won" (HT 4/6/33).

The budget-balancers were not the only ones to whom Lippmann was listening by 1932. In November Felix Frankfurter sent him a copy of the letter from the British economists to the London *Times* (D. H. MacGregor et al.) urging greater public expenditure (attached to Frankfurter to WL, November 16, 1932, WLPIII F816). Arthur Holcombe, his old and trusted friend in the Harvard Government Department, wrote him to suggest the desirability of deficit finance in the emergency. "The construction of public works upon public credit, as you properly indicate in your article, is the sound measure for permanent relief. The more useful the works the better, but public works of any utility whatever are infinitely superior to idleness. The government must borrow and repay when prosperity returns. Hence, as you wisely say, the need for courage as well as wisdom" (Holcombe to WL, April 29, 1932, WLPIII F1064). But Lippmann insisted on more "wisdom" before he could fall behind as radical a public policy as this, and he replied to Holcombe: "I don't feel at all sure about the public works aspect of the matter because I am afraid that probably quantitatively the amount that could be done is too small to make any impression" (WL to Holcombe, May 4, 1932, WLPIII F1064). Without the concept of the multiplier, deficit spending on public works remained unpersuasive to Lippmann. Yet he seemed to be having some second thoughts, and he was moved to ask his friend the lawyer William M. Chadbourne whether he "knew of anyone who has collected a reliable estimate of projects which are not too wasteful that could be undertaken, with some estimate as to the direct and indirect employment which they could create" (WL to Chadbourne, April 22, 1932,

WLPIII F407). Chadbourne suggested Virgil Jordan, an economist at McGraw-Hill (Chadbourne to WL, April 27, 1932, WLPIII F407). When Judge Frank B. Kellogg of the World Court urged Lippmann to remain firm in opposition to public works through deficit finance, he replied: "There is a point where financial Puritanism would become a grave social danger, and I think we are at that point now" (WL to Kellogg, May 25, 1932, WLPIII F1199).

The year between June 1933, when he left for the London Economic Conference, and May 1934, when he delivered the Godkin Lectures at Harvard University, was intellectually very productive, even a conversion experience, for Lippmann; over that time he developed a personal philosophy of macroeconomics that was much more radical than the one he had expounded over the prior three years and that remained substantially unchanged thereafter. He laid out the questions that he wanted answered in a column published while he was en route to the conference. He explained in simple terms the essence of the socialist-calculation debate that had been ongoing for a decade and described the two alternative paths he discerned from this debate to deal with the depression. The socialists claimed that the modern market economy was too complex and too flawed to leave to market forces. Serious failures and inconsistencies arose and could be dealt with only by a central planning bureau. Their opponents agreed about the seriousness of macroeconomic problems but insisted that only the disaggregated decision making that took place in competitive markets could achieve solutions to market inconsistencies and preserve human freedom at the same time. He quoted Benjamin Anderson, chief economist of the Chase National Bank, as an effective critic of the socialist position. "When he pointed out that 'to regulate the business of a country as a whole and to guide and control production there is required a central brain of such vast power that no human being can be expected to supply it' he spoke the simple truth. When he said that such centralized control would almost inevitably produce political logrolling rather than genuine economic planning, he was on the sure ground of experience" (HT 6/22/33).

But Lippmann did not like facing a sharp choice between completely free markets on the one hand and socialist controls on the other, and he thought of them both as unacceptable options. Real-world imperfections of all kinds had made the presumption of perfect competition no more than a theoretical possibility in "the imaginary world of the classical economics" (HT 6/22/33). "This does not seem to me to be very illuminating. For it is an attempt to solve very real difficulties by offering us a choice between two unreal alternatives. It is unrealistic to the point of being wholly misleading to assume that 'the co-ordination of the multitudinous elements' now takes place through 'the markets.' Nothing has been more clearly revealed during the course of the depression than that there is no longer an effective 'co-ordination' by 'the markets.' That is why some prices have fallen so much less than others. The three years of the depression have demonstrated, I think, conclusively, that the modern industrial economy simply does not 'co-ordinate' itself, as Dr. Anderson thinks it should, by the action of supply and demand. At a thousand vital points the system has become rigid through contracts, gentlemen's agreements, virtual monopolies, trade union rules, legislation and other devices for interfering with the law of supply and demand. Had that not been the case, the 'markets' might have co-ordinated us rapidly and successfully to a new and lower price level, and we should have made our recovery by completing the deflation" (HT 6/22/33). The notion of a central planning structure as it was understood in Soviet Russia applied to the United States was, he said, simply absurd. It was as far from reality as was the assumption of free markets: "Where is such an economy contemplated, except perhaps in Russia, and who that has any instinct for reality supposes that a system of control, which may work in the simple and relatively primitive Russian economy among a people habituated to political absolutism, could be initiated in the United States? It does not seem to me to throw any valuable light upon our own problems to ask us to choose between Adam Smith on the one hand and Lenin on the other" (HT 6/22/33).

He called, as he had been doing since his college days, for empirical study of the American economy with its special circumstances. "Is it not possible, in fact is it not altogether probable, that our own study of our own experience and our own needs may produce measures which differ from those contemplated either by an eighteenth century thinker in Scotland or by a twentieth century revolutionist in Russia? I do not think we have to choose between the devil and the deep blue sea, the frying pan and the fire, or between two systems which in relation to our own actual life are equally imaginary and equally unrealizable. . . . Where and when direction and management are necessary, how they can be organized, how far they must be carried, how made responsible, how kept informed and flexible,—these are the problems which we shall be dealing with all the rest of our lives" (HT 6/22/33). And it was these problems that Lippmann was himself setting out to explore, not for the rest of his life but at least for a year or two, starting with a summer in England.

At the World Economic Conference in London in 1933, initiated by President Hoover before leaving office, Lippmann remained deeply troubled about the proper role for government in the economy. He was uneasy about the number of sacred institutions he faced when contemplating economic policy reform, and he was puzzled especially about how everything might fit together. He had already reaffirmed free trade, rejected the gold standard, and argued for a managed money supply. But there were still questions about fiscal policy and about how government, so ill-informed about economic theory and policy, could put together a coherent program. One of the objectives of the conference was supposedly to find a way back to the gold standard, and many of the delegates were startled and angry when in his letter of instruction Roosevelt said that he was not yet ready to make a decision on this matter. In fact Lippmann too was not ready, and his strong recommendation was that this conference, which was "misconceived, disorganized, and badly timed," be adjourned as soon as possible so that everyone could rethink their positions (HT 7/5/33). When a delegate to the conference asked him what to read in order to understand the problems, his advice can be assumed to reflect his own reading. He wrote: "Cassel's recent Oxford lectures on the monetary crisis. On the whole, taking the last fourteen years together, Cassell has been more nearly right on monetary questions than any economist in the world. I think you would find a good deal of insight into the British view by reading [Ralph George] Hawtrey's 'The Gold Standard in Theory and Practice.' I do not know of any book by an American author on the monetary problem which is really first rate.

While you're in London you ought to be sure to get the London Economist and read it carefully. On monetary questions as distinguished from tariff questions it more nearly represents the views of the British Treasury than any other publication. Leith-Ross, when he was here, told me that Layton [editor of the *Economist*] spoke their ideas much more accurately than Keynes or Salter. On the tariff there is very little in the way of books that has not been made antiquated by the course of events. One thing, however, I think you should read, not because you will wholly agree with it perhaps, but because it represents to my mind at least a very deep insight into the direction which protectionist thought is taking in this country and the rest of the world. This is the address delivered by Dean Donham of the Harvard Business School" (WL to James M. Cox, May 18, 1933, WLPIII F529).

It seemed clear to Lippmann that in a relatively short time the parameters of economic policy formation had changed fundamentally. Above all the "people" had become accustomed to expressing their views about economic issues through the voting booth, or on the streets, and were not willing any longer to let others sacrifice their jobs and personal welfare in the name of sacred cows like the gold standard. It was necessary for leaders at all levels to stand back and rethink the broad objectives of policy and how it might be implemented. The questions should be not just about technical economic matters but also about social philosophy and how to design a just and efficient economic system. If they did not do so, they would be replaced. Take the British case. "Now it is perfectly true that Britain was forced off the gold standard. But what forced her off? It was not, as is usually said, her foreign creditors. It was the British working class which would not submit to a reduction in wages" (HT 12/13/33). The questions about the economy that were raised at this point in history were precisely the ones that appealed most to Lippmann and that allowed him to bring together and use the disciplines with which he was most at ease: philosophy, political science, psychology, and economics. He settled down for hard thinking over the next twelve months.

Two factors in particular help to explain the outcome of Lippmann's critical year. First was his friendship with John Maynard Keynes, which was strengthened by their participation together in the World Economic

Conference as well as meetings over the summer of 1933. In advance of the conference Lippmann and Keynes took part in "the first International two-way series of radio broadcasts" arranged by the National Broadcasting Company and the British Broadcasting Corporation and intended as "a most important step in bringing international exchange of ideas into a more advanced form" (Keynes 2010, and Fred Bate to WL, April 14, 1933, WLPIII F1578). Lippmann's first reports from the conference told of the unique contributions Keynes was making to it. He described "the Keynes plan," by which the United States would initiate a coordinated devaluation of currencies within a 20 to 33 percent range and thereby raise price levels, as having "more of the character of a decisive and a possible action, than anything which is being considered" (HT 6/29/33). The devalued currencies would be "stabilized provisionally and flexibly in relation to each other," thus averting the very real danger of competitive currency depreciation (HT 6/29/33). The scheme, Lippmann thought, would stimulate expenditure and lead ultimately to more flexible exchange rates: "It would appear that the plan offers a possible way of reconciling the divergent purposes of the French and of ourselves by achieving in one project the double result of raising prices and stabilizing currencies. . . . Yet the plan is not the happy-go-lucky panacea of an amateur. It is the proposal of the leading economic thinker of our generation. Mr. Keynes speaks with authority. The events of the last fifteen years have demonstrated dramatically that his economic insight is more truly prophetic than that of any living man" (HT 6/29/33). Later Lippmann cited Keynes on such subjects as the need to keep short-term interest rates low to stimulate investment (HT 1/25/34) and the likelihood that humans would lose interest in gold (HT 1/26/34). During the summer of 1933 Lippmann seems to have grasped quickly the essence of the evolving Keynesian doctrine that to understand and find a solution to the Great Depression one must focus on the determinants of aggregate demand. When, many years later, Lippmann congratulated John Kenneth Galbraith on his account of how Keynes came to America, he explained, "It goes without saying that I always found his great book unreadable, but nevertheless, I have managed to be an ardent, amateur Keynesian" (WL to Galbraith, December 25, 1965, WLPIII F853). Although Lippmann admitted that the London Economic Conference failed, he joined Keynes and Salter in never doubting that international cooperation would be essential for the return of prosperity in the long run (HT 7/20/33).

The second important factor in the development of Lippmann's thinking, after the London Conference, was a long vacation he took in Maine during which he read widely at his celebrated breakneck pace. He was supplied with books by the library of Harvard University where, by this time, he was an overseer and chairman of the visiting committee of the Economics Department. He had still to treat the rapidly unfolding economic events in his thrice a week columns, but for him this was a time also to "think big." He believed others should be doing so as well. "For a large part of the mischief and folly of the world comes from rushing in, taking a position, and then not knowing how to retreat" (HT 10/10/33). There were frequent indications in his columns during these months that he was hatching new ideas. While he understood and admired within limits the vision growing out of the competitive market model he concluded that there must be flaws within it because of the unsatisfactory state of the economy at that time. He suspected that the trouble might lie in the psychology thought to motivate the self-interested optimizing economic agents. The behavioral postulate of simple utilitarian rationality might not be the best one for imagining anything other than some kind of utopian economy. He speculated that the popularity of this postulate might explain the tolerance toward pervasive conflict of interest among leaders in the private and public sectors and the inattention to business ethics. The assumption of optimizing behavior made it seem natural to cheat. "My own view is that the capitalist system cannot be preserved unless the principle of disinterestedness governs the conscience of the leaders of that system. Unless bankers and corporate executives realize that these vast modern enterprises can be administered only by men whose judgment is not confused by ambiguous private interest, they will be unable to operate modern business and finance successfully, and some other form of collective operation will take its place" (HT 12/8/33). He returned to this concern after World War II in his book *Essays in the Public Philosophy* (see Chapter 11). At the time he was writing, the head of one of the largest commercial banks had been found to be taking regular side payments from the bank's customers, and Lippmann suggested that this kind of corruption extended even to the scholarly world. "A professor of economics who is on the payroll of a public utility loses the right to pretend that his observations on utilities are scholarly" (HT 12/8/33). He looked forward to a time when businessmen would be required to operate by a code of ethics at least as strict as that supposedly required of those in the public sector: "The men who conduct these large enterprises are not in the position of proprietors who can trade for personal profit; they are salaried employees who resemble public officials far more than private business men. It is no exaggeration to say, I think, that the future of these capitalistic corporations whether they are to be broken down, or absorbed by the state, or permitted to be largely self-governing, depends upon how quickly and how thoroughly the men who control them recognize and act upon the conception that they are for all practical purposes public officials" (HT 12/29/33).

Economists in Government

In November 1933 Lippmann wrote about how over the past two decades politico-economic systems had come to be dominated by single ideas: simple democracy under Woodrow Wilson, communism under Lenin, unfettered capitalism under Calvin Coolidge, fascism under Benito Mussolini. Now was a time when liberal democracy must rethink and defend its own doctrine. It was unlikely that liberalism would sweep the world or that it would be completely swept away. What had happened in Russia and Italy was not likely to happen in many liberal democracies, although liberal governments for the foreseeable future were likely to be limited to a few countries in Europe and North America where the tradition was strong: "In France, in Switzerland, in Scandinavia, in the British nations, in the United States, there are peoples with a very different history and, therefore, with very different habits. It will be for them to say what is the future of liberalism, how it is to be preserved and where it is to be modified" (HT 11/16/33). It was necessary now to explore all aspects of life in a liberal democracy. For example, different economic groups had been affected very differently by the depression. Could this be tolerated? "From 1929 to 1932 there was a great decline in the total national income. But in the course of this decline salaries and dividend payments fell slowly at first. Interest payments fell very little. Among labor incomes salaried men were favored as against wage-earners, and of course wage-earners as against the unemployed. Relatively speaking, property incomes increased" (HT 1/30/34). These differential impacts were of more than casual interest: "The mass of people have gone to school, are conscious of their powers and will not passively accept the destruction of their standards of life. The modern economic system does not have the safety valve of free land and free migration of peoples, and the peoples themselves are no longer willing to look upon social calamities as beyond human control. The consequence is that any prolonged and violent change in the distribution of wealth, whether by inflation or deflation, is a profound threat to the whole social order and the existence of political in-stitutions" (HT 1/30/34). On this ground alone he came increasingly to be-lieve that some degree of planning was necessary for the survival of the free market system (HT 2/1/34). But how much, and of what kind?

Lippmann praised Roosevelt for his willingness to experiment and to embrace new ideas that might be the salvation of liberalism, but he worried about the quality of the men who surrounded him and about the more gen-eral problem of equipping government with bright people to deal with the modern economy. He was sorry to report that no one in the Brain Trust, or anywhere else in government for that matter, was able to explain effectively the policies of the New Deal. "There is no book by any members of the Brains Trust which throws light on more than an aspect of the immense undertaking in which the President is engaged. There are indicators of di-rection, there are attitudes, dispositions, and ideals. But no one has yet done for the New Deal what Adam Smith and Jeremy Bentham did for En-glish liberalism in the nineteenth century" (HT 11/21/33 and 4/26/34). At the same time Lippmann urged his readers to be open-minded and to hear all sides of the question. Two of the most thoughtful men in the New Deal, Rexford Tugwell and Lewis Douglas, at opposite ends of the ideological spectrum, were, he observed, being vilified as revolutionaries at a time when their moderate ideas should be given thoughtful consideration. This was no time to be chasing scapegoats. "And if there is not a real villain around, we invent one. We have now reached the point where Professor

Tugwell is being fitted out with horns to frighten ladies and gentlemen of property, and Mr. Lewis Douglas is being set up as the personal devil who is opposing the children of light. Professor Tugwell, it appears, is leading a sort of personal conspiracy to subvert the American scheme of things, and Mr. Douglas is the hard-hearted wretch who stands guard at the Treasury and is blocking the millennium which, but for him, would be just around the corner. If these things were true, it would certainly save a lot of time and trouble. You get rid of Tugwell, and then we all move along happily and prosperously in the good old way. Or, you get rid of Douglas and, before you know it, the New Deal has been dealt and you have made a grand slam" (HT 12/14/33).

One of the most influential commentators for Lippmann on "the better organization of economic thinking in Washington" during this period was Arthur Holcombe, professor of government at Harvard and his close friend with whom he often visited when in Cambridge. Holcombe was engaged during the 1930s with the President's Committee on Administrative Management, charged with proposing ways to make the federal bureaucracy more effective. He discussed with Lippmann various approaches to this question, including creation of "an organ of economic thought more or less fashioned after the model of the War Department General Staff" and attached to the Bureau of the Budget, the Treasury Department, or the Federal Reserve System. Holcombe observed that the creation of the military general staff had "increased the authority of trained military experts and put military administrators on a sounder professional basis than ever before." The same might be done for economics by the creation of a "central fiscal staff" (Holcombe to WL, September 19, 1936, WLPIII F1064). To Holcombe's suggestion that such a new economics unit be placed in the Bureau of the Budget Lippmann responded: "The problem in Washington is to make coherent the credit and monetary policy of the Federal Reserve Board, the tax policy and the expenditures Etc. Etc. It is clear that the coordinator of all that has to be the president himself, but that he is not equipped for the task and that his cabinet is not truly representative for the purpose. I have toyed with the idea of building up a presidential secretariat. It is just as possible, however, that the same thing could be done by your proposal to build up the office of the director of the budget" (WL to Holcombe, September 22, 1936, WLPIII F1064). Lippmann agreed in general with Holcombe's suggestions to strengthen the president's staff, and he added: "A presidential secretariat should be more than an agency of supervision and coordination of administrative policy. It should sift, analyze, and prepare for the President's judgment all the questions that come up for decision. We treat the President as a man in our government, when as a matter of fact he is an institution, like the Crown. The presidential form of government will be workable in the long run only if the presidency operates as an institution and not merely as a one man show" (WL to Holcombe, October 7, 1936, WLPIII F1064).

In April 1934 Lippmann reflected in some depth on the economic advice flowing to FDR and how it was delivered. He acknowledged that there was no shortage of advice, and there were no monsters delivering it, as was sometimes charged. The trouble was that the advice was not evaluated or integrated. He could discern at least the following kinds of advisers from Wall Street: inflationists and deflationists, gold standard enthusiasts, supporters and opponents of the National Recovery Administration (NRA), free traders and protectionists. From the academic world there were "old-fashioned American individualists" (Warren), collectivists (Tugwell), and trust-busters (Frankfurter). The result was a cacophony. "Improvisation and haste, a patchwork of different theories, a lot of talk about planning one thing and another, but a lack of planning for the effort as a whole: these are the serious criticisms which can be brought and must be met" (HT 4/3/34). Now, with remarkable prescience, Lippmann called for establishment of a council of economic advisers to assist the president. "The real trouble has been that the President has lacked a council of advisers who had a common conception of recovery and reform, and the leisure to consider carefully the program as a whole. The brains trust has been too busy to be a brains trust" (HT 4/3/34). Lippmann was worried that even greater ignorance of macroeconomic issues was present in Congress than in the White House. In particular, congressional leaders more than the President were getting recovery from the depression confused with reforming the economic system in pursuit of some vague objectives. Not knowing any better, Congress was anxious to jump ahead to permanent reform of taxation and expenditures before recovery had been accomplished. "It is only when this process of recovery has been completed, that is to say, when the national income is restored and the government's *whole* budget is in balance, that taxation aimed to change the distribution of wealth can really be made effective. Then it will be wise policy to tax heavily the profits of prosperity and to apply them to a reduction of the national debt" (HT 4/17/34). All in all Lippmann found macroeconomic thinking, both inside government and outside, to be much more sound in Britain than America, and this might help to explain Britain's more rapid recovery. "In pursuing this policy Great Britain has had the advantage over us in certain important respects. The liberal economists, led by men like Keynes, Hawtrey, Salter, Stamp, Layton have understood the mechanism of the capitalist system far better than most of the economists in the so-called Brains Trust, and they have not gotten themselves into a muddle about the role of profits, or the relation of costs to profits, such as we see exemplified in the N.R.A. On the other hand the Conservatives, in the Treasury, the Bank of England, and the City of London have understood the mechanism of capitalism in the post-war era better than have most of ours. They have not been haunted, as most American sound money men, by the ghost of William Jennings Bryan [populist Democratic candidate for president who ran on a platform of 'free silver'] and the echoes of 1896" (HT 4/19/34).

During his year of study Lippmann softened his views toward an active fiscal policy, and questioned the orthodoxy that balanced budgets were essential for the restoration of "confidence." By the end of 1933 he had become sympathetic to the Roosevelt policy, which he interpreted as follows:

> Its fiscal policy rests on two principles: one is that the ordinary expenses of government, including interest on the debt, must be covered by revenue: that the routine budget must be in balance. The other principle is that having achieved this, the government can and should borrow and spend in sufficiently large amounts to overcome the inertia caused by lack of private spending on the part of the consumers and investors. The unemployed have no money to spend. They must be supplied with money. The farmer, the home owner, the railroad or industrial corporation, cannot renew a mortgage at the bank or in the capital market; the government must do the work the bank is unable to do. Enterprise is at a

low ebb; men will not or cannot borrow to build; the government must start enterprises of its own. This is the theory on which the Administration has been working in so far as it has been dealing with the depression as a product of the business cycle. It is committed to financing the recovery until such time as the resumption of private spending and private investment relieves it of the burden. (HT 11/22/33)

This description of macroeconomic policy sounds remarkably like Keynes, but his name is not mentioned.

By the spring of 1934 Lippmann was entirely comfortable endorsing a mixture of what he called orthodox and heterodox macroeconomic policies. He saw Roosevelt's program by this time as very close to what he could support wholeheartedly. It was, "in all its essential principles, in its mixture or orthodox and unorthodox measures, virtually the same program of recovery which has been resorted to in Australia, in England, and other free countries where a managed recovery has been undertaken" (HT 4/17/34). He was searching for effective ways to explain budget deficits and debt to his readers and to himself as more than an extension of the principles of the household budget to the nation-state. One approach he used was to picture the federal government as a temporary banking system that had to be rushed into place when the regular banking system failed. The need would disappear with the return of prosperity: "This is, I believe, the real meaning of the huge increase in the national debt. It is not an ordinary deficit. The Federal government is not now running an ordinary deficit. It is engaged in a huge banking operation which has come about because local government and private enterprise are unable to borrow or the banking system unable to lend. If this is the truth, then, certain broad conclusions follow. The first is that the remedy for the increase of the Federal debt is not to be found by demanding that the Federal government cease borrowing. It is to be found by restoring the credit worthiness of local government and of private enterprise on the one hand and the efficiency of the banking system on the other" (HT 12/28/33).

By early 1934 Lippmann had made a complete reversal from his position of a year before and was comfortable in saying that "the gigantic expenditures of this year are being made to stimulate a business recovery based upon private enterprise for reasonable profit" (HT 1/9/34). He wondered even if this stimulus by Roosevelt was being reduced too soon based on the government's overconfident prediction of a revival of private sector spending, and especially investment spending, in 1935. "The promises of his budget message cannot be kept unless the capital market is revived. That is what his promises mean" (HT 1/9/34). Lippmann denied that investors' perception of opportunities for business investment had been lost, what he called "the psychosis of investment," and that increases in effective demand had now to be achieved only through consumer expenditures. Yet it was not at all clear that business spending was ready to expand as rapidly as predicted and would not do so until the climate for investment improved. Contraction of government stimulus too soon would cause the tragedy of a double-dip depression. "This being the case, the success of the Roosevelt Administration depends upon the clear-headedness and decision with which it does those things that have to be done to stimulate private enterprise and private investment. For otherwise, when the government financing and government expenditure taper off and stop next year, a slump is inevitable and such a slump would be a moral disaster for all the reforms and hopes of the New Deal" (HT 1/12/34). For those among his conservative friends who claimed deficit finance was simply another term for public extravagance he explained that "pump priming" would not only increase consumer spending but when monetized by the Federal Reserve increase the money supply, reduce interest rates, increase the potential for net profits, and increase investment (WL to Leonard Ayres, May 15, 1935, WLPIII F137).

The Method of Freedom

In May 1934, after his year of study and reflection, Lippmann delivered the Godkin Lectures at Harvard University. They were printed in his columns soon after and were reprinted as a small book by Macmillan entitled *The Method of Freedom*. Although it is one of his most significant publications, this work has been neglected by commentators on economic thought during the Great Depression. His objective was to present "a statement of the principles by means of which, as I see it, a nation possessing a highly developed economy and habituated to freedom can make freedom secure amidst the disorders of the modern world" (vii). The influence of Keynes is evident throughout, and chapter 4, part 1, even has the same title, "The End of Laissez-faire," as a famous pamphlet by Keynes published by the Hogarth Press in 1926. For reasons about which we can only speculate, Keynes's name does not appear in the book at all. Perhaps Lippmann did not wish to associate the main ideas in his lectures with the radicalism of Keynes. Yet despite John Kenneth Galbraith's claim that Keynes came to Harvard, and to America, first with publication of the *General Theory* in 1936, a case may be made that the influence began at least two years before, through Lippmann in these lectures (Galbraith 1971, 43–59). Lippmann waited until February 1937, when discussing the developing monetary and fiscal policy of the Roosevelt administration, to make the following claim in a column: "The man who has done more than any other living person to develop a scientific basis for this policy, and to popularize it, is Mr. John Maynard Keynes. Few economists have ever exerted as wide an influence on practical affairs in their own time" (HT 2/6/37).

Lippmann wrote optimistically in *The Method of Freedom* that the present was truly revolutionary, a time in which the old order was unquestionably dying and people were willing to listen to unfamiliar ideas about what might replace it. The totalitarian systems of communism and fascism had been substantially discredited among right-thinking people. They were not efficient economically, and they were inconsistent with human freedom. "It is no accident that wherever and whenever planned collectivism has been instituted, in all countries during the war, in the post-war dictatorships, it has required censorship, espionage, and terrorism to make it work" (WL 1934, 44). The nineteenth-century vision of a system based on perfectly free markets also seemed at this point to be merely quaint: "the gospel of laissez-faire, which men treated as a revelation of the very nature of the universe, in fact reflected quite temporary conditions" (WL 1934, 13). And, of course, genuinely free markets never existed: "In a realistic view of the old capitalism, it is not far from the truth to say that free competition existed in so far as men were unable to abolish it" (WL 1934, 27). Capitalism had, in fact, been on trial since the 1890s and, with the increase in political power of the masses, was tolerated without much enthusiasm only so long as it could deliver the goods. "Private capitalism was allowed to proceed without radical interference as long as it could produce a rising standard of life for the mass and profitable careers for the more energetic and talented individuals. . . . The price of toleration was prosperity. In 1896 it was the full dinner pail. By 1928 the price had risen. It had become the two-car garage" (WL 1934, 15). World War I was economically sobering. "Within two or three years a highly militarized form of planned and regimented state socialism was set up all over the western world. The separation of political and economic power, which was the cardinal tenet of the old order, was suddenly and swiftly abolished" (WL 1934, 16). After the war the old order did not return, and nations and communities sought security through insulation from each other. "Confronted with chaos in the Great Society as a whole, men retreated into the smaller societies with which they were familiar, convulsively insisting that in them they would establish for themselves oases of order and well-being" (WL 1934, 21). The notion of "the economy" as an entity for which the state had special responsibilities, rather than "a mere congeries of separate interests which it serves, protects and regulates," was quite recent and in the United States began with President Hoover. "To this conception of the government's duty he adhered throughout his term" (WL 1934, 28 and 31). Enfranchisement of the working classes led to a focus on business fluctuations as an intolerable feature of the modern economy. Workers would no longer accept the proposition that "periodic depressions are the necessary correction of the accumulated misjudgments of the previous era of prosperity" (WL 1934, 34). New macroeconomic responsibilities had been simply thrust upon the state. "The modern state has to prevent unemployment. It has to protect the standard of life of its people. This compels it to assume a responsibility which it has never yet attempted to discharge before the era in which we are living. The task of insuring continuity of the standard of life for its people is now as much the fundamental duty of the state as the preservation of national independence" (WL 1934, 35).

A whole new approach had to be taken by the modern state to its macroeconomic responsibilities. There had to be a balance between the need for some collective control on one side and human freedom on the other. "I shall call it the method of free collectivism. It is collectivist because it

acknowledges the obligation of the state for the standard of life and the operation of the economic order *as a whole.* It is free because it preserves
within very wide limits the liberty of private transactions. Its object is not to
direct private enterprise and choice according to an official plan but to put
them and keep them in a working equilibrium. Its method is to redress the
balance of private actions by compensating public actions. The system of
free collectivism originates not in military necessity but in an effort to correct the abuses and overcome the disorders of capitalism" (WL 1934, 46).
In the first instance it takes the form of measures that set limits within which
private initiative is confined and fix standards to which it must conform
(WL 1934, 46). The method of freedom would encompass the functions for
the state that had been envisioned by Adam Smith, the American Institutionalists, the Fabians, the progressives, and John Maynard Keynes altogether. "Thus it comprises measures to prevent fraud as between buyers
and sellers: honest weights and measures, the enforcement of equitable
contracts, the suppression of counterfeiting and the misrepresentation of
goods. It comprises measures to equalize the bargaining power of the consumer and of the employee: the regulation of public utilities, factory laws,
and minimum wage laws. It comprises measures to break up monopolies, to
discourage harmful enterprises, to prevent nuisances, to restrict speculation, to repress a too rampant individualism in the use of property. It comprises measures to insure the weak against the hazards of existence and to
restrain the strong from accumulating excessive wealth and power" (WL
1934, 46 and 47).

The distinctive feature of the new method would be its macroeconomic
responsibilities, which were required because of the complex social psychology of the human agents who made up the economy. The voice of Keynes
can certainly be heard in these words. But Lippmann goes further than
Keynes. His doctrine is more like a melding of Keynes with William James,
his old psychology teacher. To the extent that he was familiar with Keynes's
theory, soon to be spelled out in *The General Theory of Employment, Interest and Money* (1936), Lippmann was sympathetic to the idea that "in order
to make public affairs comprehensible to the human mind, men have to create for themselves some kind of mental image, some sort of model, some

hypothetical pattern which is simpler and more familiar than the reality."
At the same time he may have thought the Keynesian model too reduction-
ist to explain the world that "William James used to call the buzzing,
blooming confusion of the actual world" (HT 12/20/35). Lippmann was
looking for government in its macroeconomic role to do more than simply
balance fluctuations in investment by adjustments in government expenditure. He saw the economy as unstable in many of its aspects because of the
complex nature of human behavior, which could not be understood simply
by postulating rational actions. In the following statement can be seen the
influence of the psychologist Wilfred Trotter's *The Instinct of the Herd in
Peace and War* (1919) as much as anticipations of *The General Theory of
Employment, Interest and Money* (1936). "The classical economists over-
estimated the enlightenment which is based on self-interest and the forti-
tude based on self-reliance. The event has shown that the individual judgment upon which they relied exclusively has in the crucial cases meant that
the individual followed the crowd. Imitation, the herd instinct, the conta-
gion of numbers, fashions, moods, rather than a truly enlightened self-
interest, have tended to govern the economy. The submerging of individualism in mass behavior is the consequence of the increasing complexity of
the economic order" (WL 1934, 49).

Because of their own personal characteristics the price humans must
be prepared to pay for individual social and political freedom was macroeconomic intervention by the central government. "It follows that if individuals are to continue to decide when they will buy and sell, spend and
save, borrow and lend, expand and contract their enterprises, some kind of
compensatory mechanism to redress their liability to error must be set up
by public authority. It has become necessary to create collective power, to
mobilize collective resources, and to work out technical procedures by
means of which the modern state can balance, equalize, neutralize, offset,
and correct the private judgments of masses of individuals. This is what I
mean by a Compensated Economy and the Method of Free Collectivism"
(WL 1934, 50 and 51). Monetary intervention had proved to be an important tool already. Fiscal policy showed great promise but had yet to be per-
fected: "It is not only through the central banks that the modern state can

assert compensatory control. It can act directly upon the various markets. This method is also recognized and has been tested experimentally. The state is itself a great employer, a great consumer, a great investor, and a great borrower. It can in theory,—and with experience it can probably learn how actually to do this,—time its operations so as to offset and balance the actions of private employers, consumers, investors, and borrowers. This involves the long-range planning of public works of all kinds, and action in accordance with those plans as circumstances require. . . . An ideal system of taxation would, therefore, be flexible so that rates rose when business was tending toward a boom and fell when it was slowing down. It would also be discriminating so as to encourage or discourage saving with a view to preserving the equilibrium between saving and investment" (WL 1934, 53–54). To those who kept insisting that deficit finance would inevitably cause inflation Lippmann pointed out this would not be a problem so long as private expenditures were not enough alone to sustain full employment. Inflation could certainly become a problem if the government stimulus was continued after private spending had revived: "As long as private industry is not borrowing in normal amounts, the government borrowing merely takes up part of the slack and is not producing and cannot produce a credit inflation. But if private industry starts borrowing, if the private capital market reopens, then a large volume of private borrowing plus large government borrowing would produce credit inflation. However, when private industry starts borrowing it must absorb the unemployed; that will decrease the need for government borrowing to give work to the unemployed" (HT 1/8/35). Like macroeconomists who followed him, Lippmann became annoyed that so many critics of deficit finance kept shouting "inflation" when there clearly was no danger (HT 5/23/35). They seemed not to appreciate that restoring the old price levels by increasing aggregate demand, "reflation" as he still called it, was the best hope for ending the depression.

> It seems to me that several things have been overwhelmingly demonstrated in the past six years of depression. The first is that recovery is impossible through the classical method of deflation, that is, by liquidation, bankruptcy, wage-cutting and government retrenchment. No coun-

try has been able to cure the deflation by more deflation. The second is that deflation cannot be stopped by regimentation as exemplified in the N. R. A. codes and in a thousand devices tried in all sorts of places to peg prices and wages by fiat. The third is that reflation works. It is the going policy of the leading nations of the world. It has worked all over the sterling area. It has worked in the United States. The fourth is that it works best where bankers, business men and government believe in it, understand it, and do not let themselves be led up a blind alley like the N. R. A. or into other restrictionist schemes. (HT 6/18/35)

Lippmann did not feel limited to conventional monetary and fiscal policy to combat the depression. The situation was so serious he was prepared to consider all kinds of experiments. "Another powerful instrument is the state's control over the rates charged by common carriers and public utilities. . . . Such mechanisms, in conjunction with a strong central bank which was clear about its function, would provide an enormously powerful system of compensatory control" (WL 1934, 54-55). Lippmann was prepared in 1934 as a last resort, and if the situation were dire, even to consider controlling international trade as a means of sustaining aggregate demand. "The state will be concerned not only with its own domestic budget but with the balance of payments across national boundaries. It will seek to regulate those payments through a manipulation of tariffs, bounties, and through public control of the volume and at least the general direction of foreign investments" (WL 1934, 55-56). The main message conveyed by Lippmann at this time was that available macroeconomic tools, if used correctly, could at the same time preserve human freedom and achieve economic efficiency, in contrast to the emerging collection of interventionist devices coming out of the New Deal. "Thus economic progress is determined by technological advance, by private enterprise, and by what might be described as the perpetual plebiscite of the markets. The object of the state's intervention is not to supplant this system but to preserve it by remedying its abuses and correcting its errors. The intervention takes the form not of commands and prohibitions but of compensatory measures" (WL 1934, 58).

The problems with implementing his method of freedom, Lippmann appreciated, were of two kinds. First, there were problems of devising and constructing macroeconomic tools that really worked. These problems, he was confident, would be solved in time. "They are difficult now, not because they are in principle insoluble, but because we lack experience and have not yet the will to deal seriously with them" (WL 1934, 73). Far more serious was the interference with macroeconomic policy making for the public good by interest groups that depended on special treatment. New firewalls had to be devised to protect the policy makers from such pressures. "A free collectivism using the compensatory method of control would, under democratic institutions, be subject to constant conflicting pressures from organized interests. There is no use disguising or minimizing the seriousness of this difficulty, and for my part, I am prepared to concede that free collectivism is as incompatible with political democracy in its present manifestations as are the planned economy of communism or the corporate state of fascism" (WL 1934, 76). The obvious solution to this problem was to design new political structures that would be insulated from special interest pressures. "To discharge its new responsibility public authority has to be reasonably independent of transient opinion and organized pressure. . . . The managers of the compensatory devices would have to be independent of the currents of contemporary politics. They would have to enjoy an independence roughly comparable with that of the federal judiciary and of healthy central banks" (WL 1934, 78 and 79).

Lippmann readily admitted that the political reforms likely to be required for his method of freedom would be fully as challenging as the economic ones. Yet they must be faced, and he was confident that they could be worked out. "It is the great problem of government and there is no short and easy solution. Yet if we admit that the problem is insoluble we are in a vicious circle. For in one form or another the state is compelled to intervene deeply in the economic order; if it cannot achieve sufficient independence from the pressure of special groups and of temporary opinions to govern in the general interest, it cannot meet the obligation which under modern conditions it cannot escape" (WL 1934, 88). One answer to the problem might lie with the countervailing powers of conflicting pressure groups, which would be examined by John Kenneth Galbraith after World War II. "The real problem is not how to abolish these interests or how to silence them. It is how to keep them manageable, how to prevent them from becoming intransigent and irresistible. If that can be done, the diverse groups will tend to check each other, and it is then not impossible to frame policies which compromise their demands and reconcile their claims" (WL 1934, 92). Lippmann concluded his discussion of his method of freedom by emphasizing that his intent was only to show a way for modern capitalism to be viable in the long run and to save it from the totalitarian alternatives that were gaining so much prominence in so many countries. "This is not a project to abolish private property and to make all the people servants of the state. On the contrary, it is a project to make the mass of the people independent of the state: that they may be free citizens, who need not be fed by the government, who have no impelling reason to exploit the government, who cannot be bribed, who cannot be coerced, who have no fear of the state and expect no favors. For their livelihood and personal security rest upon private property and vested rights, not upon the acts of officials" (WL 1934, 100).

Threats to Recovery

By the middle of 1934 Lippmann had arrived confidently at a strategy for recovery that contained what he thought was the proper role for government in monetary, fiscal, international, and regulatory policy. It seemed obvious to him that if government acted clearly and responsibly and followed his strategy the depression could be brought to an end quickly and prosperity restored. The tools to achieve recovery were there, and the experts knew how to apply them. Yet, inexplicably, government dithered and the depression lingered. Marriner Eccles, governor of the Federal Reserve Board, by this time saw in Lippmann such a kindred spirit in support of an active monetary and fiscal policy that he suggested that Lippmann fly a trial balloon about subsidized construction of public works: "if you should decide to write upon the general suggestion covered by my memorandum, I would be glad to know what kind of reaction you get from the country" (Eccles to WL, March 12, 1935, WLPIII F683). Lippmann found it necessary in 1936 to assure Eccles that his mounting criticism of the interventionist parts of the New Deal in agriculture and industry had not shaken his faith in active fiscal and monetary policies. "In fact, there have been two contradictory philosophies at work and my impression is that if your philosophy had been applied consistently, leaving the other aside, it would have worked twice as effectively. At that, it is pulling us out of the hole and overcoming the damage done by the other policy as well" (WL to Eccles, May 17, 1936, WLPIII F683).

Over the next several years Lippmann kept asking why, in the face of this new understanding of how to manage the economy described in his Godkin Lectures, there had been so little improvement in macroeconomic performance. He came up with a number of answers. One was that perhaps the apparently slow recovery was an illusion. The reduction in aggregate demand following the Great Crash had not resulted immediately in the lay-offs that were expected. Only when cash reserves were exhausted did employers terminate treasured employees. Consequently in the trough of the depression the level of unemployment was understated, and when during the period of recovery some layoffs did take place they masked the amount of reemployment that was occurring. As he wrote in one of his columns in 1936: "Though we have no accurate count of the unemployed, the fundamental fact seems to be that up to recent months re-employment has lagged behind recovery. The reason for that seems now to be clear. It is that unemployment was never so great as business was bad. In other words more men were kept at work in the bad times than were actually needed. So until recently the recovery has consisted mainly in increasing the work of men who had kept their jobs" (HT 10/6/36).

But there were other, deeper reasons for the slow recovery. One was that the forces that had caused the depression in the first place remained powerful and had been weakened very little by governmental policy to date. In particular, reforms that had been promised by leaders of the stock exchanges to make them more stable and less prone to wild speculative fluctuations had not been implemented (HT 6/8/34). Despite the evident social costs of speculative bubbles and the dramatic collapse of 1929, new bubbles still were forming regularly and bursting with audible reverberations. Indeed, the markets experienced a minor boom and collapse in the summer of 1934, stimulated by the evident unwillingness of government to manage the money supply appropriately and to impose new restraints on speculative stock purchases on margin. The more he studied the matter the more Lippmann became convinced that the gambling instinct was so strong in humans it would take a concerted effort by government to impose effective restraints. This was a problem that could not be solved simply by making markets more free and competitive.

> While the fundamental cause of the extremely unhealthy speculation has been the indecision and indetermination of the Administration's monetary policy, an important contributing cause was the excessive efficiency with which American markets are organized to encourage the deep speculative instinct of the American people. Our love of speculation has its roots deep in our history. A nation which has expanded as we have expanded upon the richest natural resources in the world is naturally and inevitably bullish. There is no reason to be astonished that speculation is easier to incite in America than anywhere else in the world. On the whole and in the long run speculation for a rise has always seemed to justify itself. But the instinct to speculate has cost much in the past. In the present, when the economic machinery has become so intricate, speculation is by way of becoming a dangerous vice. This is why it has become necessary to seek out measures to restrain it. It is not easy to devise such measures and even less easy to have the courage to employ them. But the main facts are perfectly clear. It is altogether too easy to buy on the exchanges and much too easy to borrow in order to buy. (HT 7/25/33)

If the stock market were just like a horse race, Lippmann wrote, society might safely leave it alone. The compulsive gamblers on the race could do little harm to others. But the stock market had close links to banks, and banks created most of the money supply, so the wild gyrations of the market had serious effects on liquidity throughout the economy. Despite the damage caused in 1929 government had done little to control the excesses. The resistance was intense. "If all that happened on the exchanges were that the lambs were shorn, one might say that gamblers must take their losses. But this form of gambling which we indulge in is far more dangerous than horse racing, or roulette, or poker, or the national lotteries which are common in other countries. Our gambling is inextricably entangled with business and agriculture, and whenever it becomes serious it endangers the whole system by which men earn their living. It is so thoroughly infectious that when the fever is on banking and business and political judgment are betrayed, as they were on a grand scale in 1928–1929, on a smaller scale in the past thirty days. For it might as well be admitted that the same fear of 'hurting business' which prevented the Coolidge and Hoover Administrations from acting in time has in some considerable measure prevented the Roosevelt Administration from taking control" (HT 7/25/33). Lippmann dismissed what he considered naïve market theory that pictured the stock market as approaching perfect competition and as relatively independent of the rest of the economy. This flawed thinking was used to impede reform and feather the nests on Wall Street. Fundamental problems growing out of what we would call today asymmetrical information between buyers and sellers needed to be corrected immediately, as they were impeding recovery. "The orthodox theory has always been that the Stock Exchange is merely a market place and that the brokerage houses are merely agents through whom orders to buy and sell are executed. . . . But the indubitable truth is that the Stock Exchange is more than a market place. It is a guild of brokerage houses who, in time of public participation, are for all practical purposes investment or speculative advisers to the owners of securities. The responsibilities of this relationship cannot be sloughed off. It is a fiduciary relationship, and therefore it has become imperative that the exchange, as a corporate body, should have standards and should enforce them, which will protect the public against rigging, manipulation and ignorance. . . . The question as to how far public regulation of a public institution like the Stock Exchange is to be carried is now solely a question of how promptly and how effectively the exchange regulates itself" (HT 8/4/33).

Structural imbalances created during the 1920s, Lippmann thought, might be still another reason for the persistence of depression. The extended boom during the decade might have led to creation of an investment goods sector that could not be sustained by current demands for investment goods. Stimuli under the NRA, which came into effect in 1933, encouraged monopoly in various ways, and suspended the antitrust laws, were directed toward consumption, and these did not increase the demand for capital goods, at least in the short run. Data he obtained from the Department of Commerce "show that the main body of the industrial depression—in human terms nearly seven out of the ten million unemployed—does not lie in the industries which the N.R.A. has stimulated by increases of pay rolls. The deeply depressed industries are those which depend directly not upon the purchasing power of pay rolls but upon the purchasing power of invested savings and bank credit" (HT 10/11/33). "Apart from credit which government agencies are employing, there is only the most miserable trickle of capital expenditure in the form of new corporate financing and mortgage money. Here are the reservoirs of credit full to overflowing and almost no one, except local and Federal government, comes forward to draw upon them" (HT 10/12/33). Investors simply did not see ways to make a profit even with very low interest rates so long as the depression remained in place. "What is the matter? The obvious answer is that the spirit of enterprise has not been revived. Now what is it that makes men enterprising under a capitalist system? It is confidence that they can produce something at a profit" (HT 10/12/33). Some critics of the New Deal were crying now for removal of all constraints on business so that it might rebalance itself and flourish once again. Lippmann was more cautious. He urged Roosevelt to resist the extremists and to retain and strengthen those constraints and safeguards that were essential for the successful performance of a free market system. "It is true that the confidence of business men needs to be restored. But it is also true that another kind of confidence needs to be restored—the confidence of the mass of people in the justice, the efficiency, and the social responsibility of democratic institutions" (HT 10/12/33).

Still another reason why the recovery had stalled, Lippmann concluded, was because the various and distinct objectives of economic policy were often tangled together and confused in the minds of the policy makers. In an important series of three columns ("The President's Task") in October 1933 he pulled his own thoughts together on this subject. His terminology changed from time to time thereafter, but he played often with the relationships among words beginning with "R." *Recovery* from the depression and *re-employment* of labor, he insisted, should be given absolutely first priority; yet, unfortunately, they were confused too often with *"reform"* and *"reconstruction"* and even *"redistribution"* of income and wealth. And, of course, in a democracy there was always looming the problem of *"re-election."* He was pleased with Roosevelt's position during the early days of the New Deal because he kept his eye firmly on the challenge of recovery alone. Programs like the Civilian Conservation Corps and the first wave of public works, even though not carefully planned in all cases, were bold and imaginative experiments designed to get people back to work. They demonstrated the power of "authority" to make things happen when "rules" would not do so. The later New Deal, however, was another story. Programs undertaken then, like the NRA, which operated within individual markets, contained restrictive features intended for reform and reconstruction that conflicted with the primary goal of recovery. Improvements in employment and production were actually constrained by these fumbling efforts at reform. "For the New Deal unmistakably implied a different distribution of income and financial power than that which prevailed before the crash, a much stricter policing of private enterprise, and a far-reaching attempt to reduce the competitive and enhance the co-operative motives in American life" (HT 10/12/33). These features discouraged entrepreneurial activity, which was at the root of job growth. The objectives of the recovery should be short run, to get everyone back to work as quickly as possible by increasing total demand and sustaining price levels. Unfortunately, many reforms of FDR were long run and might involve reducing or stabilizing demand. Keynes wrote an "Open Letter to the President" in the *New York Times* on December 31, 1933, in which he developed Lippmann's point about the need to accomplish "recovery" before "reform" (Barber 1996, 52). On this there is no way to determine in which direction influence may have flowed, from Lippmann to Keynes or vice versa.

Lippmann reviewed the macroeconomic record of earlier presidents and found that most of them, notably Theodore Roosevelt, had not jumped the gun and had waited to pursue reform until recovery was well under way. Unfortunately, this president was an exception. "Franklin Roosevelt has been setting up his measures of reform while recovery is just beginning" (HT 4/6/34). The NRA proposed to relieve the depression through myriad interventions in many markets. But a macroeconomic problem like the depression could not be solved at the microeconomic level. To explain this to his puzzled readers Lippmann came up with yet another metaphor. "N. R. A. tried to stop the water from running through the sieve by plugging each hole in the sieve. That was and is beyond human power. To attempt it required a detailed intervention in every factory and store. But no act of Congress could define that intervention. Because no act of Congress could define just how each hole in the sieve was to be plugged blanket power had to be delegated to the President. . . . For a central government the only effective method of general social control—the only constitutional method—is not to plug the individual holes in the sieve but to control the flow of the water." FDR's reform projects were intended to make the economy more efficient and equitable in the long run, and were not to be scorned. At issue was their timing. "They have to do with the deeper problems of American life, with the future of agriculture, with the relations of capital and labor, with the regulation of industry, with the conservation of natural resources, with the setting up of new financial standards, with the control of speculation, with the distribution of national income. They are concerned with the possibility of a better life, of greater equality and more justice, with the protection of the social order, the stabilization of our economy, with efforts to control the next boom and mitigate the next depression" (HT 2/27/34). Unfortunately, they impeded immediate recovery.

As the years passed Lippmann grew increasingly concerned that the confusion of policy tools and objectives in the New Deal made it difficult for citizens to comprehend even the essential objectives and limitations of economic policy making. He wrote in 1936: "No age can be so unsettled as to make it no longer true that if the people produce less wealth they will have less wealth, that they cannot eat more cake by eating less cake. In fact it is this very belief held not only by the President but by protectionists, monopolists, trades unionists, planners, price stabilizers, price fixers, that has done more than any other thing to unsettle the age" (HT 4/16/36). Of even greater importance than the confusion created in the public mind, the microeconomic constraints imposed by the New Deal on price adjustments in factor and product markets worked against the macroeconomic policies of stimulating aggregate demand. The result sooner or later would be unnecessary inflation. "Thus there is a gigantic stimulation of the demand for goods. At the same time a large part of the workers are kept out of production, being employed on public works making goods that are not for sale, and among the privately employed workers production is restricted. This combination of an artificially expanded demand and an artificially restricted supply is bound to produce an inflationary boom" (HT 12/22/36).

Lippmann appreciated and was sympathetic to Roosevelt's underlying political dilemma. "He has come into power with a two-fold mandate from the people: to raise the country out of the depression and to inaugurate a New Deal. He is commanded to bring back better times, and he is also commanded to bring in a different order of things. So he must have Recovery and he must have Reconstruction, and unless he is to arouse disappointment and revolt, he must set them both going simultaneously" (HT 10/10/33). But Roosevelt was slow to comprehend that the two objectives could be inconsistent unless pursued in sequence. "While he is trying to stimulate recovery he must also respond to the conviction of the mass of the people that the old order of things up to 1929 needs drastic renovation. He must give evidence that he is installing new controls and collective standards. This discourages enterprise and so retards Recovery" (HT 10/10/33). Lippmann did not join with those who demanded complete neglect of reform by FDR while he was pursuing recovery. He might have favored this separation in principle, but he recognized that it was not possible in political practice. "Those who bring this charge do not, I believe, appreciate as well as he does the circumstances which compel him to work out, step by step, a combination of an ordinary capitalistic recovery and a rather far-reaching social reconstruction. What is the principle of an ordinary capitalist recovery? It is, I believe, that private initiative based on the expectation of private profit revives when the deferred demand for goods exceeds the accumulated supply, and the cost of producing new goods is low enough to be profitable" (HT 12/6/33). For the time being, at least, voters, while attentive to both norms, were focused more on recovery than reform and were conscious that the latter might stand in the way of the former. "In other words, the country has accepted the policies which stimulate enterprise and it is increasingly distrustful of those which restrict it. The more effective the stimulants show themselves to be, the more the controls are disliked" (HT 4/10/34).

The NRA, whose full implications for the economy were beginning to be realized by 1933, was the instrument of change that worried Lippmann the most. Regrettably, it tried to combine inconsistent objectives of recovery and reform in one package, causing confusion all around: "the mystic letters N.R.A. signify not merely National Recovery but National Reconstruction, and the Blue Eagle [the symbol of the NRA] , if it were accurately symbolic, would be a bird with two heads" (HT 10/12/33). The act introduced monopoly and restriction into the system, precisely the opposite of what was needed for recovery. It sought to allocate demands for goods and services fairly through government intervention, rather than increase these demands, the only way Lippmann thought to achieve true recovery. At least at the start Lippmann did not reject the NRA out of hand, and he thought it was well intended. However, it responded to the mistaken but understandable human belief that when employment and production were in short supply the fairest response would be to share. Lippmann, of course, believed that all efforts at that time should be directed not to sharing but to expanding the product and increasing supply and demand: "the hasty stampede into codes [the control device] was proclaimed as a major measure of recovery, when as a matter of fact the N.R.A.'s contribution to recovery is modest and mixed in result, whereas its contribution to Reconstruction may well prove to be epoch-making" (HT 10/10/33). His best hope was that when the depression began to ease the American public would rebel against the philosophy of restriction embodied in the NRA (HT 12/19/33). An explanation for the slow recovery, and for the popularity of such restrictive programs as the Agricultural Adjustment Administration (AAA) and the NRA, lay in social psychology. From his readings in history and psychology he found that "every great and prolonged trade depression" had experienced in the early phases a "typical hypochondria, the low spirits of melancholy," "the feeling that the great days of enterprise are over and that the country is hopelessly choked by unmanageable overproduction" (HT 12/21/33). This "optical illusion" of overproduction lay behind passage of most restrictive legislation. "It is not at all unlike the state of mind of a bedridden patient during a long and slow convalescence. He does not think he is ever going to get up again and walk, and secretly he hardly wishes to" (HT 12/21/33). He called the economists Sismondi and Carroll Wright victims of the optical illusion of overproduction in their own time. In one of his columns most critical of the New Deal, Lippmann called the "destructive contradiction" between stimulative monetary and fiscal policy, on the one hand, and the restrictive "price and labor policy" of the New Deal, on the other, as "the economy of bedlam" (HT 3/28/34). With luck the madness should recede with a return to prosperity.

At the end of 1935 Lippmann concluded that, despite repeated warnings of impending inflation, recovery from the depression had still not been achieved: "though there is the theoretical possibility of credit inflation, in fact the country is still deflated . . . at this moment our trouble is not inflation, but a deflation which has not yet been completely overcome—a deflation manifest not merely in the small volume of private credit, but in the existence of unemployed resources and unemployed men" (HT 12/19/35). But with signs of improving economic activity he believed the case had grown strong for a return soon to free markets as the best way to achieve a permanent recovery. By early in 1937 Lippmann concluded that recovery had, indeed, arrived and it was time to reduce stimulative programs and give competitive markets a chance to heal themselves as they neared full employment. The failure of the Democrats to follow his advice and give up their popular new programs caused him to conclude that perhaps he had discovered a potentially fatal flaw in compensatory fiscal policy. Anticipating later public choice theorists, he asked whether it could be that once politicians discovered the joy of cutting taxes and increasing expenditures during a slump they could not easily be persuaded to give up these guilty pleasures in a boom. If so, countercyclical fiscal policy made sense economically but not politically. "The question is not whether it was necessary to spend in the depths of the depression but whether it is possible to reduce the expenditures in the course of the recovery" (HT 10/3/36). This meant that sooner or later inflation would be inevitable. "This means a boom. For there is a boom when effective purchasing power outruns the productive capacity of capital and labor. Then prices and wages begin to rise together, speculation runs ahead of real investment, a vicious inflationary spiral is set in motion" (HT 11/24/36). With the monopolies throughout the economy strengthened by the New Deal, inflationary pressures were likely to become increasingly difficult to contain. "There is, or at least there will shortly be, more purchasing power than there are goods to be purchased. . . . This combination of an artificially expanded demand and an artificially restricted supply is bound to produce an inflationary boom" (HT 12/22/36). Yet the government faced this likelihood of price inflation with as little planning as they had faced the possibility of a double-dip recession. "The situation is serious because we are now in a period of full recovery, on the verge of a boom, and an Administration which is unable to balance its budget in good times is in effect confessing that it can never balance the budget. If it cannot reduce expenditures when private business is running close to capacity, if it cannot levy sufficient taxes when the national income is big, then when can it hope to balance the budget?" (HT 4/20/37).

Another reason Lippmann suggested for the hesitant policy making he observed through the 1930s and for the persistence of depression was the continuing and growing power of special interests in the policy-making process. He saw labor, business, farmers, veterans, and a growing number of other groups flexing their muscles so that policies favored their members rather than the common good. He worried about corruption even of the Federal Reserve Board of Governors, and he wondered if guaranteed pensions might make the governors more independent and focused on the public interest (HT 2/9/35). He blamed Congress especially for giving in to the special interests, and as a reform he recommended that initiation of all legislation be reserved for the executive branch. "In the equilibrium between these two powers, of the executive to ask and the Legislature to grant funds, lies the hope of constitutional liberty" (HT 3/16/34). Special interest pleading and pork barrel legislation were threatening the political and economic health of the nation. "The power of the legislature to force expenditure upon the executive is a perversion of representative government" (HT

3/16/34). As soon as some special interests demonstrated that they could manipulate the system, others tried, and before long a coherent fiscal policy was impossible. "If one organized minority can terrorize Congress into forcing an enormous expenditure upon the President who is charged with the preservation of the national credit and the management of the currency, then other organized minorities can imitate the example and follow the precedent. That way lies chaos and the destruction of liberty. That way we must not go" (HT 3/16/34). The problem was accentuated by the opportunity to finance the pork barrel through monetized public debt that would be inflationary. He wrote to the Boston lawyer Laurence Curtis in 1939: "In my own study of the problem, I have been coming to think more and more that the chief danger lies in the fact that the deficit financing can be carried on by the Federal government through the politically painless method of inflationary bank credit. In other words these deficits are financed, not out of real loans, but out of a disguised form of printed money. As long as that condition can exist, I don't believe Congress will be seriously interested in balancing the budget, even if it had to vote specifically on each loan; so I have been exploring the possibility of cutting off this inflationary bank credit and compelling the treasury to finance its deficits out of real loans" (WL to Curtis, December 7, 1939, WLPIII F560).

Finally, an obstacle that Lippmann believed was standing in the way of ending the depression was the continuing shortage of skilled economic talent in Washington and elsewhere in the policy discussion. The facts and the theory were known, but it took smart people to apply them to the real world and recommend effective policy. More talented economists were needed both to suggest and evaluate new ideas and to keep under control the nut cases such as "the technocrats" with their foolish nostrums (HT 1/26/35, 4/6/35, 4/13/35, and 9/26/36). Macroeconomics was not easy to grasp, and a problem with much good macroeconomic policy was that it was counterintuitive and had to be explained carefully and repeatedly to the citizens. In this concern he was harkening back to worries about responsibilities of citizens in a democracy set forth in his first two books before World War I. He praised Brookings and the National Bureau of Economic Research for helping with clarification of some economic questions, but by their nature they were rather far from the seats of power (HT 5/29/35). He found ad hoc advisory bodies such as the President's Committee on Economic Security, with Edwin Witte as executive director, to be useful, but they came and they went (HT 1/19/35). Business advisory councils definitely did not perform their avowed function of providing balanced advice (HT 5/11/35). Lippmann was not a fan of Roosevelt's economic adviser Rexford Tugwell; but at least Tugwell was a serious intellectual, and he defended Tugwell vigorously against unfounded attacks by his critics. Tugwell was a man who struggled hard to understand and explain policy issues, and this was rare indeed. The conspiracy theories propounded in the 1930s about the supposed role of the Brain Trust in totalitarian plots were largely nonsense. His defense of Tugwell gave him an opportunity to reflect on the wider issue of the place of professional social scientists in government. He wrote in 1934:

> There is in the first place no Brains Trust as popularly conceived. There are in Washington somewhere between fifty and seventy-five young and middle-aged academically trained men who would in England rank as upper civil servants. They have no common philosophy. They are not an organized group.
>
> But they represent something new in American politics, something which is probably permanent, that is to say men who are professionally trained in the field of political economy. We have become accustomed to academically trained men in the scientific bureaus and, of course, in the legal departments. But professional economists are an innovation here, though Theodore Roosevelt used them continually in his Bull Moose days, and they are so common as to pass unnoticed in England, France, Germany or any other country with an established civil service. . . . So the presence of professors in government posts is a sight to which we shall probably have to accustom ourselves. (HT 6/13/34)

It is often difficult to determine whether Lippmann was leading the thinking on this subject or whether he was simply reflecting currents in the discussion with which he was comfortable and familiar. It is striking that repeatedly during the 1930s, as one way to cope with the paucity of analytical talent in Washington, he advocated creation of a body very similar to what would become the Council of Economic Advisers in 1946. He wrote in 1934: "There would seem to be two possible ways of meeting this situation. One would be to create a small committee of the Cabinet, relieve its members of administrative responsibility and forbid administrators to announce policies until the Cabinet committee has approved. This would, however, require a change in the personnel of the Cabinet, for such a committee would be useless unless it consisted of the President's most trusted advisers. It may, therefore, not be feasible. The other way would be to enlarge the White House staff by adding to it men competent to examine proposals and advise the President. These advisers would stand behind the President, not in front of him. The heads of departments would still be dealing with the President, which is what they really insist upon doing. But the President in dealing with them would be advised by men who are not harassed by office routine and are not concerned with the prestige of departments" (HT 12/18/34).

At the end of 1937, when Lippmann's frustration on many fronts was at a high level, he virtually exploded at the lack of serious study of macroeconomic issues. He observed that the problems were becoming steadily greater because of the growing powers and wishes of governments everywhere in the world to interfere arbitrarily with price signals, increase unrestrained monopoly power in product and factor markets, and encourage a steady weakening in public commitment to the competitive market system (HT 10/21/37 and 10/26/37). But macroeconomic problems should be solvable if more bright minds like that of Maynard Keynes were applied to them. It was tragic that with another serious recession at hand, as predicted by the stock markets, no one knew much more with confidence about what to do than they had known eight years before. "It may well be that the consensus of opinion reflected in the stock markets of the world is truer than the opinions of any individual trading in them or commenting upon them. What these markets seem to say is that the whole recovery of the past two years at any rate was insubstantial and impermanent, that it represented, not a true revival of the production of goods for exchange but a governmental boom, subsidized by paper money, and devoted to armaments, public works and doles. They seem to say that here and abroad, for one reason and another, a genuine recovery beyond the levels of 1935 has been prevented. The stock markets seem, in other words, to be responding not to the mechanical effects of monetary inflation but to be reflecting the realistic judgment of business men on the prospects of private business" (HT 8/19/37). As he would say repeatedly over the next few years, the tragedy lay rooted mainly in bad economic and political ideas that led to poor policy, or to no policy at all.

> The fundamental fact of the matter is that there does not exist any dependable scientific knowledge of the business cycle. The whole subject is still obscure; the data have never been fully ascertained and the theory is still very much unsettled. In the study on "Prosperity and Depression" just made for the League of Nations by Professor Gottfried von Haberler of Harvard University 158 pages are required in order to summarize the divergent theories held by reputable and competent economists. We are obviously moving in a region, therefore, where nobody knows clearly what he is talking about, in a region not yet brought securely within the frontiers of human knowledge.
>
> But the matter is complicated further by the fact that the economic process, which no one understands very well, is today in every part of the world subject to the management of politicians, mystics, demagogues, prophets and soldiers, who do not understand it at all. In the nineteenth century, although no one knew much about the business cycle, recovery used to come after a while because no one interfered with it. But nowadays nearly every government has taken charge of its own sector of the economic system, and what we are experiencing is neither a natural recovery nor an administered recovery, but a bad combination of the two. (HT 8/19/37)

The Dreaded Double Dip

Almost immediately after his macroeconomic epiphany of 1933–1934, Lippmann began to express concern about inattention to the slow pace of recovery and the possibility of a return to full-scale depression. Mainly he just mused about the causes of policy inaction, but the stock market collapse

in the summer of 1937 and subsequent declines in aggregates such as employment and production led him to conclude that his worst fears had been realized and once again his duty was to figure out what had happened and what
should be done about it. A widespread reaction from commentators was
that "pump-priming" had demonstrably failed and the obvious policy now
was to return to the tried and true orthodoxy of balanced fiscal budgets and
laissez-faire. Lippmann disliked the simple-minded pump-priming metaphor that was used in the 1930s to represent the contribution of macroeconomic intervention, but now he felt an obligation to sort it out. He may have
been looking for a homey way to explain the Keynesian multiplier when he
pointed out that a continued flow of expenditures, rather than just a single
"prime," was needed to achieve recovery. Anyone who had had any contact
with farming knew that pump-priming referred to the occasional need for a
small slug of water in a farm's hand pump to lubricate and swell the gaskets
so that the pump would operate smoothly thereafter. However, the economy was not like a pump. One infusion of public spending on its own might
well not sustain the level of aggregate demand beyond the term of that
spending. The follow-up was critical: "The true criticism of the Administration policy in the past year is not that it decided to spend money to start
activity, but that the spending policy was accompanied by other policies
that discouraged the revival of activity. It was right to have the government
go into debt to stimulate activity, it was wrong for the government to lock up
the private capital market, to tolerate or encourage semi-monopolistic price-
fixing, and to increase labor costs faster than volume of business. The danger has not been in the spending policy as such: it has been in the accompanying policies which neutralized it. For if the government spends huge
sums to 'prime the pump' but won't let the pump work, then it is faced with
endless spending" (HT 7/6/34). He pointed out repeatedly that "pump
priming" was a short-term and finite response to depression. This had to be
followed by a long-term program to sustain recovery. "It is reasonably clear
what the American policy ought to be. It can be stated in simple terms by
saying that we must prime the pump vigorously with government expenditures and let the pump work by encouraging private enterprise to take hold.

Without these expenditures it is unlikely that private enterprise is as yet strong enough to overcome the ravages of what was the severest deflation ever experienced by the capitalist system" (HT 7/13/34). In other words, after the initial governmental stimulus vigorous efforts had to be made to bring private enterprise fully on board.

From the start Lippmann held that the best policy to deal with a macroeconomic crisis was to move down two paths. Along the first, short-run path, efforts must be made to revive production and employment using bold and imaginative stimulative devices such as those used in the early New Deal. These would include increased public works and public employment as well as unemployment insurance and various transfer payments. Along a second path, steps must be taken to create the environment in which private investment would revive and take the place of the short-run governmental infusion. The demand for consumption goods had quickly to be supplemented by demand for investment goods to replace the temporary demand for public goods. Lippmann did not accept the claim often heard in the business community that actions on the short-run path would destroy the confidence required for accomplishing the longer-run goals of business recovery and therefore would be futile in the aggregate. At the same time he did denounce what he considered to be certain foolish actions in the short run, such as some taken by Roosevelt that had damaged confidence and retarded long-run recovery. Indeed, he claimed that Roosevelt's threats of an excess profits tax, encouragement to organized labor, the NRA, the AAA, attempts to pack the Supreme Court, and increased regulation of various kinds had struck terror in the business community and retarded investment. He warned as early as 1934 that inattention to the long run could be fatal: "The recovery since November has been dependent upon the artificial stimulation of government expenditures . . . the recovery will not be dependable until it is evident that private investment will take the place of government spending" (HT 5/25/34). He estimated in April 1935, with back-of-the-envelope calculations from data gathered by his friend Colonel Ayres, that no more than 80 percent of the aggregate demand needed for full employment was then in sight without resort to government

stimulus (HT 4/20/35). The confusion caused by the succession of complex
New Deal programs had clearly damaged the confidence needed for investment. "It is only natural that business men, their lawyers, their bankers,
and their brokers should be in a state of bewilderment" (HT 6/28/34). One
particular source of confusion for investors was that some long-run components of the New Deal seemed to be fundamentally inconsistent with the
short-term ones. Which foretold the future? Lippmann denied that balancing the budget would necessarily help to end the depression but, on the
other hand, an end to the depression would solve the problem of budget
deficits by encouraging private investment, increasing taxes, and reducing
expenditures: "The way to bring the budget into balance is to bring the
national economy into balance. In other words to balance the budget and to
fail to take the measures that will promote recovery will get you nowhere. A
continuing depression will again undo the budget. But if the measures are
taken that will promote recovery, then the budget will come into balance
and stay there" (HT 12/29/34).

The question to be answered for recovery then was how to make economic relationships stable for the long run. "The economic system has
been thrown violently out of balance and it cannot recover until a balance is
once again achieved. The question is where and by whom the adjustments
are to be made" (HT 2/21/35). Having seen so many chaotic responses from
government early in the decade Lippmann began to think by 1935 that it
might be time to clear the decks of antidepression programs and see if free
markets alone could restore prosperity after all. "The good doctor and
the good statesman are those who know how big a dose of stimulants is necessary and, above all, when to stop giving them. Taking the situation as a
whole, it seems to me very clear that the time has come to say that the dose
now being administered is the last one and that the next budget is to be balanced" (HT 8/14/35). It was especially necessary to restore to the United
States the strength of its free market economy as the country prepared for
another world war, which was just over the horizon. At the very least such a
new policy of encouraging free markets would release President Roosevelt
from the claims that he was using a smorgasbord of special programs to
conceal an overall collectivist agenda.

The main problem of the Federal government today, it seems to me, is not how to stimulate recovery, provide relief, or institute reform. It is how to reduce the scope and the procedure of government to a workable scale, how to restore the normal Constitution, and how to encourage the resumption of that local and private self-reliance upon which depend not only the vitality but the essential liberties of the American people. . . . A program of restoration, not a mere breathing-spell, alone can save the country and the Administration from becoming confused in a tangle of unreal problems. Once it is determined that the situation calls not for a pause on the road to higher and vaster projects but for a restoration of the normal balance of powers in the government and a resumption of local and individual responsibility, the specific issues at home will become fairly simple. It will not be difficult to balance the budget if it is decided that relief is again to be primarily a local or a private responsibility. It will not be difficult to bring about some sort of decent feeling between government and business if it is determined that business is to operate under considered statutes and judicial procedure rather than under administrative fiat and political crusading. (HT 12/3/35)

By 1936 Lippmann thought the evidence suggested the depression might at last be winding down, and the main problem soon would be how to restrain inflation. "This means a boom," he said. "For there is a boom when effective purchasing power outruns the productive capacity of capital and labor. Then prices and wages will begin to rise together, speculation runs ahead of real investment, and a vicious inflationary spiral is set in motion" (HT 11/24/36). Business firms were likely to start raising prices and accumulating profits. The first task should be to persuade them to keep prices stable and distribute profits, as recommended by the Brookings Institution. Trade unions should also show restraint and not limit entry into the skilled trades (HT 11/24/36). Government should consider raising taxes and reducing public expenditures and encouraging an increase in competition in all markets (HT 3/13/37 and 4/8/37). But none of these recommendations was followed. Both government and participants in the market were happy to see monopolies flourish and expensive programs continue, and they seemed to have forgotten how closely linked competition is with human liberty overall.

Lippmann did not have to worry for long about how to cope with a boom. The double dip of 1937 brought him back to the issues he had studied in 1933–1934, and he remained unshaken in his fundamental faith in a modified Keynesian response. Macroeconomic policy required travel down two roads, one leading to more consumption in the short run and the other leading to more investment in the long run; the latest crisis was the result of neglecting the second road. The New Deal had moved down the short-run road but had ignored the long run. He rejected the judgment of the *New York Times* that government spending had been decisively discredited by this return of recession. What the double dip showed was simply that success required coordinated travel down the two roads together. Roosevelt's programs in the later New Deal had crippled antidepression policy. "Having noted that the signs point increasingly to the adoption of another spending program to overcome the depression, 'The New York Times' on Tuesday made a formidable attack on spending as a remedy for a business depression. The argument is impressive. But from such observations as I have been able to make in Washington it does not seem to me that such argument can be effective. For I think 'The Times' does not give adequate weight to those human and political factors which in a situation such as this finally make government spending seem the only practicable remedy" (HT 2/10/38). He did acknowledge that implementation of a program of effective public spending was more difficult and complex than first imagined. But any recognized alternative was unthinkable. "The normal remedy for depression in the past has been bankruptcy and wage reductions. That is to say, when prices declined fixed charges and wage costs were forced downward till at the lower price level business enterprise could once again earn a profit. It was the prospect of profit that 'revived confidence,' in other words, made men willing to invest capital. Now the depression which began in 1929 and is still with us has been marked primarily by a general refusal in all classes of society to go through the agony of the normal remedy" (HT 2/10/38). It would be tragic if after all the pain of the past nine years government could not find a better response to this new crisis than the old one and could not restore prosperity without more of the suffering the country was still experiencing.

The position today in the spring of 1938 is ominously like what it was in the spring of 1931. Again we are deeply depressed. Again enterprise is stagnant. Again the army of the unemployed is growing. Again beneath the surface of the monetary controls, the disturbing symptoms are evident to those who are not afraid to see them. And again we have an administration in Washington that is afraid to act, rationalizing its hesitancy and inaction by telling itself that because it has instituted a few trifling reforms, like the insurance of bank deposits, the thing cannot happen again.

It can happen again. And it is about to happen again unless Washington moves promptly and decisively to take those measures which the emergency demands. (HT 3/17/38)

This time around the sharp focus had to be on the long term and on ways to stimulate investment in the private sector. "For there is almost no doubt at all, I think, that the stoppage of capital investment is the main cause of the depression in America. No doubt there are other contributing causes—such as uneconomic prices and wage rates in special industries like building and railroads, such as the political deadlock over the utilities. But the fundamental and general cause is that private investment did not increase when public spending diminished" (HT 3/29/38). If President Roosevelt wanted truly to bring the country out of depression and onto an upward growth path he must create a climate in which business could perceive profit; otherwise short-run public spending would do no more than secure short-run gains. He must demonstrate that he really cared. "Though no one could say that Mr. Roosevelt is a full-blown socialist, his mood is almost invariably anti-capitalist. Thus his concessions do not encourage enterprise which is the essence of capitalism. They are merely pauses, truces, reprieves, and men will not confidently invest their money in the expansion of industry if all the assurance they have is that for the time being, for this month or for the next six months, their government is willing to yield on this or that grievance" (HT 11/27/37). As Lippmann became increasingly sensitive to problems of human behavior he worried that a serious problem lay in Mr. Roosevelt's "rather lordly and aristocratic contempt for people who, as they say in England, are 'in trade.' Mr. Roosevelt is the country gentleman turned tory socialist. Thus he has a genuine sympathy with those who work the soil and a sincerely philanthropic attitude toward the poor in the cities. But the enterprising business man and the trader he distrusts as the landed nobility have always distrusted him. Mr. Roosevelt is anti-capitalist. But his anti-capitalism is only about two parts Karl Marx popularized and the remainder is about ninety-eight parts the broad acres of Hyde Park" (HT 1/20/38).

Lippmann warned that this double dip could easily turn into a major depression on the scale of the early 1930s. A slightly hysterical note had crept into his columns by April 1938. "The indications are that we are either on the verge of, or that we have already entered into, something worse than a business depression, into a viciously deflationary process which will, if not arrested promptly, have catastrophic consequences. In the past few weeks the trend of events has become ominously like that of the spring of 1931. . . . Let us not forget that the catastrophe of 1931 opened the way for the rise of Hitler, and that it weakened, apparently beyond repair, the foundations of public law and international order throughout the world" (HT 4/2/38). It was as if the terrible experience of the Great Depression had dulled the public consciousness to the dangers ahead. Certainly government was unprepared. "And what are we doing about it all here? We are doing nothing. Incredible as it sounds, the New Deal does not have any program, good, bad, or indifferent. . . . The crisis has now become intensified to a point where ordinary remedies will not cure it. . . . We can afford to do nothing less than to fix our whole attention upon the serious crisis which is in the making and to forget all other issues until the crisis is resolved" (HT 4/2/38).

By 1938 Lippmann found that there was little stomach anywhere for more deficit finance, even though with interest rates at all-time lows deficits were almost the only weapon available to fight recession. After seven years in which deficits had been used to buy time with no good result, everyone seemed afraid of more. "Because Mr. Roosevelt failed to retrench in the good years, he does not really dare to prime the pump in this bad year. So he is adding no important positive stimulus through government expenditures. He is merely negatively refraining from carrying out the retrenchments that he talked about hopefully a few months ago. He is pretending to prime the pump, and rather hoping to create the impression that this is what he is doing, when, in fact, he is merely proposing to continue spending and taxing at the high level which he reached about the time of the 1936 elections" (HT 4/21/38). And still there was little attention to the problem of making the private sector profitable enough to stimulate investment spending.

> For a time the New Dealers tried to believe that enough government spending would pump enough 'purchasing power' into the community to create such a demand for goods that corporate investors would find it profitable to expand. This has been the theory of Mr. Eccles [Fed chairman]. But it does not work because the profits that government spending offers are not great enough to overcome the risks that investors fear.
>
> These risks are of two kinds. There is the risk of new political measures which will create new burdens. And then, there is the fact that even if men were enterprising and took real risks the government will seize the larger profits by taxation if they win but will give them no relief if they lose. (HT 3/2/39)

A note of resignation as well as of frustration can be detected in Lippmann's discussion of macroeconomic policy at this point. In his view what should be done was clear, but it was equally clear that for a variety of reasons rooted in human character the appropriate actions would not be taken, with regrettable consequences. "And they will be serious consequences. For an unrelieved depression embittered by official agitation can end in only one way—in the deepest and darkest reactionary movement this country has ever known" (HT 4/12/38).

During 1939 Lippmann moved on from Keynes and became intrigued by the secular stagnation thesis of Alvin Hansen, which suggested that over the long run, even during periods of full employment and prosperity, private investment spending might not be enough to make up the gap between consumption plus normal government spending and the amount of effective demand needed to sustain full employment. Because of stagnation, supplemental and increasing governmental spending would be needed year in and year out to sustain employment. However, he seems not to have been fully convinced. In May of 1939 he was still decrying continuing fiscal deficits for their demoralizing effects throughout the economy. Deficits were like narcotics; they had powerful and beneficial therapeutic value—but they were also addictive. Both politicians and voters became unable to go cold turkey during periods of prosperity. "The fact of the matter is that the real evil of the system of deficit financing is not that it is about to produce bankruptcy, inflation, and financial collapse. If it were about to produce such a spectacular disaster, the American people would be quite capable of rising up to deal with it. The real evil of the deficit spending is that it is slowly and subtly demoralizing to the whole nation, to the recipients and to the lenders and to the politicians, that it disintegrates the fundamental civic virtues. And, therefore, if it continues, the financial crisis which will come, not for some years but eventually, will find our political system so demoralized that a normal cure will no longer be possible" (HT 5/11/39).

Yet only one week later, after examining testimony from Hansen and Lauchlin Currie before the Temporary National Economic Committee, he speculated that there might have to be deficits each year as a continuing fact of life (HT 5/18/39). By mid-1939 Lippmann concluded that Roosevelt's policy advisers, and especially Adolph Berle, had come to accept the danger of secular stagnation and were preparing a massive new public spending program that would be the next phase of the New Deal: "The new spending policy, of which the public has had as yet only a sketchy outline, is no temporary measure. On the contrary, it is intended to be permanent, and it will embrace nothing less than public expenditure and public control of perhaps as much as half of the national savings. The Mead bill, which would provide credit to small business under government guarantee, is only the first stage of this program; the scheme outlined by Mr. Berle, would make the Federal government the great investment banker for Federal, state and local governments and for all kinds of public enterprises, is a fair outline of what the New Deal now aims at" (HT 6/3/39). Lippmann himself found the Temporary National Economic Committee testimony so compelling that he believed in time even the harshest skeptics might be brought around. "I know this is a large assertion, and it may seem rather simple-minded these days to believe that there is such a thing as truth which can prevail over prejudice and partisanship. But, nevertheless, I believe that violent and irreconcilable controversy would give way to constructive debate among men be they economists, Republican businessmen, or New Dealers, who have studied and digested the Hansen and Currie testimony" (HT 5/20/39). It was not hard to calculate the potential gap in aggregate effective demand left by weak investment. "According to disinterested calculations which are not, I think, disputed, the annual capital investment in the United States needs to be about 18 billions a year. This was the average for 1923 to 1929, and with that much capital investment the nation will be prosperous, its income will be between 75 and 80 billions" (HT 5/20/39). So would that amount of investment take place spontaneously? It was hard to see why. "Broadly speaking, the problem of recovery is, therefore, the problem of getting 18 billions invested each year. That is what is worrying Wall Street and that is what is worrying the New Dealers who are putting their minds on the subject" (HT 5/20/39). The failure of Congress to confront this problem was testament to its ineffectiveness. "There is a human delinquency in Washington today in which suspicion and vindictiveness, personal animosity and pride, are being paraded as doctrine and submitted for policy. The moral responsibility for remedying this condition rests on the conscience of one man. That man is the President of the United States" (HT 5/21/39). He warned that too much attention to the supply side of the problem could lead to neglect of the demand side and of the goods that could be produced if the economy were running at full steam. "The production of goods is the primary fact. Without production there would be nothing in the shop that the customer could buy. And without production there would be no purchasing power in the customers" (HT 5/25/39).

He had his own agenda for how the funds should be spent, which would respond to the problem of secular stagnation, an agenda very similar to that of the Democratic Party in the twenty-first century. "The country would understand and gladly support a program of public investment in conservation, in technical education, in the development of power and the improvement of roads and markets if the whole effort were consciously and clearly dedicated to improving the productive capacity of the people" (HT 5/25/39). Those who were skeptical of the secular stagnation danger and the power of deficit spending to deal with it should, he suggested, recall that since World War I there had been no prosperity that had not been supported by

an increase in public or private credit, and this was essentially deficit finance. "The great point for everybody is that in both periods there was an
increase of indebtedness. The local and private debts of the 20s led
through prosperity to a crash. The Federal and public debts of the 30s
have given us a partial and an uncertain and unsatisfactory recovery. The
problem is whether the country can achieve a genuine recovery without
the private credit inflation of the 20s and without the Federal credit inflation of the 30s. For there has been no prosperity in the post-war era which
was not accompanied by, and was not dependent upon, a great increase in
debt of one kind or another" (HT 2/8/40). The main opponents of a policy
of maintaining full employment in the short and long run through managed public expenditures were Republicans in Congress using three "illu-
sory arguments."

> Thus they have based their oratorical attack against the spending policy
> on at least three illusions. The first was that national bankruptcy was
> near enough to frighten the voters. It is not. Europe's experience shows
> that governments can spend a much larger proportion of the national in-
> come than we do and carry on more or less indefinitely. The second was
> that the spending policy does not induce recovery. The fact is that
> enough spending does induce some recovery and, while morally and po-
> litically it is an exceedingly dangerous method, it does work. The third
> illusion was that the Republicans could declaim against spending in gen-
> eral without having to face particular issues with the pressure groups.
>
> The three illusions put the Republicans in a position where they
> first prophesied disasters that were not happening and then failed to take
> a stand to prevent the disasters they were prophesying. That is not very
> competent politics. (HT 5/27/39)

In sum, as E. A. Goldenweiser at the Institute for Advanced Study in
Princeton (who had been hearing about secular stagnation from Lippmann
for some years) pointed out to Lippmann, if incomes were distributed more
equally, consumption expenditures would rise, public expenditure would
not be needed, and inadequate aggregate demand would no longer be a
problem (Goldenweiser to WL, February 17, 1947, WLPIII F1120).

As it turned out, Lippmann in 1938 had even less time to worry about a catastrophic double dip than he had to worry about a boom in 1937. The prospect of war solved the problem in little more than a year as demand increased rapidly. In December 1939 he estimated that there were still five or six million unemployed, but they were rapidly being absorbed in preparation for war. "It will soon be demonstrated that our unemployment today, unlike that during the years immediately after 1929, is not due to overexpansion. It is due to underdevelopment during the latter years of the depression. And since it takes considerable time to enlarge plants, to construct industrial machines, and to train experienced workers, we must expect for some time to see much unemployment in the midst of booming business" (HT 12/19/39). He predicted correctly that rearmament and the production of war materials for the Allies were all that would be needed to generate the effective demand needed to put everyone back to work. In May of 1942 he announced that the challenge had become to reduce consumption to 1932 levels, rather than to stimulate investment, so as to make way for greatly increased wartime expenditures, full employment, and stable prices (HT 5/9/42). It would take a mixture of price control, rationing, war bonds, and higher taxes to achieve this objective. When he corresponded in 1943 with Seymour Harris, then at the Department of Commerce, they both agreed that the challenge had become an inflationary, not a deflationary, "gap" (WLPIII F2107). This was to be their conclusion for years to come, and well after Lippmann had moved on to other issues.

WALTER LIPPMANN began his columns in the *Herald Tribune* just as the Great Depression of the 1930s reached its low point. It was only natural, therefore, for him to turn his full attention to macroeconomic issues for the remainder of the decade. He had from his youth been interested in economic fluctuations and the pain they caused those who became unemployed in a downturn, but he had never before focused sharply on the subject. Now he did. He made every effort to discover the most persuasive theory to explain conditions, and he freed himself quite quickly from the dogma of the times about what might be done and what was out of bounds. Gradually he absorbed the approach being developed by his friend Maynard Keynes, especially the approach of seeing the depression through the components of gross national expenditure, and he came to reject commitments to a neutral monetary policy, the gold standard, and a balanced fiscal budget. He concluded that government had a continuing responsibility to use all the macroeconomic tools available to it to balance the fluctuations in aggregate demand that affected an economy from outside and inside. Complex human behavior lay at the bottom of most fluctuations, and it was necessary first to understand and then to discover ways to compensate for this behavior. After a period of intense study in 1933–1934 he was excited to find that, apparently, he had discovered many of the answers he was looking for, and he was optimistic that other answers would be found by smart people in the years ahead. But after he told the world what he had discovered in his little book *The Method of Freedom*, the next years were filled with disappointment. The most persuasive economists, such as Keynes and Lauchlin Currie, were too often ignored or dismissed. But of greatest importance, politicians of the time seemed neither to understand nor to be willing to follow the increasingly good advice that was available to them. They seemed to act both from ignorance and from a narrow conception of their own self-interest. Apparently, achievement of consensus about how to deal with macroeconomic challenges would have to come later. The depression persisted but recovery was coming soon, not through intervention based on "reason" but through the accident of war, ironically a war that had been caused, he was convinced, by macroeconomic policy failure a few years back.

6

Reform I: Redistribution

WALTER LIPPMANN was a kind and generous man in his relations with family, friends, and even relative strangers. He volunteered to help the less privileged as a student, and he made a substantial (and anonymous) contribution to a private committee set up at the beginning of the depression to help the unemployed (WL to Emergency Unemployment Relief Committee, November 9, 1931, WLPIII F708). He even paid the tuition of neighbors' children when the neighbors ran out of money. So there is no reason to expect that he would be opposed to all redistribution of income and wealth. Indeed, he did believe that some acts by government were required to make income distribution more equitable. He wrote to Felix Frankfurter in April 1932: "I regard the present distribution of income in the United States as wholly undesirable and I greatly desire to see it leveled down. But so far as I know the only tax which can do it is the inheritance tax" (WL to Frankfurter, April 5, 1922, WLPI F816).

Lippmann never doubted that he lived in an imperfect world that could be improved, and that he could assist through advice and action. His awareness of economic problems that needed solving did not grow less as the years went on, but his faith in the accepted ways of dealing with them was severely tested. He understood the marginal productivity theory (called

then "wage worth" theory) of income distribution and the socialist theory
of surplus value that attributed inequality to extraction of the surplus from
the working class, but he rejected both as explanations of the world around
him and as normative guides to public policy. His respect for socialist doctrine melted after working for a socialist mayor, and his research on Wall
Street for Lincoln Steffens convinced him that you could not understand the
payments to the current "masters of the universe" by calculating their marginal contributions to their firms or to society. So he could not see any good
reason why there should not be some redistribution of income and wealth
when conditions called for it. The questions were from whom? to whom?
and how much? He looked for answers to these questions throughout his
career, and he began early.

Need: The Poor and the Unemployed

In 1915 Lippmann wrote a long and detailed lead article for the *New Republic* on proposals for minimum wage legislation that would affect mainly
women factory workers. He mocked the critics of these proposals for claiming "with more piety than wisdom that wages are determined by natural
laws which man must let alone" (WL 1915c, 1). He demanded that incomes
of workers be stabilized above the poverty level, and he rejected the notion
that in the labor market free competition necessarily yielded economic
justice:

> [T]alking about wages depending upon 'wage-worth,' is using a catch
> phrase and a neat theory which in practice mean literally nothing at all.
> The kind of women's work to which the minimum wage would apply has
> no standard by which wages are fixed. Women get what they get, by the
> custom of the shop, by the whim of the superintendent, by arbitrary deci-
> sion. No law of supply and demand, no sense of 'wage-worth,' determines
> that a 'stripper' in order to earn fifteen cents an hour must paste paper on
> the side of about one hundred and fifty boxes, and a 'hand-dipper' must
> coat about seven hundred and twenty pieces of cream candy with choco-
> late, while a hand-ironer in the laundry will earn twenty-five cents by
> pressing four plain shirts. (WL 1915c, 3)

He examined the experience of wage arbitration in Australia and found that employers there suffered little but society became more humane. "What we are struggling for is a minimum that shall be a living wage, a minimum which is yet so low that in all conscience it is a little above the slave-owner's standard, a minimum which shall enable a woman who works all day long to earn enough to sustain her health, buy decent food, clothes and lodging, and secure a little recreation" (WL 1915c, 6). On this subject of minimum wage legislation, which would remain controversial over the next century, Lippmann concluded modestly:

> Yet it would be absurd to assume that minimum wage legislation is a kind of omnibus for paradise. To fix a "living standard" would be a great advance over what we have, but by every civilized criterion is a grudging and miserable thing. In those moments of lucidity when we forget our hesitancy before brute obstruction, it seems like a kind of madness that we should have to argue and scrape in order that we may secure to millions of women enough income to "live." . . .
>
> We may fail to secure that. So far as the press is concerned, the issue hardly exists. It lies at the moment stifled in platitudes and half-truths about "not hurting business." From the little comment there is, we might think that a business was sound if it rested on the degradation of its labor; might think that business men were a lot of jumpy neurotics ready to shrivel up and burst into tears at a proposal to increase their wages bill a penny or two on the dollar; might think, from the exclamations of Mr. Brown and his friend John Smith, that a campaign against sweating [sweatshops] would do no less than ruin the country.
>
> But you cannot ruin a country by conserving its life. You can ruin a country only by stupidity, waste and greed. (WL 1915c, 8)

Later in 1915 Lippmann reviewed a lengthy report from the National Association of Manufacturers that among other things devoted eleven pages to quotations from scripture that it said refuted public interference with wage rates. He was scathing: "This at least is certain. The temper and tone of the report can inspire no confidence whatever. From the idiotic interpretation of the parable about the vineyard to the blank assertion that the minimum wage has 'invariably failed,' the report is a mass of undigested assertion, unsupported argument, and appeals to prejudice such as one would expect from an illiterate quack, not from representatives of supposedly intelligent manufacturers" (WL 1915b, 222).

The earliest picture of ideal human economic agents detectable in Lippmann's writings is of intelligent, self-interested persons, sensitive to others in society and responsive to opportunities to help their fellow men, in some degree at least. This vision had roots in his appreciation of Santayana's life of reason, the progressives' plans for moderate social reform, and the Fabians' wish to engage the wider public in planning for social progress. This vision also lay behind his first two books, where the message was that improvement in human affairs could be achieved simply by clever people suggesting and then implementing good works. Lippmann's experience in government and the military in World War I, however, shook his faith profoundly in any simple road to social improvement. He came, instead, to appreciate Lord Acton's dictum that power corrupts, and he saw that humans were as easily misled by well-intentioned people as by corrupt ones. His progressive faith was shaken further by the Harding and Coolidge administrations during the 1920s, when selfishness and corruption ran rampant. So he arrived at the 1930s and the Great Depression with his own empathy intact and a willingness to consider ways to achieve social justice, but with a growing cynicism about the motives of others and caution about reformist schemes that required action by government.

Unemployment, and the poverty and misery that it caused, were seen by Lippmann as terrible consequences of the Great Depression, and he believed that unemployment must be examined and dealt with unhesitatingly even before the causes were fully understood. Whether the unemployed should be assisted at all was not a question he was prepared to consider. The answer was unambiguously "Yes." He wrote in one of his first columns for the *Herald Tribune* in 1931: "While there has been argument about the way in which the unemployed who are in need should be helped, there is not and never has been any question about helping them. They are a first charge upon the resources of the American nation. The resources are adequate. They will be made available, voluntarily if it can be done, by taxation where necessary. For it is not debatable that those who have must give to those who need" (HT 10/20/31). At the beginning he looked mainly to private sources for assistance and to the lowest levels of government for action. "A person is in need. He may be helped by his friends and neighbors. If they can't or won't help him, he may be helped by private organizations. If their funds are insufficient, he may be helped by public authority in his local community. If the local public authority is not equal to the need, the State must assist it. If, in extreme cases, the State itself cannot cope with the problem, there remains as a last resource to assist the states the Federal power" (HT 10/20/31). Only when all other alternatives had been exhausted should the federal government consider stepping in. "Yet great as are the dangers of departing from the principle of local and voluntary relief, the American people will face these dangers rather than allow the needy to go hungry and cold" (HT 10/20/31). Lest citizens came to believe that somehow relief from Washington was less costly than funds from closer to home, he reminded them that "it must be remembered, though it is easily forgotten, that Washington has no money for relief which it does not take from the people who have money. Washington cannot create money. It must get it" (HT 12/31/31).

By 1932 Lippmann realized that the problem of the unemployed had become dire. It was no longer reasonable to write about a private or local solution. Washington had to step in, and the main issue was how best to do so. There was talk of a bond issue. But "that kind of easy policy would at once divert attention from the essential problem. That is the problem of Federal and local extravagance" (HT 5/13/32). Another option was direct appropriations from the federal treasury, but "this method once adopted will by all previous American experience create a new pork barrel which vested political interests will control and exploit. It seems to me, therefore, that the Federal aid to these exhausted communities ought to take the form of Federal loans at a nominal rate of interest. It might be well to consider the creation of some kind of emergency commission which under proof of need would have power to grant loans to states. Some such procedure as this would make the necessary money available without all of the obvious dangers and disadvantages of direct grants out of the Federal treasury" (HT

5/13/32). His thinking continued to evolve. With the prospect of a cold and hungry winter he insisted in 1932 that action must be taken immediately. However, as he contemplated the magnitude of the need for relief he came to conclude uneasily that perhaps this should not be treated as a one-time problem. It seemed more and more like a permanent one, endemic to an advanced industrial society that generated cyclical movements and had lost much of the capacity to protect citizens against periodic hardship through family and friends. Even if this immediate incident of the Great Depression were successfully dealt with, it could be presumed with confidence that another similar incident was just down the road and would have to be dealt with soon. This was a moment to consider how to prepare the American economy to face this continuing problem of unemployment.

> The difficulty of the problem this winter lies in the fact that an unprecedented need has to be met by an antiquated machinery. We are organized on the assumptions of the early Nineteenth Century when it was still a fact that the unemployed man could go west and found a new home. Our system of relief is based on a denial that cyclical unemployment is a characteristic of modern industry. The denial is obsolete. Although the system cannot be changed this winter, it is not too early to recognize the fact that there is a business cycle and to plan accordingly.
>
> For it can no longer be doubted that with the best wisdom anywhere available there is no likelihood that the next period of good times will not be succeeded by a period of bad times. And if that is the truth of the matter, is there any escape from the conclusion that insurance funds should be accumulated in the good times and a machinery set up for distributing them? (HT 9/20/32)

But for the moment, where should funds be found to aid the unemployed? Lippmann had still not broken the shackles of balanced budget doctrine when he first addressed this problem, and as an alternative to deficits he proposed having relief distributed only as payments to laborers in the construction of self-liquidating public works. Projects that would have been undertaken in due course, such as construction of government buildings, roads, and highways, would be moved forward and ultimately would be charged to regular government budgets. In this way relief could be included in some sort of capital budget. It would simply bring about an acceleration of good works that society would have done eventually. "If the principle of self-supporting public enterprise, as distinguished from subsidized public enterprise, were understood by the voters, and accepted as a controlling policy, it would be possible for cities to carry out needed improvements, perform the social services, provide some stimulus to business and employment, and yet reduce the burden of the taxpayer" (HT 9/28/32). Like others who examined the unemployment problem in later years, Lippmann found that "the unemployed" were not a homogeneous population and needed to be understood within a set of categories. There were those who suffered temporarily from the continuing adjustment of a dynamic industrial economy. Others became redundant through technological change and needed retraining; still others found difficulty reentering the labor market after years away. Some regions of the country prospered while others languished, and this required painful decisions about whether the most affected regions should receive aid that might retard their adjustment. Ideally private and local public services should take care of most of the temporarily troubled and unemployed. "The social work of normal times is an attempt to deal with the physical, mental, and moral maladjustments of the young, the helpless, and the unknowing, who are unprotected by their families and friends. The uprooting of human beings from the land, the concentration in cities, the breakdown of the authority of the family, of tradition, and of moral conventions, the complexity and novelty of modern life, and finally the economic insecurity of our industrial system have called into being the modern social worker" (HT 10/20/32).

The sudden onset of a great depression, however, was another matter. Then the acute needs of a large part of the labor force might quickly overwhelm and permanently damage the regular social services. Public provision for the unemployment of this second kind was critical. "For the policy of depending upon private charity in the emergency has no foundation in principle. In so far as private gifts are adequate it is expedient not to raise the political question involved in a resort to public funds. But as the depression has continued and deepened, as the need has grown and

private resources have diminished, the burden of emergency relief has in
fact been shifted more and more from private donors to the taxpayers. It
will undoubtedly have to be shifted much more this winter, and wherever
the continuance of normal social work is threatened by the need for emergency relief, there the point has been reached where public money is unmistakably necessary" (HT 10/20/32). By the end of the winter of 1932–1933,
when destitution among the unemployed reached heart-wrenching levels,
Lippmann wrote that his earlier notion of a public-private partnership to
deal with the crisis was no longer sound. From then on emergency unemployment relief, which had hitherto been supported about 70 to 75 percent
from public funds, would have to be supported wholly from public funds
(HT 2/7/33). And there should not be any whining from the taxpayers. Support for unemployment relief must be based not on any economic calculation but on the social sympathy that should motivate the concern. "This tax
is necessary in order to meet a debt of honor. It is owed to our neighbors.
We have incurred it for the simple and conclusive reason that they are our
neighbors and are in need. . . . Indeed there are no reasons which can be
set forth in a lawyer's brief or in an accountant's balance sheet. The true
reasons for giving are deeper than the calculations of our intelligence. For it
can do little more than to explain what an instinctive chivalry of the human
spirit declares is the only possible basis of human relations" (HT 12/7/33).

If a community could not care for its own members during a time of
trial and suffering then perhaps that community was doomed. Lippmann
emphasized that the losses incurred by the working class through unemployment and wage reductions had been much greater than those of other
social classes. Speaking to a group of businessmen, he synthesized the results of a study conducted by the U.S. Department of Commerce and the
National Bureau of Economic Research. "From 1929 to 1932 there was a
great decline in the total national income. But in the course of this decline
salaries and dividend payments fell slowly at first. Interest payments fell
very little. Among labor incomes salaried men were favored as against wage-
earners, and of course wage earners as against the unemployed. Relatively
speaking, property incomes increased. Among various occupations the
order in which the force of the depression was felt was, first, construction,

then mining, then manufacturing, then agriculture, then transportation, then finance, then personal services and professions, then trade. All of these had incomes of not more than 65 per cent of 1929 levels and most of them far less. Three large occupations were well sheltered. They were the power industry, at 93 per cent of 1929 in 1932, communications at 88 per cent, and of course government, which was 105 per cent" (HT 1/30/34). If indeed these data showed correctly that in a depression parts of the modern economy suffered unequally, this alone was justification enough for income redistribution. Lippmann suggested that the political consequences of inaction in these circumstances should be taken into account as well as the inherent injustice. "The truth is that the maldistribution of the three bad years, which was becoming progressively worse, was subversive in the highest degree. If the disease had not been arrested, and a beginning made in restoring the balance, we should not be here tonight talking quite so calmly. For the thing which a modern democratic commonwealth cannot stand is suffering poisoned by a sense of injustice. Men can and will endure hardship. But masses of men will not endure hardship combined with a growing sense of injustice" (HT 1/30/34).

Beyond the political dangers, unemployment posed serious social and psychological dangers for the workforce, something like what would later be called post-traumatic stress. Government and business could become as traumatized as the workers. "That was the condition last winter. It reflected itself in the complete paralysis of government and in a lack of confidence in public institutions, in banks and in the normal processes of American life. That was why the President could not have succeeded had he followed the advice of conservative economists and taken only those measures which in the cold theory of the business cycle are supposed to promote recovery. He had a people among whom there was not only suffering but fierce resentment against those who in the calamity had been sheltered or had even improved their relative position. And as he was President of the United States, and not a theorist dealing with abstractions, his primary task was to weave together the torn fabric of the national mind, and unite the nation by giving it not relief from misery but relief from resentment" (HT 1/30/34).

The best way to administer relief from unemployment remained a puzzle for Lippmann. In general he preferred some form of what would later be
called "workfare" rather than simple welfare or "the dole." Payments for
labor on public works should be no higher than current market rates rather
than at the predepression levels that were demanded by some of the unemployed and their unions. Increasingly he was worried about incentives.
Would workers go through the job search process if they received unemployment insurance payments anywhere near the market wage? He found
some useful guidance from the work of the President's Committee on Economic Security, directed by Edwin Witte of the University of Wisconsin,
and also from the works of Williford King at New York University. He was
glad that there seemed to be a consensus that regular welfare payments,
before the workers were required to go to the public works programs,
should be at rates well below current labor rates and should be limited to
fifteen weeks. After that the unemployed should have the opportunity to
work on government projects at wages below union scales (HT 1/19/35). It
had always to be remembered, he wrote, that the objective of this policy
was to alleviate the sufferings of the depression without crippling the adjustment mechanisms needed to end the depression. The level of unemployment relief, recognizing that the higher it was the slower the adjustment
was likely to be, was a moral question as much as an economic one. "The
relief load could be cut down by cutting down the criterion of relief and by
restoring the stigma of relief. If the country wishes to say, for example, that
the average need a month should be $18 rather than $28, and if it wishes to
say that the $18 shall be given in such a way as to humiliate the recipient, the
relief load will diminish drastically and immediately. *In the last analysis the
size of the load depends upon how generous the country feels it can afford to be
and how generous it thinks it wise to be*" (HT 4/16/35, italics in original). On
this point, "The fundamental issue is not financial and not political. It is
moral. It is the question of how much you can help others without ruining
their capacity to help themselves" (HT 4/16/35).

Lippmann worried by 1935 that unemployment was declining at an un-
acceptably slow pace. This was a serious problem for the government and

for the unemployed. Around five million were still on relief, and this number had fallen only slightly over the previous year. "The burden of relief now constitutes for all practical purposes the whole Federal deficit. But for relief the budget would readily be balanced. What is more, the cost of relief in terms of human self-respect and its effects upon standards of personal and social responsibility, and in its political implications are, though they cannot be measured, immense" (HT 4/16/35). One explanation for the stubborn maintenance of the high unemployment rate, he thought, might be that some of the unemployed did not appeal for relief, and therefore were not counted as unemployed, until their personal resources were exhausted and they were compelled to ask for help. Thus, even though new jobs were being created, new additions were being made at the same time to the numbers of the destitute unemployed by the addition of workers who had lost their jobs as much as five years before.

Lippmann took care to distinguish between the essentially uninsurable risk for the individual of massive unemployment in a major depression, and the insurable risks of old age and survivor needs that were being dealt with in legislation that was working its way through Congress in the Social Security bill. Ad hoc unemployment relief in response to a crisis was the more flexible countercyclical tool of the two kinds of public assistance, but taking into account the dangers of corruption, demoralization, and administrative costs, he preferred programs that were automatic in their operation. Overall, he favored shifting as many as possible of these programs to the states, which would be most likely to handle them efficiently. As the years went on Lippmann became more and more critical of welfare cheats who could discredit a whole program. He wrote in 1936: "Few who stop to think about what unemployment really means will begrudge the cost. But there are also the minority who instead of having their self-respect preserved by public relief, lose it and become demoralized and would rather be on relief than take a job" (HT 3/21/36). If relief were administered at the lowest levels of government the likelihood would be greatest that corruption could be prevented and those who abused the system intercepted. "In the small communities their neighbors can and do know this, not with perfect justice and sympathy by any means, but with the nearest approximation to it obtainable. In the large cities the social workers know the truth more or less" (HT 3/21/36).

It seemed to Lippmann that President Roosevelt and his advisers accepted sound doctrine about unemployment assistance, but he was depressed that they were so inept at translating ideas into legislation and explaining the justification for government intervention to the American people. "The country would like to follow the President, but the President himself must recognize that the time has passed when it will follow him blindly. He will be misjudging the temper of the country, and jeopardizing his own leadership if he does not generously concede the right of the Congress and the people to be better informed than they now are" (HT 2/28/35). For example, he concluded that industrial education was a program that would stand the nation in good stead in the short and the long run but had been neglected under the New Deal. He told an editor of the *Yale Review*: "The problem of training men for jobs seems to me extremely important. The more I think of it, the more I feel that one of our greatest mistakes in the relief program was our failure to provide industrial training" (WL to Helen McAfee, December 29, 1936, WLPIII F2289).

Lippmann interpreted Roosevelt's second inaugural address in 1937 as, in essence, a declaration of war on poverty, a quarter of a century before the better remembered declaration by Lyndon Johnson. But he wondered whether FDR simply strengthened misconceptions about how such a war could be won rather than setting forth a campaign. Citizens should be told the truth that in fact little could be accomplished through redistribution; a reduction in poverty depended upon increased production, increasing the size of the pie rather than altering the size of the slices. "It is necessary that the people should produce wealth in abundance beyond anything ever produced before. For no matter how strong the government is made, no matter how brilliantly it is led, no matter how unselfish the people become, these high hopes will be disappointed unless the productive powers of the nation are stupendously increased" (HT 1/23/37). Lippmann was never certain whether Roosevelt was being candid with the voters about the real costs of a war on poverty or whether he was just confused or misinformed. If he understood the real costs of such a war he was silent about them; was he just telling his audience what they wanted to hear? Lippmann insisted that the only defensible position on redistribution as a general issue must be that equality among members of the labor force should be achieved at the start of their careers, and not in the middle, or at the end.

Roosevelt's plan for a major increase in federal aid to education was consistent with this position, but a major increase in the excess profits tax was not. "The great difference between the democratic theory of equality and the communist theory (which is not in force in Russia today) is that democracy aims at equal opportunity, whereas communism aims at equal rewards. The democrats would like every one to have an equal start and an equal chance under the rules of the game, and then to let the natural and real inequalities of men assert themselves" (HT 2/26/38). Lippmann was happy to note that Governor Robert La Follette of Wisconsin, one of the founders of the national Progressive Party, held to these views about the importance of increasing production rather than proposing to achieve greater equality through redistribution. It was to be hoped that leaders in the current federal government would follow suit. "For the first time in a decade a recognized American progressive has realized and said with the utmost emphasis that in this country the primary problem is not the distribution of income, but the production of wealth on a scale commensurate with our exceptional opportunities. For the first time in many years a man who might be the leader of a progressive movement does not imply the remedy for poverty is to move as rapidly as possible toward the public administration of the country's business. For the first time, I think since Wilson, a possible progressive candidate for President is interested in using the power of government not to supplant, but to liberate, private initiative" (HT 4/30/38).

At the end of the 1930s, with a real war looming, not just one on poverty, Lippmann remained pessimistic about the fate of the unemployed, although now his view was more nuanced than at the start. He saw unemployment as made up of two parts. There were those who became unemployed in the trough of the business cycle; their problem could be dealt with through monetary and fiscal policy. But now he discerned a second part, which he

called "the disemployed," meaning those who were laid off when their employers became part of some monopolistic price-fixing arrangement that
established prices higher than competitive norms in product and factor
markets, thus constraining quantity demanded and output. Unless something were done to restore competition throughout the economic system, it
was quite possible that many of these disemployed people would never find
employment again. "We have to think, I am afraid, that in the prevailing
economic philosophy of all responsible groups in America, a permanent
mass of unemployed is, so to speak, ordained" (HT 1/21/39). This was a
point at which the several parts of Lippmann's policy concerns came together. The growth of monopoly pricing in both the public and private sectors stood in the way of speedy recovery after recession, the development of
a more efficient and vibrant economy, and even modest income redistribution to achieve more justice and a stronger commitment to democracy.

Greed: The Veterans

In the exploration of the first public policy question after starting his column in the *Herald Tribune*, how to meet the needs of those in great want
either because of cyclical unemployment or some other reason, the most
discouraging discovery Lippmann made was that people for the most part
when addressing this question were not as generous and public spirited as
he perceived himself to be. Even when shown that a path ahead was best for
the common good, they would seldom take it if they thought some other
path might be preferable for them individually. This suggested to Lippmann
that a policy regime that conformed to socially selected norms, such as hu-
manity, community, or equity, would be difficult to achieve. The first, and
most poignant, manifestation of this social selfishness he found, paradoxically, among the veterans of World War I, of which he was one, those who
presumably had been motivated by patriotism during the war but now, a
decade later, were prepared to hold their friends and neighbors hostage
and for ransom while demanding unreasonable transfer payments. He addressed the issue of special treatment for veterans first at the beginning of
the 1930s, before he had been converted to Keynesian concerns for aggre-

gate demand, and when he still accepted the conclusion that the most promising road to recovery lay in strict economy and balanced budgets: "the balancing of the Federal budget by reducing expenditures and by increasing revenues is the fundamental and indispensable problem before Congress" (HT 1/5/32). Reduction of, rather than increase in, the "fantastically extravagant" payments to the veterans seemed a good place to start. Elimination of those programs for veterans that he thought were unjustified would substantially reduce the current budget deficit. The veterans—many of whom, he noted sarcastically, had never heard a shot fired in anger—were demanding extended medical care and were even fabricating disabilities to obtain pensions. Now in the national crisis of depression the veterans, egged on by the Detroit firebrand Father Charles Coughlin, were calling for early payment of bonuses that had been promised to them by Congress for a later date. If paid in advance, Lippmann asserted, these bonuses would necessarily expand the deficit and lead to inflation. Coughlin told Congress that the $2 billion bonus payment "would go to the grocers and those who have been rendering credit to the jobless veterans. It would go into channels of trade and commerce and help revive business" (HT 4/14/32). On the contrary, Lippmann said, such irresponsible expenditure would destroy confidence, threaten the stability of the government, and damage the credit of the United States, worsening the depression even more. Instead of achieving the modest "reflation" to the 1920s price levels that Father Coughlin promised, the bonus might even lead to more deflation: "a flight from the dollar would produce runs on banks, which in turn would force banks to call loans, which in turn would depress prices. Thus instead of helping 'to revive business' the measure would prostrate it" (HT 4/14/32).

Using statistics gathered by Charles Merz, his old colleague at the *New York World* now working for the *New York Times,* Lippmann showed how the veterans deserved a large share of the blame for exploding the budget, in contrast to the situation in the United Kingdom, where the veterans' political power was declining. "The great difference between the two countries in regard to payments to individuals is that in Britain the cost of the veterans has declined while the cost of social services to the whole population has increased, whereas, in the United States the whole increase has gone to the veterans. In other words, in Britain the veterans are being re-absorbed into the civilian population whereas in the United States they are increasingly a specially favored class apart" (HT 4/26/32). Lippmann called Congress craven for making the veterans "a privileged class" on whom they could count for votes, "a class of men who have rights which no other citizens possess" (HT 5/4/32). The financial commitment to the veterans was based entirely on the lowest form of politics and not on any valid argument, and now it was proposed that the special status be extended to the dependents of veterans. "If the country agrees to the hereditary principle, it will have created a new class of voters who will hang together because they have a common interest in appropriations from the Treasury. Because they hang together they will terrorize Congressmen. In addition to the veterans' bloc we shall then have the widows' bloc and the guardians of orphans' bloc. That ought to constitute a large enough body of voters to make it impossible for Congress to resist any demand from the veterans' lobbies" (HT 5/4/32).

He applauded efforts by the National Economy Committee, which included some of his friends, to reverse some of the veterans' entitlements, which he claimed had reached 10 percent of the federal budget (HT 5/6/32). He had no sympathy for the bonus marchers when they converged on Washington in 1932 demanding early payment of funds promised for 1945. He complained the marchers did not understand compound interest and that the current value of their future commitment was far less than the face value. The most financial assistance he would sanction was "transportation home to those already there, unattractive relief for those who stay on, and a refusal to admit those who come after it has been made clear that there is no lawful way in which the demands can be satisfied" (HT 6/9/32). Anything more for the veterans would effectively threaten the survival of democracy. "For of all the forms of corruption to which a republic is susceptible the most deadly is to hand money out of the treasury because a group of voters have become too strong to be refused. This is the ultimate corruption of popular government. It is the corruption of the electorate itself. Against predatory interests the final remedy is an aroused electorate. But against a predatory electorate there is no remedy by the ordinary methods of democracy" (HT 9/14/32). Lippmann was relieved that candidate Roosevelt rejected the request for accelerated payment of the veterans' bonus, but he wished that this had been done on grounds of principle rather than financial exigency (HT 10/21/32). He showed no sympathy when the veterans were rousted from their camps in Washington by a military force headed by Douglas MacArthur and including Dwight D. Eisenhower and George S. Patton.

In 1933 Lippmann urged Roosevelt, by then in power, to maintain commitments "to men actually disabled in battle, to men suffering from diseases directly arising from the war, and to the widows and orphans of men who died in the service" (HT 6/20/33). But beyond that "the Administration can with a clear conscience and with overwhelming public support resist any further attempts by Congress to put men on the public pay roll who have no better claim as against other citizens than that they once wore a uniform" (HT 6/20/33). Payments to the veterans, and to the bonus marchers in particular, would simply add to the extravagance of big government, which had to be curbed. It would also be evidence of how, unless citizens were vigilant, democracy could degenerate into a collection of special interests receiving rewards determined not by any principle but by sheer political power, most of which was administered by lobbies invisible to the public.

> Congress is operating under a system whereby the benefits it confers are visible and the burdens it imposes are invisible. There does not exist, therefore, any effective check on the spending power. . . . The veterans are by no means the only organized interest which dominates Congress in this way. The tariff, as operated in the United States, is the oldest and the greatest example of the same principle. Almost any producer can write his own tariff rate because the tax levied by the tariff is invisible and indirect. The consumer cannot see it and is hardly aware that it exists. . . . It is plain that unless some way can be found to make the costs as visible as the expenditures, the power to spend will be exercised irresponsibly and will be at the mercy of pressure groups. There is no way to keep expenditure in check if the people do not realize that they are paying the bill. (HT 2/4/36)

The veterans remained Lippmann's nemesis for years to come. After reviewing the circumstances yet once more he commented to Felix Frankfurter: "It seems to me that you seem to imply that the wickedness and selfishness that pervade society come entirely through bad example from the top, but it also works up from the bottom" (WL to Frankfurter, March 8, 1933, WLPIII F817). When in 1936 Congress paid a bonus by adding to the deficit and monetizing the amount through increases in the money supply he called the veterans a "financial vortex" into which the national product fell and disappeared. "If the government prints the money that the veteran uses, that printed money is nothing but a tax bill against the national income" (HT 2/4/36).

Salt of the Earth: The Farmers

For the most part Lippmann accepted the Jeffersonian American identity story that the farmers were the firm foundation on which American civilization rested. Farmers were pure of heart and less corrupted than city dwellers. Of course, he hardly knew any farmers. He visited gentlemen's farms on weekends, but there is no evidence that he ever talked seriously with a western fruit farmer, a midwestern grain grower, or an eastern dairyman. He liked the country and he spent several weeks each year on Long Island, in Florida, or in Maine; but during these periods the object was to get away from people, and his abundant correspondence contains few letters with those who actually tilled the soil. Nevertheless, he was attuned quite early to the suffering of farmers in the early days of the depression and especially to their inability to make their mortgage payments. He wrote to Senator Cordell Hull in January 1933: "The problem is one which interests me greatly and is, I think, of the greatest importance" (WL to Hull, January 19, 1933, WLPIII F1104).

Some of the earliest proposals for radical reform of the farm economy in the 1930s worried Lippmann a great deal. He thought they were deeply flawed in principle and might cripple competition in agricultural markets permanently while offering no constructive alternative in their place. He was especially concerned that reformers had set out to solve the problem of falling prices in agricultural markets by limits on the supply side rather than increases on the demand side. These were attempts to solve a distressing problem—suffering on the farms—by using a flawed economic practice, monopoly. The farm bill before Congress in 1933 was, he said, "a measure to establish a temporary dictatorship for the relief of the producers of wheat, cotton, tobacco and hogs" (HT 1/5/33). He admitted that the bill was well intentioned; however, it was based not on economic analysis but on a romantic misconception. "The theory of the bill is that if these particular groups of farmers are given a monopoly of the domestic market, the dictator can force prices upward by any desired amount if he can reduce the supply and also levy any tax that may be necessary" (HT 1/5/33). The notion of price "parity" embodied in the bill implied that farmers might regain the "pre-war status of agriculture" with respect to manufacturing simply by constraining free markets. "That is the Golden Age to which they propose to return, if it takes a dictatorship to do it. The answer can be seen in Mr. Frederick C. Mills's profound study of 'Economic Tendencies in the United States.' Mr. Mills shows that in the years between the opening of the twentieth century and the outbreak of the World War the real worth of farm products and raw materials was advancing and the real worth of manufactured goods was declining" (HT 1/5/33). The balance shifted in the other direction after the war, and "[n]ow these tendencies for real farm income to fall have been fantastically exaggerated by the depression. Since 1929 there has been a collapse of world prices. But in this collapse the prices of raw materials have fallen much further than the prices of manufactured goods" (HT 1/5/33). With the restrictive practices proposed in the farm bill Lippmann was convinced the farmers were being sold a nostrum that would not achieve the desired objective. The only real solution for the farm problem was to bring an end to the depression; unless this was accomplished with dispatch it could be expected that other foolish proposals to dismantle the competitive market system such as this one would follow. "But important as it is to realize the desperate character of this measure, it is even more important to make the effort to understand the desperate need which inspires it. The introduction of this measure is a signal, like the tolling of a bell, that unless concerted measures are taken promptly to deal with the great obstacles to recovery, unless the domestic and the international readjustments, which every reasonable person now knows are necessary, are courageously and decisively carried through, this country will enter one of the great political crises of its history" (HT 1/5/33).

Lippmann was intrigued by the intellectual origins of the 1933 farm bill (the Jones bill) because they might give warning about other aspects of policy reform ahead. He found that the idea behind the bill came not from some selfish market manipulator, a lobby, or an agricultural special interest, but rather from a succession of intellectuals who seriously wanted to make the world a better place for farmers, though they seemed not to understand the damage their proposals might do to a delicate price system for which there was no viable substitute. "The Farm Bill in the House is a very good example of what happens to idealists when they fall into the hands of politicians. The original idea of paying a bounty to farmers to control and reduce production seems to have been invented by the late Walter J. Spillman, formerly chief of the office of farm management in the Department of Agriculture. From him it is said to have been passed on to Professor John D. Black of Harvard and to Professor M. L. Wilson of the Montana State College. Professor Wilson seems to have developed a committee which at some time in the last year or so came into intimate contact with Governor Roosevelt's agricultural advisers, with such able and disinterested men as Henry A. Wallace of Iowa, the editor of *Wallace's Farmer*, Professor Rexford Tugwell of Columbia University, and Mr. Henry Morgenthau, Jr., New York State Conservation Commissioner" (HT 1/13/33). The original scheme was, first, to decide upon an amount of reduction in agricultural production that would maintain or raise prices the desired amount, then to tax purchasers and users of the commodities, and finally to use the tax revenues to induce the farmers to reduce production. Production quotas would be established for each county in the nation, and federal agents would enforce the reductions. Lippmann found it hard to conceive of a more ridiculous plan. "Let us try to imagine Federal agents sent out from Washington with certificates redeemable at the Treasury which they may give to farmers when they, the agents, are satisfied that the farmer has reduced his acreage by 20 per cent over a five-year average. Has anything like this ever been proposed by men in their right minds? The scheme could not be administered if every one of the three thousand-odd agents were a hero, a saint, and a sage. To think of attempting to administer it through ordinary human beings, to think of giving thousands of officeholders the power to hand out public money in this fashion, to expect them to be accurate and fair, to suppose they could withstand the pressure of local opinion, is sheer madness" (HT 1/13/33).

The farm bill did not recognize that the problems of the farmers, like those of other producers throughout the economy, did not lie in the markets for their individual products but with the depression overall. "If the general deflation continues this bill will not stop it and reverse it. It will fail, as Mr. Hoover's farm relief failed, because the downward pull of general economic forces is too strong. But if the general downward pull no longer exists, then with rising prices a limitation of supply may raise farm prices a little higher and a little faster than they would otherwise rise" (HT 3/21/33). Lippmann did not question the sincerity or integrity of those who proposed and advocated this legislation; but he did find them naïve and innocent of the world. Their claim that the farmers liked such a plan should not be taken as any indication of its virtue. "For they will have accepted the preposterous notion that a majority vote among those who have a vested interest is binding upon the majority of the whole people" (HT 12/20/34). Lippmann concluded that "if this bill goes into effect, Mr. Roosevelt will be in for trouble compared with which Mr. Hoover's experience in farm relief will seem comparatively tranquil and pleasant" (HT 1/13/33).

By 1934, when the exceptional drought in the Southwest was rapidly becoming the second economic catastrophe of the decade, Lippmann claimed that the plight of the farmers was becoming analogous to that of their city cousins, rendered unemployed by natural disaster rather than manmade calamity. Both were victims of what amounted to uninsurable risk. In the countryside as in the cities there was now a prima facie case for public assistance. "For the people affected it is a disaster which they are quite clearly unable to meet with their own resources. They are stricken by a natural catastrophe after years of impoverishment due to the world depression. There will, therefore, be no question as to their need or as to the duty of the Federal government to provide relief. Fortunately, the government is organized, as it has never been before, to act promptly, intelligently and adequately" (HT 6/5/34).

Lippmann noted that some were opposed to any help for the farmers because they were, for the most part, small entrepreneurs and must become accustomed to taking the bad with the good.

> The traditional view is, of course, that farmers must take the weather as it comes. Relying not at all upon government devices, they become the self-reliant independent stock from which the nation renews its vitality. In this view a paternalistic policy for the farmer is undesirable not so much because it costs money, but because it softens him as an individual. There are few persons who would not feel that while there is something in this view, it is infected with a kind of moral blindness. Is the modern American farmer the same kind of farmer around whom there has grown the ideal of complete self-reliance? The traditional view is an ancient one based upon the experience of farmers working their own land for their own needs and for a neighboring community. But the wheat farmer in the Dakotas and Kansas and Nebraska does not live that kind of life. He produces for a world market and he supplies his own needs out of a world market. He is no longer even approximately self-sufficient. Can he then be expected to be wholly self-reliant? (HT 6/5/34)

The conclusion to be drawn was that the western farmer, as much as the urban unemployed factory worker, was deserving of relief. "Today his real income fluctuates spectacularly due to causes which he cannot control by his own prudence, thrift, or industry. These are the underlying reasons why we now recognize that to protect the farmer against great natural calamities or economic convulsions is a social duty. If he is to be self-reliant, he must be more or less self-sufficient; in so far as he is not, he must either be led back to self-sufficiency or insured against those forces of nature and of society which self-reliance alone cannot deal with" (HT 6/5/34).

For Lippmann the logic of the situation was clear; public assistance of some kind for the farmer was a social obligation. "The difficult aspect of the matter is to know where to draw the line and then to have the political courage to draw it. The farmer, being only human, will expect more protection than society can afford or that he is really entitled to have. But the rule which ought to govern in these affairs is reasonably clear, however hard it may be to apply it in many particular cases. Taking into consideration its resources in the light of its obligations to other groups in the nation, society ought to attempt to insure men against those risks which a reasonably prudent man cannot be expected to avert or to deal with single-handed" (HT 6/5/34). Paradoxically, those who demand responsible individual response to economic challenge must be prepared to accept a relief role for the state. "If the virtues and values of individualism and self-reliance are to be preserved, we must not put upon the individual person burdens that are greater than he can by self-reliance carry. This is the surest way to kill individualism: by making it intolerable. . . . For that reason it can be said that those who are laboring to distribute justly the social risks of our immensely complicated society are the true defenders of individual liberty against the diseases of paternalism and the dangers of tyranny" (HT 6/5/34).

By the time most of the main elements of the New Deal had been proposed and implemented in the mid-1930s, Lippmann's attitude toward farm policy softened somewhat, mainly for three reasons, which all reflected his reluctant acceptance of the second best. Because the overall plan for the New Deal seemed to be to create a national economy built on monopoly and fixed prices it was unfair to ask one sector—agriculture—to play by the rules of competition and equilibrium prices. If balance among the sectors of the economy was to be maintained, then the powers of economic intervention had to be distributed evenly. Lippmann seemed to be moving toward a concept similar to John Kenneth Galbraith's later notion of "countervailing power." This point had been pressed on him by Bernard Baruch as early as 1927 (Baruch to WL, March 7, 1927, WLPI F117). As another world war seemed increasingly probable it was necessary also to think of the strategic importance of commodity production. If agriculture was to be sustained for emergencies such as war in an economy of restrictions it must have the power to balance the monopoly of other sectors. Otherwise it would be crushed. "If the power to close our economy through industrial tariffs and to make it rigid through big business and labor unions exists under the

Constitution, then the power to protect agriculture and give it equal economic status must also exist" (HT 7/20/35).

Finally, although he remained deeply critical of recovery schemes like
the Agricultural Adjustment Act of 1933, which set out to support prices by
curtailing production, in agriculture at least the system worked smoothly.
This was partly because Roosevelt, with his patrician background from
Hyde Park, was more sympathetic to agriculture than to urban life, and
partly because the Department of Agriculture, in contrast to the National
Recovery Administration, was well run by experienced professionals who
had been on the job for years. "No one can doubt that the department is
manned by officials who really understand agriculture, that they are seasoned and on the whole extraordinarily competent career men. It is one of
the departments at Washington which most nearly approaches the ideal
which civil service reformers have aimed at. . . . One may dislike the program. But no one can seriously deny that it has been effectively executed,
that it is a very remarkable feat of administration. The contrast with the
N.R.A., for example, has been devastating" (HT 12/14/35). Lippmann was
especially appreciative of Mordecai Ezekiel, economic adviser in the Department of Agriculture, who provided a continuing stream of data and
commentary on agricultural policy as it evolved. He counted upon Ezekiel
to explain farm issues to him throughout the 1930s (e.g., Ezekiel to WL,
December 5, 1932, January 16, 1933, January 24, 1933, January 26, 1934,
February 10, 1936, WLPIII F725). All this said, Lippmann was relieved
when the Supreme Court declared the AAA unconstitutional in 1936 (HT
1/9/36). Although a "justifiable expedient," it had become "an economic
and political monstrosity" (HT 1/14/36). At least the way was open again for
a farm policy that would be fair, workable, and respectful of the functions of
competitive markets (HT 2/6/36).

One of the dangers in accepting the principle that farmers should be
helped by stabilizing prices through constraints on supply, Lippmann
thought, was that there was no clear line of demarcation indicating where
the principle should end. One extension in particular that worried him was
to raw materials of all kinds. Surely, on the face of it, the coal miners deserved the same special treatment as the farmers. "The coal problem is not

essentially different from the farm problem. In effect one of the most illuminating things ever said about it is that coal mining is, in its technique and its economics and its social history, a branch of agriculture rather than an industry" (HT 5/23/36). The example of agricultural policy had opened up price fixing as a way of helping almost any disadvantaged group and threatened the survival of the competitive market system. "It is one thing to say that government may regulate prices to cure the evils of a monopoly, and a diametrically opposite thing to say that it may regulate prices in order to confer and enforce the privileges of a monopoly. The one form of regulation is for the benefit of all: the other for the special benefit of a particular group" (HT 5/23/36). There was no obvious end to this kind of market intervention defended as a means of assisting some impacted groups in depression. Who would be next? Railways? Automobiles? Hydroelectricity? And once in place powerful lobbies would rise to defend such schemes and they would become extremely difficult to terminate: "it is into such absurdities that a society must fall when it seeks to stabilize itself by making every one a privileged monopolist" (HT 5/23/36).

By the end of the 1930s Lippmann was far less comfortable with the notion of redistribution of income and wealth than he had been at the beginning of the decade. His discomfort grew not from selfishness about the possibility of having to contribute himself, nor from some new ideology that Greed is Good. Indeed his social empathy and commitment to a humane society remained intact. His problems with redistribution grew from observing the difficulties in implementing such a policy. In each of the groups for whom redistribution was contemplated in the 1930s serious obstacles appeared to a successful outcome. For the unemployed the issues were how much relief to make available on grounds of social justice, and how to prevent the payments from weakening incentives among those without jobs to find work. The veterans demonstrated to Lippmann just how selfish and demanding one group in society could become if they saw the possibility of extracting resources from government. They conjured up for him the possibility of a democracy with many groups of cunning mendicants all looking to exchange their votes for payoffs. In the case of the farmers Lippmann saw a large segment of society, unlike the veterans, with genuine suffering and obvious need. But how should they be helped? He found the farm problems happy hunting ground for irresponsible intellectuals with a glint in their eye and untested schemes to bring salvation to the farmers. Here the problem was not the opportunities presented to scoundrels but the danger that could be done by well-meaning amateurs to the survival of a free market economy when burdened by ideas like "parity" that were fundamentally inconsistent with competitive markets. Lippmann often scolded those who called the redistributionists of the 1930s authoritarian and even fascist. To him this misrepresented the problems of the depression. He returned often to the observation that foolish but well-intentioned reformist ideas were far more of a threat to the American economy than were the totalitarian doctrines gaining strength elsewhere in the world.

When summarizing his position on redistribution late in the 1930s, Lippmann conjured up an image of more and more mendicants sidling up to the public trough with few ways seemingly available to move them away. He talked of "the siphon principle," by which at the moment five strong siphons from favored groups were attached to the federal treasury, sustained by active lobbies, with funds flowing through them in exchange for votes: the veterans, the farmers, the Civilian Conservation Corps, the unemployed, and local governments. Attempts to create a more just society had morphed into the creation of entitlements through "the pressure of powerful interests," and there seemed no obvious way of turning back (HT 1/21/36).

7

Reform II: Monopoly

LIPPMANN BEGAN HIS CAREER as a journalist at the end of World War I with the optimism of the young progressive intellectuals of his day. He was a reformer but not a revolutionary. He believed that the democratic polity and competitive market economy were far from perfect, but they could be improved and they could be saved. These systems should not be replaced if for no other reason than because no better alternatives could be discerned. Lippmann believed that society was populated in the main by reasonable people of goodwill who would do the right thing if it were pointed out to them persuasively. For the most part these people pursued their own narrow self-interest, which usually and coincidentally was in the public interest, but they would act with restraint if the reasons for doing so were spelled out, such as the existence of positive or negative externalities from their actions. The decade of the 1930s tested Lippmann's progressive faith severely. Above all he discovered to his regret that his commitment to democracy and the competitive market was not as widely shared among his fellow citizens as he had supposed. Leaders in the public and private sectors were often quick to adopt schemes that moved the state from democracy to authoritarian, or even totalitarian, systems. At one extreme were the new dictators: Benito Mussolini, Adolf Hitler, and Francisco Franco; at the other were well-meaning bureaucrats who were willing gradually to chip away at personal freedoms with restrictive schemes justified in the name of "planning."

So, over the course of the decade Lippmann moved from an emphasis on creative social improvements that required government involvement to rejection of market concentration of any kind and a spirited defense of liberty across the board. Increasingly Lippmann became convinced of two reasons for an emphasis on competitive markets. First, most human liberties depended on vigorous competition; where there was monopoly there would be, sooner or later, government intervention and constraints on free choice and behavior. Second, many people, while professing allegiance to competition, were in fact surprisingly willing to abandon it. Sadly, this was true for leaders of capital, labor, and government. By the end of the 1930s, monopoly had become for Lippmann like original sin. All were cursed with an unquenchable desire for it, and the best policy makers could do was to find ways to constrain it. Straightforward laws to prohibit monopoly usually did not work, just as prohibition had not reduced the taste for alcohol. The challenge for economists was to find ways to solve the monopoly problem without making it worse.

Capital

Lippmann, like many others, began by thinking that leaders of business and finance were the natural defenders of the free market. Typically, free markets and competition were part of the business creed, and business leaders could surely see that they would suffer under any other kind of economic system. The wonders of the free market had been spelled out clearly to him by Thomas Nixon Carver in the Harvard classroom before World War I, and Carver's other graduates and those of like-minded colleagues in the boardrooms of America could surely be expected to make the same case for competition in their subsequent careers. But they did not. Increasingly, Lippmann saw monopoly as widespread and growing and causing serious problems at both the micro and macro levels. He expressed a view accepted by many American Institutionalists, such as John Maurice Clark, that to deal with the depression "the essential problem is to decide what to do about the deep and pervasive tendency to monopoly which is characteristic of modern business. For this monopolistic tendency makes prices, and overhead costs rigid, prevents any easy adjustment of the economy, and accentuates the violence of the business cycle" (HT 5/30/35). To those who said that the business community had the answer to the depression, he replied sarcastically: "There is a very good reason why the business men are unable to formulate a program for dealing with unemployment. It is that within the realm of business there are two sharply contradictory policies at work and two opposing philosophies. One of these is the old fashioned scheme of increasing business by lowering the price, by giving more value for the same money or the same value for less money. The other is politely called stabilization: it used to be called monopoly and restraint of trade" (HT 4/30/36).

So it was not surprising that Lippmann saw the widespread support of monopolistic practices in the American economy as a betrayal of the true economic faith. Would-be monopolists did not seem to appreciate that any constraint on the market was the first step toward government "planning." Businessmen often talked a good line in public about the evils of monopoly, but they were equally ready to pursue it for their own purposes if given a chance. "Much is said by certain orators about individualism, free competition, and the laws of supply and demand. These ancient and excellent principles are being rapidly suppressed in modern industry, and not by a few visionaries in the so-called Brains Trust, but by business men themselves" (HT 5/30/35). If the free market could not count upon a genuine defense from the business community, he lamented, where could it turn? "If big business men try to practice a private socialism, inevitably they will push the country into some form of public socialism. The real propagandists of collectivism in America are not the Marxian orators but the promoters of private monopoly" (HT 4/29/37).

Most depressing for Lippmann was his observation that pressures for monopoly were visible across the private sector. Certainly this was true of Wall Street, where his work with Lincoln Steffens had demonstrated the dominance of the House of Morgan. He welcomed the efforts of the Pecora investigation by Congress to discover "whether the system under which savings are converted into capital investments is properly managed and sufficiently regulated." Since there had been heavy losses in 1929 the matter was urgent. It would appear that there could be only two possible answers to the question "Why had the capital market failed?" The first answer was that "[t]here is a Money Trust directed by J. P. Morgan and Co." The second answer was "that the business is in fact highly competitive and dangerously chaotic. In developing public policy, and in fixing personal responsibility, it is of first importance to know which of these two diagnoses is the true one" (HT 5/26/33). In either case it appeared that Wall Street was far from being really competitive, and without voluntary internal reforms the case for some kind of governmental intervention was strong. Even if it were determined that Wall Street, dominated by Morgan, was not an "organized monopoly," it was still something other than competitive. The psychological hold of Morgan, whether or not a tight monopolistic one, affected investment decisions across the country: "The main investment market is decisively influenced by the state of mind in Wall Street. This influence is particularly strong at a time like this, on the bearish side. When the captains of finance are discouraged or apprehensive, their sentiments infect investors, bankers and speculators in all the financial centers of the country" (HT 10/19/33). A better way of thinking about Wall Street than using the competitive market model might be to see it as a sovereign entity within the nation-state. "Therefore, we have had, since March 4 [1933, the inauguration of FDR], what might be described as a rupture of diplomatic intercourse between Washington and Wall Street" (HT 10/19/33). The kind of reform of the financial sector that made sense to Lippmann in 1933 was not simple outlawing of monopoly, but rather insistence on ethical behavior, transparency, and avoidance of all conflict of interest: "unless the moral principle itself is understood and generally upheld, particular rules will have little effect because they will easily be circumvented" (HT 12/8/33).

The emotional tone of much of the discussion of monopoly at both extremes of opinion also worried Lippmann. Monopolists and their critics were equally shrill and uncompromising, yet a consensus was required to form good policy. He applauded a report of the American Bankers' Association as striking just the right tone, nicely in the middle, when reacting to criticisms of the banking sector. In agreeing to the need for greater competition among banks, the report was "clearly effective," and through "an appeal to reason" and a willingness to accept constructive criticism it gained the public confidence. By contrast, statements from the utilities were filled with vitriol and empty of reason. "They would find, I believe, that if they suspended their somewhat hysterical outcry that they are about to be murdered and presented a reasoned brief stating just exactly what it is they think should be changed in the Rayburn bill, they would protect their legitimate interests more successfully than they are now doing. They would raise up allies among disinterested men in the Administration, in Congress, and among the people who are today immobilized because they will not help those who terrorize public opinion and cannot help those who are too excited to state clearly what they want. It is true that the method of reasoned appeal will not commend itself to those who believe that to protect the legitimate interests of public utilities is to serve Mammon. Nor will it commend itself to those feudists who do not feel that they have started the day right until they have brushed their teeth and sung their hymn of hate against the Roosevelts of Hyde Park" (HT 3/30/35). Lippmann's general comments about the character of the debates over monopoly were in the best tradition of his mentor Santayana: "To appeal to reason is still an effective method of arguing a case in this democracy. In fact, there is ground for thinking that the brazen voices and the screamer headlines and the intoxicated adjectives are loud but indistinct and that they who speak quietly and with composure and with consideration are best heard by those to whom their words are addressed" (HT 3/30/35).

Unfortunately, through their advocacy of the NRA and the AAA, the New Deal leaders had lost much credibility as trust busters, even though there were certain cases where they could hardly lose. Aluminum was one, where Alcoa and Andrew Mellon had done everything to create and sustain a monopoly in the sale of aluminum in the present and for the future. Surely the Justice Department could dust off the Sherman Act and win the aluminum case easily. Despite the nearly universal rhetoric in favor of competition, apparently just about nobody was willing to step up in its defense

when they themselves were directly affected. "The restoration of competition is the only possible alternative to socialism, and it would be useless, as
well as hypocritical, for any one to object to the collectivism of the New
Deal and yet to cry out that an unmistakable economic monopoly should be
tolerated by the law. If one company is to be allowed to be the sole producer
of pig aluminum in America, and by virtue of this monopoly, plus tariff protection plus understandings with foreign producers, is to be able to fix the
price in the American market, then the competitive system is dead in the
aluminum industry, and some kind of government management of the industry is ultimately inevitable" (HT 4/27/37).

Lippmann's greatest disappointment with the private sector was with
its efforts to impede international free trade and to use protective tariffs
as a device for sustaining its monopolies. As with so many policy issues
that he addressed, he saw serious political and social costs well beyond the
economic ones. The fragmentation of the world economy caused by tariffs
was of course a source of inefficiency, a cause of the depression, and an obstacle to recovery, but it was also a barrier to the progress of civilization in
the societies that were isolated when cut off from trade. "In the hundred
years between the battle of Waterloo and the battle of the Marne, the spiri-
tual leaders of the west came to think it self-evident that there would be a
steady progress toward a universal civilization. And it is by this criterion
that the generation which knew the pre-war world judge the condition of
the present world; because their hopes were pitched so high, their discour-
agement has sunk so deep. Yet, as events seem to declare, we must for our
generation give up the hope of a steady and predestined advance toward a
universal civilization. We can at least remember that it is our hope, perhaps our illusion, that we must revise" (HT 12/25/37). When war appeared
on the horizon in 1939, Lippmann even blamed the impending conflict in
part on economic and political fragmentation caused by tariffs to support
monopolies.

By rights it should be presumed that leaders of the Republican Party, as
representatives of the business community for the most part, would rise to
defend the free market. But they did not, and especially when it came to
protecting the narrow interests of their constituents. Senator Henry Cabot

Lodge of Massachusetts was, Lippmann thought, one of the worst offenders. Lodge was glad to advocate all kinds of restrictions, including fair labor standards legislation, to protect northern manufacturers from southern competition. "Senator Lodge inherits and firmly believes in the tariff philosophy of his party. And he saw much more clearly than the liberals who supported the bill, that in effect it means the establishment of an internal protective tariff system within the United States" (HT 8/3/37 and also 5/21/38). Once the basic principle of market freedom was contravened there were no limits beyond which the monopolist-protectionist would not go: "before they have finished, Senator Lodge will be in favor of building a Chinese wall around the Back Bay to protect it against the competition of South Boston" (HT 8/7/37). It was ironic that those who pushed most aggressively for tariff protection that would surely cripple the free market system were also spokesmen for global competition. Sadly, there were only a few courageous political leaders, such as Paul Van Zeeland, former prime minister of Belgium (HT 1/29/38), and Secretary of State Cordell Hull (HT 11/19/38 and 3/14/39), who spoke up loudly for freedom. "Whereas Mr. Hull's principles, if consistently applied, make for freedom, productivity and peace, the collectivist principles of the farm and labor bills make for despotic interference, for arbitrary government, for general impoverishment, and for parochial bitterness" (HT 11/20/37). Although somewhat unpredictable in his approach to economic policy generally, Senator Borah on occasion was one of the few in Congress willing to take on the monopolists. "Mr. Borah is doing an inestimable service to the country by reminding it that liberty is not the liberty of the monopolist, that non-interference by the government in business is not a license to business to regulate prices privately" (HT 6/2/36).

By the end of the 1930s Lippmann concluded that, faced with the apparent growth in popularity of business monopoly, planning, and authoritarian rule, the best hope for the survival of economic and political liberty lay with recovery of the "lost wisdom" of the eighteenth century, in which the enduring threat to freedom from the growth of bureaucracy and the crippling of free trade was clearly recognized. He sounded a lot like Friedrich Hayek and other classical liberals at the time he wrote. "The lost

wisdom of our forefathers was in their discovery, during the experience of
the eighteenth century, that the way to make men free is to replace the
decrees and commands of a ruling class by a system of equal laws. . . .
They discovered also that the way to unite free men in larger and larger
political unions is not to construct new, gigantic and overpowering centralized governments but the very opposite of this: to remove the barriers,
to repeal the privileges, to disestablish the monopolies, which interfere with
the free exchange of goods and services, and thus separate men into warring,
jealous groups each with its vested interest. These were the two cardinal
principles by which our forefathers were guided: that the individual becomes free by the development of law, and that men become united by freedom of trade" (HT 11/25/39).

Labor

At the *New Republic* in the early days of World War I, Lippmann expressed
support for labor unions, even if they were in the business of controlling the
sale of labor as monopolists. In 1915 he submitted to Theodore Roosevelt
Jr., for the use of his father, a long memorandum defending "faith in the labor movement," by which he meant that organized labor could be an instrument for educating the working class and leading them to "industrial democracy." "As I see it, it is a belief that workingmen will learn industrial
citizenship from the exercise of industrial power; that the only way the
habit and intelligence for industrial democracy can be developed is by the
increasing exercise of industrial responsibility. If that faith is pretty strong
in us we have got to be prepared to understand failure, disappointment,
corruption, and all the other bad qualities which labor shows in such a startling parallel to the political citizen" (WL to Roosevelt, February 18, 1915,
WLPI F1065). When pressed to explain what he meant by "industrial
democracy," he replied: "I am really stumped to give you a definition of industrial democracy. It is so much easier to say what some of the elements of
it should be. I should say that industrial democracy exists when every adult
has enough education not only to do a job but to know why he is doing the
job, and what the circumstances are which make the job necessary; where

every adult is sufficiently insured for the primary needs of life so that he is capable of making some kind of free contract with other men. On a basis like this it would not be difficult to erect machinery for the different kinds of control which may be devised. Sufficient education and a sufficient stake in the community are necessary to what in the modern sense we call a free man" (WL to Robert C. Valentine, March 17, 1917, WLPI F1227).

Lippmann thought the time was near when some brave new experiments should be undertaken with industrial democracy, involving all of the stakeholders:

> The time is coming when certain industries ought to make an experiment in representative government. Some far-sighted railroad man, for example, ought to try a radical reorganization of the method by which a board of directors is chosen. It seems to me that the proper representation now would be one director from the stockholders, one director from the bankers, one director from the shippers (elected perhaps by the chambers of commerce in the section which the railroad serves), one representative of the working force, and one representative of the executive, who would be the President. Such an experiment if honestly carried out would give us a chance to test our theories and would be a practical demonstration of what we mean by our faith in labor. (WL to Roosevelt, February 18, 1915, WLPI F1065)

He wished the state, at a minimum, to create a satisfactory environment in which collective bargaining would take place peacefully: "The first item there, it seems to me, is the organization of the labor market by a system of nationally federated labor exchanges. The second, is the development of sickness, accident, and unemployment insurance. The third, is the development in parasitical industries of minimum wage boards. The fourth, is drastic legislation against child labor, overwork, bad sanitary conditions, and so on" (WL to Roosevelt, February 18, 1915, WLPI F1065). By 1915 Lippmann had gained such a reputation as an expert in this subject that he was invited by the United States Commission on Industrial Relations to ghostwrite their "findings and recommendations" (Basil W. Manly to WL, June 10, 1915, WLPI F785). He declined.

During World War I Lippmann had some responsibility in the War Department for aspects of labor relations in the defense sector, and he emerged from that experience somewhat less starry-eyed about the prospects for unions. Indeed, he recoiled at the prospect of decades ahead of industrial strife unless some sort of remedial action were taken. He sympathized with organized labor, whose relative strength and impact were often less than was understood by the public: "labor's power cannot be asserted without disturbing the routine of life, whereas the obstinate employer's power always seems to be asserted in favor of the tranquility of the state" (WL 1920a, 226). At the same time it had to be faced that "machine industry is so organized that determined minorities can paralyze it and that injunctions, legal or moral, cannot revive it. Indeed the more self-conscious men become about their place in the industrial system, the smaller becomes the minority which can paralyze that system" (WL 1920a, 224–225). Moreover, the problem was getting steadily worse. "In what is usually called the democratization of industry, the power of the strategic minority is likely to increase rather than to diminish, unless new and better methods of social control are devised" (WL 1920a, 225). The only solution Lippmann could envisage at this date was an experiment with a radical new "legal process" that might restore labor peace. He proposed seven governing "principles" for this process, which included limits on job termination, wage determination in "conference" on the advice of "expert investigators," profit sharing with workers, representation of employees in management, excess profit taxation, and grievance procedures.

It was a puzzle to Lippmann that so many leaders of the business community who shared a broad perspective on the economy still supported free markets in word but not in deed. He was less surprised that leaders of organized labor adopted this posture, as their jobs depended upon their behaving as monopolists. Few of them had a vision that went beyond the narrow interests of their union members. He agreed with Alfred P. Sloan that at General Motors labor leaders were probably more enthusiastic about aggressive collective bargaining than were the rank and file (Sloan to WL, June 22, 1934, and WL to Sloan, June 26, 1934, WLPIII F1956). Early in the 1930s, using data from his friend the labor economist Leo Wolman, he concluded that unions as they then existed might be an anachronism and were in fact in decline; he thought he could see real strength among them only in five industries (HT 8/3/33). This evolution might solve the problem of labor strife. But then to his dismay he watched government encouraging the growth of unions, and grow they did. "It can be shown, I believe, that this effort, while well meant, has been misconceived and misdirected" (HT 3/23/34). The result of this government engagement with unions was certain to mean that one more segment of the market economy would ultimately fall under public control. "If the government makes it its business to create unions, to foster them and guide them, it will become responsible for what they do. Let there be a series of great strikes in the vital services and how is the government to resist the clamor that it must control what it created" (HT 3/21/34). By 1934, after reading a volume entitled *Business Annals* by Willard Thorp, published by the National Bureau of Economic Research, he warned the nation to expect increased labor disputes "in the last phase of depression and in the first phase of revival" (HT 5/29/34). To cope with this prospect he called again for a "constitutional system" to bring capital and labor together under a system of law, and he suggested that to bring this about the political scientist and military strategist might have more to offer than the economist. He worried that when concentrated industry faced organized labor in a market economy the result could be destructive chaos and violence leading thereafter to a loss of freedoms. He thought that the model for the peaceful and orderly solution of labor disputes could be diplomacy in international affairs between two contending nations, where the conditions in which negotiations were conducted were as important as the substance of the difference. In essence he claimed, rather surprisingly in light of his concern about the growth of government, that peaceful and productive industrial relations could take place only in conditions thought of now as the welfare state: "There is the profound realization of wage-earners that they are the most exposed, the most vulnerable, the most insecure group in the nation. Who can deny it? Who can fail to recognize that for their sakes, as a matter of social justice and social decency, for the sake of the nation as a whole, the modern state must assume the obligation to overcome this insecurity? For that reason this is the proper time to take [make?] a national commitment to establish protection against the hazards of unemployment, of sickness, old age, of technological displacement, of sweating and exploitation" (HT 5/30/34). Presumably the price that workers would be asked to pay for such security would be labor peace.

A general strike in San Francisco in 1934 was a severe test for Lippmann's faith in the prospects for quiet diplomacy on the labor front. He quickly lost patience with the unions, and he called for the strike to be stopped by the government: "the general strike is not industrial but political. For by calling a general strike they [the unions] force the government, which protects their right to strike against political employers and is neutral in their particular disputes, to abandon its neutrality and break the strike" (HT 7/17/34). Still, he did not want to poison the waters in which a new constitution for industrial relations had yet to be negotiated. "A general strike ought not to be allowed to succeed: but its failure, once demonstrated, should not be made the ground for reprisals" (HT 7/17/34). As the strike dragged on, however, his patience with the unions grew even thinner, and he began to see a work stoppage as something like an ultimatum from a group of holdup men. "At no time in modern history has it been more important to assert the authority of government against organized private force. Democracy is gravely threatened in many parts of the world. Its defense requires a profound and scrupulous and unhesitating support of its basic principles" (HT 7/20/34).

The main problems that were emerging in collective bargaining, Lippmann concluded in 1935, grew, like so many other economic problems of the time, out of thoughtless meddling in markets by officials of the NRA, in this case under the infamous Section 7-A of the National Industrial Recovery Act, which stated that in covered industries "employees shall have the right to organize and bargain collectively through representatives of their own choosing" (HT 3/21/35). But what exactly did this mean? "It really says that we are to have compulsory voluntary agreement, which makes no more sense than to say that a man and a woman shall be compelled to fall in love with each other for the purpose of marrying. The authors of Section 7-A made it inherently unenforceable by lumping together and muddling up two distinct things: the right to organize on the one hand and collective

bargaining on the other" (HT 3/21/35). When this provision was incorpo-
rated later in a wage bill with the added requirement that employers must
"bargain in good faith," Lippmann pointed out again that the conditions
were contradictory and could not be resolved except through compulsory
arbitration. "How does one compel men to bargain in good faith? This act
does not merely protect an old right—the right to organize. It creates a new
duty—the duty to bargain in good faith. There is no more hope of enforcing
a duty to bargain in good faith than of enforcing a duty to think the authors
of this bill are a herd of pink elephants" (HT 5/21/35).

As one industry after another went on strike in the 1930s, dashing
Lippmann's hope of a peaceful constitutional solution to labor conflict, he
bemoaned the absence of any kind of effective market process that would
enforce restraint and yield a solution based on reason rather than naked
power. In 1936 he saw labor problems in the steel industry as a test case of
current industrial relations and what might happen in the future. Three
outside entities were all vying to gain control of the wages and working conditions of the steelworkers and in effect create a huge monopoly in the sale
of a certain kind of labor: the craft-based American Federation of Labor
(AFL), the industrial Congress of Industrial Organizations (CIO), and the
manufacturers' own company union, the American Iron and Steel Institute.
"In this conflict between vertical unions, horizontal unions, and company
unions, all three contenders are outsiders in the sense that they seek to formulate the labor policy of the whole industry rather than to let it be worked
out in each plant. All three seek to supersede the actual workers and actual
managers in the mills where steel is manufactured by subjecting them to a
national policy directed from Washington or New York. They are all for a
united front differing only as to who shall be the master. It is against this
sort of thing that American opinion is in rebellion when it applauds those
who denounce monopoly" (HT 7/4/36). Labor costs were too large a part of
steel prices, and steel prices too crucial to the national economy, for government to allow any of these three outsiders to gain control. The inevitable
result of inaction would be that another sector of the economy would fall
under governmental jurisdiction and act like a monopoly, not through the
efforts of energetic planners in the public sector but because of short-sighted

actions by leaders in the private sector. "The labor leaders and the gentlemen of the [American Iron and Steel] Institute between them are following
a line of action which leads directly to a collectivist economy. No private
power can for long hope to be allowed to regulate nationally an industry
like steel" (HT 7/4/36). An alternative effort must be made "to move effectively and decisively to restore a free market in the industry, independence
and self-government in the plants, decentralization of control" (HT 7/4/36).

Although most of the labor monopolies were in the private sector,
Lippmann believed that they would have little power to enforce their demands if they were not protected by government. "Without very special assistance from the government, the organization of the unorganized is not
likely to proceed fast or far" (HT 11/17/36). The New Dealers were clear in
their minds that they were justified in assisting labor organization by strengthening unions' monopoly position, but they should examine more carefully
the results of their actions. In particular, they should remember the old wages
fund doctrine that labor's share in the total product was more or less stable at
any one time and if some workers got more, others were likely to get less:
"The total income of labor cannot be fixed by any kind of collective bargaining. What can be fixed by collective bargaining is the relative income of some
groups of wage-earners. Unions can to a certain degree determine how total
wages shall be distributed among workers at different levels of employment.
But unions cannot determine what should be the total wages to be distributed" (HT 11/17/36). As Lippmann laid out the case, government had no reason to support trade unions that simply benefited their own members at the
expense of nonmembers, and indeed it had good reason to restrain them.

The image, and even the language, of collective bargaining, Lippmann
thought, were often a distortion of what was actually taking place. The process was less like peaceful negotiation than simple warfare. The outcome
was the result of the exertion of brute force and depended on which party
was stronger. He saw in the General Motors strike of 1937 little evidence of
consultation, negotiation, and compromise. Rather he saw demands, coer-
cion, and a struggle for conquest and sovereignty. "The General Motors
strike must have brought it home to many how primitive is our whole system of industrial relations" (HT 1/12/37). He thought that something like a

system of compulsory arbitration with a tribunal composed of distinguished civic leaders might arrest the movement toward greater monopoly then under way in the labor market. "Those men would have a great opportunity. They could lay the foundations for law in the one region of society where primitive anarchy is still the rule" (HT 1/12/37). As the GM strike dragged on, with violence on both sides, Lippmann called for "industrial disarmament" leading to negotiations and a viable new system for setting wages outside the market (HT 2/20/37).

When strikes in steel and automobiles seemed finally to be coming to an end Lippmann suggested that the widespread feeling of frustration in the country with the current arrangements might lead to some final solution to what had become in effect economic warfare. "It was the recognition, which is increasingly general, that a complete, sincere and thoroughgoing choice has to be made, and made at once, between peace and war, between the psychology of the class struggle and the psychology of democratic persuasion and consent" (HT 3/6/37). Initially big business had believed that by remaining uncooperative they could destroy the unions once and for all. Now with that hope evaporating they seemed resigned to search for some way to settle issues of income distribution without conflict.

> As long as big business stood entrenched behind its Pinkertons and its dogmas, it was in fact imbued with the psychology of class war, however much it might deplore the idea when openly preached from a soapbox. The refusal to recognize the unions and to negotiate with them could not by any possibility be described as an attitude of peace; among nations the equivalent is a refusal to have diplomatic relations, an act just short of war which generally leads to war. This war-like state of mind had to be overcome and radically reversed if the country was not to be drawn into a destructive struggle between so-called economic royalists on the one side and Bolsheviks, or whatever the epithet is, on the other. The time had to come when stubborn suspicion and animosity gave way to matter-of-fact dealing between men. (HT 3/6/37)

Lippmann concluded optimistically that just as warfare among nations could be reduced by new institutions and agreements, so industrial relations could be systematized and placed under a rule of law, with strikes and boycotts replaced by arbitration as the civilized way to settle disputes: "We shall repeat the history of all other industrial communities and we shall see that the full legal recognition of labor unions has as its logical consequence the gradual outlawry of the strike in all its forms. Just as no one has any sympathy with the bootlegger, now that we have repeal, so public sentiment will turn against strikes when the unions are organized and recognized" (HT 4/6/37).

It seemed to Lippmann that at last all branches of government were determined to discover the means whereby labor disputes could be settled without substantial damage to the American economy. "For that reason, on any long view, the deepest interests of labor now lie in preserving the essential constitutional balance of the government, and above all in preserving an independent judiciary" (HT 4/15/37). There were certainly still leaders of business and of labor who would rather fight than settle differences peacefully. But happily "between them stand the employers who are willing to negotiate contracts, and the labor leaders who mean to enforce the contracts they sign. It is to these employers and these labor leaders that we must look for the solution of the problem, that is to say, for the development of an orderly procedure in making agreements which can be relied upon" (HT 6/12/37). He was always looking for helpful analogies to cast light on current problems, and here he compared American industry to a new nation attempting to establish constitutional government. "The condition of these industries in respect to labor relations is very much like that which prevails in a politically backward state where neither the voters nor the public officials understand constitutional government or have acquired the habits of mind and character needed to make such a government work" (HT 6/24/37).

Lippmann was anxious to develop a constitutional relationship between capital and labor, apart from government, to eliminate the need for yet more concentration of economic power in Washington. He was opposed to the imposition of any labor policy by Congress, the Department of Labor, or a separate labor relations board. He was glad for government entities to conduct research as background for labor negotiations, but the conduct of them should remain in private hands. He thought that the National Labor Relations Board (NLRB), set up under the National Labor Relations Act (Wagner Act), was a good example of a government agency co-opted (later called captured) by a special interest (the AFL and CIO). It had none of the functions, powers, or responsibilities that its name implied. Rather, it was an agency whose function was to press for a certain philosophy of labor-management relations that amounted to monopsony meeting monopoly. "While it is generally supposed that the board was set up in order to regulate the relations between employers and workers. In fact the board has no power to do anything about the promotion of industrial peace. That is still the function of the Department of Labor. The board has no power to conciliate, to mediate, or to arbitrate; it has no power to deal with working conditions, or with wages, with strikes, with lockouts, with the equity of labor contracts, with their interpretation and enforcement. It is sailing under false colors when it calls itself the National Labor Relations Board. For it is no such thing. It is a special agency designed to enforce the theory that the constitutional right of labor to organize in unions means that all labor in the industry must be represented by the union selected by a majority of the workers" (HT 5/5/38).

He thought that the NLRB might better be called "bureau of legal aid" for the labor movement with offices in the Justice Department (HT 3/4/39). The misnamed NLRB was not merely harmless, however. It reduced the freedom of choice of workers in the labor market, and it pointed toward some form of compulsory arbitration of prices and working conditions in a corporate state. "As a matter of fact, once the government passed from the protection of the right to organize to the compulsory promotion of particular forms of labor organization, it has started on a road which leads far afield. Compulsory unionism means compulsory employees' association, and once labor relations have become compulsory, there is no likelihood of stopping short of compulsory arbitration. Perhaps that is the way we are going. But it is the way taken by the corporative state, and if we are going that way, we should know it and go there with our eyes open" (HT 1/9/40). It is hard to tell how much of Lippmann's dislike of organized labor was based on the threat it posed to freedom of choice in a large segment of the market economy and how much it grew out of his distaste for some of the

early labor leaders, who he thought were a little like gangsters holding up the
nation for as much as they could extract. By 1941, with war looming and
mobilization impending, Lippmann was somewhat relieved after all by the
improved status that labor had obtained.

> As compared with its position in the first World War and in the 1920s,
> labor has made three great social gains. One, labor has achieved a status
> in American life. Whereas in the past employees had the legal right to
> organize and to bargain collectively, they have in recent years gained not
> only the active protection of this right but also the recognition as a matter
> of public policy that the exercise of this right is in the national interest.
> Where formerly unionism was tolerated now it is preferred; where for-
> merly the representatives of labor were acting as a pressure group on the
> outside, today they are on the inside, participating directly and continu-
> ally in the shaping of national policy. Second, labor has achieved a new
> security in that protection against destitution and helpless old age is a
> recognized public obligation. Third, labor, when employed, has gained
> considerably higher rates of pay per hour of work. (HT 1/11/41)

Government

Lippmann began his life as a columnist not deeply concerned about the
monopoly problem. He appreciated the economic benefits of the free market but, like many progressives, he saw monopoly as having complex consequences that went well beyond just scale economies to incentives, innovation, environmental impacts, and other effects. Moreover, monopolies, like
all other human institutions, were constantly evolving and could be judged
only at a point in time. Each monopoly should be evaluated on its own, and
if socially destructive behavior were discovered, there were a number of responses that could be considered, from outright public expropriation to
regulation, licensing, restraining orders, taxes, and subsidies. The reading
and research that Lippmann undertook in the 1930s, as well as his interactions with people throughout the economy, nevertheless made him increasingly suspicious of monopolies and anxious to discover if they received the
attention they deserved from society.

Lippmann began by thinking that in light of the Wall Street collapse and the apparent role of monopoly in the financial world Congress would be prepared to take a strong hand and confront the special interests. However, it soon seemed clear that the political process had been deeply corrupted and every scheme for reform would be resisted. "Against every tax proposed there is a lobby. Against every economy proposed there is a lobby. The arguments pro and con are interminable and inconclusive and not Solomon in all his wisdom could judge justly each complaint" (HT 4/22/32). Surely the nation should see that now was the time when the special interests must be rooted out. It would be painful, but it was essential. "The country can help Washington by making up its mind to swallow its bitter medicine cheerfully. For the more confusion there is as a result of resisting the medicine now offered the more trouble there will be and the stronger the medicine which will have to be swallowed later" (HT 4/22/32). The root of the problem was that members of Congress had come to perceive themselves as simply the representatives of special interests, and what the special interests wanted above all was monopoly. There was practically no one charged to see the nation's problems and needs writ large. "The American people has forgotten that if it is to have good government it must elect men not to perform errands for their constituents, but to use their judgment freely, and freely to speak and act upon that judgment" (HT 5/17/32).

Lippmann suggested that monopoly was like drunkenness. It was not likely to go away if it were simply forbidden. Prohibition under the Volstead Act had proven that, and so had the Sherman Act with monopoly: "to make laws that are too strict for human nature and too noble to be sustained by public opinion is simply to invite corruption and hypocrisy" (HT 4/5/34). Initially Lippmann was pleased with some early successes of the New Deal that were bold and imaginative, and he was optimistic about prospects for the longer term. He thought that Congress had wisely instructed Wall Street to clean itself up and suggest appropriate legislation rather than taking punitive action itself. This sword of Damocles had been more effective in prompting Wall Street to act than attempts at reform by congressmen or bureaucrats in the Justice Department would have been. He wrote in 1934, "Let the sword remain suspended over Damocles for another twelve months, and let the spirit of reform in the exchanges have a chance to show what it can do" (HT 4/5/34). The Securities Exchange Act of 1934 that created the Securities and Exchange Commission was the outcome.

A cooperative spirit was especially important in constructing effective reforms. This had been demonstrated in the Wall Street case and gave reason for optimism that a better mood could be sustained across the economy in the implementation of reform. Initially government and the Wall Street firms had been at daggers drawn, but steadily relations improved. He explained in June 1934: "In Washington men were moved by righteous indignation; in the financial communities men were terrorized and sullen. In the past three months this mood has given way to a realization in Washington that reforms must work and in Wall Street that reforms are necessary" (HT 6/8/34). It seemed to Lippmann that in the first New Deal the Roosevelt administration in some of its programs was pursuing a sensible and imaginative policy toward monopoly, for example with its efforts to break up large holding companies among the utilities. He rejected the arguments of the utilities that the holding companies were necessary to distribute risk. At the same time he was puzzled and disturbed by other government programs that actively encouraged monopoly, notably the NRA and AAA. By 1935 he was increasingly alarmed by this apparent inconsistency in philosophy: "The thing everyone is discussing —the dissolution of certain kinds of giant holding companies—is an attempt to recover some of that individualism and economic freedom which we hear so much about. That is why those of us who have disliked mightily the monopolies fostered by N.R.A. and A.A.A. and have looked upon them as leading to the kind of directed and dictated economy which is unsuitable to American conditions must, if we are to be at all consistent, welcome this evidence that Congress and the Administration now believe, as the President put it, that the 'destruction of private socialism is utterly essential to avoid government socialism'" (HT 3/14/35).

In addition Lippmann worried about the governmental practice of denouncing monopoly in a rather mindless fashion, even while promoting it in various places. Monopolies were a complex phenomenon; some were good while most were bad, but each case required thoughtful scrutiny. The utilities were again a case in point. He conceded: "The industry is a natural monopoly, and there can be no question of the right and of the duty of the government to regulate it and to stamp out its abuses. There is no doubt also that the President and Congress have a mandate from the people to see that the industry is regulated in the public interest and its abuses prevented." But to accuse all the utility firms of being equally guilty of abuses, as the president had done, was mistaken and unfair and certain to bring about a powerful negative response from the most responsible firms. "In place of an opposition without much moral credit, the President created an opposition in which the sincere grievances of the better men became the protecting shield for the inferior men" (HT 12/21/35).

Conscious as he was of the problems as well as the potential benefits of public ownership of public utilities, Lippmann set out for his readers with clarity and simplicity the issues that they should take into account when making up their minds about the matter. The main issue, of course, was what price would be charged consumers under different regimes. Referring, perhaps, to the recent political movie *Gabriel over the White House* (1933), which he had reviewed, he suggested that even the angel Gabriel living in Hollywood needed protection from a predatory monopoly. "It could charge whatever it thought Gabriel Angel could be made to pay. It could even turn off his electricity if it wanted to. And so, because he has no protection from competition in the open market, because the company is a monopolist unrestrained by competition, Gabriel's end of the bargain has to be protected by law. That is the reason why utilities, as distinguished from automobile companies or grocery stores, are regulated by the law. The government intervenes because ordinary commercial competition does not exist" (HT 11/11/37). But what price for electric power would be fair to both Gabriel and the electric company? There were two ways to answer the question. One was to calculate a price that would yield a fair profit on the value of the utility company at its original cost. Another was to calculate the price for power from what it would cost to build the utility today. In the deflationary climate of the 1930s the first approach would benefit the company, the second the customer. Under inflation the reverse would be true. To answer the question Lippmann suggested that some sort of compromise be achieved.

The second difficult question related to publicly owned utilities was how to devise an effective scheme for management and control. For an exploration of this question in 1938 Lippmann used the case of the Tennessee Valley Authority, which he regarded as perhaps the most successful institution devised to concern itself with the conservation and responsible use of natural resources. The main objective of the TVA was to encourage economic development in a blighted section of the country with low electric power rates achieved through economies of scale. "It is a principle, incidentally, which stems not from Karl Marx but from Henry Ford. It cannot be too strongly emphasized that the T.V.A. is not even claiming to demonstrate that the government can provide cheaper power than the private companies. It is demonstrating, and in a local area using its authority to compel the demonstration, that more power can be sold more cheaply than less power, that large volume at a lower price is a sounder economic principle for a standardized product like electricity or a popular automobile than small volume at a high price" (HT 2/25/36). The question remained, all the same, of how to organize such a huge undertaking as TVA to work effectively. It could be seen as a test case if America wished to turn more and more to public monopolies as a corporate form.

An effort had been made to duplicate the structure of a private corporation with a three-person board of directors to control the management and to guard the public interest in the way the board in a private corporation attended to the interest of the shareholders. The problem with this prototype public corporation was that the board members had unceremoniously appointed themselves the managers and the external oversight disappeared. This situation was unsustainable. "It would be a thousand pities if T.V.A. failed and were discredited because it was badly organized and was mismanaged. For in any long view the T.V.A. is the prototype of a public agency that the nation must learn how to make successful if it is to conserve and to develop wisely the basic natural resources of the nation" (HT 3/8/38). He was sad to report that when the forces of competition were absent it seemed distressingly difficult to achieve a satisfactory economic result (HT 1/25/38). He continued to believe, in the tradition of Teddy Roosevelt, one of his early heroes, that government had a crucial role to play in protecting "the national patrimony" (HT 2/13/36). "For it is only on the foundation of great natural resources that a free economy can perpetuate itself. To conserve those resources is to defend the foundations of democratic capitalism; to let them be destroyed is to make a free economy impossible to maintain" (HT 2/25/36). Naturally, therefore, he was distressed to find that the TVA model of the large public monopoly was not an effective instrument to achieve this objective. Lippmann's assignment of such a large role for government in economic development as late as 1936 must have made some of his liberal friends cringe. His critique of the TVA was based not on principle but on what he took to be incompetence in the New Deal. "What makes T.V.A. a great experiment is that it is a practical test of whether it is possible to develop a new organ of government to which a democracy can safely entrust the management of large economic enterprises. This experiment will have been proved to be a failure if the President succeeds in demonstrating that T.V.A. is not a new organ of government but just another department of government under his personal control" (HT 3/24/38).

Lippmann concluded that not only was the federal government unable to constrain the destructive tendencies of entrepreneurs who were willing to damage the free market with monopolies simply for their own selfish interests, but through its own actions government too often strengthened these special interests with differential concessions embodied in "pork barrel" legislation (HT 1/31/35). In fact, he claimed that by 1936 so much pork had been distributed that any kind of coherent planning to conserve competition was no longer possible (HT 6/30/36). Especially in depression, competitive markets were under threat from frightened participants who, seemingly, would do anything to protect themselves. "When severe deflation is taking place, men always seek to save themselves by government protection and private monopoly. They are afraid of competition. They believe that there is over-production which must be stopped by force" (HT 6/30/36). There was not likely to be much hope for recreating a competitive environment until the recession had eased: "When the deflation is conquered, when prices rise and the burden of debt diminishes, the spirit of enterprise revives. Then it is opportunity, not mere security, that men desire. Then they are prepared to attack monopoly because it limits opportunity and to turn away from government protection because it suffocates initiative" (HT 6/30/36). Looking ahead, the American people must recognize that "the only alternative is to restore the effectiveness of free competition. That can be done only by withdrawing the legal privileges which foster monopoly and enable concentrated corporate control to dominate the markets in which prices and wages are determined" (HT 6/30/36).

Sadly, the leadership seemed lacking in both political parties to mobilize against interest group politics and special interest monopolies. The doctrinal position of President Roosevelt was hard to pin down: "it is almost certain that President Roosevelt has never been a convinced socialist. But it is also certain that he has never been a deeply convinced liberal. . . . For the liberal maintains that unless these vital decisions are made by the markets they will be made first in the offices of corporations and eventually in government bureaus. And the liberal argues that the power to fix prices is the ultimate power over the life and labor of a people, and that no system of liberty can survive under the private or public administration of prices" (HT 5/1/38). Yet salvation did not lie with the Republicans either. Alf Landon, the Republican candidate in the campaign of 1936, seemed as willing as FDR to bestow monopolies and sacrifice the free market for votes. If this philosophy prevailed for long, the vision of a truly free and efficient democracy would be dashed forever. "For if it becomes the accepted practice, American national politics will become degraded into a struggle of pressure groups, centering their demands upon Washington. Such a centralized scramble for favors always has corrupted, and would here corrupt, not only the government but the electorate itself. That is the most dangerous disease of a democracy" (HT 10/1/36). When Lippmann set forth a "birds-eye view" of Washington, the only politician he could discern with a truly liberal philosophy was Secretary of State Cordell Hull. "Whereas Mr. Hull's principles, if consistently applied, make for freedom, productivity and peace, the collectivist principles of the farm and labor bills make for despotic interference, for arbitrary government, for general impoverishment, and for parochial bitterness" (HT 11/20/37). By 1938 Lippmann had lost faith in his old comrades the progressives because of their willingness to sacrifice the free market for a nebulous path to prosperity through monopoly. "It is, I believe, an accurate description of post-war progressivism as made articulate in 'The Nation' and 'The New Republic,' in the speeches of men like Mr. Tugwell and even in certain of the President's speeches, to say that it accepts the Marxian idea that social progress is the outcome of class conflict. The practical consequence of this idea has been the alignment of the progressive intellectuals in support of almost any demand made by a pressure group among the farmers or workers. They have either approved, or at least tacitly sanctioned, the whole vast distribution of doles, subsidies, monopolies and special privileges provided only farmers or labor leaders were asking for them" (HT 4/30/38).

Lippmann had high hopes that perhaps the Temporary National Economic Committee, which began hearings in 1938, would cast light on the problem of monopoly, but his attention and theirs was soon distracted by the prospect of war. Lippmann appreciated the economic benefits of the free market, but like many progressives and especially the Brain Truster Adolph Berle, he saw monopoly having complex consequences, some good and some bad. Happily, he thought, there were many paths to reform or control of monopoly: regulation, public ownership, dissolution of the monopoly, licensing, taxes, and subsidies, even moral suasion. Monopolies should be regularly scrutinized and their negative behaviors penalized. However, the investigation, reading, and discussion he undertook in the 1930s made him increasingly gloomy about monopoly. Everyone, it seemed, wanted to be his own monopolist, and the standard devices used to restrain the phenomenon were distressingly ineffective. Rent-seeking seemed to be a universal human characteristic. Moreover, he came to see monopolies as a deeply corrosive political and social force whose ill effects were steadily growing. Many proclaimed the virtues of the free market like a catechism, but few were willing to make sacrifices in its defense.

What was to be done? Lippmann was especially distressed by the behavior of President Roosevelt and other leaders of the Democratic Party. They failed to articulate a grand vision for a free market economy and by their actions seemed intent on creating an economy based largely on monopolies: "the true New Deal vision does not look to a society of competing individuals; it looks to a collection of industrial, agrarian, and labor

monopolies co-ordinated, planned and managed by the Federal government" (HT 12/31/37). What prospect could be less appealing? As World
War II was breaking out in 1939, and Lippmann concluded that a strong
and centralized government was needed to implement mobilization, he
still did not forget the ever-present threat of monopoly to an economy in
either war or peace. After a decade of depression, proposals for market
concentration seemed as widely popular as ever, perhaps because of the
weakness of the defense presented of the free market: "when social conditions are bad, false ideas will flourish where true ideas are lacking" (HT
11/9/39). With this in mind he provided his readers with a final ringing defense of market freedom.

> For almost every one today is possessed by the idea that his security and
> his income can be improved by a privilege which restricts the free ex-
> change of goods and services and gives him some degree of monopoly.
> The domestic producers want tariffs. The producers for export want sub-
> sidies. The manufacturers and farmers want combinations which control
> the market and fix the price and exclude competition. Employers, em-
> ployees, merchants and others want state tariffs and all manner of devices
> for restricting the competition of outside goods and labor. The trade
> unions want wage rates which disemploy the less efficient workers. They
> want apprenticeship rules which obstruct the training of new workers.
>
> The philosophy of restrictionism is almost universal. It is the philoso-
> phy of every interest, of every pressure group, and of every politician who,
> as Professor W.H. Hutt has put it, allows "private interest to triumph over
> social interest" by following the policy of "Beggar my neighbor." The com-
> bined effect of all these restrictions—tariffs, subsidies, Cartels, combina-
> tions, price-fixing and wage-fixing—is to restrict and constrict and con-
> tract and to strangle the production and the exchange of wealth. And so
> in the midst of the plenty of nature and superb technical possibilities, we
> have the unemployed, the disemployed, the idle resources, the half-used
> plant, the idle capital, and a gathering anger that the economic system does
> not do what it ought to be able to do. (HT 11/9/39)

Lippmann was ready for a new approach.

8

"Regenerated Liberalism"

THE LAST HALF of the 1930s was an especially dark time for Lippmann. The Great Depression would not go away. Dictators were strengthening their positions in Europe. The economic and political ill effects of World War I had not been dealt with satisfactorily. The various conferences set up to achieve peace, disarmament, and a more satisfactory world economy had been unsuccessful. Even the League of Nations seemed to have failed. In the United States Roosevelt was elected to a second term despite his apparent disregard for free markets and civil liberties. The New Dealers in his administration kept coming up with schemes that would damage the competitive market system and threaten human freedom, undeterred by negative reactions from the Supreme Court and Congress. As Lippmann had long feared it was now clear that the progressivism of Teddy Roosevelt and Woodrow Wilson had been hijacked by irresponsible reformers in the New Deal. He wrote in 1937: "Some months ago I ventured to say that the cause of American progressivism was in the hands of inexperienced and short-sighted zealots who, unless they were soon checked, were destined to discredit progressivism and to provoke a violently reactionary temper; and that in the ensuing conflict the ruthlessness of the Right would be much more than a match for the ruthlessness of the Left" (HT 6/23/37).

The situation was bad in other countries as well as in the United States. Political leaders everywhere seemed inexplicably reluctant to accept and implement the macroeconomic policies of John Maynard Keynes that might
finally bring an end to unemployment. A new world war seemed increasingly probable. And Lippmann's marriage of two decades was failing.

In addressing the many economic problems that afflicted the nation in
the early 1930s, Lippmann's posture was initially optimistic. Intelligent analysts could understand the problems, he thought, and well-intentioned politicians would implement solutions. But then he turned pessimistic. What
frustrated Lippmann most was the behavior of economic actors at all levels
that impeded the recovery and reform. When economists finally came up
with persuasive monetary and macroeconomic theory and policy, politicians did not follow through. When the question of redistribution of income and wealth arose, potential recipients were so greedy that the process
degenerated quickly into a test of strength rather than a resort to reason.
Monopoly appeared first to Lippmann as a set of tractable problems but
ended up, like redistribution, as a series of struggles among selfish people
that usually required governmental intervention, as in the bitter contests
between large corporations and organized labor. Moderate, sensible, public-
spirited behavior seemed absent everywhere. Even in government the experts on public policy did not inspire confidence about their grasp of the
problems. "There are some of the President's critics who think that he is
dominated by advisers who are conspiring according to a systematic revolutionary plan. I do not myself think there is anything to this notion. So far as
I can make out the most radical of the theorists to whom he listens are rather
reckless experimenters and intellectual adventurers than men with a coherent and dogmatic purpose" (HT 1/11/38). There was an increasing danger
that, backed by "transient popular majorities" in Congress, these theorists
might seriously threaten the free society: "if we are to have democracy in fact
as well as in name, we must not monkey with the dangerous notion that transient popular majorities, however impressive, can give to any American
President a personal mandate to rule this country" (HT 11/13/37). It was no
surprise that by the middle of the decade Lippmann thought less in terms of
discrete economic policy problems and more in terms of the possible degen-

eration of the entire system of free markets and personal liberty upon which Western culture depended. As his focus broadened to systemic failure his tools of analysis expanded also to include political theory, social psychology, modern history, geography, and even creative literature.

Occident and Orient

Lippmann's new macro approach to the crisis of the economy appeared first in 1935 in one of his occasional reviews of the state of the world entitled "Watchman, What of the Night?" There he speculated in apocalyptic terms that some bad "thing" had happened to the Western world as a result of the importation of a body of thought "alien to western civilization. . . . It is the idea that the security and happiness and glory of the individual man are to be found in surrendering to the compulsion of mass feeling and the dominion of omnipotent states. This idea, as I read history, is native in the eastern world and has inspired the long series of oriental despotisms from the Egyptian Pharaohs to the present day. It took root in the later Roman Empire and destroyed the republics of the Graeco-Roman world. Again and again western society has had to repulse the advance of the idea and of armies carrying it with them. Once more in our time western men have had to face this challenge to their belief that the state is their servant and that the state is not the master of their lives, their labor, and their consciences" (HT 1/1/35). Lippmann saw a clear demarcation between the liberalism of the West, the Occident (meaning mainly Western Europe, North America, and Australasia) and the despotism of the East, the Orient (meaning most of the rest of the world). South America was seldom mentioned. It is possible "oriental" as a term of disparagement came easily to him because it was used often to describe the eastern European working-class Jews arriving in the United States, who were so distasteful to middle- and upper-class German Jews of New York City like himself (Steel 1980, 7). Russia and Germany on the eastern flank of the West, he asserted, were under constant pressure to give way to the "fanatical unreason" of the East. "It was in this borderland that bolshevism and fascism appeared. They are two sprouts from the same stem. Though they employ some of the same apparatus of western civilization, in their essence they are nothing but another manifestation of the ancient despotism of the east" (HT 1/1/35). The appeal of "omnivorous governments claiming jurisdiction over every interest of man" led to the rise of Hitler and Lenin. In this description of systems of ideas distributed geographically Lippmann may have been influenced by works such as *National Life and Character* (1893), the immensely popular book by the British historian Charles H. Pearson that, through its emphasis on distinct regional and national characteristics, is often given credit for the White Australia Policy and other racially discriminatory practices.

The year 1935 was one of thinking and reading for Lippmann. His new semi-racist argument that the problems in the American economy were the result of foreign ideas filtering in from corrupted thinkers abroad permitted him to shift the blame somewhat for problems in the domestic economy from his earlier emphasis on human greed and corruption to the intellectual equivalent of the Black Plague spreading across borders. But he did not turn away from local developments. He tended usually to be optimistic when given the opportunity, and he thought he detected in 1935 the possibility that Roosevelt had at last seen some light about the dangers of collectivism. Perhaps then the free society could be preserved at home after all. He was glad to find that in the budget message of 1935 there were plans for a "regenerated liberalism," inspired perhaps by success in other parts of the Occident. This new liberalism depended upon "a new form of social control: one which is neither laissez-faire nor collectivism, is neither rugged individualism nor a planned and directed economy but is a method which calls for the use of power of the government to preserve private enterprise by regulating its abuses and balancing its deficiencies. It is a policy which has been tried out in principle in a number of free nations, particularly in Great Britain, Australia and in the Scandinavian countries. But nowhere else has it ever been adopted so clearly and so boldly as in the program which the President is now disclosing. It is a reasonable conviction, I believe, that this is the policy of a regenerated liberalism, that this is the affirmative method which liberalism has evolved as the alternative to the old deal, to communism and to fascism" (HT 1/8/35). This new program guaranteed to citizens "the opportunity to work" but was not a "planned economy." "It is conservative. For it presents no threat to personal liberty, and preserves private property, private initiative, and private profit as the dominant characteristics of the social order. It is the only known positive alternative to fascism or communism which can hope to create personal security without regimentation" (HT 1/8/35).

For the moment, then, Lippmann was cautiously optimistic once again and thought he saw a turning away from the ideas of the Orient. "These ideas are alien to western civilization and have been rejected by the genius of all those from Socrates through St. Thomas Aquinas to the English and French and American thinkers who have made articulate the western way of life. At various moments, in troubled times, the struggle with these ideas has to be renewed and it is from another such struggle that western society is, I believe, now emerging." For reasons that were not clear Lippmann concluded that the struggle between East and West had, at last, been virtually won by the West. "I believe that during this year a decision has been reached and that the tide of these alien ideas has begun to recede" (HT 1/1/35). But it was not long before his optimism gave way once more, and he prophesied the apocalypse again. In an address to the Harvard chapter of Phi Beta Kappa that was printed in full in the *Herald Tribune* in lieu of a column, and that was widely noted by his readers, he expressed deep frustration that while the sensible path forward was well understood, leaders of the private sector still refused to cooperate and show the way; they called for free markets and competition in their public statements while they pressed for monopoly in their private affairs. By so doing they opened the way for those dreaded collectivist ideas from the East. As Lippmann's words on this occasion are not easily accessible today, and because they read so much like an updated old-style progressive manifesto, they are cited here at some length. The rich and powerful were at the root of America's dilemma, he insisted, and they must be confronted. About the "industrial and financial leaders of America," he wrote:

On the major issues of the modern world they believe in an ideal of masterly inactivity. That is the ideal. That is the ideal they would have the schools and colleges profess. To the young men asking how they can serve their country—how they can mitigate booms and depressions, maintain a healthy relation between agriculture and industry, conserve and develop the natural resources, prevent the congestion of population and the concentration of wealth and power, the orthodox answer must be that these matters are not the concern of the state and that the only sound policy is to have no policy. . . . Is it astonishing that a doctrine which is not practiced should lack vitality and authority? Sermons on the danger of interfering with economic laws are somehow unimpressive when they are preached by men who in their own markets have suspended those laws. It is intellectually confusing to live in an age when the dominant tradition is so deeply at variance with the dominant practice. . . . The basic question is not whether we should have state socialism, regimentation, inflation, or a flexible and competitive economy. It is whether we can have any coherent and working economy by having no conscious policy, allowing those who are strong to escape automatism in their own efforts and to subject others to its intensified consequences. (HT 6/22/35)

At the end of his talk Lippmann returned to the theme of his earlier columns: that the American economy was threatened by dark forces abroad and the youth of the country must not be told simply to let well enough alone but must prepare intellectually and physically for a bruising struggle ahead. "Let us rather tell them the truth, that our civilization is in peril and that they have a great duty, a duty comparable in its grandeur with that of any generation that ever entered the arena of events. For theirs is the duty in an age when darkness is again setting in elsewhere, and the barbarians are again at the gates, to make invincible on this continent a commonwealth that invites the soul of men" (HT 6/22/35). Discussion of the Occidental-Oriental conflict did not appear very often thereafter in Lippmann's writings, but it was never forgotten. In 1946, at the start of the Cold War, he warned his readers that the forthcoming "ideological contest" was not just between capitalists and communists, as many of them undoubtedly thought, but was between East and West: "the contest is not laid in the west; it is laid in the east, where men have not known liberty but tyranny, caste and exploitation, and where plenty except for the ruling classes, is entirely unknown" (HT 2/28/46).

From 1935 on Lippmann was especially sensitive to the problem of how to constrain bureaucrats and politicians who had a voracious appetite for interventions of all kinds in the market economy. For example, he advised Mayor La Guardia to be satisfied with a much shorter policy agenda for New York City than he had presented to the public. "What is the good of denouncing the despotism of Europe if here at home we cultivate the idea that anything may be done which at the moment seems good to those who are in office? Is it not evident that this is the very doctrine which destroys all the defenses against tyranny? For was there ever a tyrant who did not profess a profound interest in the future of the race or one who did not temporarily persuade a large group of persons that he knew how to insure the welfare of the race?" (HT 12/10/35). Lippmann told a meeting of seven hundred physicians that they, more than members of the other professions, recognized good government because they treated human beings not as machines but as they actually were, not as they might like them to be. The eccentricities and preconceptions of humans should be considered data, not frictions to be removed or ignored. He worried that the methods of the engineer, seemingly creeping into economics, were dangerous in constructing public policy.

> There are some who think that government should use all its powers of coercion to make the social order correspond with their own ideal of a nobler and more satisfying social order. But this is as if a doctor dealt with a patient on the assumption that he must use drastic medication if he finds that his patient is not as strong as Hercules, as beautiful as Apollo and as wise as Zeus. . . . Society is not and never will be a machine that can be designed, can be assembled, can be operated by those who happen to sit in the seats of authority. To know this, is to realize the ultimate limitations of government, and to abide by them, is to have that necessary humility which, though for the moment is at a discount in many parts of the globe, is nevertheless the beginning of wisdom. (HT 12/20/35)

A continuing problem with the performance of government in the economy, Lippmann maintained, was the large number of well-meaning and enterprising bureaucrats, such as Roosevelt's Brain Trust, who kept on generating ill-thought-out schemes supposedly to improve the economy and who used the excuse of the depression to put them in place. Since these schemes were the bureaucrats' babies, they fought for them tenaciously. In recent months, he was relieved to note, "[t]he critics have caused the Brains Trust, if this metaphor is not too mixed, to practice birth control" (HT 3/19/36). But this restraint could not be counted on forever, and he was depressed at how few leaders of the country joined him in defending "the liberal tradition." He deplored the "common vice of the New Era [Hoover] and the New Deal [Roosevelt]. They have both stood for protection, privilege and monopoly" (HT 6/4/36), and no one has stood up for freedom. He praised a manifesto issued in 1936 by two of his close friends, the former Wilson and Roosevelt cabinet members Newton Baker and Lewis Douglas, asking for "a course radically different from both political traditions, one which leads to the reduction of tariffs and other special privileges, the dissolution of private monopoly and the restoration of a competitive economy under a free decentralized and limited government" (HT 6/4/36).

Increasingly during the second half of the 1930s Lippmann turned again to economic geography to explain what was taking place, but this time not to the flow of economic ideas across frontiers. Now he was worried about the social consequences of the concentration of economic and political power in large cities. At this point in his thinking he found it impossible to separate economic issues from political ones, and his approach became very much what is called today "political economy." Concentration of economic activity, he claimed, led inexorably to monopoly and authoritarian rule. It was the natural ambition of bureaucrats to consolidate their power even though this threatened both the performance of the economy and freedom of individuals, and this could be achieved best in large cities. Most of the advocates of big government centered in Washington did not appreciate the panoply of forces they set in motion with such concentration:

> There is a fatal blindness in the men and women who call themselves liberal and progressive when they are eager to use centralized power in order to do good works more quickly. They are preparing a bad future for themselves and for the things they care about. They are failing to see that if you centralize in order to carry out progressive measures you will

precipitate a struggle for power on a continental scale. They are flying in the face not only of the deepest democratic and liberal traditions of this Republic but of the unmistakable lessons of European despotism and insecurity. These dazzled humanitarians, so intoxicated for the moment with the wine of power, will, if they are not set down and set back now, prove once again how hard it is for the wise to undo the mistakes of the merely good. (HT 10/22/36)

There seems also to have been some use by Lippmann of social psychology in attempting to understand this danger in large and concentrated numbers. People in crowds were dangerous, he had been advised, especially those in large crowds. "One of the world's greatest psychologists" had told him that there are "in all societies a group of persons who are not medical cases and are yet emotionally and intellectually maladjusted and unbalanced. He estimated that under normal conditions they might be about 10 per cent of the population, and that politics remained decent and rational as long as the other 90 per cent were unaffected. But wars, inflations and deflations increase the number of the unbalanced and maladjusted, and when their number rises to, say, 25 per cent of the population the ordinary processes of law and of reason tend to break down" (HT 9/26/36). This breakdown was most likely to occur in concentrated places. He wrote in 1936: "the movement toward collectivism, whether it be Communist, Fascist or extemporized, improvised and confused as in the New Deal, is leading the world to civil struggle, poverty and war" (HT 9/15/36). Lippmann has been accused of rejecting democracy. It was more that he thought the public themselves might cast off their own freedoms.

Given the weakness of the public and private leadership of the economy it was a good thing, Lippmann thought, that there were circuit breakers like the Supreme Court to restrain the "transitory majorities" of democracy. "We recognize, in short, the simple truth that we are human, not very wise, not very far seeing, likely to do foolish things, and that it takes time to find out what we really mean, and to correct our mistakes" (HT 11/26/36). The courts were an essential device to protect citizens from themselves. The first few years of the depression provided ample evidence that people

were willing in their own narrow self-interest to take actions that were destructive of the community overall, even though if acting together all would
be better off (the problem now called the prisoner's dilemma). "From the
top to the bottom of western civilization the struggle for existence became a
stampede in which nations, special interests, and individuals sought to
make themselves self-sufficient and secure by tariffs, embargoes, subsidies,
monopolies, restraint of trade, restriction of output, the destruction of exchange and the hoarding of wealth" (HT 1/19/37). Therefore it was desirable to slow down such actions as much as possible and to search for new
institutional arrangements that would prevent them entirely.

The court-packing proposal of FDR was especially foolish, Lippmann
thought, because it would reduce the breaking effect of the court on executive and legislative action and because it threatened the security of property
on which the whole free market system depended (HT 2/20/37). It must not
be forgotten, he wrote, that the judiciary was the cloak under which the
economy, the polity, and society were protected. "What we wish to do, it
seems to me, is to preserve intact against all sudden gusts of popular opinion the fundamental civil liberties and the democratic structure of the government. We do not wish to make it easy for any passing majority to impair
religious liberty, the freedom of the press, the right of assembly, and other
human rights, or to change the term of office or the manner of electing officials or to destroy the independence of the judiciary. On the other hand, we
do wish to make representative government more effective, more able to
regulate the economic life of the country, and to make the Constitution
more flexible in this sphere" (HT 3/9/37).

Moving from social psychology to individual human psychology,
Lippmann noted regretfully that almost all humans when given personal
power want more, and so a critical structural problem was how to restrain
this proclivity while retaining an effective economy and polity. "So close
are we to this development of personal government that as yet we barely see
the forest for the trees. But if we look at it as a whole we must be startled at
the extent to which the restraints of free government are being destroyed"
(HT 5/6/37). Perhaps the answer might lie in the public nourishment of a
stronger civil society. "In one way or another, perhaps by inventing some

sort of public endowment based on the inheritance tax, we shall have to invest large sums in enterprises that politicians do not control, though ordinary politicians will not support them unless they do control them. Just as we have in some measure succeeded in making the administration of justice independent of political control, so we shall have soon to deal with the problem of making publicly supported cultural activities independent of political control" (HT 5/25/37).

The Good Society (1937)

More than by any other book, Lippmann is remembered today among economic thinkers by *The Good Society*. Before the book, a draft was published in the *Atlantic Monthly*, and there was discussion of publishing 250,000 copies of an abridgment by the Sloan Foundation for "key people in the country," but nothing came of that (WL to Edward Weeks, January 8, 1938, WLPIII F119). The book is widely perceived now as one of the building blocks of "neoliberalism." It received effusive praise from such prominent liberal thinkers as Friedrich Hayek, Lionel Robbins, Henry Simons, Fritz Machlup, William Rappard, Louis Rougier, and Wilhelm Ropke. Even the notoriously dyspeptic Frank Knight, in a nine-page review in the *Journal of Political Economy*, called the book as "important in content as it is finished in form" (December 1938, 864–872). Of *The Good Society*, Rappard wrote: "It is from all points of view a most remarkable work, and one the publication of which will, I am sure be a real landmark in the history of our times" (Rappard to WL, September 11, 1937, WLPIII F1773). Lippmann paid effusive thanks to the Austrians for their inspiration. He wrote to Hayek in 1937: "In a crude way I had discerned the inherent difficulty of the planned economy but without the help I have received from you and from Professor von Mises, I could never have developed the argument" (WL to Hayek, March 12, 1937, WLPIII F1011). Hayek returned the compliment. "Although my mind has been moving more and more in the direction of regarding the inevitable restriction of intellectual freedom as the main design of collectivism, and although I have been planning an essay on the subject, you have brought out this cardinal and new point so much better than I could hope to do, that the credit belongs entirely to you" (Hayek to WL, April 6, 1937, WLPIII F1011). A gathering in Lippmann's honor was held in France to celebrate the publication of the book in French (the Colloque Lippmann), a meeting that led some years later to formation of the Mont Pelerin Society. One may wonder whether the book was all that influential with those luminaries gathered at the colloque or whether they were simply thrilled to find many of their ideas expressed in the work of a man with millions of readers. The book may be examined through a variety of lenses; what is offered here is a reading by an economist.

In the prologue, Lippmann called the book an examination of attempts to reconcile the two most important affirmations of the time. "The first, and the more fundamental of the two, is that the politics, law, and morality of the Western world are an evolution from the religious conviction that all men are persons and that the human person is inviolable. . . . The second affirmation is that the industrial revolution which still engages the whole of mankind and poses all the great social issues of the epoch in which we live, arises primarily from the increasing division of labor in ever-widening markets; the machine, the corporation, the concentration of economic control and mass production, are secondary phenomena" (WL 1937, x–xi). He began with the strong assertion that "the premises of authoritarian collectivism have become the working beliefs, the self-evident assumptions, the unquestioned axioms, not only of all the revolutionary regimes, but of nearly every effort which lays claim to being enlightened, humane, and progressive" (WL 1937, 4). In consequence, the life of a truly liberal scholar had become a lonely one. "Unless he is authoritarian and collectivist, he is a mossback, a reactionary, at best an amiable eccentric swimming hopelessly against the tide. It is a strong tide" (WL 1937, 4).

Advocates of a collectivized economy argued that market concentration was necessary because of machine technology: "the beneficent promise of modern science can be realized only through the political technology of the pre-scientific ages" (WL 1937, 9). This he denied vociferously. "We belong to a generation that has lost its way. Unable to develop the great truths which it inherited from the emancipators, it has returned to the heresies of absolutism, authority, and the domination of men by men. Against these ideas the progressive spirit of the western world is one long, increasing protest" (WL 1937, 21). The appeal of a planned economy had become so strong because the mixed economy of the time was understood so poorly. This was a failure of the modern social sciences. Both data and theory were lacking. "It is not merely that we do not have to-day enough factual knowledge of the social order, enough statistics, censuses, reports. The difficulty is deeper than that. We do not possess the indispensable logical equipment—the knowledge of the grammar and the syntax of society as a whole—to understand the data available or to know what other data to look for" (WL 1937, 33). It was necessary to confront the unproved claims of the collectivists that authoritarian control was necessary to limit chaos and to organize for the production of plenty. "For more than two generations an increasingly coercive organization of society has coincided with an increasing disorder. It is time to inquire why, with so much authority, there is so much less stability; why, with such promises of greater abundance, there is retardation in the improvement, in many lands a notable lowering, of the standard of life; why, when the organization is most nearly complete, the official idea of civilization is least catholic" (WL 1937, 39).

Perhaps thinking of Otto von Bismarck's rise to power in Germany, Lippmann dated the decline of widespread support for liberal ideas to about 1870, when "freedom ceased to be the polestar of the human mind. After 1870 or thereabouts men thought instinctively once more in terms of organization, authority, and collective power. To enhance their prospects businessmen looked to tariffs, to concentrated corporate control, to the suppression of competition, to large-scale business administration. To relieve the poor and lift up the downtrodden, reformers looked to an organized working class, to electoral majorities, to the capture of the sovereign power and its exploitation in their behalf" (WL 1937, 47). Now, it seemed clear, the experience with the collectivist vision had been unsatisfactory. "So it may well be today that the beginning of the end is at hand, that we are living at the climax of the collectivist movement, its promises already dust and ashes in men's mouths, its real consequences no longer matters of theoretical debate but of bitter and bloody experience" (WL 1937, 48). Prominent American collectivist intellectuals like Stuart Chase and George Soule reflected the sad state of collectivist doctrine. When their projects failed, all they could propose was more of the same. "The application of their principles creates such disorder that they are never without warrant for redoubling the dose. Without abandoning their central doctrine, how can they refuse to invoke the state as savior when there is obviously so much evil that should be remedied? They have no other principle they can invoke" (WL 1937, 53). The most extreme collectivists, the communists and the Fascists, had nothing to contribute to the search for solutions to current problems. "In short, communism, when it abolishes private property in productive capital, establishes a new kind of property in the public offices which manage the collective capital" (WL 1937, 83). Total war, when the norm of the economy became simple, was the only condition in which authoritarian planning had any appeal. In peacetime, when the economy was required to satisfy complex and ever-changing human needs, a collectivized economy could not do the job.

Early in the book Lippmann begins a chapter with the now-famous Keynes quote from *The General Theory* (1936), published in the previous year, that both "practical men" and "madmen in authority" were "usually the slaves of some defunct economist." But, in fact, Lippmann bases his argument about the continuing decline of collectivism not on the appearance of a more persuasive rival but upon the failure of this doctrine to meet its goals. The socialists lost the debate about planning in his eyes not because the Austrians had triumphed but because the socialist experiments had failed. Since no persuasive rival doctrine defending the free economy in a democracy had been constructed on the other side, economic policy formation now was at the mercy of the special interests. "Because a democracy cannot adopt a plan for collectivism, the practical initiative in each measure of its gradual advance comes not from the energy of a general ideal but from organized interests seeking protection and privileges. In practice gradual collectivism is not an ordered scheme of social reconstruction. It is the polity of pressure groups" (WL 1937, 111–112). The Hawley-Smoot tariff of 1930 and the Agricultural Adjustment Act of 1933, two products of creeping collectivism, were examples of policies that came into existence because liberals had no effective vision with which to combat them. Even innocent-seeming projects to correct market flaws became the tool of powerful lobbies. "The social-security laws providing for insurance against unemployment, for example, and the laws to promote collective bargaining give protection to well-established, strategically placed, and highly organized groups. They are quite unable to give the same degree of protection, let us say, to domestic servants, or to casual workers" (WL 1937, 116). Special interest distortions were now so common that they often counteracted each other. Tariffs protected manufacturers but raised input prices to farmers. So limits were placed on agricultural production, which raised farmers' incomes and also raised input costs to manufacturers. That was why in countries like the United States that were undergoing gradual collectivization, "particular interests will be found advocating protection for themselves and free trade for those with whom they transact their affairs" (WL 1937, 121). Ironically, Lippmann quoted his Harvard teacher Thomas Nixon Carver, so much maligned by him in his youth, to the effect that no economy could be improved by setting up a system of special privileges (WL 1937, 125). On the contrary, the overall effect of positive responses to special interests that characterized gradual collectivism was to make an economy poorer. "While it is not easy to discern the effect of every measure, the total effect of raising prices and wages by restricting markets and limiting the division of labor is to reduce the production of wealth" (WL 1937, 127).

Lippmann tried to understand the gradual self-destructive path of collectivism in the western world by examining economic history. He found this revealing. Adam Smith had demonstrated that division of labor in free markets increased total output. But he discovered also that unconstrained markets introduced substantial uncertainty into the outcome, and some gained while others lost: "there is a very large margin of error, which in human terms means personal misery, arising from the fact that choice of careers and the investment of personal savings are long commitments; whereas the short-term fluctuations of prices are often misleading, and yet sufficiently violent to wreck many lives before men can readapt themselves" (WL 1937, 171–172). Humans do not like uncertainty and often over the course of economic history it became too much to bear. "It is easy to understand, therefore, why almost all men have felt that they must escape the ruthless dictation of the open market. The collectivist movement in its many manifestations is, I believe, precisely that—a rebellion against the market economy. . . . Men begin by seeking protection from or mastery of the market. They end by rejecting the whole conception of an economy in which the division of labor is regulated in markets. Instead they adopt the conception of regulation by intelligent authority" (WL 1937, 172–173).

In part 3 of *The Good Society* Lippmann examines the history of economic ideas about liberalism. He thought that Adam Smith and the other eighteenth-century political economists understood markets well and the policy questions surrounding them in their time. But times changed, and classical economics went downhill quickly as an explanatory device and within a century was obsolete. In the nineteenth century the influential thinkers of the western world abandoned "the debris of liberalism to the vested interests, and then they attacked those vested interests with a body of learning constructed on socialist premises. This would appear to indicate that at some point in its development the liberal philosophy became scientifically untenable, and that, thereafter, it ceased to command the intellectual respect or to satisfy the moral conscience of the leaders of thought" (WL 1937, 184). It was in the nineteenth century that, tragically, liberalism became associated with a public policy of "laissez faire." "At this point, as so often happens among old and triumphant revolutionists, the dynamic ideas which had brought the liberals to power were transformed into an obscurantist and pedantic dogma" (WL 1937, 185).

The failure of liberalism in the second half of the nineteenth century was at two levels. The first was at the level of policy making. There "the progress of liberalism was, I am convinced, halted by the wholly false assumption that there was a realm of freedom in which the exchange economy operated and, apart from it, a realm of law where the state had jurisdiction. The consequences of the error were catastrophic. For in setting up this hypothetical and nonexistent realm of freedom where men worked, bought and sold goods, made contracts and owned property, the liberals became the uncritical defenders of the law which happened actually to prevail in that realm, and so the helpless apologists for all the abuses and miseries which accompanied it" (WL 1937, 191). As a result the liberals refused to join in the search for a better society through policy reform. "It became impossible for the latter-day liberals to ask the question, much less to find the answer, whether the existing law was good and how it could be reformed. That is why they lost the intellectual leadership of the progressive nations, and why the progressive movement turned its back on liberalism" (WL 1937, 192). So, for Lippmann, this is where liberals stood in the second half of the 1930s. "It is the unfinished mission of liberalism to discover the guiding principles by which this revolutionary readaptation of mankind can proceed" (WL 1937, 194).

Lippmann saved his sharpest critique for economists of the late nineteenth and twentieth centuries whom, following Keynes, he called "classical." His main complaint was the familiar one against what others have called "the Ricardian vice," that the classical economists worked from models of competition with many simplifying assumptions and then moved too easily from the models to policy conclusions for the imperfectly competitive world. "This seemed so delightful that the classical economists forgot that they had deduced from their hypothesis the conclusions which they had put into it. . . . The economists, alas, did not protest very loudly when they found themselves promoted to the status of oracles. For it was a pleasant role, full of dignity and honor, and, moreover, they were profoundly confused" (WL 1937, 199). One of the strongest recommendations of *The Good Society* was for a reformed and reconceived economic science upon which an effective defense of liberalism could be constructed.

> Instead of the classical economics being an apologetic explanation of the existing order, it is, when properly understood, a searching criticism of that order. It is a theoretical measure which reveals how far short of the promise, how unadjusted to the needs of the division of labor, is the actual society in which we live. Had the liberal economists realized this implication of their own hypothesis, they would have embarked at once upon the task of exploring the legal, psychological, and social circumstances which obstructed and perverted the actual society. They would not have left the criticism and the reform of society to those who did not understand, or were determined to abolish, the new mode of production. They would have seen that the mission of liberalism was to develop the

principles by which mankind could readapt its habits and institutions to
the industrial revolution. They would have carried on the tradition that
Adam Smith founded, and, like him, they would have been the critics of
the status quo and the intellectual leaders of its necessary reform. (WL
1937, 201–202)

Since his college days Lippmann had been torn by the tension between the
logic of classical economics on the one side and the appeal of socialist and
Institutionalist thought on the other. Now he concluded that this intellectual schism had become deeply tragic for the modern world.

For the liberals are the inheritors of the science which truly interprets the
progressive principle of the industrial revolution. But they have been unable to carry forward their science; they have not wrested from it a social
philosophy which is humanly satisfactory. The collectivists, on the other
hand, have the zest for progress, the sympathy for the poor, the burning
sense of wrong, the impulse for great deeds, which have been lacking in
latter-day liberalism. But their science is founded on a profound misunderstanding of the economy at the foundation of society, and their actions, therefore, are deeply destructive and reactionary. So men's hearts
are torn, their minds are divided, they are offered impossible choices.
They are asked to choose between the liberals who came to a dead stop—
but stopped on the right road up to wealth and freedom and justice—and
the collectivists who are in furious movement—but on a road that leads
down to the abyss of tyranny, impoverishment, and general war. (WL
1937, 204)

Lippmann gave a list of policy areas in which economists could make contributions if only they would approach them with a foundational commitment to the preservation of human liberty and free choice and with a concern always for those who could not cope with modernity: "the conservation
of land and of all natural resources," including the zoning of urban and agricultural land (WL 1937, 212 and 213); slum clearance; and adjustment assistance for those affected negatively by technical change. "There is nothing
whatever in the necessities of the new economy which compels society to be
indifferent to the human costs. There is no reason whatever why some part

of the wealth produced should not be taken by taxation and used to insure and indemnify human beings against their personal losses in the progress of industry. . . . For if it is properly devised, such a system of social insurance would facilitate the necessary technological changes, and reduce the very human resistance which comes from those who now see themselves the appointed victims of progress" (WL 1937, 223–224). Capital must be made more mobile so that it, rather than labor, could become the factor that moved most often when technical change required it and workers might remain in their "ancestral homes" (WL 1937, 223). The reinvestment of profits by firms should be discouraged so that the most profitable enterprises could find capital in open markets at competitive rates (WL 1937, 216). Profits distributed to stockholders would be supplied to the capital markets rather than reserved for the use of firms that had generated them. Every means must be explored to sustain competition in markets of all kinds: "The improvement of the markets must be a subject of continual study in a liberal society. It is a vast field of necessary reform" (WL 1937, 221). Some unearned income should be redistributed for public purposes. "It would be recognized that while an unearned income which is reinvested replenishes the capital goods of the whole society, unearned income spent on consumable goods is sheer privilege" (WL 1937, 227).

Macroeconomic policy requirements seemed clear to Lippmann. As he had explained in his Godkin Lectures three years before, government had the responsibility to seek full employment by making sure that investment was equal to saving over time. "The evil effects and the dangers of the business cycle need no elaboration. It is clear that social controls are required which will keep the real savings and the real investments of the community equal to each other" (WL 1937, 219). Among other things, this macroeconomic commitment required government to manage the money supply. "Monetary reform, and what is now called monetary management, are, therefore, necessary" (WL 1937, 220). In the event that, over the long run, private investors did not wish to make use of all loanable funds (Hansen's stagnation thesis), "the use of the taxing power is indicated in order to pump the surplus funds of the rich out of the ordinary capital market and into public investments. . . . Unless the excess savings are publicly invested they will be hoarded and wasted" (WL 1937, 229).

A point that Lippmann makes repeatedly throughout the discussion of his extensive agenda for policy reform is that he is calling not for creative and heroic action by people in government, as had been experienced under the New Deal, but for a revision of legislation, of the rules that govern the economy, so that improvements could take place spontaneously. There must be respect for the rule of law above all else, not arbitrary decision making by members of an executive, a legislature, or a bureaucracy. A primary function of the liberal state must be "to adjust the social order to the economy," not to leave open opportunities for the arbitrary exercise of power. Social control must be by the rules of the game: "In the debacle of liberalism during the delusion of laissez-faire, this method of social control was unappreciated and then forgotten. The reformers forgot it when they multiplied officials instead of revising the rules of the game; the conservatives forgot it when, in effect, they announced that the existing rules were immutable" (WL 1937, 266). If only the subject were examined further it could be shown that a large amount of social control could be implemented simply by changing property rights. He posits a man who has invented a mousetrap. In response the state may introduce a clever system of property rights to minimize the need for bureaucratic intervention in exploitation of the invention. "Though the state has not undertaken to direct the invention or to administer the manufacture of mouse traps, it is not letting me 'alone' without social control. The change is brought by a readjustment of the rights of my neighbors and of myself. Impressive social changes may have been effected—and the public health improved, a new industry brought into being, I prevented from becoming a millionaire, my neighbors relieved of a bitter grievance, good feeling promoted. But these things have been done without appointing new officials empowered to issue commands to anyone" (WL 1937, 272).

In 1947 Lippmann helped Henry Steele Commager, historian of liberal thought, sort out just where *The Good Society* stood in that history. Lippmann wrote:

You are quite right in saying that *The Good Society* was an attempt to resolve the dilemma of the choices between anarchy and despotism. You are right in saying that I went back to the 18th Century for foundations, because I do believe that that is when the foundations were correctly laid and most clearly understood. You are quite right also in pointing out that the main contribution of the book, as I saw it, was the attack on the perversion of classical economics which masquerades as liberalism. You are very right in pointing out that it was not the substance of the New Deal, but the method of the New Deal which I have objected to, and that my constructive purpose was to show a method by which the objects of liberalism and indeed of socialism could be obtained while preserving the essential principles of liberty. I like particularly the phrase "the reformation of the economic order through the reconstruction of the legal." (WL to Commager, May 31, 1947, WLPIII F486)

It is dangerous to speculate about the extent to which Lippmann anticipated important ideas ahead of his time. But perhaps this summary of his economic thinking in *The Good Society* may close with a few extracts that suggest that by this date he may even have been on the trail of the new subdiscipline of law and economics:

> The prospects of freedom depend very largely upon whether the intellectual leaders of the modern world can recover the intellectual habit of looking for a solution of social problems by the readjustment of private rights rather than by public administration. In the debacle of liberalism this habit was lost, and the art of free government has been almost forgotten. (WL 1937, 282)

> It follows that the temper of officialdom in a liberal society must be *predominantly* judicial; that holds not only for the judges themselves but for the legislators and executives as well, indeed for all who wish to serve the public interest. . . . In relying whenever feasible upon private actions, the law tends to get itself enforced when the offense causes real damage rather than when it is a merely theoretical departure from an abstract rule. (WL 1937, 284 and 292)

> A state commanded by finite men cannot afford to have a more grandiose purpose than to dispense justice. When it confines itself to that, the state will arouse no false expectations. (WL 1937, 296)

In 1948 Lippmann discussed with McGeorge Bundy, who had recently completed work on Henry Stimson's autobiography, the possibility of coauthorship of a "revision and modernization" of *The Good Society,* taking into account ideas contained in an unpublished manuscript he prepared soon after the original publication and entitled "The Image of Man." But they both concluded after working on the project for several months that it had been a tract for the times and was not suitable for revision (WLPIII F327). Lippmann was not sorry for the decision. He told Ralph Albertson in 1948 that "[t]he book was written in anticipation of the war but it is a book for the post-war period and I think that the substance of it has held up through the development of events" (WL to Albertson, July 6, 1948, WLPIII F25).

There always seemed a possibility in the 1930s that Lippmann might take a position at the University of Chicago, both because of his friendship with the president, Robert Maynard Hutchins, and with Vice President William Benton, and because of the congruence of his views about higher education with those of the university. He found much in common with prominent Chicago economist Henry Simons, to whom he wrote in March 1936: "I have read with great interest and profit your article on 'Rules versus Authorities in Monetary Policy.' I have been engaged for a long time in a study of liberal policy and had come to much the same conclusion as you do, namely that we must not go in the direction of management and authorities but in the direction of fixed rules, so I am very grateful for your article and for the illumination it gives. May I ask you to send me a copy of the Positive Program for Laissez-faire? I have mislaid my copy and I should like to have another one as soon as it is possible to get it here" (WL to Simons, March 19, 1936, WLPIII F1949). The possibility of an appointment at Chicago was pursued more vigorously after publication of *The Good Society.* Discussions began when he delivered a series of lectures there in 1935, and there were conversations around the question of how the university should respond to complaints by C. R. Walgreen, president of the drug store company, about the "communistic influence" to which his daughter had been "insidiously exposed" while she was a student at the university (Hutchins to WL, April 10, 1935, WLPIII F1113). After the dust had settled and explanations had been accepted Walgreen made a generous gift to the university, and these subsequent discussions concerned whether Lippmann might come to the university on a regular basis, deliver lectures, write, and advise on expenditures from the Walgreen fund.

The notion appealed to him for a while because he contemplated writing two more books: the first, a major examination of American government, the first since James Bryce's *The American Commonwealth* (1888), and the second book on liberalism for which *The Good Society* would be an introduction and prospectus. Hutchins suggested that Lippmann spend ten weeks each year in Chicago and try the arrangement for a year; Walgreen was enthusiastic (Hutchins to WL, March 17, 1938, WLPIII F1113). But Lippmann began to get cold feet and agreed finally to deliver only four lectures and perhaps spend ten days in Chicago advising on the Walgreen gift. He favored spending the money on fellowships for "advanced students and more or less proven scholars" (WL to Hutchins, April 19, 1938, WLPIII F1113), which should be rather simple and take little time. Discussions about a continuing connection seem not to have gone further; the lectures were delivered in March 1939 and became a small book entitled *Some Notes on War and Peace* (Macmillan, 1939). It appears from a letter of Henry Simons to William Benton (n.d.) that "several prominent persons" attempted to block "Mr. Lippmann's selection for the Walgreen Lectures and to prevent his selection for more permanent appointment under the Walgreen Fund" (George Stigler Papers, University of Chicago Library, Box 25). This unpleasantness may have played a part in Lippmann's final decision not to pursue the matter.

A Vision of Liberty

Those who found that in the second half of the 1930s Lippmann went through a conversion from progressivism to conservatism and, perhaps, even to libertarianism, did not read *The Good Society* carefully. Indeed, during this decade he became anything but conservative. He was seeking a new liberalism appropriate for the twentieth century. He came to believe that social thought over the past century, which he described as a mix of collectivism and laissez-faire, had in the end been a disaster and was at the root of current problems. The collectivists had seen too large a role for the state, the laissez-faireists none at all. The American progressives from whom he himself sprang, while manifesting an admirable if too enthusiastic reformist spirit, had neglected the liberal values that must lie at the foundation of a democracy. The partial and narrow attempts at social and economic reform that had characterized the preceding century had not responded effectively to the possibility of a loss of liberty. Neither the collectivists nor the "liberals" of the nineteenth century had constructed an appealing vision of a truly free society, and the last thing needed now was to conserve this old thinking. What was needed was creative and imaginative thinking of the kind that had led to the formation of the United States of America in the eighteenth century out of a set of disparate colonies.

The historian Harry Elmer Barnes, who claimed to have been "an almost reverent admirer of you and your writings when you were a leader of liberal thought," wrote to Lippmann in 1937 complaining of his "current apostasy" (Barnes to WL, January 5, 1937, WLPIII F165). Lippmann replied: "As for the matter of liberalism, my view of course is that the apostasy is on the part of those who once were liberals and have now become collectivists. But as a matter of fact, apostasy is something within the realm of faith, whereas all of us I think have been having rather a difficult time adjusting our ideas to the facts of the modern world. In the task of that adjustment there ought to be no more question of apostasy than there is in the realm of the natural sciences where men feel perfectly free to revise their theories without being terrorized by their friends charging them with apostasy" (WL to Barnes, January 8, 1937, WLPIII F165). Lippmann sought out as correspondents those few whom he thought reflected his own perspective on the future of liberalism. At the other extreme from Barnes he found Professor W. H. Hutt, the South African economist, who had prepared "the most penetrating discussion of my book that has appeared anywhere" (WL to Hutt, January 6 and October 28, 1938, WLPIII F1114).

In all the problem areas that he addressed, Lippmann found that current thinking was too narrow, repetitive, and unpersuasive. To move forward, thinkers must be engaged and educated once again in the methods of the Enlightenment. A new agenda for research in the humanities and social sciences was needed. He told those gathered at the Lippmann Colloquium in Paris in 1938 what perhaps some of them did not want to hear:

> We take a wrong turn whenever we attach ourselves to one of the numerous liberal sects, every time we confuse the cause of liberty with doctrines like those of natural law, popular sovereignty, the rights of man, parliamentary government, the right of self-determination, of laissez-faire, or of free trade. These are concepts that men have used at certain times and in certain historic circumstances. Often they have served to forge and win a partial emancipation. But they have not been the first cause or the motivating force, and the fate of freedom is not tied to any of the liberal theories. That is why we should reserve the right to review the premises of all the liberal theories and not grant to any of them a definitive and dogmatic value.
>
> For what we are attempting is not to revive a theory but to discover the ideas which will allow the impulse toward freedom and civilization to triumph over all the obstacles due to human nature, to historic circumstances, to the conditions of life on this earth. It is a long-term task which requires sustained efforts, extended cooperation, and the noble patience of those who sincerely and humbly seek the truth. Before it is finished, I believe humanity will have gone through a very profound and very vast religious experience; it will have to reevaluate science and its relationship with philosophy and ethics, it will have to review the idea of the State, of property, of individual rights, and the national ideal. Civilized men will have to reexamine the conceptions that seemed new before the war, determined to discover which ones are and which are not compatible with the vital necessities and the permanent ideals of humanity. It is to these vital necessities and these permanent ideals, not to the doctrines of the 19th century that we must refer in order to undertake the reconstruction of liberalism. Thus we seek not to teach an old doctrine but to contribute within our means, to the formation of a doctrine of which none of us has more than a vague notion at the present time. And we should think of liberalism not as an accomplishment of past time and now outmoded but as something still unfinished and still very young. ("Walter Lippmann Colloquium" 1938, 16)

The question remained, of course, of how to achieve this vision and these goals.

By the end of the 1930s some of President Roosevelt's severest critics were comparing him to Lenin and Stalin. Nonsense, said Lippmann. Lenin had a vision, even if it was flawed; Roosevelt had none at all. "Mr. Roosevelt is not in the least like Lenin; if there is one thing he does not possess, it is a dogmatic and coherent philosophy. He has consistent sympathies with the poor and perhaps more or less fixed antipathies against certain kinds of rich men, particularly against the more newly rich ones. Mr. Roosevelt does not, however, have a definite, a closely reasoned and deeply held, social philosophy. He has never acquired one and probably would not like it if he had. He did not begin to bother his head greatly about the fundamental difficulties of modern civilization until about 1930. Before that he was predominantly an ardently regular Democratic partisan with a strong hankering to be on the side of the angels" (HT 11/18/37).

Rather than a coherent vision of some sort, Roosevelt expressed simply confused economic thinking. "For the President seems to say that the way to bring about this vast increase of material things is to control farm surpluses and fix minimum wages. . . . Yet that must be a delusion for is it really possible that more wealth is produced by producing less wealth, or that higher prices for a smaller quantity of goods and services will result somehow in a greater quantity of goods and services? Surely the President is confusing now, as he has for five years, a different distribution of the national income with an increase of the total national income" (HT 1/4/38). There were several reasons why Lippmann regretted the absence of a coherent vision in FDR. One was that, without a vision, debate with him was so difficult; it was like debating a pillow. Another was that neglect of civil liberties, such as protection against arbitrary arrest and seizure, followed almost by accident from the president's incoherent ad hoc doctrines. This last failing made annoying institutions such as the American Civil Liberties Union especially valuable in a free society. The ACLU made the critical point that "[t]he most effective way for any one to do his part in protecting the liberties he cares about is to defend the liberties he does not care about" (HT 12/15/37).

Lippmann continued to believe that the tasks of government must necessarily be substantial, but they must be carefully weighed and thoughtfully formulated. Among his most confident findings were that human behavior was not easily predictable; humans were seldom well informed and did not often venture beyond narrow conceptions of self-interest when taking action. This suggested that humans should be constrained as much as possible by the system of laws from doing foolish things, and their opportunities for independent action should be limited when they could do damage to others. The best way to constrain destructive human action in the long run was to strengthen and preserve the judiciary as an essential and protective part of the policy making and implementing process. Another path to reform led through broad liberal education and research, making use of whatever insights might be revealed by the natural and physical sciences, the social sciences, humanities, the arts, and the professions. Areas of policy research that frustrated him through the decade of the 1930s, and which he believed now could be enlightened by a creative visionary approach, included Keynesian macroeconomics, the discovery of a regime through which peaceful industrial relations could be achieved, construction of new institutions to maintain free markets at home and abroad, the distribution of income and wealth according to the principles of justice, and the support of socially desirable but politically unpalatable activities such as environmental protection and encouragement of the arts. After the start of World War II he insisted that the study of war must go well beyond the activities of the military. Following publication of *The Good Society*, Lippmann's columns addressed the need for broad systemic reform more than the details of particular policy issues. He explored ways whereby he himself might help to stimulate the kind of thinking that he had come to believe was essential for the achievement of peace and prosperity.

He kept on searching for the true nature of a liberal society. Above all he rejected what he took to be the economist's notion that personal liberty was desirable mainly to sustain free markets. Human liberty was to Lippmann above all an end in itself and must not be seen a means to anything else; its protection was the purpose of the rule of law. He examined sacrifices made for such documents of freedom as the British Magna Carta and the American Bill of Rights, and he insisted that their appeal could not be understood as a means to utilitarian ends. "These struggles are at once too general and too passionate to be explained on the ground of calculated self-interest. Men respond to the cause of liberty who can never hope to enjoy its fruits. So it must be that the tree of liberty has its root in some deep and abiding need of man. The founders of our liberties knew this. They knew that the need to be free, once awakened in man, is as imperative a passion, and almost as universal a passion, as hunger and love" (HT 12/14/39).

Often he turned back to classical literature or to history to make his point. As a practical matter he became convinced that free markets were an essential element of freedom; but true freedom involved much more than markets. For example, people who lost their independence and means of support in the presence of competitive markets were never again truly free, and they deserved help. Despite his own lifelong residence in large cities he believed that the Jeffersonian ideal of small independent entrepreneurs, as free as possible from the trammels of government, was a good one for America. But in the modern world the requirements for such independence were different from Jefferson's time, when a worker threatened with dependence could simply move westward and try again. "To have economic independence a man must be in position to leave one job and go to another; he must have enough savings of some kind to exist for a considerable time without accepting the first job offered. . . . The more I see of Europe the more deeply convinced do I become that the preservation of freedom in America, or anywhere else, depends upon maintaining and restoring for the great majority of individuals the economic means to remain independent individuals. The greatest evil of the modern world is the reduction of the people to a proletarian level by destroying their savings, by depriving them of private property, by making them the helpless employees of a private monopoly or of government monopoly" (HT 7/16/38). Independent individuals who were not simply cogs in a great, suffocating machine were essential requirements of a successful democracy, and ways must be found to sustain them in the face of urban unemployment and rural depopulation. "Now it is, I believe, in this ever-widening separation from the elementary facts, the elementary truths, and the elementary necessities of human existence that the profound confusion of modern man originates. All over the world, but most particularly in the countries where civilization is supposed to be most advanced, there are collected in great cities huge masses of people who have lost their roots in the earth beneath them and their knowledge of the fixed stars in the heavens above them" (HT 11/3/38). As time went on Lippmann became increasingly impatient with the terminological questions about economic systems that fascinated some people, and especially about the true meaning of liberalism. In 1946 he advised the young Gabriel Pressman, a veteran who was in graduate school at Columbia, about how to proceed in thinking about the subject. "I wouldn't start by defining these terms; I would start by ignoring them and try to describe concretely how you and other veterans feel about the political scene" (WL to Pressman, November 21, 1946, WLPIII F483).

Demonstrating how far he was in fact from being a libertarian, Lippmann insisted that wide and even redistribution of property was required for human independence, and for sustaining a sense of patriotism. How to achieve this distribution while at the same time preserving security of property, another condition of freedom, was a major challenge for government.

> It is always true that the object of policy within a state must be to protect individuals and natural communities in the property on which and by which they earn their living, and thus to attach them to the state not by commands and doles and slogans but by their immediate and self-respecting interest. It is always true that the accumulation of property is an evil whether it be in the hands of a plutocracy or of a Socialist or Fascist state. For it is always true that the arrival of masses without property will in the end destroy a civilization.
>
> It is always true that a society of free men is a society of men with secure and sufficient property. It is always true that individuals cannot be free if their community is not independent. It is always true that independence has to be maintained by the willingness to fight and die for it. And finally it is true that men will not have the will to live or the courage to die if they have ceased to believe that they are in communion with things that transcend entirely their personal affairs. (HT 11/3/38)

Lippmann turned back to the classics of political and social thought to help understand the crisis in democracy that had its origins in the desperation of the poverty-stricken farmers and the urban unemployed. How could the country be kept together with such suffering? He turned to the writings of his old mentor George Santayana, who said that "a democratic order will work when all concerned are agreed on ultimate objectives, when no sizeable number of voters are revolutionary and irreconcilable, and when men are willing to change their minds and modify their actions as a result of debate with their opponents" (HT 11/8/38). America seemed far from that condition in 1938. Perhaps the problem lay deep within human character. On the puzzling problem of fundamental evil in society he turned to the church fathers (HT 1/7/39) and, as he had done in earlier writings, to Plato. "But if thoughtful men have differed about the psychological springs of malevolence, there has been no difference of opinion among the great teachers of the western world that there is in human nature a disposition to evil, that government is not government which cannot restrain it, and that religion is satanic that does not seek incessantly to overcome it. Long ago Plato fixed the image of man's moral problem as that of a charioteer who drives a pair of winged horses: 'one of them is noble and of noble breed, the other is ignoble and of ignoble breed.' And living as he did in an age of disaster and disorder, Plato added that 'the driving of them of necessity gives a great deal of trouble to the charioteer' " (HT 11/15/38). At this stage Lippmann was groping for the ideal form of government to confront successfully the tragic circumstances of the time. He was glad to report that his old comrades the progressives remained agreed on the virtues of capitalism, but they too were puzzled about its reform. "It is the widespread realization among American progressives that after all the indictments of capitalism have been drawn up, the capitalist system is indissolubly bound up with democracy and human freedom. The spectacle of Russia and of Germany has put American capitalism in a new perspective" (HT 12/13/38).

Beyond directing his columns toward a wider consideration of fundamental issues in the economy, as he did in the second half of the 1930s, what could Lippmann do to reach his objective of "regenerated liberalism," the only way he believed personal freedom and economic efficiency could be achieved together in modern society? He proposed three things: improvement of American education, a national debate over matters of great moment in public affairs, and a gathering of right-thinking persons to take the leadership in the perpetuation of liberal values. In none of these efforts was he obviously successful, suggesting that his strength was more as a journalist than as a public policy entrepreneur. But his efforts are worth remembering.

Throughout the 1930s Lippmann spent a substantial amount of his precious spare time encouraging reform of American education. In the secondary schools he bemoaned the loss of history from the curriculum. But he devoted most of his attention to the teaching of college undergraduates. He described as tragic mistakes the separation of the arts and humanities from the social sciences, and allowing the social and behavioral sciences to hive themselves off from the others into ever more narrow specialties. He regretted especially the isolation of economics from political science, history, psychology, and philosophy; the result had been that those trained in economics paid so little attention to values and to the determinants of human motivation that they were ill equipped to deal with the real world. He occasionally wrote to people in power about the poor work produced under their authority, and he seldom missed a chance to blame the social sciences. For example he wrote as follows to Donald Stone, assistant director of the Bureau of the Budget in 1943, about a memorandum from a staff member with which he disagreed: "The writer of the memorandum is, if I may say so, under the bad influence of American social science in the present generation, which has produced men entirely uneducated in the military-diplomatic realities" (WLPIII F2011).

He tried valiantly to reverse the tide of specialization at Harvard University with, by his own admission, little success. He supported the Hutchins great books experiment at the University of Chicago, and he was an enthusiastic advocate of the disciplinary integration at St. John's College in Maryland. He told Averill Harriman in 1941 that the St. John's experiment was "the most important thing happening in American education" (WL to Harriman, January 29, 1941, WLPIII F995). It was tragic, he believed, that leaders of America were less able to address fundamental problems than were the Founding Fathers. "For they have inherited great and noble institutions from their forefathers who made them. But because they have not inherited the knowledge which enabled their forefathers to make these institutions, they do not really know how to preserve them, repair them, and improve them" (HT 12/27/38). A "revival of learning" was needed so as to retrieve and make available to the young the great works of earlier ages. "We have emptied education of rigorous training in the arts of thought, and having done that, we are no longer able to read in any language the classical masterpieces of the human mind. Between ourselves and the sources from which our civilization comes we have dropped an iron curtain of false progress that leaves us to the darkness of our whims, our vagrant opinions and our unregulated passions" (HT 12/27/38).

Although he never developed the idea fully, Lippmann seems to have envisioned something like a great national colloquium to address and settle around a consensus the enormous questions about the economy and society that emerged in the 1930s. He became increasingly certain that the work of academics, bureaucrats, congressional committees, journalists, and think tanks, each acting alone, could not lead to persuasive answers to questions about economic planning, stabilization, industrial relations, entitlements, the world economy, income distribution, and preservation of the environment. He did not expect that grand debates of the kind he had in mind would lead to immediate agreement among the stakeholders. That would imply settlements based simply on strength. Rather he wanted solutions that were right and just and perhaps emergent from brilliant analysis and imaginative and creative thinking by participants in the debates. The model he seemed to have in mind for such engagement was the debates leading up to adoption of the American Constitution. He thought that the alternative visions for the role of government in the economy that had been put forward then by Thomas Jefferson and Alexander Hamilton were useful still, and he hoped that some new juxtapositions of this kind could be proposed. But what could be done to advance this debate by a journalist writing three columns a week? Unfortunately, he discovered, not very much.

Lippmann used the many opportunities presented to him in his relations with editors of books and magazines to encourage the publication of works that would enrich the public debate. In addition, he did explore one possible experiment in publication of this kind on his own. When in 1933 he was nearly deluged with commentary on alternative monetary and fiscal policies, he proposed clarifying the debate in six magazine articles that would review and appraise the relevant professional literature in economics and make it available to a lay audience. But he needed professional help. Using the same method that Lincoln Steffens had employed to discover him two decades before, he contacted friends for the names of the best advanced graduate students in economics who might like to make a little money as collaborator. His good friend Archibald MacLeish, then editor of *Fortune* magazine, wrote that he had found "the perfect man for you. He is a youngster in the Yale Graduate School named Richard Bissell who has just completed a year in the London School of Economics and who is considered by the Yale economic faculty the most promising young economist they have had in this generation" (MacLeish to WL, October 30, 1933, WLPIII F1421). Lippmann's subsequent dealings with Bissell reveal his apparent unfamiliarity, and impatience, with American graduate education. As might have been expected, Bissell, in the midst of a PhD program, was able to produce in a month no more than what amounted to a literature review in outline form of macroeconomic theory at that time (WLPIII F232). A month later he sent an extended review, which Lippmann found to be useless for his purposes. He wrote to Bissell: "You have tried to be thorough but the result is obviously something which cannot be made intelligible and interesting to a lay audience," and to Bissell's dismay he terminated the project (WL to Bissell, December 20, 1933, WLPIII F232). Bissell went on to a career at the Ford Foundation and the Central Intelligence Agency, where he became the deputy director responsible for, among other things, the Bay of Pigs invasion of Cuba and the U2 spy plane.

The most intriguing effort undertaken by Lippmann to help shape a great debate over fundamental economic issues was referred to by him and his collaborators variously as "the project" and "the Group." The earliest plan seems to have been for some sort of joint American-European collaboration. He wrote to Hayek in April 1937: "Your suggestion that it might be worthwhile to consider some sort of closer cooperation among liberals interests me very much indeed. I should be more than ready for it, though I do not know just how one would go about it. I suppose the best beginning would be to identify the genuine liberals and begin to correspond with them and get them in touch with each other" (WL to Hayek, April 8, 1937, WLPIII F1011). Hayek replied with a list of the "real liberals" in America "quite untainted by collectivist ideas." There were not many: B. M. Anderson, Henry Simons, H. F. Gideonse, F. Machlup, and Gottfried Haberler. He had considered including Leonard Ayres, Jacob Viner, Alvin Hansen, and C. O. Hardy but thought better of it. Hayek wondered if those on the list might collaborate in "some sort of international journal entirely devoted to the problems arising out of the rational reconstruction of a "good society" (Hayek to WL, June 11, 1937, WLPIII F1011). He kept Lippmann informed of his progress on *The Road to Serfdom* and sent a draft for Lippmann to read in June 1943 (Hayek to WL, June 13, 1943, WLPIII F1011). Hayek and Lippmann remained in continuing contact, and when the former's *Constitution of Liberty* was published in 1959 he wrote to Lippmann that the "trend of thought" reflected in this book "may be said to have started twenty-two years ago when I read *The Good Society*" (Hayek to WL, December 18, 1959, WLPIII F1011).

Considering how close they were on so many issues it is a puzzle why Lippmann declined to write the introduction to *The Road to Serfdom* when invited to do so. Fritz Machlup was the unsuccessful intermediary (Machlup to WL, February 7, 1944, and WL to Machlup, February 8, 1944, Hayek Papers, Hoover Institution). The answer may lie in Lippmann's colossal miscalculation of the salability of the work. He wrote to Raymond Everitt at Little, Brown in 1943 about the possibility of publishing *Road*: "I have a personal obligation to ask you whether you would consider it, but I must be honest with you and tell you that you would be doing a very disinterested thing if you publish it, because I am afraid it would have few readers" (WL to C. Raymond Everitt, July 27, 1943, WLPIII F1351). Everitt showed equally bad judgment in replying: "It is such a valuable point of view that it is a pity that it's presented in what one might call such a 'turgid' manner. I really doubt that we could publish it with success, meaning get real attention on it and the ideas" (Everitt to WL, August 9, 1943, WLPIII F1351).

For some reason the "project" and the Group soon became confined to Americans. There were informal meetings of Lippmann with several of his closest friends, people with whom he could feel fully comfortable. The first of these was Lewis Douglas, whom he had met when Douglas arrived in Washington at the end of the Hoover administration as the sole congressman from Arizona. Over the next years Douglas became Director of the Bureau of the Budget under FDR, a Wall Street businessman, principal of McGill University, and ambassador to Great Britain. Throughout, he kept up a steady correspondence with Lippmann. The second was Walter Stewart, an extraordinary figure who moved from a professorship at Amherst College to the Federal Reserve Board in Washington in 1922, where he set up the research department; then in 1926 to the investment securities firm of Case Pomeroy in New York, where he rose to be president; economic adviser to the Bank of England, 1928–1930; Institute of Advanced Study at Princeton, 1938–1955; wartime service at the Treasury Department in Washington; and ultimately membership in President Eisenhower's Council of Economic Advisers, 1953–1955 (Yohe 1982). The third was Leo Wolman, a friend of Lippmann's since the 1920s and perhaps the most prominent labor economist in the United States. Although Wolman was settled at Columbia University, Lippmann had tried to persuade him to come to Harvard (see Chapter 3). The fourth was Robert Warren, a close colleague of and aide to Stewart (discussed in Yohe 1990, 471 and 478). All five in the Group were nominally Democrats, but they all wished to distinguish their positions on public policy from political allegiances and regional prejudices. There were occasional suggestions of other members for the Group, including Admiral Richard Byrd, who manifested his admiration for Lippmann by suggesting that he run for president and bringing back a flag for him from an Arctic expedition (Byrd to WL, March 24, 1933, and May 20, 1935, WLPIII F353).

All members of the Group were united in their dislike of the New Deal and their conviction that it was a betrayal of true liberal values. But they did not make this the centerpiece of their interactions. This is one reason why, while praising and congratulating the European liberal thinkers, they seemed uneasy about the Europeans' close identification with politics and with political causes. These Americans were more at ease arguing a case and reaching conclusions without some predetermined outcome established by outside political authorities. Douglas wrote to Lippmann in 1936: "My conception of the project is that it would be most effective if there could be held in St. Louis, or Kansas City, or Denver, or Louisville, a meeting of Democrats from various parts of the country which would approve of a calm and deliberate document indicting the basic fallacies of the New Deal, pointing out, however, that they are but the logical result of Republican Post-War policies, and reaffirming a faith in the basic philosophy of the Democratic Platform of 1932" (Douglas to WL, March 23, 1936, WLPIII F640).

The five corresponded on various topics from the beginning of the 1930s and may have discovered then how similar their core values were. Above all they were in favor of global free trade, and they opposed monopoly in all its forms. For example, Douglas wrote to Lippmann while he was still director of the Bureau of the Budget, rather indiscreetly it would seem: "I fear that the Administration is drifting into a policy of isolation. There are a good many inconclusive, but indicative signs. I hope that I am wrong, but I feel very strongly that, in this highly industrialized age, isolation leads to economic destruction; or, to state it in a less exaggerated form, I believe that for ourselves in America isolation must inevitably reduce our agricultural population to a status of peasants and create a permanently unemployed class of several millions" (Douglas to WL, June 27, 1933, WLPIII F640). In general this statement of principles was Lippmann's position for the rest of the decade.

The first project of the Group was undertaken in 1936, and it seems not to have had much impact through an abundance of caution. Their policy target was Lippmann's nemesis: monopoly in all its forms, especially restriction of domestic production, tariff protection, and trade unions. Their first thought was to have a meeting of like-minded people to discuss "a declaration of principles signed by a very limited group of men" on this topic;

but then they thought of the presidential election coming up and that this might seem like just an anti-Roosevelt attack (Douglas to WL, March 23, 1936, WLPIII F640). Lippmann concluded that they should, instead, produce "a declaration which men like Hull and even Wallace [secretaries of state and agriculture] would genuinely subscribe to" (WL to Douglas, March 27, 1936, WLPIII F640). They ruled out participation in their affairs by those who took extreme positions, like members of the Liberty League. Lippmann composed a work entitled "(Tentative) Draft of Declaration of Principles" on monopoly that was intended to provide the background for a national debate (see Appendix) and might have become the model for later declarations, but the group got cold feet, fearing that it too could have an impact on the election.

In 1938 Wilhelm Ropke of the Graduate Institute of International Studies in Geneva and Alexander Rustow, then at the University of Istanbul, prepared an eleven-page memorandum for Lippmann and his emerging "project" entitled "The Urgent Necessity of Re-Orientation in Social Sciences" that called for "Synthetic Interpretation of Current Economic Problems, including Radical Dissatisfaction and Unrest of the Laboring Classes, Economic Instability and International Economic Disintegration" (Ropke to WL, September 15, 1938, WLPIII F1837). Lippmann read the memo over dinner to Stewart, Wolman, and Douglas and sent copies to Raymond Fosdick at the Rockefeller Foundation and Abraham Flexner at the Institute for Advanced Study (WL to Ropke, September 27, 1938, WLPIII F1837). Lippmann wrote to the French social scientist Louis Rougier in October 1939, that he, Stewart, Warren, and Douglas "have agreed to meet regularly and begin to develop some kind of center for the study of liberalism," but the war put an end to these plans (WL to Rougier, October 17, 1939, WLPIII F1848).

The Group continued to meet whenever they found themselves in the same city, and by 1939 they had agreed that a new topic should be "the problem of organizing a federal union in Europe and the American relationship to such a union" (WL to Stewart, November 21, 1939, WLPIII F2009), a plan that was being actively explored by others in Britain and France. They proposed to meet with Lord Lothian, the British ambassador; the

French ambassador; Adolf Berle from the Roosevelt administration; and others who might have interesting things to say on this subject. In his column of November 21, 1939, Lippmann argued that such a union could have salutary political and economic effects by discouraging nationalism and encouraging free trade. The union, he presumed, "will have in effect a common currency and a common budget of appropriations for their respective imports. Within their own territory, and within that larger area which embraces the British Commonwealth, the dependent empire, and the French empire, they will practice a division of labor so as to obtain 'the best use in common interests of the resources of both countries in raw materials, means of production, tonnage,' and as the statement adds significantly, 'etc.' This will have to mean in practice a decided movement toward Franco-British free trade and away from restrictionism and nationalistic self-sufficiency" (HT 11/21/39). After the war this European Union should welcome Germany, purged of Hitler and Nazi doctrine. Evidently the course of the war caused this project to be put aside by the Group.

What Lippmann's plan for the production of documents and encouragement of debate by distinguished liberal thinkers accessible to the ordinary lay person lacked was an intellectual entrepreneur like, for example, his close friend Abraham Flexner, and some institutional infrastructure like Flexner's Institute for Advanced Study, which might have maintained the momentum of projects and resisted the inevitable inertia that came with busy careers.

9

War

LIPPMANN WAS REVOLTED by war. It was the antithesis of the peaceful and efficient Good Society, to which he looked forward throughout the 1930s. War was wasteful, in most respects irrational, and destructive both of goods and services and of human freedom. He had seen war up close in the War Department in 1917 and as a commissioned officer, and he was especially conscious of how truth and candor were replaced by propaganda. He had been disgusted at how the war effort was turned over to those who knew little about it or how to conduct it. At the start of the Great War in 1914 a human capital interpretation of warfare caused him to be optimistic, at least for a short while, that a cost-benefit calculation would keep the United States out of the conflict. The common man had become too valuable, he thought, to be slaughtered in the trenches. He wrote:

> Human life will become more valuable as we invest in it. The child is worth bearing, nursing, tending and rearing, worth educating, worth making happy, worth building good schools and laying out playgrounds for, worth all the subtle effort of modern educational science, is becoming too valuable for drudgery, too valuable for the food of cannon. It is

because for some years we have been putting positive values into life that
this war appalls us more than it would have appalled our ancestors. . . .
This is the best internal defense against those amongst us who may be
dreaming of aggression. Every dollar and every moment of care devoted
to increasing the individual importance of people, all skill and training,
all fine organization to humanize work, every increase of political expression, is a protection against the idle use of military power, against
any attempt to convert legitimate and necessary preparation for defense
into any instrument of conquest. (WL 1914b, 14)

But this optimism did not last long after he himself was brought into the
war and saw how little rational calculation explained events.

Thinking about War

When the war finally ended he agreed with those like Keynes who concluded that the Paris Peace Treaty would not really bring peace but had,
instead, set the stage for another war; economic conditions now would invariably become powerful causes of further conflict. He corresponded
throughout the 1920s with those who shared this view, but neither he nor
they were sure what should be done. One of his regular correspondents was
Allyn Young, the distinguished Harvard economist who had been his colleague in Colonel House's Inquiry. Young, while planning an International Economic Conference for the League of Nations in 1927, wrote to
Lippmann: "Sir Arthur Salter has asked me to see to it that among the various memoranda prepared for the Conference, one at least shall deal effectively with the economic causes of war and with the possibilities of economic peace. It is the kind of thing which is worth doing if it can be done in
a thoroughly impressive fashion. I discussed some topics of the matter in a
recent presidential address before the American Economic Association. In
that address I leaned very heavily upon yourself and John Dewey, for the
things which you and Dewey have written seem to me to come a little closer
to the heart of the matter than anything else that had been done. I really do
not know how to go about it, but I wish very much that in some way your

services could be enlisted. You write more effectively than anybody else I know" (Young to WL, July 13, 1926, WLPI F1316).

Yet intermittent warfare had punctuated human history, and Lippmann remained skeptical of the various utopian schemes that were proposed in the 1920s to prevent conflict by such devices as nonaggression treaties, arrangements for international conciliation and arbitration, and agreements to outlaw war. He was critical of much of the thinking that went into these plans, as for example the campaign against the trade in arms. Although in 1926, while working at the *World*, he had suggested that the paper consider what sounds like a very modern endeavor—"a crusade against the manufacturers of guns, aimed to bring them under very strict Federal regulation as to sale, to break up their very powerful lobby at Washington and in various State Legislatures" (WL to Mr. White, October 15, 1926, WLPI F899)—he concluded that this approach would not work on a global scale. He pointed out in 1934 that embargoes on international arms sales might simply drive more countries to become self-sufficient in arms production and thereby worsen the problem of arms proliferation (HT 5/24/34). The critics of arms sales seemed not to realize that the problem was demand, not supply. Lippmann was aware of the irony that increased demand for war materiel could have positive effects in the domestic economy by increasing aggregate demand and employment; but he observed that this increased output would not be for consumer goods and therefore would not increase consumer welfare. "For there is no escaping the fact that [in a closed economy] nations cannot consume more than they produce. No national mysticism and no kind of political demagoguery can suspend that inexorable law" (HT 8/20/38).

By 1935 Lippmann could see that the prospect of another war was very real and rearmament should be contemplated. He worried for his beloved Great Britain and for the survival of western (Occidental?) civilization, which was for him the pinnacle of human existence. At this date he was not certain what should be done to stave off war. "The only precaution that the American people can take is to make sure that these momentous decisions are thoroughly examined and carefully debated, that they are not taken absent-mindedly and casually by over-worked officials and accepted inattentively by the public" (HT 12/3/35). In 1936 he concluded that suffering caused by the depression was the main force driving parts of the world to contemplate warfare, and the best strategic policy for the United States was to press for macroeconomic reform and a return to prosperity:

> That the tensions of Europe can be relaxed only by opening up the channels of trade, has been demonstrated by the experience of many countries. The effect of the contraction of trade by exorbitant tariffs, by monetary disorders, by embargoes, quotas, bounties, and what not, is to set the people fighting each other at home and abroad in a desperate struggle to keep their share of a diminishing national income. The rise of communists, fascists and extremists of all sorts is due to the fact that men resort to violence when their standard of life is being depressed. A liberal and generous and democratic society is one in which men feel free, generous, and friendly because they have opportunity; it is depression, deflation, restriction of opportunity that arouse violence, intolerance and fratricidal enmities. (HT 5/30/36)

By 1937 Lippmann's sense of urgency had increased markedly. Continuing depression, he observed, had driven nations into the hands of the "lunatic fringe" and had silenced the voices of the "cool-headed and practical-minded." He told an audience at the Drake University commencement that "[t]he surest sign of a really dangerous crisis is that the people of the middle are being forced to choose between one lunatic fringe and the other. At such times in human affairs the spirits of men become subject to a law very much like what is known as Gresham's law about the circulation of money. Gresham discovered, you will remember, that if there is good money in circulation, say, money made of gold, and if then a cheaper money is also put into circulation the cheaper money will drive the better money out of circulation. During a great social crisis something like this happens to men's opinions. On the right the decent conservatives who wish to preserve property, but recognize that property must be used in the public interest, are steadily and rapidly overwhelmed by reactionaries who want to make property absolute. In the end ordinary conservatives find themselves supporting and following men of fascist temper. On the left the progressives who wish to modify the rights of property and remove privilege and make opportunity more equal, and to do all these things by democratic methods, find themselves compelled to go along with men of a revolutionary temper" (HT 6/8/37).

Lippmann did not doubt that macroeconomic mistakes were the driving force behind both international and domestic conflict and would be the ultimate cause of another world war. They, not the Marxian claims of exploitation by the bourgeoisie, were the source of the mounting class war that could soon break into a shooting war. "There can be little doubt that in the western democracies the parties of the Left are now imbued with the philosophy and the spirit of the class war. This philosophy and this spirit, rather than the specific measures of reform, are the reason why the conservative classes are today as sympathetic as they are to the fascist advance" (HT 11/9/37). The economies of countries on the brink of war in 1938 were so fragile that even a small addition to their suffering could bring an end to their democracy and to their peaceful state. "Here, for example, a strike is a strike, costly, inconvenient, angry, but nevertheless an episode which in no ultimate sense touches the national independence or the constitutional order of the American people. But in Europe almost any large strike carries with it the danger of a general catastrophe, either of a convulsive class struggle within or of a new invitation to aggression from abroad. Here again the problem of the government finances is serious and may have large consequences in the long future; but in the remaining free countries of Europe, the collapse of government finances is not only a more immediate danger but it may well involve the system of representative government and the essential liberties of the citizen" (HT 10/11/38).

Even after Munich and the rapid strengthening of Hitler's military power Lippmann continued to believe that the best hope for peace was through restoration of prosperity at home and abroad: "A genuine full recovery in the United States is the greatest contribution that can now be made to the prevention of war. Recovery in America is in fact indispensable to the defense of law and order in the outer world, to the consolidation of that determination, which is now manifest in every country, to defend the peace against aggression and revolution. . . . The American economy represents approximately half of the commercial capacity of the world. For that reason depression and prosperity in the United States have an enormous, and probably a decisive influence upon the economic life of all the other nations that depend, much more than we depend, upon normal international trade" (HT 3/7/39). Only import growth by the United States could enable the free nations to rearm and at the same time to reduce the anger and frustration of their own people. U.S. foreign policy must both stimulate investment in its partner countries and increase effective demand for their goods and services. For this he endorsed a radical proposal. "The only thing which will surely bring that about quickly is to offer investors and speculators the inducement of profits large enough to overcome their inertia and their fears. The stroke of policy most certain to do that would be the repeal of the capital gains tax" (HT 3/7/39). Lippmann worried that Roosevelt's advisers appreciated too well that if the private economy were able to generate enough aggregate demand on its own to sustain full employment and balance the fiscal budget, the justification for many New Deal programs would disappear (HT 3/28/39).

By 1938 a major war in Europe seemed imminent, and the big question for Lippmann became not the cause of the war but how to plan for it. He recognized that the United States would not be persuaded easily to join in, and he had to be careful not to appear as a war monger. All the same, war planning, even if only in the broadest sense, had urgently to be undertaken. He treated war planning as similar to peacetime economic planning. In fact the two seemed largely identical; just the objective changed. War, like satisfaction of consumer wants or maintenance of full employment, involved an objective to be achieved, victory, and limited resources with which to achieve it. Questions were how best to allocate and employ the available resources to reach the goal. This realization that some sort of planning, the process dreaded by many of his liberal friends, was now desperately needed caused Lippmann to think as deeply about war as he had about the Great Depression in 1933–1935. Indeed, he found there were important parallels between the two crises. After some reflection he suggested that there were at least six "systems of thought," meaning economic thought in the broadest sense, by which people could address the war, but unfortunately only one of these was helpful at the moment. He did not present these systems in a list as given here, but he covered all of them in his columns.

The first approach was to picture the United States as a large island with the capacity to live within this island-world, cut off from all the rest of the globe. When facing war, just as when facing depression, this reasoning ran, the wisest strategies were to encourage isolation from the outside world and increase insulation from potential enemies. Under this approach, building artificial walls around the United States to supplement the natural barriers of the two oceans seemed the most sensible tactic. Support a strong navy and do not worry very much about an army or air force, since you would never be called upon to fight on land or in the air. Some extreme isolationists thought even these naval preparations were unnecessary; just turn your back, they thought, and people won't bother you. Forget about what was happening in Europe and Asia. Let the countries over there have their squabbles, and stay out of them. Lippmann found the origin of this isolationist approach to military threat, as he had found the isolationist approach to problems in the global economy, in the American sense of exception that went all the way back to the American Revolution. Various myths supported this doctrine. America was felt by the isolationists to be different from the Old World; it had been settled by peace-loving immigrants who were escaping persecution by moving to the New World, and with the most bountiful natural resources anywhere to convert into a great civilization. The American republic was righteous, uncorrupted, and able to do perfectly well on its own. The American sense of exception was given strength by selfish interests that supported the myths to justify devices like tariffs and embargoes, which protected their own private activities.

The policy of isolation was especially dangerous where macroeconomics and international relations came together. The mistaken belief in the United States at the end of World War I and after the onset of the depression that domestic prosperity could be achieved by reducing international trade and increasing war debt payments had contributed to the deepening of depression around the world. Economic and political isolation was pursued by the United States as a package, and the results were tragic on both dimensions. Economically desperate people around the world turned to dictators and military aggression as a way out of their misery. "With the best of intentions but with a deadly misunderstanding, we all adopted the isolationist view of disarmament and separateness," Lippmann wrote nine months before Pearl Harbor. "We stopped the growth of our own navy. We induced Britain to let her own navy become dangerously weak. And we took the fatal step of breaking up the association with Japan, imposing upon Japan a policy of isolation which was the beginning of Japan's increasingly restless imperialism. . . . Then having obstructed the reconstruction of the world, and having seen the ensuing anarchy produce the revolutionary imperialist dictatorships of Russia, Italy and Germany, we tried to protect the failure of isolation by the policy of insulation—by the neutrality acts which were to keep us safe by renouncing our rights" (HT 2/27/41).

One of the consequences of the exceptionalist myth of American uniqueness was ignorance of most things international in the United States. Why learn about parts of the world that were inferior on all levels and from whom it was best to maintain a safe distance? Even though Americans understood little of the world economy, they knew even less about issues of global security. Many of America's leaders regarded participation in World War I as an unfortunate aberration in American foreign policy resulting from President Wilson's strange internationalist pretensions, which were not shared by the mass of the people. Refusal to take part in the League of Nations was seen as the true expression of the American view of the world. The lesson drawn by these isolationist leaders from World War I was "never again, just build the walls higher." And after the conclusion of the victorious war, "it was the isolationists who forced the United States to make a separate peace and to withdraw from all further association with other democracies to keep the world safe for democracy. It was the isolationists who insisted on that sudden breaking of economic collaboration and that helter-skelter demobilization here and among the Allies which caused the first great post-war depression. This they followed up by insisting on the first of those destructive tariff bills which, with ever increasing severity over the years, imposed economic isolation and a cutthroat competition upon the nations of the world. It was the isolationists who set their faces against a workable solution of the debt problem and imposed upon us and upon the Allies the devastating policy of collecting uncollectable reparations and debts. It was the isolationists who wrote the laws which forbade us to lend money to our old friends and Allies but left the way open to the wild lending of the '20s. It was the isolationists who capped this obstruction to economic reconstruction and recovery by the Hawley-Smoot tariff in Hoover's administration and by the wrecking of the world economic conference in the first Roosevelt administration" (HT 2/27/41). Lippmann did not encourage planning for a war economy using the isolationists' system of thought.

A second system of thought that Lippmann found to be embedded in American thinking by the end of the 1930s was derived from programs of the New Deal, especially the NRA and the AAA, which insisted that macroeconomic challenges could best be met by supply restriction and monopoly to sustain market prices. Foolish as this principle was in peacetime, Lippmann wrote, it certainly could not be sustained in wartime, when maximum production of war material was the objective and inflation rather than deflation was the threat. Still, the adjustment in thought was not easy. "Had we not spent ten years of depression closing down plants, paying people not to produce, shortening the hours of labor, subsidizing unemployment, and generally trying not to be choked by the productivity of the country? Then suddenly we find ourselves in a position where everything is reversed" (HT 7/15/41). Another aspect of New Deal thinking was to treat businessmen, and especially entrepreneurial ones, with suspicion as potential exploiters of the working class. By contrast, a challenge in fighting a war had to be to gain the support and cooperation of the business community to produce the particular goods that were desperately needed. "It is not astonishing that American business men have been slow to believe that after twelve years of being on the defensive they have in fact been called back to leadership and high responsibility" (HT 1/9/41). Better relations of government with the business community had to be an objective when preparing the economy for war, and the system of thought embedded in the New Deal was not likely to make this happen.

The third system of thought that Lippmann found to be inappropriate for planning for war was what he called "laissez faire" of the free-trade Manchester School type, and what might be called today "libertarianism." Under this system the implication was that if citizens wanted defense, or

even such a narrow objective as victory in a war, they could express their
demands through their votes and thereby allocate their resources and those
of the government optimally to satisfy their preferences. Competitive bids
could then be taken for defense projects, and monopoly or collaboration
among suppliers would not be tolerated any more in defense projects than
in others. Creeping collectivism should be resisted vigorously in war as in
peace. Lippmann thought this too was an impossible approach to a national
crisis like war. If this approach were taken the war could be lost before mobilization was ever achieved. It was his view that in the emergency of war it
would be necessary for government to go to General Motors and Ford and
Chrysler and say not "Will you please submit bids?" but rather "We need so
many tanks. Who can and will produce them, and how quickly?" The day
after Germany invaded Poland, the beginning of World War II, he wrote:
"Men may disagree about many things. But none will deny that in a time like
this there should be a national government, that there should be a united
people, that no policy can be executed except as it is backed by strength, that
there is no safety and no honor in division, in helpless inaction, and in forc-
ible words which are accompanied by feeble deeds" (HT 9/2/39).

The fourth system of thought about how to address preparing for war
was politics as usual. Lippmann had developed a cynical view of politics
from his close engagement with government over almost thirty years. Like
public choice economists down the road, he saw actions taken by bureaucrats and politicians as reflecting mainly their perceived individual self-
interest, and the special interests of those who supported them, rather than
reflecting anything that might be called "the public interest." Lippmann
had seen how corporate interests, trade unions, and campaign contributors so often called the shots. From this perspective a war effort for those in
government was like building a highway. In so doing you took care of your
friends, your constituents, and yourself. Sadly, after long experience, many
citizens had come to accept this way of thinking. "The whole thing is still
seen by the people generally not as a national undertaking but as a commercial job, like a contract to build a house, which is being carried out for them
by Mr. Roosevelt and Mr. Knudsen [CEO of General Motors] and others."
And therefore "[i]t is not strange that our minds have not adjusted them-

selves rapidly enough to the new facts" (HT 7/15/41). But adjustment must come quickly, and the objectives and behaviors of public servants had to adapt to a new reality. He claimed that the American educational system had contributed to the widespread acceptance of the inevitability of a government dominated by self-interest and had discouraged virtues like self-sacrifice and patriotism. He singled out for a good deal of the blame Charles A. Beard's *An Economic Interpretation of the Constitution of the United States* (1913), because it pictured even the founders of the Republic as motivated mainly by self-interest. "This book has had an immense influence upon the writing and teaching of American history and upon the outlook of the generation that was educated in the interval between the two great wars. It would hardly be an exaggeration to say that this book is the classic which set the fashion for the debunking historians" (HT 10/3/40). It was the recent historians more generally who had helped to create the impression that politics could do no more than enrich the participants. "Our own historians, who think they have explained the greatness of the American past when they have explained it away, have emptied American history of all significant meaning, of its value as a source of wisdom, of its power to teach by example" (HT 9/8/40). The result was that it was not possible to think of the challenge of war as a problem to be solved by political thinking. "Who that has read the debates in Congress or talked with recent graduates of the colleges has not been impressed by the degree to which American political thinking oscillates between cynicism and sentimentality, between despair and credulity, between an absolute agnosticism and an extreme gullibility?" (HT 9/8/40).

But it was not just the narrow selfishness pervading government in America that caused Lippmann to reject the politics-as-usual system of thinking as an appropriate way to plan for war; it was also some of the simplistic knee-jerk responses legislators had developed to complex problems. One was that passage of a prohibitory law could eliminate a practice you did not like. Examples of failures with this strategy were the Sherman Anti-Trust Act to deal with monopoly and the Eighteenth Amendment to the Constitution to deal with abuses of alcohol. When Congress discovered that passing laws of this kind did not always work, they adopted another panacea. "Having learned that the evils which afflict mankind cannot be

cured by passing laws, our political leaders have passed on to the notion
that most evils can be cured by appropriating money. They have had a lot of
practice in appropriating money, and many of them have as much faith today in an appropriation bill as the solution of a problem as they had formerly in a prohibitory law" (HT 4/29/40). In fact, Lippmann wrote, the
challenges of rearmament had become far too great to respond merely with
an appropriation: "the plants have not been built, the tools have not been
made, labor has not been trained, in order to produce armaments as quickly
as the condition of affairs in the world requires" (HT 4/29/40). Still another
aspect of party politics that Lippmann disliked was governing by public
opinion polls: find out what the voters want on every question and then
pander to them. Lippmann thought this was poor strategy in peacetime but
catastrophic in wartime. Since none of the familiar legislative practices, a
prohibitory law, an appropriations bill, and opinion polling, were likely to
be helpful in preparing for war, Lippmann rejected out of hand this fourth
system of thought.

   The fifth system of thought that Lippmann found to be unhelpful when
planning for war was, ironically, very much like that which *The Good Society* greeted with so much acclaim only a few years before. In that work he
had called for decentralization of control over economic activities among
several layers of government, and respect above all for the rights and liberties of the individual participants in the economy. The maintenance of
competitive markets, he had maintained then, was essential to the preservation of civilization and the good life of the citizens. This vision was dis-
tinctly Jeffersonian. Now he saw elements of this vision as luxuries that
could no longer be afforded. Centralization and efficiency, meaning the capacity to defeat the enemy quickly rather than necessarily to deliver satisfaction of consumer wants and protection of human liberty, were the qualities of government that must be sought above all others. Hamilton must
now be the architect rather than Jefferson. "In so great an emergency the
national interest must override all personal, factional and partisan considerations; public men must rise above their ordinary ambitions and habitual
prejudices; and the people have a right to insist that their leaders shall be
equal to the occasion" (HT 8/20/39). As war broke out in Europe he called

for a degree of concentration in the federal government much greater even than that contemplated under the New Deal. Instead of division of powers he called for bipartisan decision making by a new council made up of leaders of Congress and the executive branch. "These men should meet not occasionally but every day, if necessary all day, as a council of national defense. They should have available to them all the information which reaches the State Department, the Treasury, the War and Navy Departments. No important question of policy should be decided without their advice and consent; no policy should be proposed publicly until it has been considered by them. No proposal should be made to Congress without their agreement and their willingness to defend it on the floor of both Houses of Congress" (HT 8/20/39).

Workers in government, no matter whether politicians or bureaucrats, must be motivated no longer by their own complex self-interest. All of this must be laid aside when national survival was at stake. "Our first need, therefore, is the complete adjournment of personal, factional, and partisan politics through an agreement between the President and the responsible leaders in Congress that they will consult, decide, and work together" (HT 9/2/39). In wartime even free trade was no longer sacred; tariffs and embargoes should be employed as necessary to assist allies and punish enemies (HT 9/23/39 and 9/28/39). Perhaps addressing those of his readers who were pacifists, he suggested that by deploying economic warfare, shooting warfare might possibly be avoided. He wrote in November 1939 that "on the evidence now available, given the kind of war that is being fought, it will, I believe, soon become clear to every one that this war is not going to be decided on any battlefield and that no American army will be or could be sent to any European battlefield in this war" (HT 11/4/39). In this, as in some other predictions, Lippmann's prescience was flawed. He wrote just three months before Pearl Harbor that with a strengthened navy and air force there no longer was a need for a substantial army. "As a matter of fundamental strategy in the conflict, our role is on the sea and in the air and in the factory—not on the battlefields of Europe or Asia. Our army program, now that we have lend-lease and the Navy in action, should be made to conform to this basic American strategy" (HT 9/26/41).

Lippmann claimed that the new liberal society that he and others were groping for might some day be a sound basis from which to conduct a war, but not yet. He told the Walter Lippmann Colloquium in 1938: "even if the world were in a condition to listen to the teaching of liberals, the liberals will not be ready to guide a movement until they have revised and reconstructed their philosophy, until they have discovered a new synthesis that reconciles antitheses as those which exist between individual liberty and popular sovereignty, between order and freedom, between national sovereignty and international security, between the power of majorities and the continuity of the State, between stability and change, between private property and public welfare, between freedom and social organization" ("Walter Lippmann Colloquium" 1938, 20).

Lippmann's abandonment of the fifth system of thought, which emphasized so much human rights, especially personal freedom and rights of property, and which had characterized *The Good Society,* is significant because it helps to explain one of his most controversial positions during World War II: his expression of strong support for the internment of American citizens of Japanese ancestry on the ground that they were a threat to security. When discussing the need to respond pragmatically to problems of security he remarked: "The rule, for example, that alien Japanese are to be treated as enemies but their children [who were citizens] as patriots is the kind of ruling which just makes no sense at all in practice and on the spot" (HT 2/14/42).

By the end of 1939 Lippmann was pretty well resigned to the high probability of a second world war and the engagement of the United States in it, sooner or later. This led him to introduce a sixth system of thought, which looks like nothing more than old-fashioned mercantilism from the early eighteenth century. In fact he read Eli Hecksher's monumental and relatively sympathetic account of mercantilist doctrines, entitled *Mercantilism,* when it was published in 1935, and he recommended it to friends (e.g., WL to Bernard Berenson, March 20, 1936, WLPIII F206). He began now to construct a modernized mercantilism appropriate for a crisis in the twentieth century, piece by piece. First of all, there was the matter of war finance. Looking just a short way down the road, he declared that the depression mentality of the 1930s, which had focused on stimulation of effective demand, must now be put aside. "If we look ahead only a few months, it is clear, I think, that the problem will no longer be how to make work for idle men and idle resources, but how to produce enough to repair the wastage of the war and to develop enough armaments to make this country strong in a world that is ever more dangerous" (HT 11/28/39). The problem would soon become not how to increase government spending for conventional purposes such as public works and welfare programs, but how to constrain such spending in preparation for the huge military outlays that were imminent. In effect Lippmann was moving from Keynes of *The General Theory* (1936) to Keynes of *How to Pay for the War* (1940). In the American case Lippmann thought the best way to constrain nonmilitary public spending would be to make consumers appreciate more clearly the full costs of government programs. "The obvious way, in fact the only way, to do that is to broaden the base of the visible tax, namely the income tax, so that there may be at least twice as many voters who pay direct taxes as there are today. There is no other means by which political spending can be made politically unprofitable" (HT 11/28/39).

When interpreting and recommending wartime macroeconomic policy, Lippmann stayed close to the Keynesian position. In September 1940 he deduced that the initial effect of the war would be to bring an end to the recession at last: "it is the easiest and pleasantest phase of the armament boom, easiest because for the most part it merely takes up the slack, the pleasantest because it is the phase in which we get more guns and still get more butter" (HT 9/19/40). Yet two longer-run challenges remained. "These problems are of two general kinds: one, which is the more immediate and urgent, is how to speed up national defense production as much as possible: the second, which must be continually kept in mind though it is in the far distant future, is how to demobilize this defense economy if and when real peace is eventually restored" (HT 9/19/40). It may have been his own experience with demobilization after World War I that caused Lippmann to worry about the process even before the war had begun. What he said in 1940 he kept repeating for the next five years.

Demobilization itself will have to be administered with the exercise of great powers and the expenditure of much money. If it is not, it will produce an economic catastrophe and breed a revolutionary condition. It seems to me clear that the world returned to normalcy too quickly after the last war, and it was this helter-skelter demobilization, along with a bad peace, which made reconstruction and a sound recovery impossible. The system of free enterprise, which is I profoundly believe, alone compatible with freedom, was resumed too quickly—that is to say, before conditions were stable enough to permit free enterprise to flourish. Because it failed to do the impossible, namely to restore a civilian economy after all the nations had been under a war economy, the capitalist system suffered a terrific loss of prestige. The leaders of capitalism were unwise. They should have known that the system of free enterprise works in a stable and peaceable world. Before they returned to free capitalism they should have made stable the world in which it operated. Free capitalism requires order, confidence, security. Therefore, it will not work in war time. It will not produce a great military power. It cannot demobilize a nation after a great military effort. And we do no service to the cause of free enterprise when we place upon it tasks that are beyond its powers and foreign to its virtues. (HT 9/19/40)

He suggested that, with good luck, the economic experience of war might carry over positively into peace. "The war is a producer's dream, and the sense of power and of competence which men are finding in doing what is needed will, I believe, give to the American economy enterprise and confidence which it has not had since the opening of the West" (HT 5/23/42).

World War I had demonstrated that damage to the economy from foolish policies could be more than the actual costs of warfare, and careful steps must be taken to see that this did not happen again. "The peoples found it easy enough to repair the physical devastation of the last war; what they were never able to repair successfully and adequately was the disorganization of commerce and the revolutionary distortion of incomes, costs of production, wages and prices within the various countries. The task of economic statesmanship is to prevent that from happening again. The broad outline of the policy can, I think, already be discerned" (HT 12/7/39).

Lippmann saw two phases in the construction of a satisfactory war economy, and these must be carefully planned.

> The chief problem in the first phase is to manage the increase of production so as to avoid stoppages at natural or artificial bottle necks. By a natural bottle neck is meant, for example, the shortage of skilled labor which is due in part to the fact that during ten years of depression so many young men have not had the opportunity to learn skilled trades. The remedy here is industrial training, subsidized one might hope out of some of the funds that have been badly spent on mere relief. By an artificial bottle neck is meant, of course, monopolistic price controls, monopolistic union activity, to jack up some wage rates and to exclude new workers, and tariffs, external and domestic, designed to limit supply and restrict the market. . . .
>
> In the second phase, when demand is really greater than supply, an inflationary rise of prices cannot be stopped by prosecuting or persecuting business men and labor leaders who advance prices and wage rates. In this phase the only way to prevent inflation is to work more, to save more, and to consume less. That means that the restrictions on the hours of work and on output will need to be relaxed. It means that the taxes will have to be increased. It means that government, corporate, and private borrowing will have to be financed out of actual savings, and not out of inflationary credit created by the banks. (HT 12/7/39)

One of the major adjustments to be made in undertaking war planning was abandonment of the satisfaction of consumer wants as the criterion for economic performance. At the best of times Lippmann was skeptical about using public opinion as a guide to policy formation, but in wartime this was truly impractical. All public opinion would reveal was the variety of ill-informed private interests, most of which must be put aside. "The notion that public opinion can and will decide all issues is in appearance very democratic. In practice it undermines and destroys democratic government. For when everyone is supposed to have a judgment about everything nobody in fact is going to know much about anything" (HT 4/10/41). He reported modestly from his own experience that having studied many issues related to warfare, his opinion still should not be taken into account by war planners any more than that of the average citizen (HT 4/10/41).

In fact, selfish behavior, which would mainly be discovered from consulting public opinion, had to be replaced in wartime by self-sacrifice and patriotism. "There in a nutshell, I submit, is the answer to all our problems: the vested interest problems of business men, the labor problems, the farm bloc problems, the bureaucratic problem, the partisan politics problem, the prima donna problem, and being a newspaper man myself, I must not omit the newspaper man problem. All these problems are in essence the same problem: that of pushing the old peace-time machinery of our interests out of doors and leaving it there for the duration of the war. Until that is done, none of us will really think of nothing else but his war job" (HT 2/23/42). Americans must be prepared to give up all luxuries known to them in peacetime, "the symbols and the reminders of the soft ways into which we fell during the period between the two wars—during the years of irresponsibility, self-complacency, self-indulgence, private and public speculation and materialism" (HT 3/28/42). Long-standing practices like the eight-hour day and the forty-hour week must be forgotten. There was little in his rhetoric now that sounded like that of a decade before. For example: "Abundance, like over-eating in the individual, makes nations fat and puts them to sleep. It is in leanness and in stringency, when living is hard, and the reason for living is high, that men find their souls and their hearts are at peace" (HT 3/28/42).

A point that Lippmann made repeatedly about strategic policy was that Americans must see their participation in this or any other war as in response to their own broad national self-interest. Woodrow Wilson had made a mistake in picturing World War I as philanthropy. The result had been disappointment and "a great revulsion of feeling. It was a revulsion against the war, against war, against all that Wilson had stood for, against our allies, against armaments, alliances and strategic defense—against every element of a sound national policy—and the country passed into the disillusioned lethargy which led [left?] us unprepared and not alert to Pearl Harbor" (HT 12/26/42). Lend-lease was a transfer of military resources to an ally, and it should have been treated as an act of self-interest, not an act of charity (HT 3/6/43).

Beginning in February 1940, Lippmann wrote a series of columns entitled "Some Notes on War and Peace," which constituted a primer for his sixth system of thought, meaning essentially what must be done if winning the war was the foremost, or even the only, goal of public policy. He began with a number of "fallacies" of which the populace must be disabused, including the ease of achieving a lasting victory, the simplicity of reaching domestic agreement on what were the best tactics, and the capacity to run a war with little experience. Next he stressed the importance of having clearly in mind what was expected to constitute victory. What kind of world was anticipated after the war ended? Without such a vision military accomplishment might be simply empty. Above all, World War I had demonstrated how essential it was to reconstruct the vanquished after victory and not simply walk away. In 1919 the Allies "could have maintained their victory only by maintaining and perfecting their economic and political union, and by absorbing Germany into it as an equal partner and guarantor. They did the opposite" (HT 2/27/40). After this war the Allies must do better.

Lippmann contemplated the conscription of both labor and capital in the event of war (HT 8/24/40). The forty-hour work week must be repealed for the duration (HT 10/3/40). Wage rates must be regulated, and union rules must be set aside (HT 10/2/41). He thought that threats of a coal strike by his old nemesis John L. Lewis were close to acts of treason. "If ever there was Congressional business, this is it—to place the rights and duties of labor unions and labor leaders on a firm base of clearly declared principle. Congress has fixed the duty of corporations when their services are needed for defense. It has fixed the duty of the young men registered in the selective service act. It should now fix the duty of Mr. Lewis so that there may be no doubt left in any one's mind as to whether it is or it is not legitimate to interrupt the production of weapons for the defense of the United States. Congress wants to do this. Congress should be helped to do it, and to do it wisely" (HT 11/13/41). The traditional assumptions of the free market, for example that labor and capital had full mobility, no longer held: "Nothing would more seriously impair the regime of private property and the system of free enterprise than to permit a recalcitrant minority among business men to obstruct the national defense. Nor is it in the interest of property or of free business or of the conservation of the capitalist system to take the position that while men may now be compelled to serve the country, property may not now be compelled to serve it. . . . The very essence of the national effort consists in the obligation of all citizens to serve the nation rather than themselves, and when the great majority are serving, no minority may resist or refuse" (HT 8/31/40).

It might be thought, Lippmann reflected, that nationalization of the entire economy as in the Soviet Union would be the best way to mobilize for defense, but this was not a practical possibility. "This country knows how to operate industry as a whole through private management; it does not know how to operate industry as a whole, or any considerable part of it, by government management. To change over from the system we understand to a different system which we do not understand would simply stall the whole industrial machine" (HT 9/12/40). He warned that deciding questions like this on the basis of plebiscites or Gallup polls was no longer an option. "Our history is full of painful instances in which the public sentiment of well meaning but necessarily uninformed crowds has over-ridden the better judgment of the commanders. This is such an old story here that it is the recurrent nightmare of American soldiers and sailors" (HT 10/21/41). This mistake of responding to public opinion in wartime must not be repeated. After Pearl Harbor he was even more adamant. "We cannot too soon make it clear to ourselves that in the discipline of war, public opinion cannot control the details no matter how curious we may be to know them, that wars cannot be directed by committees and Gallup polls and rumors and mass meetings" (HT 12/11/41).

Preparing for War

Before Pearl Harbor settled the matter, Lippmann's first task was to persuade Americans that the war in Europe was their war too. He did this by emphasizing the costs of staying neutral. He wrote in May 1940: "For if the Allied power falls, there will fall with it all the outer defenses of the Western Hemisphere, and we shall be left isolated in a world dominated on both sides of our oceans by the most formidable alliance of victorious conquerors that was ever formed in the whole history of man" (HT 5/11/40).

His repeated message was that no more time could be lost in moving to a war footing without paying a heavy price. "There is no time left for trifling. There is no more time left for conducting our affairs on the basis of Gallup polls and on the hunches of office-seekers as to what the voters of Nebraska or West Virginia are going to think next November. There is no more time left for arguing as to whether this country shall have two more battleships five years hence. There is no more time left for backing and filling about whether or not this country is to start organizing itself seriously for the defense of its vital interests" (HT 5/11/40). Full speed ahead on all fronts had to be the order of the day. And above all it had to be made clear that rearmament was in the United States' own self-interest; it was not philanthropy. "The American people know now that if the allies begin to fall, there will come into being an alliance of aggressor powers—Nazi Germany, Fascist Italy, Soviet Russia, and imperialistic Japan—which the United States alone, especially in its present condition of physical unpreparedness and of mental and moral confusion, is incapable of dealing with" (HT 5/16/40).

The American people were smart enough to make the right decisions if the facts were put before them; government at this moment must forswear propaganda and be candid with the people. "They will like best those leaders who do not treat them as children, too young to be told the facts of life, or as nervous invalids who must not be shocked by the grim truth; they will wish to be treated as brave and honest and loyal men who are responsible individually and collectively for their country and its future" (HT 5/18/40). In particular, Americans must accept that their purchasing power for consumer goods would remain stable or fall over the course of the war, and there was no point complaining. "Economic stabilization in war time is arbitrary in the sense that the rule of the road is arbitrary. It is necessary to stabilize incomes *somewhere*, and keep them from rising any higher because no income will mean anything if you do not" (HT 2/11/43).

Lippmann found it necessary to combat what he considered all sorts of fallacious or misleading economic information about the security situation, for example that rearmament must be constrained by the size of the national debt. Remembering that through his columns he was helping perhaps eight million voters straighten out their thinking on questions like this, it is interesting to see what he says. "Not only may we dismiss from our minds the notion that the high national debt is in itself a handicap to the efforts we must make, but we may go further. We may say that because our debt is solely an internal debt while we possess virtually unlimited purchasing power in the form of gold and of export surpluses, we are as respects financial means invulnerable. Money is no limitation upon any effort we need to make; the only limitations are to be found, first, in our own capacity to produce, and second in our capacity to obtain delivery from Asia and Europe of critical strategic materials which we may be prevented by other powers from buying under ordinary commercial conditions in the open market" (HT 5/25/40). Just as economists discovered in the Great Recession of the twenty-first century, Lippmann found sixty-five years before that the public could become easily confused and then misled about the significance of the national debt. At both times the size of the national debt was given as an excuse on its own for reducing or terminating public expenditure. Unscrupulous people were regularly using the size of the debt to discourage sensible public policy, and he attempted to refute their claims. He wrote in 1944: "If we fix our minds upon the fact that the capacity to produce is the nation's wealth and upon the dislocation of that capacity as the supreme evil to be avoided, we shall, I believe, have hold of the saving truth. This is not the economics we were taught in school. But it is the economics we are going to have to learn in order to live in this century" (HT 1/18/44).

Public finance in wartime, he explained, had an entirely different set of functions and constraints from peacetime. He was guided in this subject by Albert Gaylord Hart, then at Iowa State University and later at Columbia. Although not appointed to do so by Lippmann, Hart kept up a steady stream of comment and suggestions, the flow sustained by regular notes of appreciation from Lippmann (WLPIII F1002). The legitimate peacetime restraints on the size of government, Lippmann began, had now to be removed, with the only criterion for size being the contribution of government operations to defeat of the axis powers. For the duration of the war public economics, rather than the economics of the private sector, mattered most. Indeed, Lippmann took a radical position: that victory could be achieved only by virtual nationalization of the economy, accepting universal service in place of the labor market and placing all productive factors at the service of the state as needed. "This can be done only by committing ourselves to the principle of universal service, to the principle of the total dedication of our resources, and to the principle that a nation can be armed only by leadership and authority" (HT 5/30/40). He reproached the labor leaders Bill Green and John L. Lewis, who claimed that this proposal was simply wage slavery (HT 3/20/43 and 3/25/43).

With breathtaking speed Lippmann dramatically abandoned the principles of *The Good Society* under the threat and then the reality of war. "Come what may, the easy-going days are over, and unless the nation is brought at once to a wholly new mood of duty, sacrifice, and honor, it will drift and be pushed and be harried down the path of disorder and humiliation" (HT 6/11/40). The competitive market system was hardly relevant anymore because the enemies employed monopoly. Their monopoly had to be fought with our monopoly. "The notion that separate and competing American firms and separate American farmers could deal separately with a continental system of monopoly under an all-powerful dictatorship is a tragic delusion" (HT 6/11/40). Conditions at home and abroad suddenly had made competitive product and factor markets defenseless and ineffective. "For private competitive trading and unplanned competitive production and private investing based on estimates of private profit in a free market will produce neither the armaments we shall need if we are isolated; nor will they give us the equality of bargaining power needed to do business with, and yet not be exploited by, the gigantic Continental monopolies of Europe and Asia" (HT 7/30/40). The long-dreaded concept of "plan" must now replace competition as the motto for the economy, while civil liberties and security of property were necessarily put aside. "An economy of peace can be converted into an economy of preparedness for modern war only under a national plan based upon authority and the power to command, upon an iron discipline, and in the broadest sense, covering wealth, non-combatant activity and military enlistment, upon the principle of universal service. . . . It will be said by some that these measures call for the suspension of many of the liberties we prize and that they are not in accord with the American way of life as our generation has lived it. That is true" (HT 6/11/40).

Worries about liberty and way of life had to be set aside for the duration. Such niceties as concerns about monopoly practices must be forgotten for the moment, and impending antitrust action against the petroleum industry should be dropped so that the oil companies could devote all their energies to production (HT 8/1/40). Lippmann made it very clear that the new system of "organization of economic life" that he was calling for was fundamentally different from those of the New Deal and the laissez-faire liberals. "To prepare for total war—and building a two-ocean Navy and a great air force and Army in preparation for total war—is impossible both under the New Deal conception of social reform and under the anti-New Deal conception of competitive private enterprise. There will be needed a new kind of planning— military planning— undreamed of by the former New Dealers and an enlistment of executive and managerial talent which they have always avoided. There will be needed a new kind of regimentation—military regimentation— which differs from the regimentation that businessmen complain of under the New Deal but differs no less from the free enterprise that they have hoped to return to" (HT 7/22/40). Lippmann was one of the first to call for military conscription, but he also went further. He wanted compulsory service from all able-bodied persons. "Without the power to compel people to go to work there is no way of getting the labor that is needed at the places where it is needed. How could there be under a volunteer system in which wages are frozen? If a man or a woman cannot be lured by profit or compelled by law how do you put him or her to work?" (HT 1/29/44).

Under circumstances of war the competitive market had become an enemy rather than a friend. No longer was it reasonable to think of bidding for critical civilian services. "Until this fundamental condition is cured, there cannot be and there will not be a war labor policy. The law of supply and demand will defeat it" (HT 1/29/44). Lippmann's apocalyptic prescriptions for wartime control of the economy were not viewed enthusiastically by everyone. Alfred P. Sloan wrote to him: "in my considered judgment, based upon a very broad experience, speaking both generally and more directly from the standpoint of General Motors, I am quite certain we will do a better job if we carry along as we are, through the process of evolution, rather than adopt your philosophy of revolution" (Sloan to WL, October 1, 1940, WLPIII F1956).

As the presidential election of 1940 drew near Lippmann argued that the main criterion for voters should be the performance of the president as commander in chief and implementer of the great new plan. "There is but one question to be decided in the Presidential campaign: who can be counted upon to organize the more effectively the military and economic defenses of the United States?" (HT 7/9/40). The sacred notion of division of powers had to be set aside for the duration. "So, if the existing facilities are not now worked to maximum capacity, it will be because the President has not yet converted his own mind to the requirements of total defense" (HT 8/1/40). As quickly as possible he must establish order and discipline in the economy and the society. "The downfall of the democracies in Europe has been due to their weakness; they have been disintegrated from within and then conquered from without because they failed to discipline their liberties and to establish authority in their democracy. Every totalitarian state has risen out of the ashes of defeat, frustration, humiliation and confusion; none has risen from an orderly establishment of authority and deliberate acceptance of discipline" (HT 8/10/40). The president should be assisted by a small body to replace the cabinet, called something like the "Supreme Council of National Defense." The model was a corporate one. "For what is needed, I submit, is not another agency alongside the existing cabinet and the existing independent offices but a small, compact cabinet which exercises all the powers granted by Congress and has full responsibility over all questions—diplomatic, strategic, military, economic and social—which are involved in the total problem of national defense" (HT 10/19/40).

Lippmann received a good deal of feedback about the apocalyptic tone of his proposals for war planning, especially from the business community. His longtime friend and conservative critic the lawyer Arthur Ballantine through a letter to the editor of the *Herald Tribune* insisted that in war as in peace the United States must operate as a free market economy. "What the Government would get by taking over all the property of the people would not be a spendable fund—the value of securities representing savings would be destroyed for there would be no market—but control and disposition of the stream of production. Is it to be supposed that with us the stream available for the support of the Government of the people would be as large under Government management as under the management of those having

direct interest and still having the impetus of voluntary effort? A complete
change of the basis of economic effort would be more likely to produce partial paralysis" (Ballantine to the HT editor, June 1, 1940, WLPIII F157).
Lippmann responded to Ballantine: "I am not proposing that the nation
should take over all of the property of the people. Here you are erecting a
straw man. I am proposing that the nation assert an absolutely prior claim
upon the services and the property of the people. This means the principle
of universal service both for the armed forces and for industrial production.
It means the power to tax to the limit of what is practicable. It means to direct the savings of the people into investments which serve the national defense. It means the power to restrict consumption, to ration materials and to
shut off all forms of purchasing power and investment which compete with
the needs of the national defense. Any other principle of rearmament is, as I
said before, the fatally erroneous principle of the [Neville] Chamberlain government [1937–1939, noted for the appeasement of Hitler at Munich in 1938].
I do not agree that the adoption of this principle is an abandonment of our
way of life. Our way of life is determined by its ends, not by the means that
are required to defend it" (WL to Ballantine, June 8, 1940, WLPIII F157).

Fighting the War

After December 8, 1941, almost all of Lippmann's columns for the duration
of the war dealt with some aspect of the war economy. He remained adamant that defense policy should not be determined by public opinion. The
public should understand, but should not be allowed to influence, policy. It
was the responsibility of people like Lippmann to inform the public of the
circumstances and their meaning so that citizens could feel involved and at
the very least not become critical of policy for the wrong reasons. He went
through his familiar three-step procedure when considering most policy
questions; first, he estimated which issues were of greatest current importance; then he learned as much as possible about them from reading and
talking to experts; and finally he decided upon the best ways to explain the
issue fairly and clearly to the public. To get the facts and sample opinion he
traveled widely: he visited war plants, went abroad as a war correspondent,

and talked with members of the military of all ranks. He engaged in contro-
versies large and small, often revealing a remarkable grasp of detail. As an
example of his position on a big issue, he argued that controversy over income distribution in wartime was unseemly and should not be tolerated.
"No one has ever worked out a just system of economic payments for the
Marines in the first assault wave at Tarawa. No one has been foolish enough
to try. Yet on the home front we go through the elaborate forms of debate
about wage rates, prices, profits and taxes as if it were possible to arrive at
any solution which is absolutely and perfectly just" (HT 12/28/43). To give
an example of a small controversy in which he took a strong stand, he supported a proposal for a new, small transport vessel called the "Sea Otter,"
which, he was informed, would be faster, less expensive, more simple to operate, more nimble, and better able to outwit submarines than conventional
cargo ships. The proposal for the Sea Otter was turned over to the Navy,
and "the fate of the new ship had been entrusted to men who did not believe
it could succeed" (HT 3/17/42). He took the U.S. Navy's quick dismissal of
this proposal as an indication of the sclerotic condition of its governance
and the need for total overhaul. But most of his attention was focused on
large questions of defense economics, which he kept on coming back to over
the first years of the war.

Lippmann selected topics for attention that he thought were critically
important, not well understood by the public, and where the best policies
were counterintuitive. The first of these was price control. He was persuaded that a successful war effort could not be conducted during a time of
rapid inflation, and like many others at the time he recalled with displea-
sure the unsatisfactory price policies of World War I. This was a topic
where the unsophisticated reactions of citizen and Congress were likely to
be unhelpful, and "there must be a clearer public understanding of the economics of price control and of inflation if any policy is to be carried out"
(HT 5/13/43). Some people were claiming that you could just pass a law that
said prices must not rise. Why do anything more? He had to explain that
the problem was really one of aggregate demand outstripping the pace of
production, that a universal price freeze would simply create excess demand in some markets more than others, which would lead to shortages

and black markets. An overall price freeze would require, at a minimum, some form of rationing to allocate scarce commodities that were no longer available in quantities adequate to satisfy market demand at fixed prices. His first response was to agree with Leon Henderson, administrator of the Office of Price Administration, that perhaps the prices and quantities of strategic materials should be controlled first while others were left to float freely and find their own equilibria of supply and demand. "This is a complex business, and since no government bureau can hope to know just what price ought to be fixed for every transaction, the wisest thing to do is to administer the supply of the strategic commodities—those vital to defense and for the necessities of life—and then, while watching the results vigilantly, to let the law of supply and demand operate among the less essential goods" (HT 10/11/41).

He thought that the economist Allen Wallis had provided the best arguments for retaining competitive markets whenever possible and not jumping into price control unless absolutely necessary. "The central control mechanism of our economy, and the inner principle of our economic liberty, is the price mechanism which enables men meeting in the market place, and not government officials in an office, to regulate production and consumption" (HT 12/22/42).

In 1940, before the war began for the United States, Lippmann downplayed the problem of inflation. "For while it is true that eventually an inflationary condition may be created, and that, therefore, the danger must be resolutely kept in mind, in fact our condition today is not inflated" (HT 11/21/40). By 1941, however, general inflation seemed more probable, and he set about to explain the phenomenon to his readers. He emphasized that the administration of public finance and inflation were closely connected.

> So the government's real problem is how to keep private citizens from spending more money than there are goods, at approximately present prices, which are available for sale to private citizens. There is nothing in the least complicated about this. In fact the main idea is so simple that it is often overlooked, and as a result policy becomes confused and may be or may seem to the public, unintelligible and arbitrary. . . . This is what is meant by inflation, and the vice of inflation is that while the prices which every one has to pay go up, not all incomes go up in proportion. So while a few may get richer because their incomes go up faster than prices,

most get poorer because prices go up faster than incomes. This is unjust. It is oppressive. It is obviously evil and dangerous. (HT 5/3/41)

Lippmann praised Marriner Eccles, chairman of the Federal Reserve Board, for explaining inflation clearly and for making the case in Keynesian terms for control of prices through fiscal policy.

> This is war finance looked at from the point of view of the individual citizen and its object, as we have seen, is to protect him against a rise in the cost of living by compelling and inducing him not to spend his whole income. The amount that individuals collectively must not spend is the amount that the government must spend. Looked at from the point of view of the government the object of war finance is two-fold: to protect the people against inflation and to make sure that the national defense has a first call upon factories, materials, transportation, managerial skill and labor. Reducing the amount of private expenditure is an obvious necessity here so that private individuals should not be bidding against the government. . . . Whatever it does, as to taxes, bonds, priorities, conscription, rationing, the central principle is the same and is very simple. In order to arm the nation it is necessary to work harder and consume less. For it is impossible to consume 100 billions of goods when 25 billions are for arms. It is possible then to consume only 75 billions. And the task of government finance is to see that the sacrifice or postponement of this 25 billions of private expenditures is made in a just and orderly and efficient way. (HT 5/3/41)

As the war went on Lippmann kept reminding his readers that nothing could be more disruptive of the war effort than uncontrolled inflation, and he began to contemplate extreme measures, such as government acting as monopsonist in markets for strategic goods and then as monopolist-seller of these goods to essential buyers. "Nothing is so violently disruptive of the social order as a run-away inflation, and the most radically effective measures to prevent inflation are, therefore, far preferable to more orthodox measures which do not work" (HT 7/19/41). With food shortages and price pressures looming he suggested controlling agricultural prices on the principle of parity, a notion that had been anathema to him a few years before

(HT 9/23/41). Over the course of the war he kept up a running commentary on matters of price control and inflation, in part at least because he perceived this to be a topic on which intuition might be a bad guide and his readers needed leadership. A point he made repeatedly was that prices controlled artificially might simply conceal the presence of strong inflationary forces, which would have to be dealt with sooner or later unless steps were taken to reduce them in time. Here are some of his reflections on this problem:

> It is a fallacy, I submit, to teach the people to believe that if prices are forbidden to rise, inflation has been prevented. It is much more important to understand that frozen prices cannot prevent inflation. . . . The true policy, I submit, must put its primary emphasis not on the control of prices but on the control of supplies—the supply of money and the supply of goods and services. It is necessary to control the supply of money in order to keep money from depreciating: when there is too much of anything in relation to other things, that thing must fall in value. The supply of money can be controlled by taxes, by contracting credit, by voluntary and by compulsory saving. (HT 4/14/42)

> Where we do not have to regiment for war we ought, I believe, as a matter of deliberate policy to put a premium on private enterprise in the belief that it can solve many problems which the government is too busy to think about. For that reason we ought in our laws to favor enterprises which develop substitutes out of materials that are not pre-empted for war. We ought to revise the labor laws to promote these enterprises. And we ought to think carefully about price ceilings in this field so as to be sure that in the rush to freeze everything we do not freeze out the incentive for invention and ingenuity and initiative. (HT 4/21/42)

Over the course of his commentary on price control Lippmann had to return repeatedly to explain that the problem could not be dealt with by a simple universal price freeze. This would make matters worse, not better. "The fallacy of the universal freeze becomes quickly apparent when we realize that it is a proposal to operate the most complex capitalistic economy in the world by removing the central mechanism of prices, which regulates production and consumption" (HT 5/6/43). He speculated that a reason

why the universal freeze was so popular was that it seemed a plausible alternative to a painful range of new taxes, which were necessary to constrain the inflationary pressures (HT 12/16/43). When in 1942 the United
States did adopt a policy something like a universal freeze he was very
critical. "As a matter of fact, the American experiment in universal price-
freezing has been from the start an economic absurdity, and in practice a
most curious deception" (HT 5/27/43). He called the amount of aggregate
demand in excess of total production of goods and services at current
prices "dangerous money" in that it could lead to inflationary pressures.
He estimated this amount in 1944 to be 10 percent of current production.
"That is still an enormous amount of dangerous money. It is an inflationary deficit nearly seven times as large as the net deficit of the government in
the year before Pearl Harbor" (HT 19/7/43). At a minimum this circumstance should be explained openly and clearly to the people by the secretary of the treasury.

One point of macroeconomic policy that Lippmann found it hard for the
American people to grasp and to which he returned often with an explanation was why under tight price controls it was necessary occasionally to provide subsidies to some firms in an industry but not to others. This practice
was often denounced as unfair. His answer was that in order to attract a relatively high-cost marginal producer into production it was necessary to create
a profit through a subsidy. This was a preferable method to breaking the
price control and increasing the profits of all producers through an increase
in product price. He wrote: "It may not be unuseful in clarifying the real issue to treat the matter as an elementary problem in economic science." Then,
after giving a simple numerical example, he concluded that "the example
demonstrates how by paying $1 in subsidy the community makes a net sav-
ing of $2 which it would otherwise have to spend" (HT 11/23/43). He did
point out that while consumers may benefit from this method of controlling
prices, producers lose by receiving less than what they would receive under
free market prices. He did concede that the subsidy as a feature of price control should be used sparingly. "To justify any subsidy the proponent must
always show a clear, overriding public reason for departing from the basic
principle of our economy, which is that goods should be bought and sold at
the prices which are set in a free and honest market" (HT 12/4/43).

Lippmann commented often on price control because he thought his readers were inclined to think it was simply a matter of passing a law. He returned often as well to the question of how to mount an effective defense effort because he feared his readers thought it was just a question of the size of an appropriation. He emphasized repeatedly that the human element in a first-rate defense was absolutely critical and could not be affected simply by expenditure of funds. In particular he was concerned that imaginative leadership was sadly lacking in the highest ranks of the military and the federal bureaucracy, and the cure involved more than simply additional funds. This was especially serious in those agencies responsible for the transport of goods to the war zones, an aspect of the defense effort so critical that it might determine the outcome of the war. "I am afraid that a new spirit of invention and enterprise needs to be infused into the agencies which now deal in transportation. They are administered we need not doubt by able conscientious and experienced shipbuilders and shipping men. But what is lacking is a full awareness that there is a radical difference between shipping in war and shipping in peace, between the economics of war and the economics of peace. The effect is to stifle invention and to delay the adoption of drastically new measures. Yet these are indispensable if we are to break victoriously out of the blockade which our enemies are imposing upon us" (HT 4/2/42). Rather than attempting to change the habits of senior staff associated with transportation, he favored "recruiting civilians and militarizing them" (HT 8/4/42). The problem was not confined to transportation; it was visible also in the selection and development of weapons systems. "Certainly it takes judgment, as well as vision and audacity, to prepare today the right weapons for tomorrow. But that is just what it takes to win the war: sound judgment in men who have bold hearts and seeing minds. If men of that sort do not come to the top, if they are not pulled to the top by our leaders and pushed to the top by the people, we shall never get the initiative in this war. We shall always be surprised by the Japanese Zero planes and Rommel's anti-tank equipment" (HT 8/6/42).

The problem was partly that creative thinking and entrepreneurship were traditionally not rewarded in the public sector and so tended to migrate to the private sector. Now, somehow, the direction of that flow had to be reversed. It was also that systems were not in place in government to re-ward creative achievement and to remove appointees when they were no longer making contributions. "It has high symptomatic value that first-rate men are not in charge. For those who are genuinely in the know there are much surer tests. Perhaps the chief reason why they are not applied sternly is that we have gotten along quite well in this country without having to in-sist upon the very highest standards of excellence in the public service. Honesty, a fair amount of industry, some public spirit have seemed good enough; we have pursued excellence elsewhere where the rewards were greater than in public life" (HT 6/25/42). Ways must be found to accelerate the generational turnover. "The vigor of the whole war effort will depend in very large degree upon how rapidly and how generously the older men learn to select and promote and season, and, finally, to give way to, the men who, because they are younger, have greater reserves of energy" (HT 12/20/41). A similar view has been expressed recently by the historian Thomas Ricks (Ricks 2013). The tragedy of poor leadership from government was that the American private sector was poised to make extraordinary contributions if pointed in the right direction and freed from unnecessary constraints. A housecleaning of incompetent bureaucrats and the appointment of distin-guished successors would do more to advance the war effort than most pro-grams that could be undertaken with new appropriations. "The President is a poor judge of human nature, and he is disregarding the wisdom of po-litical experience, if he will not see how much it would energize, and indeed electrify, his whole administration if he removed some of the place holders and then promoted younger men who are serving the country so well" (HT 7/1/43).

Finally, he was deeply critical of the educational system that was train-ing and preparing leaders for defense. He thought that the common sense necessary for successful performance in government and the military was lacking too often, and too much weight was given to various forms of tech-nical training. "In critical moments of decision the men whose judgment has been proved to be correct have been, so I have learned, those men who discounted the opinions and theories and ideologies of the moment, relying upon a knowledge of history and the logic of human behavior" (HT 1/2/40).

It was necessary to appoint and elect to leadership positions people who were accustomed to achieving goals, not the conventional American politician forever fighting and refusing to compromise. "The men who count in Washington and who will, if they prevail, save the day are not business men, labor leaders, New Dealers, or officials as such, but men who realize that the old habits which produced the old quarrels must be overcome. They are not helped by the partisan advocates, who as professed friends of labor or of social progress, or as professed friends of the business community, accentuate every difference, intensify every grievance, sharpen every controversy, embitter every suspicion between business men, treated as a bloc, and officials treated as a bloc" (HT 7/5/41). Thinking in the public sector was typically sclerotic and defended by the observation that this was always the way it had been done. But war was different and required some things to be done that had never been tried before, and done quickly. "To make the thing clear to ourselves, let us consider the planning of a program for the production of apple pies. You make an estimate that you need thirty apple pies. If you ask the cook to bake one pie a day for thirty days you will have produced thirty pies. That is one way to get a lot of pies. But there is another way, and that is to hire thirty cooks to bake thirty pies in one day" (HT 8/28/41). It was necessary to find leaders who had the mental flexibility to consider the thirty-cook option and the skill to place the option effectively before their followers.

Apart from early retirement for senior people, Lippmann did not have many specific recommendations to improve the quality of the leaders of the defense establishment. He did urge that training of the officer corps be conducted in colleges and universities so that a broad liberal education might be a component of their training (HT 1/24/42), and he insisted that the widest range of candidates be considered so as to reach the largest talent pool rather than a narrow slice of society reflective of social class. "It is, therefore, urgently necessary to democratize the training for officers and specialists at once so that when the draft reaches down to the younger men, there will be no favoritism and no grievances based on the dollar sign" (HT 7/28/42). He rejected what he took to be the emerging policy that "for the duration of the war a liberal college education can be offered only to women and the physically unfit men" (HT 2/18/43).

A third theme in Lippmann's steady commentary on the war economy was concerned with the need to keep citizens fully informed and involved in consideration of economic policy questions. Citizens must be prepared for constraints on their own economic liberties, but they must be engaged in the policy making that put these constraints in place. As the war was just getting started he discerned that the government was intent on managing the news. He found the whole idea that the public could and should be manipulated intolerable. "Indeed, it is fair to say that far from earning public confidence the elaborate and costly publicity offices are managing to get themselves disliked and distrusted. I venture to believe that the rapidly mounting irritation with the public relations experts is due to the fact that they operate on a theory which is inherently insincere, and as the temper of the people hardens because they face the issues of life and death, they find this insincerity more and more repellent" (HT 3/14/42). He condemned propaganda in the strongest terms: "A learned friend tells me that propaganda is that branch of the art of lying which nearly deceives your friends without deceiving your enemies" (HT 7/10/43).

One of the first problems with propaganda was that it seldom worked. "The net result of the whole procedure is the manipulation of public opinion by preventing an independent examination of the facts. This method of manipulation is wholly objectionable" (HT 7/10/43). He disliked censorship as much as propaganda, except in the most clear-cut cases of security need. When in doubt he favored open debate. "To combine adequate freedom of discussion with the necessary secrecy and dispatch is, in practice a matter requiring common sense, forbearance and confidence by all concerned" (HT 4/15/43). He was willing to forgo free markets, civil liberties, and security of property for the duration, but he insisted on retaining openness in the decision making of government. He wrote in July 1942: "The longer the war lasts, and there is every prospect that this will be a very long war, the more important it will be to see to it that the press and the radio are able to keep the people informed upon matters like rationing, price and wage fixing, the draft, taxes, salvage, priorities and allocations which touch directly the lives of everyone. . . . There is no other way in which any one can hope to understand why one policy, rather than some other one, was decided upon" (HT 7/11/42).

Lippmann had at least four reasons for his objections to propaganda, secrecy, and censorship. One grew out of his experience during World War I with the propaganda machine of the military and his unhappy recognition of how easily public opinion could be manipulated at home and among the enemy. Propaganda was too powerful and too dangerous a tool to be placed casually in the hands of government bureaucrats. A second reason came from his observations of human nature in a democracy and the importance of morale. Secrecy and obfuscation, he observed, led to more selfishness, rejection of patriotic acts, and reluctance to engage in cooperative behavior. It was not the case that incentives could simply be manipulated to obtain the behavior that was most desired. Most humans in wartime insisted on being part of a team in which they would be told the truth. Hence, if a certain policy were recommended to the people that was inconsistent with their narrow self-interests but with all the implications spelled out and all the arguments for and against explored fairly, that policy was much more likely to be accepted and supported than if it were presented with distortions and sugarcoating. A third reason for opposing all secrecy in government was Lippmann's observation that politicians and bureaucrats had a tendency to become autocratic if not subject to the test of transparency. This presented an important role for Congress and the media in wartime, to discover the facts and test the policies imposed against these facts without fear or favor: "Government publicity however well done, has one incurable defect; it is essentially a handout. A free people will not give full faith and credit to information of this kind until it has been subjected to some sort of independent check. The Administration, testifying in its own behalf through its publicity services, cannot hope to have the testimony accepted confidently as true evidence unless that testimony has been tested by cross-examination" (HT 3/26/42).

An example of the need for candor in the coverage of the war that Lippmann often discussed related to the devastating loss of shipping in 1942. He was convinced that a fair presentation of the situation would have made the American people appreciate better the seriousness of the situation and the need for sacrifice. Instead, the government chose to present the circumstances "through rose-colored glasses," and as a result the people were lulled into a sense of ease and lassitude, whereas "the plight of the merchant fleet is so serious that we cannot rest content until we set out to deal with it in a spirit like that of Dunkerque, where anything that floated was put to work" (HT 5/19/42). Similarly, if the people knew the real purpose of the tax system, which was to discourage their expenditures, they would be more likely to accept it readily. "Suppose then the Administration said to the people: the immediate object of our taxes is during the war to make you feel poor rather than extravagant. But the larger object of the taxes is to establish a tax structure which will support after the war the normal expenses of the government and the service of our huge national debt. If the tax structure is properly designed, we shall neutralize the national debt—which would otherwise be unmanageable—because in effect the taxpayer will pay himself the interest on his bonds with the income from his bonds" (HT 6/20/42).

This led Lippmann to the fourth reason for openness, that there were never enough bright minds to solve strategic problems. If the facts were widely known, unexpected solutions might come from unexpected directions. He went back again to his experience in World War I. "It was a group of younger officers who solved the submarine problem in 1918 and, while we wait for the delivery of enough orthodox combat ships to master the submarines, it would be reassuring if something of the same sort were at least being attempted" (HT 5/19/42).

World War II presented exceptional challenges for Lippmann, especially as his energies throughout the years just before the war had been directed mainly to devising a system in which peace and human liberty were the ultimate desiderata. But he turned on a dime and addressed quickly the problems of a planned and controlled economy, which he became convinced was needed in the short run to achieve the paramount objective of the moment: military victory.

10

Peace

A S   H E   L O O K E D   F O R W A R D   to peace on the home front even before war
had ended overseas, Lippmann brought together in his columns many of
his recommendations for peacetime made over the years about how to achieve
a good economy, together with some new ones. He emphasized at the outset
that his abiding objective was to make possible for his fellow Americans a
life based on reason, and now the objective should be to spread this tradition of the West throughout the world, a sort of newfound Manifest Destiny
for America based on ideas. He wrote in 1945: "Our power and influence
will endure only if we measure them truly and use them for the ends that we
have always avowed and can proclaim with pride. We are the latest great
power developed by and committed to the tradition of the west. We are
among the bearers of this tradition and we are numbered now among the
proudest defenders. That is the polestar by which we must set our course.
At the center of that tradition resides the conviction that man's dignity rises
from his ability to reason and thus to choose freely the good in preference to
evil. We may claim without offense that this inner principle of the western
tradition is not local, tribal, or national, but universal, and, and in so far as
we are its faithful servants, we shall, in learning how to use our power, win
the consent of mankind" (HT 9/11/45). It is striking how many of

Lippmann's proposals from this time ultimately were implemented, not primarily because of his intervention, of course, but perhaps in part.

Planning for a Postwar World

Despite the continuing objections of many of his academic and business friends, he reaffirmed his regard for a kind of economic planning, not socialist planning or the "helter-skelter" kind of the New Deal, but careful and restrained planning at both the micro and macro levels in anticipation of difficulties ahead; his ultimate objective was absolutely not the creation of a planned economy in the traditional sense, or even indicative planning, but rather a strengthening and implementation of a "compensated" free market system. After nearly a decade and a half of ruminating and writing he remained essentially a limited and cautious progressive with a strong Keynesian faith.

In February 1943, he suggested to the journalist and historian Herbert Agar that "in post war policy the order of business should be as follows: First, a convincing program of domestic demobilization covering soldiers, war workers, farmers, government officials and business men. Second, reciprocal engagements with our principal allies in the field of military security, covering such matters as trans-oceanic air and sea bases. Third, relief under Lend-Lease closely related to military necessity so that the principle of Lend-Lease remains military. Fourth, a separate authorization and a separate fund, though the administrative mechanism of Lend-Lease might be used, for rehabilitation and international public investment" (WL to Agar, February 10, 1943, WLPIII F18).

For a start, Lippmann said, there must be careful planning for demobilization. He wrote in August 1944:

> If the demobilization of the forces, the reconversion of domestic production, the liquidation of the world-wide war economy, and its reconstruction, are not planned, agreed upon at home and abroad, and firmly regulated at home and abroad, there will be a chaotic and destructive stampede of private individuals and corporations. Those of us who

believe that the world is not likely to be free, prosperous, or long at peace unless there is established a very large amount of free enterprise by individuals, —those of us who believe that—must not delude ourselves at this time. We must not imagine, as so many do, that by dismantling the "bureaus," and de-controlling the economy, a workable system of free enterprise will automatically result. What will automatically result is a scramble for jobs and sales, a feverish boom and a devastating collapse. (HT 8/5/44)

Beyond the planned conversion from war to peace there was a longer-term vision he set in place that had both macro and micro dimensions. "Our return this time to the traditionally American system of free enterprise will be judged by the results. The free economy must stabilize the business cycle and maintain reasonably stable steady and full employment, without gross poverty and gross speculative riches. It must provide reasonably stable markets and acceptable prices for farmers and the producers of raw materials. It must keep open opportunity against monopoly and special privilege. It must satisfy the social conscience and the sense of justice among the people. And it must, though it is not under the control of the government, act voluntarily and wisely in the public interests" (HT 2/24/44).

Lippmann claimed that the most important changes in public policy in the postwar world grew from the theoretical discoveries of John Maynard Keynes, equal in importance to the discovery of the operation of competitive markets by David Hume and Adam Smith in the eighteenth century. "Yet when we look back we can see that the world we were born into was profoundly affected by the discovery in the eighteenth century of the principle of the international division of labor. From the very earliest times there has been international trading. Nevertheless, the wide application of this principle as a means of increasing the wealth of nations rested on a new discovery which men like David Hume and Adam Smith were able to define and to explain. In our epoch the principle of the division of labor has been modified and supplemented by the discovery that large nations with big resources, skilled labor and progressive management can, if they insist on it, regulate the cycles of booms and depressions. Since the discovery has been made the public will no more tolerate a failure to apply it than they would tolerate hospitals which refused to use sulfa drugs and penicillin" (HT 5/20/44). Lippmann was happy to report that Keynesian doctrine was now widely accepted by professional economists and governmental leaders. "For some years before the war, in fact since 1936 when J. M. Keynes published his book 'The General Theory of Employment, Interest and Money,' the basic theory has been known. It has won wide acceptance among economists. But only gradually is it being understood and accepted by laymen, and only now at the beginning of the post-war period has it become possible and necessary to apply the new knowledge. The President's message, supplemented by the fifth report of the Director of War Mobilization and Reconversion, is based upon the findings of the new economic science of our generation" (HT 1/22/46). From this account, it can be seen that he thought it remained only for interpreters like Lippmann himself to bring the laymen on board.

A point made repeatedly by Lippmann as the war drew to a close was that with the return of peace it would no longer be an option, as some leaders took it to be in the 1930s, for government to leave the maintenance of full employment to the market. Two conditions had changed forever. Now economists knew how to restore employment, and voters had become too sophisticated to accept that long-term unemployment was inevitable. "There is not much dispute as to what is the paramount question on the home front. It is how to achieve and then maintain full employment for all who are able and willing to work. A public man fitted for the post-war world might almost be defined as one who knows that full employment is in time of peace what the national defense is in time of war: an obligation which must be met, and no excuses or explanations for failure accepted" (HT 9/7/44). The market collapse in 1929 was the result of irresponsible behavior by government and the financial sector in the 1920s. The suffering of the 1930s had made it clear that unemployment on that scale must never happen again. The achievements of the 1940s, despite the war, had shown how remarkable could be the performance of the economy if only restrictions were kept to appropriate levels and aggregate demand was well managed.

Throughout this period of peace the United States had at all times a greater capacity to produce food, raw materials and manufactures than it knew what to do with. The country was baffled, and men suffered, not because there was famine and scarcity but because there were unsalable and unusable surpluses of all the elements of economic well-being.

This paradox of poverty in the midst of plenty has become, in the literal sense of the word, intolerable to the modern democratic conscience—all the more so because we have been able to achieve in two world wars that full employment which we could not achieve in peace. This war, moreover, has shown that the American capacity to produce is beyond any previous estimate of any responsible economist or industrialist. The industrial miracle of war time is, therefore, the promise of a great rise in the well-being of the nation. But it is also a threat that if we do not conduct our economy better than we did in the '20s and '30s, the unemployment, the economic surpluses and the discontent will be greater. (HT 9/7/44)

Lippmann never lost his faith in the capacity of deficit finance to maintain full employment. He complained to Charles Collingwood during a television interview in 1963 that at that time "perhaps thirty to thirty-five billion dollars" in national product were being lost annually because of a mistaken insistence on balanced budgets. "Deficits are bad if they're permanent, but deficits over a business cycle of four or five years, and deficits in the time when the cycle is down, are good; and a lot of what is called spending and deficit is actually called by private business, investment" (WL 1965, 144–145).

The one dark macroeconomic cloud that Lippmann could see after the war was Alvin Hansen's specter of secular stagnation. The aggregate demand each year to fight the war he calculated to be roughly $40 billion. Could the peacetime economy generate such a level of demand for other purposes? "For if we do not find a civilian substitute for about half our present military expenditures, then it does not seem possible for us to have full employment. How much of that necessary $40,000,000,000 can free enterprise use, not once, but annually—assuming ideal conditions, a friendly administration, a revised tax system, and the like? And what is to be done about the portion which free enterprise cannot invest and cannot spend?" (HT 9/7/44). "If private expenditure for consumption and private capital investment cannot provide sufficient jobs, then government expenditure and public investment must make up the difference" (HT 9/23/44). In the event, Lippmann need not have worried about the capacity of the American economy over the long run to generate sufficient aggregate demand, at least in his lifetime.

Moderate as he was in conjuring up visions, Lippmann urged the proponents of the Murray Full Employment bill, which was before Congress in 1945 (soon to become the Employment Act of 1946), to be cautious about treating employment as a "right." Such a commitment was too strong. This act, he believed, would become "the most important domestic measure of the post-war period" and should not "raise expectations which the bill itself is not designed to satisfy" (HT 9/18/45). Full employment must remain an "objective," not a "right." "The true intent of the Murray bill is to see to it that in the nation as a whole, not necessarily in each community nor in each kind of employment, the conditions are such that the demand for goods and services will be sufficient to prevent any prolonged involuntary mass unemployment" (HT 9/18/45). He did worry, however, that even this loose commitment to full employment might prove unacceptable to those with property, who saw some amount of unemployment as a necessary discipline for the working class. "The underlying fact is—to put it bluntly—that in reaction against the consequences of excess employment there is a patent desire in the great middle mass of the people for enough unemployment to re-establish their lost bargaining position and to restore industrial discipline" (HT 11/8/45).

Perhaps because of his experience as an aide to President Wilson in 1918, even before the outbreak of World War II Lippmann was warning that the likely outcome of a new conflict must be kept clearly in mind before hostilities began. When the war started he was more insistent still. It was never simply a matter of winning a war; the long-term goal must be to create a world that would be stable, prosperous, and peaceful. Before mobilization was complete, a vision of demobilization must be in place. This held for both domestic and foreign policy. At home "the same basic principle—that the peace is shaped during the war—holds no less strongly in regard to the post-war economy" (HT 1/22/42). Abroad, for Lippmann, the memories still burned bright of the mistakes made during and after World War I. "The United States and Great Britain, though they fought together, had not bound themselves to remain together. The seeds of that fatal rivalry which was later to cause us to disarm one another, of the destructive competition which arose out of war debts and tariffs, were planted during the war" (HT 1/22/42).

As early as 1942 Lippmann announced that in the "great adventure" of the world after the war two changes from the decade of the 1930s would be significant. First, the United States would inevitably have to take responsibility for the welfare of the rest of the world in a way that it had never dreamt of doing before. If the nation needed to identify self-interest in this role it could reflect on the reduction of immigration pressures, and emigration possibilities that would ensue. "Many of the Americans who are now moving into all parts of the world will find a satisfying life's work in the development of the vast undeveloped regions of the globe. They will open up new frontiers as their forefathers did. Many of those who have found asylum here since Europe became a prison will go back to their homes, or to the new lands which will be calling for enterprising men with special knowledge. Only if we allow the world to sink into a morass of misery will America be faced with the dilemma of granting asylum or of condemning human beings to incalculable suffering. If, on the other hand, we use the power which victory will give us to make the world safe for the humble and open for the enterprising, we can without uncharity maintain the immigration laws, and we shall find that a strong tendency to emigration will in fact set in" (HT 11/26/42). He had high hopes that the proposed United Nations would take the lead in facilitating decolonization and global development beyond Europe (HT 3/26/45).

He insisted also that the extensive foreign aid that would be required after the war, especially for Europe, be seen not as charity but as squarely within the national interest: "What we are called upon to do will be done best if we do not think of the operation as an outpouring of relief. The much truer description of it is to say that we are asked to make available some working capital in order that these people may in a relatively short time be self-supporting once more. Relief in the sense of charity to the destitute is necessary but it is not the preponderant part of the business: the preponderant part of it is to supply them with enough working capital—food, seeds, tools, transport, drugs—to enable the Continent to get started again" (HT 11/9/43). With unpleasant memories always in mind of what he considered the mistakes made at Versailles, Lippmann urged that the same mistakes not be made again: "punishment and reparation are no longer the paramount objectives but are becoming subordinate means for promoting the economic reconstruction of Europe" (HT 3/24/45). Germany must be rebuilt as a strong and democratic member of the Western community. "Almost certainly, it seems to me, we shall find that the German economy is a ruin. We shall therefore find that the main question of allied policy is going to be not whether we should ruin it still more or should not ruin it, but how we should permit and even assist a radical reorganization and reconstruction of the elements and character of the German economy" (HT 9/26/44).

With American ingenuity at work Lippmann was highly optimistic about the potential for limitless global development. "Our greater end is to prime the pump which will, so to speak, cause the desert to bloom—to make the initial investments in the form of materials, and technical knowledge and promotion, which will start the undeveloped regions of the world on a great development" (HT 11/26/42). Every effort must be made to conquer the "fear that one man's or one country's gain is another man's or another country's loss," which "is undoubtedly the greatest obstacle to human progress. . . . It is upon this prejudice that civilization has foundered again and again" (HT 11/26/42). A vibrant world economy would, in fact, be the surest guarantee America could have of continuing peace and prosperity. America must help to maintain full employment abroad as well as at home. This was a point where domestic and foreign policy came together in what he called "the principle of prosperity" emerging from macroeconomic theory:

> This discovery is much the most important advance in human knowledge in modern times. It is the discovery that government can by the

proper use of public funds create a condition of full employment for all its
people. Heaven help the administration which refuses to apply this
knowledge in the post-war world. For the war has demonstrated conclusively that unemployment is now an unnecessary and therefore an intolerable evil. The prime lesson of the war in domestic affairs will be that by
the proper use of a small fraction of the funds now devoted to engines of
destruction, the country can become productive beyond anything ever
imagined, and on that productiveness it can maintain a high and rising
level of prosperity. In the freedom from want men find freedom from fear.
And when they cease to fear, they begin to realize their powers and to
believe, as men should when they are worth their salt, that they are only
at the beginning and that they are not at the end of the great human adventure. (HT 11/26/42)

Lippmann believed that the remarkable economic performance of the
American economy during the war, when he understood growth rates approached 6 percent, would make economists rethink their positions on
many issues of foreign and domestic economic policy. "We shall find that in
the presence of this demonstration of American productivity, the change of
scale, the new order of the magnitude of things will compel us to re-examine
all our common assumptions on such matters as taxes, the national debt,
tariffs, international commerce, finance, imports, exports and investments"
(HT 1/14/43).

Lippmann became increasingly certain that it was essential for the
nations of the world to rethink their relationships with each other and to
replace old structures, like the colonial empires, that were no longer relevant.
Even before the war began he expressed confidence that some new forms of
political union would emerge that would bring economic benefits and
would be the foundation for future civilization. Creation of a united states
of Europe must be the first priority. He wrote in 1940: "In the absence of
civilized authority, such as existed in the nineteenth century, the peoples of
Europe and elsewhere have been sinking through barbarism into a dark age
of unstable tyranny and endless indecisive violence. If this is correct, then
the great question of the war is whether there will be established a new and
durable center of civilized union and authority, capable of repulsing attack,

large enough and strong enough to exhaust the aggressors, and able in the
end to admit and absorb into its unity the civilized people of the Western
World" (HT 2/27/40). This statement had still the ring of his earlier concern for the Occidental world in tension with the Orient. But he emphasized now that his concern was not for any narrow geographic entity, and
Americans must not treat this next war as another one that would "make
the Western Hemisphere safe for isolationism" (HT 5/2/40). He had high
hopes for the benefits of global free trade and economic integration. The
lesson of the interwar years should be that the special interests, no matter
how well meant, must be kept away from foreign policy making. "Are we
not ever going to learn as a nation what we know as individuals that economic transactions are two-way affairs, and that for every sale there must be
a purchase, for every purchase there must be a sale? Yet if we let the blocs
and the lobbyists frame our tariffs, let Admiral [Emory Scott] Land [chair-
man of the U.S. Maritime Commission, 1937–1946, and administrator of the
War Shipping Administration, 1942–1945] fix our shipping policy, Mr.
[William M.] Jeffers [the 'rubber czar'] our rubber policy, the airlines our
aviation policy, they will, as a combination, though each is full of the best
intentions and the highest principles, lead us straight to a catastrophe as
great or greater than that which robbed us of the fruits of our victory in
1918" (HT 8/26/43).

Lippmann was an enthusiastic supporter of most of the wartime planning for new international organizations. He endorsed the idea of an international monetary fund to make possible fixed exchange rates that could be
adjusted from time to time. He had favored something like this as early as
the mid-1930s. "Bretton Woods recognized that stabilization loans touch
the sensitive nerve of modern nations—their social policy, their employment policy, their wage and price levels which, second only to political independence, are now regarded in all popular governments as the very essence of their sovereign control of their own affairs" (HT 3/17/45). He
denounced Senator Robert Taft and the other isolationists for opposing the
Bretton Woods proposals: "a temperate and open-minded, and in spirit scientific, approach will be all the easier if we clear our minds of the notion
that the conference is discussing a raid on the United States Treasury, and

that we must rush frantically to stop it. Senator Taft, whose record in under-standing what is going to happen is not distinguished, has just rung the burglar alarm" (HT 7/13/44). He was complimentary about all of the rec-ommendations that came out of Bretton Woods: "in so far as Bretton Woods evolves any kind of institution, be it a monetary fund, a bank for reconstruc-tion and development, or both, which enables Americans to participate in the management of the international economy, we may count it a construc-tive achievement" (HT 7/6/44). His main objection was that not enough ef-fort had been devoted to informing the public and energizing public opin-ion. "It has been impossible for the general public to obtain any idea of what the Bretton Woods conference is about. Though it is concerned with ques-tions which will affect men's lives deeply, the language of monetary policy is understood by very few men in any country. It is a little as if a conference to examine arrangements for buying and selling goods across frontiers, for re-lating international trade to domestic employment and social welfare, were to conduct its proceedings in the Sanskrit language. . . . Moreover, how-ever wise it may have been to let the experts come together and think with-out distraction in so pleasant and remote a place as Bretton Woods, the dis-advantage has been that they have been isolated in an ivory tower from the men who have to understand their work if they are to explain it" (HT 7/13/44 and see also 5/28/45 and 6/12/45). He was not pleased with the criticism of Bretton Woods from the Harvard economist John Williams, whom he took to be too close to the commercial bankers (HT 3/17/45).

Suggestions for Reform

Lippmann never wavered in his belief that education and improved under-standing at all levels would be the answer to most economic problems of production and distribution in the future. For the leaders of society in in-dustry, finance, government, and the military, he remained a committed advocate of a broad liberal education rooted in the humanities, the social sciences, and the arts, more than in technical training of the kind that was gaining popularity during the war for applied areas such as business ad-ministration and engineering. He wanted an education that would nurture the imagination, judgment, and creativity of leaders rather than one dependent on rote learning. He insisted that technical skills remain "on tap" through advisers, rather than "on top," as the alternatives were sometimes posed at the time. He complained to the industrialist Henry Dennison that "[o]ne of the things that people in England understand so much better than people over here is just this question of the power of an adviser and what's required to exercise it" (WL to Dennison, May 21, 1935, WLPIII F605).

In recognition of events that had dominated the first half of the twentieth century he called for more study of international affairs and warfare. "It is a study which has been very much neglected in our universities, and there will be some, perhaps many, to say that as a matter of moral principle, since war is evil, the study of the military art ought to continue to be ignored. But they are mistaken" (HT 10/30/43). He complained that the social sciences, in particular, misallocated their efforts among policy concerns because they found some subjects distasteful. He wrote to the assistant director of the Budget Bureau of "the bad influence of American social science in the present generation, which has produced men entirely uneducated in the military-diplomatic realities" (WL to Donald Stone, October 19, 1943, WLPIII F2011). He told his readers: "We may hope, then, that the universities will recognize that military history is history that they dare not neglect, and that research in the history of war is at least as important as research in the theory of taxation, currency, corporate enterprise, labor relations and the social services. For war, when it comes, quickly dominates all the other interests of a democracy; how, then, can a democracy be said to be fit for self-government if it is not versed in the history, the problems and the issues on which its very survival may depend?" (HT 10/30/43). He was joined in his enthusiasm for the study of history as background to the social sciences by the distinguished lawyer Charles Warren, who went on to endow the Charles Warren Center for Studies in American History at Harvard University (Warren to WL, October 7, 1940, WLPIII F2191).

Returning to the theme of his first book, Lippmann insisted that as important as education of the elite was for successful policy making, "preparing the minds" of the citizens at large for the challenges of the postwar world was equally essential. For "if we do not teach ourselves the hard lessons of the economic realities today, events will teach the lesson to us in a still more forceful way" (HT 8/5/44). He envisioned a host of problems connected especially with the first few years of reconversion to peace, and if the best solutions to these problems were to be discovered and accepted it was necessary for there to be widespread and well-informed discussion among the people. "The answer to all this is not to stop talking and thinking about the problems of peace but to agree promptly on a strong and convincing program for meeting the problems of peace. The trouble is not the talk but the lack of an adequate program to deal with the questions men and women are bound to talk about" (HT 8/5/44). Lippmann thought education in macroeconomic theory especially difficult to accomplish, in part because so much of it was counterintuitive, but it was highly important. The public had to support policies required for full employment if they were to succeed: "high-level employment is a novel and complex undertaking which can be carried forward successfully only by leadership and persuasion, not by compulsion and command" (HT 1/30/45). He was optimistic, all the same, that such public education could be undertaken successfully.

> The maintenance of a stable economy at a high level of productivity is a new undertaking in the experience of human society. Much but not everything is known about the theory of this undertaking: something but by no means enough about the application of these principles. No one can doubt that the task must be undertaken: people who have seen that there can be overemployment in time of war will not tolerate underemployment in time of peace. But no one can suppose that all the necessary knowledge exists, or that the men who would know how to apply it have been developed: the effort which must be made entails, therefore, a long time of trial and error.
>
> We cannot hope to pass through it successfully unless we can draw upon large reserves of confidence and of patience and of openmindedness. And just as the progress of preventive medicine requires a population which has learned to understand hygiene, so the progress of this idea will require a great rise in the general level of economic thought. (HT 1/27/45)

Politicians and bureaucrats needed economic education as much as the rest of the population, and Lippmann pressed for new centers of analysis and data collection in government and the private sector. He was pleased with the work of the National Resources Planning Board and of the Council of Economic Advisers created under the Employment Act of 1946, and he reviewed favorably the Council's first annual report (HT 12/26/46). He called for a new public institution, which sounded rather like an internationally oriented Congressional Budget Office, to study and report on international economic issues and to keep the public well informed while avoiding controversy as much as possible. "It would be most useful, it seems to me, if we could set up now a public institution which had the duty of reporting regularly upon our international accounts, and the right to be consulted before the Administration or Congress adopted any important measure affecting these accounts. It ought not, I think, to pass judgment on any policy, to propose policy or to veto it. It ought only to keep the score. Then we could begin to know what we are doing when we decide for or against this or that policy or project. In effect, this would establish a bureau of the budget of international payments. . . . In any event, it should have independence and a reputation for disinterestedness. It should not legislate. It should not administer. It should not judge. Its authority should be only the moral and intellectual authority it can earn for itself by keeping the whole government and the people enlightened" (HT 3/2/44). He had always made it clear that a well-informed opposition was as important as a well-informed government.

He was convinced that "no one can be trusted very far with power, and that the only way to meet the abuses is to have powerful criticism and a real alternative" (WL to William Allen White, April 7, 1936, WLPIII F2226). He was glad to see the creation of organs like the Office of Strategic Services (later to become the Central Intelligence Agency), which could make sense of international data, recognizing that competent analysts would have to be trained. "The main trouble has been in the interpretation and judgment of the information, in being able to read or as we say in newspapers to edit correctly the information brought in by the reporters. . . . We have to recognize that men prepared for these highest judgments are not to be found easily in a nation which has so long discouraged military education and the study of the art of war, which has so long enjoyed immunity from the need to have a foreign policy" (HT 12/26/44). The Department of Commerce also should strengthen its analytical capacity. "What the Department of Commerce can do is to provide the government and the nation with economic intelligence about the condition of the national and international economy: it can inform, it can warn, it can do research, it can consult, it can propose" (HT 1/25/45). The secretary of commerce might himself mobilize "the best economic intelligence of the country, to exercise a formative influence upon all who exercise power in this field" (HT 1/27/45).

One of Lippmann's continuing concerns about the formation and implementation of economic public policy was the poor quality of those who were attracted to the public sector as politicians and bureaucrats. There were those who criticized Roosevelt for creating a Brain Trust and encouraging creative thinking in government. Lippmann was not among them. His complaint was that members of this Brain Trust did not have enough brains. He found that the Harding and Coolidge administrations had brought into government businessmen who were concerned mainly with their own personal interests. Roosevelt, by contrast, had attracted people who were earnest but feckless, like Rexford Tugwell, or simply not up to their jobs, like Frances Perkins, secretary of labor, and Henry Morgenthau, secretary of the treasury. In criticism of these people in his columns he clearly called a spade a spade. For example he wrote that under Morgenthau "his Treasury experts are not fiscal statesmen, but men of very small caliber trying to score debating points. . . . The Secretary of the Treasury should be more than a good chief clerk of the Treasury Department. He should himself be the master of the problems of war finance, capable of leading opinion and shaping policy and directing his subordinates. Now the fact that the President does not have a Secretary of the Treasury upon whose judgment he can lean has meant that Mr. Roosevelt's fiscal policies have been no more than a collection of unconsidered, casual and often contradictory statements based on memoranda supplied by small subordinates in the Treasury Department" (HT 2/26/44). During the war some distinguished leaders had come into government from the private sector, but still Roosevelt "has clung to his old pre-war appointees and henchmen. That is the sufficient explanation why, while the military war is so well conducted, the civilian part of the war is so unsatisfactory" (HT 2/26/44).

After Roosevelt died Lippmann was distressed that President Truman seemed to be following in the Roosevelt tradition. He wrote in 1946: "The White House is deplorably weak, and since Mr. Truman is a modest and unpretentious man who must feel his way without benefit of much inspiration through a maze of problems, he has little hope of being a successful President if his own immediate official family remains what it now is. The blunt truth is that the men nearest him do not have enough brains, and have practically none of the wisdom which comes from experience and education, to help him to be the President of the United States" (HT 1/5/46). But it need not be this way. The U.S. government had the capacity to attract persons who could master contemporary problems if it would, but apparently it would not. "The cult of mediocrity, which is a form of inverted snobbery, is not democracy. It is one of the diseases of democracy. For what democracy demands are equal rights for all men because they are men and, at the same time, equal opportunity—so that what is best and exceptional in each man may come forth and flourish. Faith in democracy is justified by this promise that it will release talents and gifts that would be suppressed in a society of caste, and therefore that it brings into the service of the nation and of mankind men who have rich and varied and excellent abilities" (HT 1/5/46).

A continuing subject of regret for Lippmann was that few leaders of the business community had been attracted to Washington, except for the interlude of the war, when they had performed so magnificently. From his extensive contacts in politics, academia, and elsewhere this was where he thought much exceptional leadership talent resided. Perhaps their relative exclusion from power could be explained by the suspicion of those who were "in trade," so common in Britain. He thought that because of their "inventive genius and managerial ability and working skill . . . that is why the working philosophy of the American business man is destined to play so decisive a part—for weal or for woe—not alone in his future but in that of this republic and of the world" (HT 12/10/42). It was unfortunate, he suggested, that after their bad experience with the New Deal and the demands made of them during the war, American businessmen might retreat from leadership. "I do think that the American business men today face essentially the same choice as did the British and French nobles in the eighteenth century. Will the American business men assume very heavy burdens in order to continue to lead our industrial society, or will they become so absorbed in complaining about their burdens that they will not be able to lead? This is a very real question. It is the answer to this question which will determine the future of American business men and, I believe, the very future of American industrial society under private management" (HT 12/10/42). He regretted that American businessmen had such weak links with the social sciences and philosophy. He wrote to one correspondent: "I agree with you about lack of philosophy among business men, and I might add also that they seem to have an extraordinary capacity for taking as expert advisers and publicity men those who have hardly a speaking acquaintance with the evolution of economic doctrine" (WL to F. Russell Bourne, March 21, 1945, WLPIII F261). He applauded organizations like the Bankers Committee, led by Guy Emerson of Bankers Trust, which worked with government on banking legislation (WL to Emerson, July 15, 1935, WLPIII F709), and the Committee for Economic Development, which attempted to involve leaders of the business community more closely in public affairs. He found that no one benefited if government and business were simply in confrontation.

While reconstruction of the European and world economies was the main challenge that Lippmann discerned in foreign policy, the one domestic problem for which he could not come up with a solution after twenty-five years of thinking about the issue was industrial relations. How, he wondered, could the rule of reason be extended to the distribution of income between capital and labor? He was immersed too much in the real world to think that perfect competition could ever be achieved in the labor market and that payments to factors of production could be determined by marginal productivity. But he was revolted by so much violence and confrontation of raw power in the establishment of wages and working conditions, with the consumer of the product and the larger society mainly neglected. He was particularly enraged by the behavior of some unions during the war, and he felt that the problems raised had to be confronted quickly in the peace. At the very least legislation had to be introduced to prohibit strikes like those that had occurred in coal and railroads. "They had the legal right to do all this. But they did not have the moral right to do it. Having done it, nevertheless, they have proved that the law under which they have acted is antiquated and must be revised. The right to strike in an essential public service can never again be defended as one of the essential rights of man. The time has come when this right must be qualified and regulated by a formal and solemn act of Congress" (HT 5/25/46). Lippmann left for others to solve the larger overall puzzle of how the rule of reason could be implemented in the labor market. But, overall, Lippmann kept to his lifelong progressive credo that it was always possible to make society and the economy better than what had gone before. "The system of free enterprise has never meant, except to those who ignorantly or for selfish reasons misunderstand it, a general license to private interests in the presence of a helpless national government. This view is not Republicanism but a kind of nihilism, which would have horrified Alexander Hamilton or Theodore Roosevelt. For a free economy is not a natural order of things which would flourish if government disappeared or were reduced to impotence. On the contrary, it is necessary to have strong government and firm laws and a continual and progressive program of public action to establish a free economy and make it work" (HT 11/16/46).

11

The Economy of the Postwar World

LIPPMANN'S COLUMNS during the first decade and a half of publication, 1931–1946, were driven by his strong sense that the free market system was failing, especially in the United States. This meant to him that liberal democracy also was in jeopardy. At the macroeconomic level, failure was evident in the high levels of unemployment and stagnation. A democratic nation would not tolerate this suffering for long. Already, he observed, authoritarian regimes promising a brighter future had come into power in Europe, and others were just over the horizon. At the microeconomic level, schemes for "planning" and market intervention were being proposed that in themselves threatened the very foundations of human liberty. These involved monopoly in both product and factor markets, government restrictions on prices and quantities, protection from foreign competition, and half-baked schemes like the National Recovery Administration that would cripple the salutary forces of competition and make markets little more than happy hunting grounds for unscrupulous rent seekers. At the end of the 1930s, when world war again loomed, there was the question also of whether a free market system could mobilize for defense as effectively as its totalitarian adversaries for attack.

Lippmann was surprised at the beginning of the 1930s, when he first immersed himself in economic issues, to discover that few in the economics profession, whether in government or without, had convincing answers to the questions that were raised by the Great Depression. Accordingly he engaged energetically with economists of all stripes in Europe and America to find answers for himself. He took little for granted in what they said, and he insisted on being convinced by reasoned argument and data. He read the literature of economics, went to meetings of economists, and engaged lively thinkers in conversation and correspondence. He learned with the economists over the decade, rather than simply from them. Overall he emerged impressed with what he found. He was attracted especially by the broad theoretical principles that were used to explain economic problems; fine points of theory and application did not hold his attention. By the end of the 1930s he was confident in the conclusions that he had reached. He was fully persuaded by Keynes that fluctuations in the aggregate demand for goods and services were endemic in a market economy and, if not corrected, caused periodic recessions and occasional depressions. However, by attending to the four components of aggregate demand—consumption, investment, public expenditure, and net exports—government could eliminate, or at least alleviate, the worst of these fluctuations. At the market level it seemed that assiduous pursuit and punishment of monopolies could reduce the depredations of rent seekers. He understood that precise formulation of specific policies to meet problems might not be easy, but he was confident in the inventiveness of economists to work out successful strategies.

Moving to a New Agenda

After World War II, Lippmann seldom engaged economists any more over theory or policy, and the economists did not seek him out, as they had in the 1930s, to serve as their mouthpiece to a wider public. In the postwar years Lippmann often quoted Paul Samuelson on economic matters, but when Samuelson finally called upon him it was not to discuss economics but so that he could "tell my grandchildren that I was personally acquainted with Walter Lippmann" (Samuelson to WL, March 10, 1961, WLPIII, F1881). Why this change in attitude? It was undoubtedly in part because Lippmann thought the great questions facing America were no longer economic but diplomatic, strategic, and military. On these subjects, he found,

American intellectuals were sadly ill informed, and the American people were most in need of his guidance there, rather than about the economy. He was distressed especially because American ignorance of foreign affairs had become greatest just at the time when heavy global responsibilities were thrust upon them by a collapsing world order. Americans had believed up until 1941 that they could remain insulated from unsavory world affairs by their two oceans and therefore they could safely look away. Now, when they discovered at Pearl Harbor that this belief was unfounded, they were ill equipped to cope with reality. He saw that his responsibility was to help fill this intellectual vacuum. He discovered, however, that to understand foreign affairs, unlike economic affairs, he had to go back to the primary material. There was not a community of scholars in this area upon whom he could depend and with whom he could interact productively as he had with the economists. To come up to speed in international affairs he read widely in history and in the relevant public documents and he immersed himself in the current affairs of foreign nations. He also spent a remarkable amount of time on the road. During his extended trips he met with politicians, businessmen, media moguls, church leaders, and intellectuals of all kinds. He often cabled back columns from abroad, and invariably when he returned home he would provide primers for his readers on the affairs of the countries he had visited. His style remained what it had always been: clear, concise, and candid; he did not hector or patronize his readers. He warmed quickly to the new topics, and he enjoyed the role of celebrated world traveler and authority on international affairs. His trips sometimes took on the character of royal progressions, the monarch commanding audiences with all those who interested him. Few declined his invitation. Famously, when Nikita Khrushchev asked to change the time of an interview because of an emergency outside Moscow, Lippmann replied that this was impossible. Khrushchev rearranged his schedule (Steel 1980, 463).

Other factors that help to explain Lippmann's shift away from economics during this time include the move within the discipline from a literary subject, comprehensible to outsiders, to a mathematical science. Lippmann's command of mathematics was very limited. Moreover, the number of publications in economics was increasing rapidly, and while in the 1930s he could contact a prominent authority, obtain a reading list, and get up to speed on almost any economic topic in a few days, this was no longer possible. He found as well that more economists skilled at addressing the wider public, and with whose conclusions he tended to agree, were now on the scene, such as Walter Heller and Paul Samuelson. His loss of self-confidence in economics after World War II may help to explain the narrower range of economists from whom he came to draw inspiration. Now there were few references to the Chicago school of economics, with whom he had been so comfortable before the war. He did not ignore the economy entirely during the postwar years, and in particular he returned regularly to subjects on which he had felt confident during the 1930s and where his views had not substantially changed. But there was less time for economic writing. In addition to trips abroad he also regularly took long summer and winter vacations, and there were periods of illness. In the 1950s he reduced his weekly commitments from three columns a week to two. The columns on economic issues were far fewer in number than before the war. During the 1930s they had sometimes reached one hundred per year. After the war they were seldom more than fifteen.

The new economic topic that attracted Lippmann most in the immediate postwar world was what would be called today the "political economy" of the changing world system. He concluded that he had to combat the "ostrich policy" of American isolationists, who thought that there was safety in ignoring what was happening in the rest of the world: the new institutions, practices, and international agreements that were being formed and were already playing a part in world affairs. He thought the yearning for isolation among human beings in the twentieth century was universal, and certainly not confined to the United States. But it was dangerous. The New Industrial Revolution had overwhelmed the sense of confidence of humans everywhere about technological change, "from the jet engine and computers to the synthetic fibers and the contraceptives, the almost indescribable multitude of products of nuclear, electronic, chemical, metallurgical, medical, and agricultural ingenuity" (WP 11/15/66). The result was that "[m]odern men are predominantly isolationists. They are preoccupied with the more immediate things which may help or hurt them. Their state of mind is marked by a vast indifference to big issues, and in this indifference there is a feeling that they are incompetent to do much about the big issues" (WP 11/15/66). But Americans, unlike those in more quiet locations, could not afford to give in to this state of mind and to neglect world affairs. There was too much to be done.

Reform of the Global Economic System: Out with the Old, In with the New

Because Lippmann assumed that the American people had not been paying attention, his columns after World War II that deal with global issues often read like "International Relations 101." He begins by explaining that as a result of the war the European empires were crumbling and causing much pain to all concerned. The United States was being pushed to pick up the pieces but must be extremely cautious in doing so (HT 2/13/47 and 2/25/47). Regrettably, most of the imperial nations were leaving the scene in disarray. Britain was an exception. He called Britain's decolonization its "second finest hour." Prime Minister Clement Atlee and Lord Louis Mountbatten, the last viceroy, had left India "with lucidity, reason, imagination, resolution, sincerity, and good will" (HT 6/7/47). Lippmann reminded his readers that, in addition to political control, empires involved monetary cooperation, tariff protection, and provision for internal and external security. Now the question had become: Could these services provided from the metropolis be replaced? He was especially troubled by the decline of the sterling area, and he wondered how its functions might be taken up by some new structure (HT 9/13/49). As the French Empire in Indochina and elsewhere began to break down with much less dignity than the British Empire he warned against the United States acquiring dependent states from this wreckage. He worried that if the U.S. government failed to address the decline of empires directly the country might end up assuming the costs of decolonization around the world (HT 11/13/56). As his column drew to a close in the dark days of the Vietnam War, Lippmann observed sadly that America seemed willing to acquire its own empire in Asia led on mistakenly by well-intentioned and charitable instincts akin to those that had motivated the

Marshall Plan and the domestic Great Society programs. The trouble with this generous approach was that Southeast Asia was not like Europe after the war, and individual countries in Asia were not like depressed regions of the United States: "It is naïve and dangerously silly to think we can treat Vietnam as if it were another Appalachia. . . . In Asia today we are filling the vacuum left by the fall of the British and French empires, and though we do not regard ourselves as imperialists, we are playing an imperial role. As long as this continues, the Vice President's [Hubert Humphrey's] notion of political reform and economic and social development in Asia is a pipe dream which is dangerous because it diverts our attention from the realities" (WP 4/28/66).

But if a new American empire would be a mistake, what was the alternative? A network of new multinational organizations of various kinds was his answer. When explaining the purposes of such organizations he trod carefully, remembering that he was addressing an American people that had rejected the League of Nations. The isolationists were still alive and well, represented now by Senator Robert Taft (HT 3/28/50). In forging a new world order Lippmann favored exploring all available models of international cooperation with friendly nations, and relationships of a different kind with "adversaries," a term he liked better than "enemies." He rejected what he took to be George Kennan's doctrine of intransigent confrontation with, and containment of, the Soviet Union (HT 10/11/48). In general he could see some constructive role for virtually all international organizations proposed after World War II, including the United Nations and the Organization for Economic Cooperation and Development, even if when created he found some of them to be flawed in various ways (HT 1/18/47, 6/14/55, 11/15/56, 3/9/61, 3/27/62, 4/5/62). He was especially troubled by the structure of the International Monetary Fund, which was supposed to replace the institutions of the old gold standard but seemed unable to establish stability in the international currency and financial markets.

A truth that was hard for American voters to grasp, Lippmann found, was that the United States should occasionally make gifts and grants to other countries. This seemed contrary to the American belief in prudence and self-reliance. The question of transnational charity had been addressed in the 1930s when Britain needed assistance with defense procurement, and the issue had been sidestepped through the opaque concept of "lend-lease," a notion that Lippmann had a part in conceiving. After the war Lippmann kept emphasizing that a peaceful world would cost money and sometimes it was cheaper to make gifts than to buy guns. He applauded General Marshall's speeches at Princeton in February 1947 and at Harvard in June of that year, making the case for short-term assistance to a prostrate Europe (HT 2/25/47, 3/1/47, and 5/10/47). He was a consistent supporter of the Marshall Plan that followed; this, he said, gave the United States critical influence in world affairs without the responsibility of governing other countries (HT 6/21/47 and 6/24/47). He emphasized that the European Recovery Program, as the Marshall Plan came to be known, was for recovery and not for relief or defense and would be self-liquidating (HT 6/28/47). Moreover, dollars granted to European nations would return as effective demand for U.S. goods and services, employment would be sustained, and long-term trading partnerships would be established. He did not wish to frighten Congress by selling the Marshall Plan simply as a bulwark against communism, because "fright is a poor substitute for argument" (HT 11/11/47 and 1/20/48). Rather, he presented it as the prelude to a new era of peace and prosperity, with free trade among democratic countries everywhere.

Programs for assistance to developing nations that came after the Marshall Plan were, Lippmann was sorry to discover, a particularly hard sell with the American people unless they could be defended as contributing to the containment of communism. For his own part he offered an eloquent defense of foreign aid on moral grounds, to which he knew there would be strong opposition (HT 1/30/51 and 1/29/59). He also used arguments from current growth theory to make his case. Developing countries, he claimed, needed short-term bursts of public capital to reach what economic historian Walt Rostow called a "take-off" into self-sustaining growth. Lippmann conceded that foreign assistance might be wasted in some cases, especially if it went to countries without some kind of a national plan, but he argued that it was worth the gamble. In one of his periodic reviews of the Agency for International Development program during the Johnson administration he conceded: "I find myself wondering why the whole subject has become so stale. Some kind of vital spark has gone out of the argument. The annual plea for appropriations becomes increasingly a repetition of tired slogans. . . . What we must dwell on is that the problem is ceasing to be that of providing emergency relief for friendly countries in time of war and its aftermath. It has become very largely the problem of helping the less developed countries build the foundations of their own well-being. This a less exciting and a slower effort, and it is asking a lot that each year a Congress elected from constituencies where public money is very short, should allocate about 3½ per cent of the Federal budget to foreign aid" (WP 3/26/64).

But this was not to say that the issue of foreign aid had lost its salience. "The modern problem of foreign aid confronts us because about two-thirds of mankind is poor, has become aware that this is not inevitable, and is determined to overcome its misery and its immemorial servitude" (WP 3/26/64). In another of his periodic reviews of foreign aid he sounded cynical when he reminded his readers that "[i]n the American age of innocence before the United States recognized itself as a great power in the world, our national purposes abroad were served by diplomacy and arms. Only since we have adopted the role of a great power have we done what great powers have always done. We have added money and propaganda to diplomacy and arms" (WP 3/9/65). Unfortunately, he said again, the American people had seldom been presented with effective arguments by persuasive spokesmen for why they should attend to world affairs and not just leave them to the diplomats and the military. Fortunately by the mid-1960s one such spokesman had appeared, Senator J. William Fulbright, a member of the Senate Foreign Relations Committee: "he is doing wonders to make the country and the Congress begin to re-examine the encrusted deposit of ideas and ideology and prejudices under which our foreign policy labors and groans" (WP 3/9/65).

Sustaining the Health of the Liberal Economy

Lippmann never wavered in his commitment, made in the 1930s, to an economic policy for a successful free society that had three components: Keynesian monetary and fiscal policy, tight constraints on monopoly in

product and factor markets, and carefully thought-out progressive innova-
tions that would not damage the competitive market system and would respond to needs that could not be met by the market. For the remainder of
his career, unemployment, utopian schemes of reform, and the actions of
rent seekers remained for him the great economic threats to a free society.
His position on Keynesian policy was that its wisdom had been irrefutably
demonstrated in theory and practice. The only serious problem in applying
it to policy was that it seemed counterintuitive to most voters. Balanced
budgets, like good manners and personal hygiene, were taught as best practices within the family and could not easily be shaken or denied when applied to the nation-state. Nothing was more obvious to the man on the street
than that the sensible posture was to economize in bad times and spend
liberally in good ones. But of course this was the exact opposite of the best
policy for the nation-state, according to Keynesian doctrine.

Lippmann thought it would take perhaps a generation to educate
people to accept that in fiscal policy the fallacy of composition prevailed.
What was true for a member of the community was not necessarily right for
the community as a whole. On several occasions he pointed out that a comparable difficulty in public education had been encountered at an earlier
date when persuading the common man that the earth was round (WP
1/30/63). Everywhere that man looked the earth was flat. So why was this
not true for the earth overall? A similar question was asked about budget
balancing. The challenge of explaining Keynesian principles to the people
was, Lippmann saw, as great for the journalist as for the college teacher
and the politician, and he struggled with how best to do it himself over
three decades. He deplored the seeming unwillingness of some Republican leaders, notably his nemesis Senator Taft, to grapple with the challenge at all. He wrote in 1947: "Mr. Taft's problem, and the country's problem, is posed by the fact that if there is a serious decline from the present
rate of private capital investment, a serious depression is as certain as anything can be" (HT 2/15/47). He used a study by Gerhard Colm and Fritz
Lehmann to suggest that the income tax and undistributed profits tax in
place in 1938 were "operating to prevent the production of wealth" and
should be reconsidered (HT 3/5/38). He was glad that, after the war, he

found Presidents Truman and Eisenhower, if not exactly converted to Keynesian doctrine, more nuanced in their pronouncements on fiscal policy (HT 2/2/54 and 3/15/54).

By 1947 Lippmann thought that a decline in long-term investment pointed toward the possibility of the serious recession that many had predicted when the war ended. Perhaps it was only the effective demand created by foreign assistance that sustained employment for the time being (HT 6/12/47 and 6/14/47). For Lippmann the possibility of secular stagnation, much discussed before the war, was also still there, even though Keynesian economists had shown ways to prevent it. The fear was that there would not be enough demand for the cornucopia of goods that had materialized after the war. Although inadequate demand did not in fact become a problem, Lippmann might have claimed that this was because of the large unexpected defense expenditures. He thought that the fear of inflation often repeated by critics of Keynesian policy was overblown, and he accepted Colin Clark's position that inflation was unlikely so long as taxes were less than a quarter of Gross National Product (HT 1/20/55). In the 1930s he had feared that the growing power of trade unions could be the Achilles heel of capitalism by generating unsustainable increases in wages that would cause either inflation or unemployment. It was not obvious what to do about this problem of organized labor, which he called "the Riddle of the Sphinx" (HT 4/19/47). But after the war he became more optimistic about reducing union power, and thereby wage-push inflation, because the public was less willing to tolerate union power after the return to full employment, as demonstrated by passage in 1947 of the Taft-Hartley Act (Labor Management Relations Act). He credited this development, like so many others of which he approved, to the widespread acceptance of Keynesian macroeconomics (HT 5/15/47). The Wagner Act (National Labor Relations Act), passed in the depth of the depression in 1935, had been a public response to the evident suffering of unemployed workers; but with the assurance now of full employment, monopoly power of unions no longer was so appealing to the public (HT 5/9/49). In the long run Lippmann looked to wage arbitration on the Australian model to keep wages in line with labor productivity (WP 8/20/63).

Lippmann was pleased when the "Accord" between the Treasury Department and the Federal Reserve was approved in 1951 and liberated the Fed to pursue price stability in addition to interest rates as a target of open market operations (HT 12/9/47 and 12/18/47). He was opposed to wage and price controls as a means to constrain inflation because, while controls could reduce the symptoms of inflation, they could not eliminate underlying inflationary forces (HT 12/18/47 and 7/29/48). He seems to have reached the conclusion quite early that mild inflation was likely to be the inevitable accompaniment of full employment. Relating macroeconomic policy to the Cold War, Lippmann reported that those Russians with whom he talked had not yet appreciated that Keynes had shown the way to eliminate the two greatest "contradictions of capitalism," unemployment and inflation. "It was quite evident to me, judging by a few conversations I was able to have with serious Communists, that they are fascinated and puzzled by the idea that a reformed and humanist capitalism might present the world with something tremendous that is not dreamed of in the Marxist philosophy" (HT 1/6/49). He acknowledged increasingly that long-run growth must be a critical objective of a free economy: "Expansion is a continuing political and social necessity in a free and capitalist economy. The first conditions of expansion—the one inseparable from the other—are technological improvement and sufficient incentives to enterprise and investment" (HT 2/8/54). But short-term stability was equally important, and the two objectives of growth and stability need not be contradictory. "The principles that are needed for the short run of the business cycle are not in fact in conflict with the principles for the long run. They are supplementary. The tendency to regard them as conflicting is, however, a deep danger in the free world and especially in the American part of it. Yet it is only the unreconstructed New Dealers on the one hand, and the unreconstructed Old Guard on the other who believe that there is an irreconcilable conflict" (HT 2/8/54).

Over the course of his career Lippmann sometimes drew on the work of prominent economists without specific acknowledgment of them by name. This was especially true of Keynes, perhaps because of the political connotations associated with his name. He did not wish to have any label attached to him, whether "Keynesian" or any other. The most obvious example of his failure to acknowledge his sources was the Godkin Lectures in 1934, in which he set forth Keynes's policy position on a "compensated economy" without once mentioning his name. Another incident occurred in 1957, as the Eisenhower administration moved into its second term and Lippmann was feeling frustrated by the slow adoption of Keynesian principles. In 1928 Keynes had given a talk that was published two years later in modified form in the *Nation and Athenaeum* with the title "Economic Possibilities for Our Grandchildren." Almost thirty years later, possibly in homage to Keynes, but again with no mention of him, Lippmann titled one of his regular columns "On the Grandchildren's Future." With respect to the titles of their two essays it is ironic that neither Keynes nor Lippmann had grandchildren, or indeed children. The Keynes essay was not devoted to prophesy, as implied by the title, but was rather a suggestion of the economic opportunities that would be presented through capital accumulation and technological change if certain conditions were fulfilled, in particular if there were no wars and no population explosions. Keynes went on to explore the changes in attitudes that would have to take place with abundance and reduced demand for labor. Lippmann examined the same economic forces as Keynes when he looked into the future, but he added the new understanding of macroeconomics to which Keynes had been the major contributor. As one of Lippmann's most eloquent later columns, this one is worth quoting at some length.

> There have been the wars, and the rise of the United States as a world power with a great military establishment. There has been the fabulous, indeed explosive, increase of the American population. There has been not only the deep and wide technological development, but, with the organization of scientific research, a radically new pace in the application of science.
>
> There has been also, so at least it seems to me, a non-violent but nevertheless revolutionary change in the inner principle of our own social economy. This is the new principle, which goes by the prosaic name of "full employment"—the imperative that the government must use the fiscal and other powers of the state to keep the demand for labor at least equal to the supply.

Until the present generation this principle was unknown to, much less was it the policy of, the United States or any other capitalist nation. Its adoption marks a profound change. It would not in my view be an exaggeration to say that it has brought about a revolution in the West which has made the Communist revolutionary propaganda irrelevant and antiquated.

For when the government is committed to the maintenance of full employment, the bargaining power of labor is underwritten. This means a decisive change in the balance of forces within our society. . . .

Although the principle of full employment was worked out under Roosevelt and Truman, it is now national policy from which no public man, who expects to have a future, would think of dissenting.

We have not begun to see the full consequences of the new principle. But in all probability, it is the real reason why it appears that the inflation in which we find ourselves cannot be stopped by the orthodox devices of tight money and a balanced budget. It may well be that a gradual inflation is the inseparable accompaniment of the policy of full employment, and that the two together will gradually but inexorably work a great transformation in the American way of life. (HT 7/4/57)

By the end of the Truman administration in 1953 Lippmann was confident that any reasonable policy maker must insist on full employment. The Great Depression had demonstrated that the costs of the alternative were unbearably high, while Keynes had shown that there were simple remedies. During the Eisenhower years, however, Lippmann's faith in the eventuality of this policy was shaken. It seemed that the Republicans wished to maintain a moderate slack in the economy sufficient to restrain what they perceived to be an inflationary threat, and to maintain social discipline overall. Three aspects of this approach disturbed Lippmann: first, fiscal and monetary policies controlled inflation better than unemployment did; second, the human suffering involved with unemployment was intolerable; and third, the goods that were not produced were badly needed for public projects of many kinds.

Lippmann, like many others at the time, was influenced during the 1940s and 1950s (HT 1/20/49) by the writings of John Kenneth Galbraith, and especially his 1958 book, *The Affluent Society*. As with Keynes, and perhaps for the same reason that he did not wish to be labeled, despite a warm personal friendship he seldom cited Galbraith by name. Up until the 1950s Lippmann's major macroeconomic concern had been simply that unemployment was economically wasteful and socially destructive. Now Galbraith helped to convince him that pressing public needs required not only full employment but a faster growth rate and some reallocation of expenditures away from personal consumption. One of the complaints about the economists of the New Deal often made by Lippmann was that they did not appreciate how much the enormous expansion of the public sector that they proposed depended on rapid growth of the private sector, the sector that they were regularly seeking to restrain through confiscatory taxes and regulatory regimes (HT 3/12/38 and 3/29/38). Now Galbraith added to his concern. It is hard to imagine that the following, which appeared in Lippmann's column two years after Galbraith's book appeared, did not have Galbraith in the background: "For it is inconceivable, to cite a few examples, that a country which can spend what we spend on luxuries should tolerate much longer the shameful neglect and starvation of public education. It is inconceivable that this country will put up with inadequate medical care, with blighted areas in its big cities, with the pollution of the air and of water, with inadequate airports and failing railroads. The public facilities of this country are not keeping up with the growth of the population, the congestion of the cities, and the rising standards of private life. It is as sure as anything of this sort can be that in the decade of the sixties there will be a great modernization and expansion of public facilities" (HT 7/9/59). He attacked the economic policies of the Eisenhower administration using a combination of Galbraithian and Cold War arguments: "The President has adhered to a principle which would probably no longer be suitable even in a time of total peace. He has adhered to a principle which puts private comfort and private consumption ahead of national need. The President has spent his seven years in office reducing the share of the national income devoted to public purposes. The challenge of the Soviet Union has been demanding an increase, not a reduction, of the share of the national income devoted to public purposes. We are falling behind in the race because we are not allowed to run" (HT 1/19/60).

Galbraith's book gave Lippmann the opportunity to reflect on many of the neglected public goods and market failures that had bothered him since his college days. He believed that education was the public sector program that was most critical to the success of a free society, starting at the lowest level with literacy and moving upward through improved understanding of policy options to advanced science and engineering, which would facilitate rapid economic growth (HT 4/26/47 and 4/29/47). He thought segregated education was an abomination, and he condemned it at every opportunity (e.g., HT 5/20/54). Other public goods that Lippmann found to be in disgracefully short supply included hospitals and health workers, transportation infrastructure, urban renewal, protection of natural resources and the environment, and a public broadcasting system (HT 10/27/59 and 3/3/60). In 1958, with two years left in Eisenhower's second term, he expressed his frustration that little progress could be expected over that time. "For the future, which he must face for another two years, will be greatly concerned with this lag. It will be concerned with the lag in the provision of schools and colleges, with the lag in hospitals and medical services, with the deficiency of highways and the backwardness of much of our transportation, and with city planning and slum clearance. The future will be concerned with the conservation and the development of our natural resources, with the water supply of large areas of the country, with the contamination of the air, and with many other consequences of the extraordinary growth of our population, its conglomeration in big urban masses, and with the shaking up of the people's habits due to the application of modern science" (HT 11/20/58).

He believed that if economic activity were sustained at full capacity and the growth rate of national product could be increased to 4 or 5 percent, there could be a social surplus that might be taxed relatively painlessly and be used for all the public purposes he had listed (HT 3/8/60, 7/14/60, and 7/26/60). If this were not done, "we shall have to pay the price of having neglected our national needs because we were too soft and too timid to tax ourselves enough" (HT 3/5/59). With technical economics now substantially beyond his grasp Lippmann found very useful when discussing public sector needs the special reports produced at this time by the Rockefeller

Brothers Fund. By contrast he found the advice coming to President Eisenhower from his Council of Economic Advisers to be precisely wrong. He quoted Chairman Raymond Saulnier to make the point: "'As I understand an economy,' he [Saulnier] said, 'its ultimate purpose is to produce more consumer goods. This is the object of everything we are working at: to produce things for consumers.' . . . There precisely [wrote Lippmann] is the root of our trouble. Our goal is to maximize consumption. That is a very low national goal, and altogether unworthy of a great nation which has a great part to play in human affairs. The object of our economy is not to become fat with consumer goods. It is to use the wealth and the power which the economy can produce to support the national purposes which we so frequently proclaim" (HT 1/21/60).

The one continuing economic problem that Lippmann identified early in the 1950s, and that he kept on revisiting until the end, was the worsening U.S. balance of payments. The problem could not continue to get worse, it seemed to him, without a crisis; sooner or later something had to give. It seemed clear that the arrangements set up at Bretton Woods, whereby the U.S. dollar and its fixed value in gold would be the peg on which the whole global monetary system rested, could not be sustained, especially as American expenditures abroad for defense, international assistance, and other needs grew more rapidly than revenues (HT 11/1/60 and 12/6/60). One of the worrisome consequences of this unstable condition was the high domestic interest rates required to sustain the large short-term foreign borrowing. Lippmann could sense a worsening problem, but he could not reach a judgment about the various interpretations in the literature or make confident recommendations about remedial action to his readers.

The Political Economy of Policy Formation

Lippmann was reasonably certain by the middle of the 1930s that he was clear in his own mind which economic policies needed to be adopted and implemented to solve the problems of the Great Depression and open the way to a glorious economic future. But to his great consternation the political leaders of the time seemed unwilling to accept these policies. He saw

himself as a man of reason, and he had arrived at his conclusions after an
extended period of reasoned thought. Why, then, would these politicians
not take his advice or prove to him that he was wrong? He was deeply frustrated. It may be that he was politically naïve. Unquestionably he was impatient. After Harry Truman unexpectedly found himself president in 1945
and failed to pick up on some of Lippmann's recommendations, Lippmann
would not give him even the rest of Roosevelt's term before suggesting that
he resign in the national interest on grounds of demonstrated incompetence: "In plain words Mr. Truman does not know how to be President. He
does not know how to conduct foreign relations or how to be Commander
in Chief" (HT 10/12/48 and see also 4/1/48). But if the political system would
not deliver what Lippmann thought was essential to the national welfare he
must try to discover why. During the last days of writing *The Good Society*
in the middle of the 1930s he began work on another manuscript, called
tentatively "The Image of Man," which was intended to be a full-scale examination of the American political system with respect to its capacity to
construct and implement good public policy. Apparently this was the document that he hoped immodestly in the late 1930s might stimulate a debate
over constitutional reform comparable to that over the Constitution itself in
the early days of the Republic. The manuscript was not completed until the
mid-1950s and was published in 1955 as his last major book, *Essays in the
Public Philosophy*.

The political theory in Lippmann's columns over their first quarter
century is reflected in *Essays in the Public Philosophy* and may usefully be
reconstructed before examining the book. In simplified form his position
was as follows. There are three political communities in a democracy: the
electorate, the legislators, and the executive. They all face challenges and
have distinct functions. Troubles arise when these communities do not perform their appointed tasks, or worse still when they attempt to take on some
of the responsibilities and authority of the others. The responsibilities of
the electorate are to keep informed of current events and to develop the
skills necessary to identify their own interests and those of the nation. The
complexity of modern life made the tasks of the electorate demanding ones,
and it was the responsibility of the educational system and of the media to

assist them in maintaining their competence. Knowledge of basic principles in the social sciences and of some history was a prerequisite for the electorate to fulfill their obligations.

The legislators' correct function was to discover and to reflect the interests and values of their constituents and to take these into account when addressing national policy and approving legislation. Legislators should have greater sophistication in policy analysis than members of the electorate and should support institutions, in government and outside, that translated complex policy issues into simple descriptions that they could understand. Legislators had the power of the purse and must say "yes" or "no" in a timely manner to all proposals from the executive. They should not have an opportunity themselves to propose legislation; when they usurped this power the result inevitably was laws and institutions that reflected a mix of economic and ideological special interests emerging from complex logrolling among legislators. When legislators had the right to initiate legislation inevitably they bartered their votes, and the result was a congeries that reflected values of many particular interests rather than the national interest. Lippmann realized that the limited role for senators and congressmen he proposed would attract a different kind of candidate than at present, but that, he was sure, was all to the good.

Finally, the executive in a democracy had the responsibility to "govern," meaning prepare proposals for the legislature and then implement programs that were approved. The executive should contain persons with exceptional leadership skills, imagination, and capacity to manage complex systems. In his descriptions these should be like successful business entrepreneurs. As role models for leaders he had great admiration for Winston Churchill, Franklin Roosevelt (in wartime but not in peace), and especially Charles De Gaulle who, he thought, had rescued France from disaster (HT 4/21/60). He had mainly contempt for Harry Truman, who did not exhibit the required qualities of leadership, and Dwight Eisenhower, who had mainly the qualities of a retired army general. The American system had not conscripted many of the people he thought worthy of executive leadership: notably Dwight Morrow, Newton Baker, Nelson Rockefeller, and Adlai Stevenson. The chief executives had a special responsibility to remain

close to, and make good use of, the best intellectuals in the country; typically they failed in their jobs when they did not do so (WP 3/15/66). Apparently Lippmann was leaning toward a parliamentary form of government
and away from the American tripartite division of powers. But his model
seems closest to that of the large modern corporation. The political electorate were the stockholders, the legislators the board of directors, and the
chief executive the chief operating officer. Things went wrong in the polity
as in the corporation, Lippmann concluded, when the various participants
assumed the authority and responsibilities of others, and especially when
the legislature tried to "govern." Not only did this reduce the power of the
executive to fulfill its responsibilities; it also attracted the wrong kind of
people to government: self-interested manipulators and ideologues to the
legislature, men like Joe McCarthy and Barry Goldwater, and weak administrators to the executive who were willing to put up with all of the obstacles
placed in their way by the legislators.

The most dangerous part of the American democracy was undoubtedly
Congress; it could induce paralysis in government. "This being a Presidential system of government, only the President can govern. The Congress can
oppose him, it can obstruct him, and it can stop him from governing. That is
why Congressional government, as Woodrow Wilson said in his book 75
years ago, is bad government. The Congress cannot take the place of the
President in order to govern instead of him" (HT 7/9/59). And in a nutshell:
"We have here in its American form the critical disease of democratic
government—namely, the paralysis of the executive by the elected assembly" (HT 12/10/63). How could this political condition be ameliorated?
Over the years Lippmann contemplated a variety of piecemeal changes,
such as a reformed primary system, insistence that all legislation be initiated by the President, and elimination of the filibuster, which he described
as "a conspiracy to suspend representative government" (HT 12/26/63). But
by the mid-1950s he concluded it was time to take an all-encompassing look
at the entire political system and propose an overall plan for reform. That
was the purpose of his book.

Essays in the Public Philosophy is not an easy book. Those who had not
been following Lippmann's political commentary over the years must have

found it difficult to comprehend his purpose. He began by insisting, "I am a liberal democrat and have no wish to disenfranchise my fellow citizens. My hope is that both liberty and democracy can be preserved before the one destroys the other" (WL 1955, 13). Lippmann meant the book to be a plea for constructive reform, not for total destruction of the existing political system. But some did not believe him and thought that behind the complex prose an autocrat lurked who wished to turn government over to a mandarin class (Williams 2007). Certainly he made it clear that he was unhappy with the status quo and was prepared for radical change that in its sweep sounded ominous: "There has developed in this century a functional derangement of the relationship between the mass of the people and the government. The people have acquired power which they are incapable of exercising, and the governments they elect have lost powers which they must recover if they are to govern" (WL 1955, 14). It appears that he wished less to take power away from the people than to place the people in a better condition to use it. But a reader could be pardoned for not appreciating this subtlety. Some of his observations, like the following, if not viewed against the evolution of his thinking, can be easily misinterpreted. "Mass opinion has acquired mounting power in this century. It has shown itself to be a dangerous master of decisions when the stakes are life and death" (WL 1955, 20). This sounds like a proposal to disenfranchise the public when it was not. It was above all a plea for better public education in a democracy, and, as we shall see, for "faith." Public ignorance of international affairs, he found, had led inevitably to the widespread use by government of propaganda rather than reasoned argument. The government had little choice but to do so.

During World War II "it seemed impossible to wage the war energetically except by inciting the people to paroxysms of hatred and to utopian dreams. So they were told that the Four Freedoms would be established everywhere, once the incurably bad Germans and the incurably bad Japanese had been forced to surrender unconditionally. The war could be popular only if the enemy was altogether evil and the allies very nearly perfect" (WL 1955, 23). Given this condition of voter ignorance of public affairs legislators in the emergency of attack responded predictably to it with

manipulation: "Successful democratic politicians are insecure and intimidated men. They advance politically only as they placate, appease, bribe,
seduce, bamboozle, or otherwise manage to manipulate the demanding and
threatening elements in their constituencies" (WL 1955, 27). The effects on
the executive branch of public ignorance could be devastating: "The devi-
talization of the governing power is the malady of democratic states. As the
malady grows the executives become highly susceptible to encroachment
and usurpation by elected assemblies; they are pressed and harassed by the
haggling of parties, by the agents of organized interests, and by the spokesmen of sectarians and ideologues. The malady can be fatal. It can be deadly
to the very survival of the state as a free society if, when the great and hard
issues of war and peace, of security and solvency, of revolution and order are
up for decision, the executive and judicial departments, with their civil servants and technicians, have lost their power to decide" (WL 1955, 27).

To illustrate the condition of the mass of the electorate Lippmann fell
back on the metaphor of Plato's cave, which he had used successfully in *The
Phantom Public,* where the inhabitants were seen to react not to reality but
"to the pictures in their heads. Human behavior takes place in relation to a
pseudo-environment—a representation, which is not quite the same for any
two individuals, of what they suppose to be—not what *is*—the reality of
things" (WL 1955, 92). This was a condition that had to be changed; but it
would not be easy. The danger that lurked in a country where the electorate
was cut off from reality was that the voters would fall for some revolutionary
nostrum as a solution to their problems. This had thrown France into the
French Revolution and Russia into the Stalinist purges: "In the Jacobin
philosophy the world as it is must be transformed; the day is soon to come
when history, reaching its culmination, will end, and there will be no more
struggles. So Marx and Engels decided that one more, though this time the
conclusive and the final, revolution was called for, in order to achieve the
classless society" (WL 1955, 79). Lippmann considered himself a reformer
and a "meliorist" who believed confidently in improvement, but he was
never a revolutionary.

At this point in his career Lippmann was unusually discouraged at the
political prospects ahead. Unlike many democratic thinkers of the past he

took no solace in the prospect of an enlarged franchise as a solution, since then the challenge of public education would become even greater. "To multiply the voters makes it no more probable that a plurality of them will truly represent the public interest. Our experience with mass elections in the twentieth century compels us, I think, to the contrary conclusion; that public opinion becomes less realistic as the mass to whom information must be conveyed, and argument must be addressed, grows larger and more heterogeneous" (WL 1955, 39). In economic affairs the voting public had shown that they could be counted upon always to take the easy way out, when so often the hard way was most socially desirable. "It is easier to obtain votes for appropriations than it is for taxes, to facilitate consumption than to stimulate production, to protect a market than to open it, to inflate than to deflate, to borrow than to save, to demand than to compromise, to be intransigent than to negotiate, to threaten war than to prepare for it" (WL 1955, 45). The results of this attitude could be tragic: "There is then a general tendency to be drawn downward, as by the force of gravity, towards insolvency, towards the insecurity of factionalism, towards the erosion of liberty, and towards hyperbolic wars" (WL 1955, 46).

Essays in the Public Philosophy is divided into two parts. The first is essentially a synthesis of Lippmann's thinking about political theory and political events over his career. The second part is his account of what should now be done; and it is quite opaque. It must have seemed like something of a letdown to many of his readers that the reforms he suggested were so unfamiliar and so esoteric. He recommended as the foundation for political improvement the revival of faith in what he calls "the public philosophy," by which he means "a body of positive principles and precepts which a good citizen cannot deny or ignore" (WL 1955, 101). This philosophy was a part of "*natural law,* a name given which, alas, causes great semantic confusion" (WL 1955, 101). He explained: "When we speak of these principles as natural laws, we must be careful. They are not scientific 'laws' like the laws of the motions of the heavenly bodies. They do not describe human behavior as it is. They prescribe what it should be" (WL 1955, 124). By appealing to natural law he hoped to identify a code of political conduct or good behavior that had been built up through past civilizations. This code, like the common law, would specify practices to be respected and not to be challenged, a feature that seemed inconsistent with his long-standing insistence on submitting everything to reason. But he did not see an inconsistency. "This common law is 'natural' in the sense that it can be discovered by any rational mind, that it is not the willful and arbitrary positive command of the sovereign power" (WL 1955, 107). To justify this position he cited the historian of political thought Sir Ernest Barker, who claimed that "European thought has been acted upon by the idea that the rational faculties of men can produce a common conception of law and order which possesses a universal validity" (WL 1955, 104). This conception of the common practice embodied in the public philosophy would seem to prohibit behavior that was governed solely by the individual wants of the actor or by the commands of saviors who appeared suddenly on the scene. "This philosophy is the premise of the institutions of the Western society, and they are, I believe, unworkable in communities that do not adhere to it. Except on the premises of this philosophy, it is impossible to reach intelligible and workable conceptions of popular election, majority rule, representative assemblies, free speech, loyalty, property, corporations and voluntary associations" (WL 1955, 101). Through this philosophy "modern men could make vital contact with the lost traditions of civility" (WL 1955, 102).

Through his *Essays in the Public Philosophy* Lippmann did not wish merely to revive an ancient political philosophy to guide modern affairs. He wished to modernize a code that had been neglected for a century or more as a constraint on human action: "The school of natural law has not been able to cope with the pluralism of the later modern age—with the pluralism which has resulted from the industrial revolution and from the enfranchisement and the emancipation of the masses of the people. In the simple and relatively homogeneous society of the eighteenth century natural law provided the principles of a free state. But then the mode of such thinking went out of fashion. In the nineteenth century little was done to remint the old ideas. They were regarded as obsolete and false, as hostile to the rise of democracy, and they were abandoned to the reactionaries. . . . Yet, in this pluralized and fragmenting society a public philosophy with common and binding principles was more necessary than it had ever been" (WL 1955, 109).

It was more the content of the political philosophy that Lippmann proposed than the notion of an external code that startled Lippmann's readers. He seemed to be moving sharply away from his earlier emphasis on well-informed free choice in the economy and polity. Some of his comments sound like the lament of a deeply disappointed and disillusioned observer of the selfishness in his fellow citizens. "The modern trouble is in a low capacity to believe in precepts which restrict and restrain private interests and desire. Conviction of the need of these restraints is difficult to restore once it has been radically impaired. . . . In the prevailing popular culture all philosophies are the instruments of some man's purpose, all truths are self-centered and self-regarding, and all principles are the rationalizations of some special interest. There is no public criterion of the true and the false, of the right and the wrong, beyond that which the preponderant mass of voters, consumers, readers, and listeners happen at the moment to be supposed to want" (WL 1955, 114). He appreciated that this message was likely not to be well received by those it proposed to restrain. "The public philosophy is addressed to the government of our appetites and passions by the reasons of a second, civilized, and therefore, acquired nature. Therefore the public philosophy cannot be popular. For it aims to resist and to regulate those very desires and opinions which are most popular" (WL 1955, 162).

He offered dire warnings of the consequences of not attending to the need for such restraint. The success of the effort he proposed depended on "whether this old philosophy can be reworked for the modern age." Totalitarian rule in the economy and society would likely result from failure. "If this cannot be done, then the free and democratic nations face the totalitarian challenge without a public philosophy which free men believe in and cherish, with no public faith beyond a mere official agnosticism, neutrality and indifference. There is not much doubt how the struggle is likely to end if it lies between those who, believing, care very much—and those who, lacking belief, cannot care very much" (WL 1955, 161).

Strange as Lippmann's concerns may sound to modern ears, his conclusion that self-interested human behavior often did not lead to good social outcomes had some wider appeal at the time he was writing. In the field of

environmental protection soon after World War II the pioneering ecologist
Aldo Leopold, trained like Lippmann in the social sciences, described how
simple cost-benefit calculations by individuals had led to destruction of the
American landscape, and he called for the strengthening of a culturally determined "land ethic" that bears some strong similarities to Lippmann's
"public philosophy" (C. Goodwin 2008). Lippmann was appealing for
something like a culturally determined economic ethic.

Lippmann was discouraged by the unenthusiastic and uncomprehend-
ing responses he received to *Essays in the Public Philosophy*, and he suffered
a breakdown that lasted several weeks (Steel 1980, 493–496).

The Tragedy of the New Frontier,
the Great Society, and Vietnam

Not long after painting this dark picture of the possible future of western
civilization in *Public Philosophy,* things began to look up. At last the depressing two-term presidency of Dwight Eisenhower was coming to an end,
and the Democrats turned for leadership to the youthful senator John
Fitzgerald Kennedy, who was surrounded by advisers from among Lippmann's
close Cambridge friends: McGeorge Bundy, John Kenneth Galbraith, Arthur Schlesinger Jr., Paul Samuelson, and others. After complaining that
under the Republicans the executive branch had become weak and out of
touch with the intellectuals, here was the promise of a sharp turnaround.
Moreover, following a decade in the political wilderness Lippmann himself
was again near the seats of power. He was consulted on the wording of the
Inaugural Address and about cabinet appointments, as Kennedy assembled
around him what David Halberstam would later call "the best and the
brightest" (Halberstam 1972). Lippmann was delighted with the orienta-
tion of Kennedy's thinking: "Kennedy is a conservative of the age he lives
in. His views are addressed to the contemporary scene, not to the dead past
and not to an imaginary future" (HT 12/20/60).

He liked especially the way Kennedy dealt with the talent he had gathered. He kept the intellectuals as advisers, but he placed the government
itself in the hands of seasoned administrators. "It is not an Administration

made up of professors drawn out of an academic life of scholarship and research. It is, for the first time in our history, an Administration manned primarily by professional public servants—by men whose primary careers have long been the public service. They will need public support. They will need a lot of luck. But I do not know of any Administration in our time in which the level of competence has been so high" (HT 1/19/61). In commenting on the Inaugural Address Lippmann observed that in domestic affairs the Kennedy team demonstrated that they were exceptionally competent; in foreign affairs, by contrast, they had a lot to learn: "While the domestic section is founded upon a well known and well tried modern economic philosophy, there exists as yet no comparable statement of American foreign policy in the new world situation—of Russian nuclear parity, of the prospective achievement by China and others of nuclear power, of the emergence of new nations out of their colonial past, of the spread of what has been called the revolution of rising expectations to the Western Hemisphere. . . . In the domestic field the Kennedy Administration is able to draw upon a mature body of doctrine. In foreign affairs it has an obsolescent body of doctrine with which to face the world, and it has before it the task of restudying, and revising, and re-educating before the hand-me-downs and the leftovers from other times are discarded" (HT 1/31/61).

Lippmann took a position even before the election of 1960 on what would become one of the most contentious economic issues in the Kennedy Administration, whether it was desirable to administer macroeconomic stimulus to the economy. He was strongly in favor of doing so. Soon after Kennedy took office Lippmann quoted Paul Samuelson, whom he described as the oracle on such matters and from whom he had heard privately, in support of his position: "Professor Samuelson does not hold any public office. But in many ways he is the economist to whom the Administration economists listen most closely. He has just written an article for a Japanese newspaper, the 'Nihon Keizai Shimbun.' The article discusses the Kennedy program as it has been formulated to date. Professor Samuelson thinks that 'when you come to add up in quantitative terms what the whole package of programs can be expected to accomplish, you realize how limited the total package really is. . . . It is a fair inference from Professor Samuelson's article in the

Japanese newspaper that he is now rather expecting that a supplementary package will be needed. These ideas stem from the belief that the present recession, following upon a poor recovery from the recession of 1958, and coming at the end of several years of sluggish economic activity, is much more serious than Congress or the mass of the people who are not unemployed have yet realized. 'It is well' says Professor Samuelson, 'to have no illusions about the magnitude of the proposed (Kennedy) measures'" (HT 3/1/61).

Since well before the election of 1960, Lippmann's attention in macro-economic affairs had shifted from the maintenance of full employment, which he thought any sensible person now could take for granted, to economic growth. He even collaborated with the MIT macroeconomist Francis Bator on an article for the *Saturday Evening Post* (November 1960) stressing the need for rapid economic growth. Was it enough to make sure everyone was working and the economy was operating safely within the speed limit, he asked, or should there be targeted stimuli that would increase the growth rate so that the economy would proceed "at full throttle?" He thought there should be an additional stimulus, but he thought also this was the ideal time for a national debate on this question, of the kind that he had been contemplating since the 1930s. Kennedy, he noted, was an effective orator who could explain the merits of a stimulus, and the experts were lined up nicely on the two sides of the question. Soon after Kennedy took office Lippmann spelled out the question once again to his readers. "The issue in the debate is whether the economy will, if left to itself, achieve a full recovery or whether it will need to be stimulated by tax reduction, additional spending, or some combination of the two. In this momentous debate, which is being carried on in a highly civilized fashion, there is on one side Mr. Arthur F. Burns, who was President Eisenhower's economic adviser during his first term. On the other side are to be found President Kennedy's economic advisers, Mr. Walter Heller, Mr. Kermit Gordon, and Mr. James Tobin" (HT 5/30/61). What should happen next seemed obvious to Lippmann. President Kennedy must announce that he favored the stimulus and then the two sides could engage in a vigorous exchange over this proposal; the argument would end when the experimental tax cut had achieved its objective, or had not.

Lippmann was discouraged to discover that President Kennedy, like other presidents before him, was not always ready to accept his advice. Kennedy waffled on whether to implement a tax cut and was wishy-washy on the subject when addressing the public. Initially Lippmann was prepared to be tolerant for a while because he recognized that fiscal policy was counterintuitive with so many people: "The administration is operating within the Eisenhower slogans and stereotypes about the budget. This is not because the Kennedy men believe in them but because there are a large majority in both parties who do believe in them. . . . But the President has not yet braced himself to the effort of explaining to the public the difference between balancing the budget annually and balancing it over the business cycle. Yet most of what he has promised to do, most of what for the long pull urgently needs to be done, depends on explaining this theoretical issue to the people. . . . It is a complicated thing to explain why the earth is round. It is a complicated thing to explain that the Federal budget is not only an accounting of revenues and expenditures. It is also a great fiscal engine [a metaphor he had taken from the economist Otto Eckstein] which as a matter of national policy has to be managed in such a way as to promote a stabilized growth of the economy. It is a make-weight which has to be swung from deficit to surplus and from surplus to deficit to compensate for the ups and downs of the business cycle. There is nothing sinister or mysterious in this idea. But it is a new idea, new at least to a great many people" (HT 3/30/61). When Kennedy still did not take action to administer the stimulus after more than a year in office, Lippmann's disappointment increased, and he announced: "There is mounting evidence that those economists were right who told the Administration last winter that it was making the mistake of trying to balance the budget too soon" (HT 5/31/62).

He was worried that Kennedy was beginning to look a little too much like Eisenhower. "The President's first priority is to get the economy moving" (HT 6/12/62). At least, he wrote thankfully, Kennedy was not exhibiting the fatal flaw of Franklin Roosevelt, of attempting social and economic reforms before recovery had been achieved. He appreciated that Kennedy faced the same obstacles to implementing a stimulus as earlier presidents had faced, especially the unfamiliarity of the American people with even the simplest principles of modern macroeconomics. "It is this work of re-education which the President began [in his speech] at Yale. It was a very good beginning. But, of course, one speech will not do what needs to be done—which is to close the cultural gap and put American public opinion and American political debate in touch with the realities of the modern age. This re-education is not a fight between good men and bad men, between rich men and poor men, between Republicans and Democrats. It is, like all education, a search for enlightenment in which all who participate bravely will be the winners" (HT 6/14/62). Using his own knowledge of macroeconomic lingo he estimated the current deflationary gap at thirty billion dollars, the income multiplier at 2.5, and a required stimulus therefore of at least ten billion (HT 7/19/62). He made it clear that he wanted a stimulus large enough not only to reduce the unemployment rate but also to increase the growth rate: "The choice before Congress is not between the tax program on the one hand and on the other a contented and complacent sluggishness. The tasks of the American nation and the increasing needs of the people have made the economic sluggishness an evil and a peril. The compulsions and the necessities of our time will demand that in one way or another the economy be made to work at or at least near full capacity" (WP 1/16/63).

Lippmann was delighted that, to some extent at least, discussion of budget policy had caught up with macroeconomic theory and the process of educating the electorate had begun. The "chronic sluggishness" that had characterized the American economy since World War II was finally to be confronted in 1963. "This, the second Kennedy budget, differs from all preceding budgets in that it expresses openly modern economic theory as developed in this generation. Other budgets, even some of Eisenhower's budgets, have reflected the theory without acknowledging it. But this budget makes the theory explicit. We should add that the application of the theory is very moderate and cautious. The nub of the theory is that in the modern economy, the first objective is not to balance the government budget itself but to balance the economy; when the economy is balanced at full capacity and full employment, the budget will itself tend to come into balance. The budget cannot be balanced successfully without unacceptable hardship if the economy is not balanced. . . . Since all of this is not what the older generation was taught in school and college, it will need a lot of explanation and demonstration. The President and his Council of Economic Advisers have made a very good beginning" (WP 1/23/63). Lippmann reminded his readers that Keynes himself had taught that the effects of a tax cut would be reduced if the wage level were not kept constant (WP 1/30/63). Looking always for new metaphors that would help his readers grasp the economic theory, he suggested now that the tax cut could be understood through a mechanical analogy. "A measure which will stimulate economic growth is the hub of the wheel from which all the spokes radiate" (WP 4/16/63), from rebuilding the educational system to reducing racial tensions.

Lippmann was devastated by the assassination of President Kennedy in November 1963, an act that he called "murder most foul" (WP 11/26/63). An administration that had so much promise had been nipped in the bud. But initially, at least, he was very optimistic about Lyndon Johnson. Here was a shrewd political veteran with a program similar to that of Kennedy and with many of the same staff, who might just be able to overcome the "critical disease of democratic government" that he had discussed in *Essays in the Public Philosophy*, "the paralysis of the executive by the elected assembly." Lippmann urged that the various procedural reforms that he had long recommended now be implemented so as to make Johnson's task easier: elimination of the filibuster and dependence on seniority, restraints on unnecessary spending in the districts of influential members, and, very specifically, "[l]et each house of the Congress pass a rule that any measure proposed by the President, and certified as important, must be put to a vote by some specified date or within some specified time" (WP 12/10/63).

Lippmann was ecstatic about some of Johnson's early moves, especially his declaration of a War on Poverty, including improvements in education and an end to discrimination. He was delighted that Johnson had accepted the idea that the surplus from economic growth at full capacity should be shared among all segments of the society. This idea was "transforming not only capitalism as it was known a generation ago, but it is transforming also socialism and communism as well" (WP 3/19/64). He was confident that the War on Poverty could be won. "There is no reason to doubt that, if we take the measures to counteract the causes of poverty, we shall in some degree reduce it. The effort will pay off well not only for the poor but for all of us. For there is nothing so good for a nation as to become interested in doing good works" (WP 3/19/64). Johnson had the skill to mobilize a national consensus, which Lippmann defined as two-thirds of the electorate, behind a cause that was so compelling. "As the realization becomes clearer that the internal progress of the republic is a vital matter, there will come also an understanding that the costs of internal progress are not painful liabilities but are in fact highly productive investments. Poverty, ignorance, discrimination, disease and ugliness exact a far higher sacrifice from us all than the initial costs of investing to overcome them. The country will not become poorer by fighting poverty. It will, on the contrary, become richer" (WP 12/15/64).

He thought Johnson had the capacity, rare among Democrats, to persuade those with wealth that class warfare was obsolete and everyone would gain from victory in the War on Poverty. "Here in the United States, as in most of Western Europe, this is the post-Marxian age. That is why President Johnson is able to wage a war against poverty and at the same time win so much confidence among the well-to-do" (WP 5/26/64). It was now clear that the sources of poverty in America were poor education and difficult home life, and the solution did not lie in simple redistribution: "the cause of the poverty which still remains is not the maldistribution of wealth but a shortage of education. The children of the poor are hard to educate because their homes are so cramped and so meager and because they go to schools which on the whole are more crowded and have less skilled teachers than the children of more fortunate families" (WP 10/15/64).

The apparent success at last of the innovative Kennedy/Johnson tax cut of 1964 seemed finally to have eliminated the "chronic sluggishness" of the American economy and at the same time helped to pay for the War on Poverty. Acceptance of Keynesian macroeconomic doctrine, for which Lippmann had been arguing for thirty years, was now about to make possible a series of progressive programs that he had been advocating for even longer than that. The tax cut "was taken on the new theory, accepted by most but not by all economists, that a big expansion of consumption and capital investment was necessary to overcome the chronic sluggishness of the American economy during the past ten years, with its high rate of unemployment and its rather low utilization of industrial capacity. For the sake of the record we must recognize that this planned deficit on top of an unplanned deficit is an innovation that goes beyond anything the New Deal ever did under Roosevelt and Truman" (WP 6/23/64). The many skeptics were about to be proved wrong. "Thus, confronted by the new tax law, many have prophesied that it would mean inflation, a flight from the dollar, destruction of confidence, bad business, and increased unemployment. These fears can now be examined against the concrete evidence which is now coming in" (WP 6/23/64).

By October 1965, Lippmann thought it almost too good to believe that "an authentic progressive, Lyndon Johnson, was also the most experienced and effective legislative leader of the century." Now both progressive impulses and Keynesian macroeconomics would be accepted once and for all without any fear of inconsistency, and the prospects ahead for the nation were limitless. "The country which did not believe it was possible has had a demonstration that by the use of modern economic doctrine, which originated with Keynes, it is possible to manage prosperity. It takes wise and skillful men to do this. But it can be done. We cannot, to be sure, as yet be absolutely certain that it can be done continually and indefinitely, and a certain conservative skepticism is still very much in order. What we do know is that the American economy has been expanding for 55 months and that nothing like such sustained prosperity has ever been enjoyed before" (WP 10/21/65).

Yet only two months after this burst of euphoria Lippmann's mood turned to gloom, and almost to despair. It seemed to him that the enormously promising Johnson presidency was about to be derailed by a condition that he had warned about a decade ago, innocence about international affairs. In Vietnam the United States was becoming increasingly embroiled with the wreckage of the collapsing French Empire, and misled throughout by the lessons of Munich in 1938 and a strategy that related everything to the containment of communism. The terrible tragedy, Lippmann was convinced, was that there were not enough resources to fight both the good war at home and the foolish war overseas. "The real pinch comes from the fact that money will not buy enough technicians and trained men, qualified administrators and commanders, nor will it buy the morale and the attention and the variegated energy which would be needed to carry out effectively and successfully all the commitments at home and around the globe. Only those who suffer from the delusion of omnipotence will think that this country can reconstruct its own society, can fight a major war in Asia, and can police the world from Berlin to Korea, from Central Asia to South America" (WP 12/21/65). Lippmann did not mince his words: "high policy today is in the hands of men who know the value of freedom, peace, righteousness, and justice in human affairs but are all too little aware of the price that must be paid to defend them and promote them. For this there will be a reckoning" (WP 12/21/65).

Lippmann reminded his readers repeatedly in 1965 that one of the great achievements of the first half of the 1960s had been to demonstrate that through macroeconomic management it was possible to have rapid growth with full employment and price stability. The story as he told it had become familiar, but it is worth repeating here one last time:

> This great expansion was managed successfully under the direction of Mr. Walter Heller, and supported by a consensus of the preponderant majority of the leading economists in the country.
>
> The story of this expansion, for which there were few tested precedents, is very heartening to those who dare to believe that reason and rational method and rational discussion can be made to prevail in human affairs. Forty years ago none, except perhaps a few solitary thinkers in Europe, believed that the capitalist system of private property and free enterprise operating in markets could proceed without severe ups and downs. The business cycle of slump and boom was regarded as being, like the cycle of the seasons, beyond human control and something to be accepted as inherent in the human condition.
>
> This fatalistic view was first challenged effectively in the Western world by John Maynard Keynes, though he himself drew on the teachings of others, notably Knut Wicksell, of Sweden. Keynes began to write in the 1920s—between the depression after the first world war and the Great Depression of 1929. Keynes was long regarded as hereti-

cal, subversive, even sacrilegious, in that he refused to bow with the accepted nature of things. However, Keynes' teachings made their way here and abroad in the universities, and from them into the finance ministries of every advanced industrial nation. In the last five years a new generation of American economists, all of them descended in one manner or another from Keynes, have been at the center of policy making and decision. . . . These economists have now achieved such high authority and public respect that politicians will not easily overrule them nor will they be easily obscured by the propaganda of special interests. (WP 3/15/66)

But now, Lippmann reported, these macroeconomic authorities discerned trouble ahead. President Johnson's decision to go forward with the purchase of both guns and butter, without new taxation, promised inflation just down the road. Walter Heller, back at the University of Minnesota, "spoke calmly but he raised the question as to whether 'further restrictive action is needed.' Professor Samuelson has been more emphatic . . . 'The issue' says that high authority, Professor Samuelson, 'is no longer growth versus stagnation. It is maintainable long-term growth versus frenzied and self-defeating scrambling for limited resources'" (WP 3/17/66). In May 1966 Lippmann wrote that Gardner Ackley, current Council of Economic Advisers chair, as well as Heller and Samuelson, were all calling for a tax increase, but the administration refused with the midterm elections pending. Johnson was counting on exhortation of price makers to constrain inflation. "The attempt to do by propaganda what should be done by monetary and fiscal measures is unfair and it will not work" (WP 5/5/66). By July 1966 Lippmann concluded that all of the products of economic growth promised by President Johnson for the War on Poverty were now being consumed by "the costs of the global crusade into which he has plunged us" (WP 7/12/66). The results were social and political as well as economic dangers. "The real cost is that the surpluses of an expanding economy have been swallowed up and this has removed the lubricants and the cushions against the conflicts of interests and the rivalry of ideologies. We are moving more and more into sharp and raw confrontations. This is the tragic consequence of one of the most serious miscalculations in our history" (WP 12/29/66).

To the degree that the Great Society programs had been put in place by 1967, problems with them were swept under the rug because of the war (WP 1/24/67). All of the obfuscation that followed had contributed to what Lippmann called a "credibility gap" between what President Johnson told the media and the people and what they believed (WP 3/30/67). Johnson, it turned out, was enraged by these criticisms from one who only a short time before had sung his praises, and Lippmann became persona non grata throughout Washington. On May 25, 1967, he announced that after thirty-six years this would be his last column. He promised to experiment with new ways to make his voice heard, and he continued to write for *Newsweek*, but his voice was now effectively muffled. He sold his large home in Washington, where he had lived since the 1930s, and with his wife, Helen, tried to start a new life in Europe, first in Italy and then in France. When this proved unsatisfactory he returned to New York and spent his last years in an apartment hotel. After a period of ill health Lippmann died on December 14, 1974. His wife had died in February of that year.

12

The Good Economy

WALTER LIPPMANN BEGAN HIS CAREER as a newspaper columnist having devoted little time or attention to economics. As a student he dismissed classical economics as mainly a tool of the ruling class, and then he became disillusioned quickly with socialist doctrine. The new Institutionalist economics that was emerging during the early years of the twentieth century did not seem to answer many of the questions that troubled him. Yet by the end of his first decade and a half as a columnist he had arrived at a confident position on the several major economic challenges that faced the nation. One of his main objections to the received economic wisdom was that it ignored many of the social, psychological, and political variables that he thought were crucial when searching for answers. He set out to redirect the attention of the discipline.

When he began to write his columns in 1931 he was acutely aware of the destructive consequences of unemployment, and the economics that he explored told him little about how to solve it. More than simply the lost production and the degradation of skills concerned him; there were also the psychological damage to those who were unemployed, the social costs to their families, the destruction of their communities, and the political dangers from the growth of dictators, authoritarian governments, and irresponsible reformers in the democracies. He appreciated the division of labor and increased competition that came with free trade, and he found that a healthy, open, world economy strengthened and sustained political freedoms. Consequently he was worried that isolationist and protectionist tendencies among Americans during the 1930s were a serious and continuing threat to the global economy and world peace. But greater world trade alone would not put everyone back to work. Lippmann quickly abandoned macroeconomic orthodoxy in the early 1930s and accepted first a monetary explanation for the Great Depression and then the new Keynesian economics, which seemed to meet his needs. No longer, he thought, could anyone see unemployment as inevitable or insoluble. Now it was only a matter of will to eliminate the scourge of unemployment once and for all. It was the responsibility of the journalist in the good economy to direct and strengthen this will. He was delighted when during the Kennedy years it seemed that macroeconomic policy had finally caught up with Keynesian theory.

The Journalist in the Good Economy

One of Lippmann's continuing fascinations was with the complexity of human behavior, and he made some of his most memorable scholarly contributions in this area, notably in his book *Public Opinion*. But this was also where he became most disillusioned. He believed that in a good economy the right balance must be maintained among self-interest, moral conscience, and a willingness to cooperate in the endeavors of the community. Yet everywhere he looked he saw mainly overdeveloped and destructive self-interest. He felt deep empathy for those who were suffering in the depression, but he discovered that when assistance was given, the recipients—symbolized by the veterans—simply wanted more. Suffering gave way to greed and a sense of entitlement. Similarly, when competitive markets for commodities, manufactured goods, services, and factors of production were needed to preserve personal liberty and free choice, too many of the market participants opted instead for monopoly. They seemed unable to grasp that economic, social, and political freedoms were indivisible, and when one was lost you would likely lose the others. Concentration of power in markets and in government became for Lippmann the great enemy of the good economy, and one of his main goals was to point this out. Some thought that Lippmann's analysis had led him to favor rule by an intelligent and moral elite. Quite the contrary. He concluded that what the good economy and society had to have was not a governing elite but an informed and relatively sophisticated citizenry, guided ideally by a culturally determined economic ethic. And so Lippmann saw a crucial role for the journalist in explaining microeconomic challenges in the good economy as well as macroeconomic ones.

Early in his career Lippmann concluded that a modern liberal democracy needed people who could do what he then set out to do himself, provide citizens with a balanced understanding of complex economic, social, and political problems and their possible solutions. Then the citizens could guide their political representatives and make sensible and informed decisions in the voting booth. Knowledge, if widespread among the citizenry, could eliminate what otherwise would be a strong case for rule by philosopher kings or some other form of omniscient authoritarian government. An informed electorate could restrain politicians and bureaucrats from overstepping their bounds, making foolish decisions, and endangering personal liberties. Possibly no one before or since has done as successfully what Lippmann wanted done. He was more than a journalist in the sense that the term is used today. He had a relationship to his readers that was a mix of trusted adviser, teacher, confidante, mentor, and friend. He did not report on the social sciences as some journalists do today, or from within them as some social scientists do as well. He wrote successfully outside the social sciences yet with a high degree of authority and familiarity with them. Until World War II, at least, he seldom lacked the self-confidence to survey the state of opinion on a topic in the social sciences that interested him and reach a judgment about which parts were valuable. After the war he found the social sciences less penetrable and he was more ready to defer to the "experts."

He used the social sciences as tools, not as ends in themselves. His agenda was set by the policy challenges of the time, not by the puzzles in the disciplines. Yet he gained perhaps the highest level of repute ever achieved in the social sciences by a newspaperman. What were his secrets in reaching this eminence? Here are a few. First of all, he was enormously talented and intelligent, and he used these gifts carefully. He did not boast, or patronize his audience. He depended on quiet persuasion, and he accomplished this with impressive skill. He could read with great speed and master material quickly so that on a complex problem he could write from the commanding heights while the problem was still evolving. He was fearless intellectually and would take up any subject from scratch with the expectation that he could grasp the essentials before very long. He consulted widely with experts and often confronted one received opinion with another until he became confident of their relative merits. To the dismay of some of his admirers he was resolutely nonideological. He seldom approached a new issue with his mind made up. He listened to recognized authority but did not accept it unless he was convinced by the theory and evidence. He felt free to develop his thinking in public and to change his mind when this seemed called for. This posture helps to explain the stories of his inconsistency and flip-flopping. He was determinedly nonpartisan, swinging often back and forth in an election between parties and candidates. He understood that it was not adherence to a single party or body of doctrine that brought him to so many breakfast tables each morning. He tried hard, not always successfully, to stay free from identification with orthodoxies. The "neo-liberals" of the late 1930s, 1940s, and 1950s in particular were anxious to call him their own, but he kept them, like most others, at arm's length. He declined to join the Mont Pelerin Society.

Some of Lippmann's critics chastised him for being a journalist responsive mainly to the bureaucracy and the experts, one who neglected Congress and the people and their needs for information and guidance. The good economy, they said, required journalists whose reach was wider than the elites. Felix Frankfurter complained in 1932 that Lippmann was mainly the journalist for the intellectuals, few of whom then took responsibility to educate the masses or their representatives. "You berate these fellows in Congress a good deal. And they are pretty poor things. But what about us intellectuals? What have we done all these years, what are we doing now, to give public men a body of knowledge or insight based on massive experience to guide them in their perplexity? Think of the whole economics fraternity, with all their 'new era' and two fat volumes by [Edwin] Seligman to prove that installment buying is sound, and even the labors of the Wesley Mitchells and the [Edwin] Gays. What have they done to enlighten what is obscure or to speak out with courage that which privately they know? They are poor things in Congress because they are so poorly equipped for the vast demands which we make upon them" (Frankfurter to WL, April 7, 1932, WLPIII F816). Frankfurter accused Lippmann of giving the impression that "Congress is an awful nuisance, and that the Jack-in-the-Box ought to be shut up. It ought all to be left to the Great White Father" (Frankfurter to WL, March 15, 1933, WLPIII F817).

But it was not the failure of Congress to understand problems that worried Lippmann the most; it was that they did not wish to understand. Members responded to the narrow, parochial interests of their constituencies while increasingly the problems facing them were national and global. The political scientist Heinz Eulau wrote of Lippmann's supposed "dislike of the 'masses,' distrust of democratic processes, and dislike of the main currents of American life" (Eulau 1956, 439). Yet Lippmann never objected to educating the "the masses"; he simply had little faith that this education could be achieved in a short time and during an emergency. When the New Deal was just getting under way he wrote to Frankfurter: "I agree with you that the public needs education in the factors relevant to wise decisions. But I do not frankly believe it's possible to educate the people on all the factors that are relevant to all the wise decisions that have got to be made in the next few weeks. It is utterly impossible to perform such a feat of education. The matters are too intricate, prejudices are too deep and complex, the necessary technical knowledge is too lacking" (WL to Frankfurter, March 14, 1933, WLPIII F817). The need to move quickly in an emergency was no excuse to neglect public education, but it was necessary to appreciate that "the process of reason in public affairs is necessarily a very slow process." In the economic emergencies of the 1930s and 1940s he thought it was sensible mainly to focus educational efforts on those who could grasp the complexity of the problems and help in their solution. By 1941, at least, Frankfurter agreed with Lippmann that the formation of public policy by consulting Gallup polls ("poll mischief") was a great mistake (Frankfurter to WL, April 10, 1941, WLPIII F818).

logic and theory and formulae, are usually the guiding elements. To
some temperaments a close view of the conduct of affairs will, therefore,
be discouraging. Looking for a sense of definite direction and clear purpose, they will find only arguments and practical expedients: they will
see not a revolution and a reconstruction but a very active and energetic
example of muddling through. To other temperaments the character of
this movement will be neither astonishing nor discouraging. They will
recall that the method of muddling through is the classic method of the
English-speaking peoples, and that using this method these peoples have
succeeded, as no other peoples have, in riding out the storms of history
and remaining free. (HT 8/11/33)

Although in time, after savoring the experiments, Lippmann became an intense critic of the National Recovery Administration, the centerpiece of the
New Deal, he still appreciated the method of trial and error that was employed. "Enlightened men must know that the basic conceptions of the
N.R.A. represent a necessary evolution of modern industrialism. But they
know also that the working out of that evolution calls for long adjustment
and contrivance and compromise" (HT 10/12/33). His later complaint with
the NRA was not that it had been tried but that it had been continued when
the costs were found to exceed the benefits.

In addition to feeling free as a public economist to change his mind on
policies as new data and arguments appeared, Lippmann was not shy
about proposing ideas very tentatively. For example, in 1934, as major reforms of economic policies were taking place in many areas, he suggested
that some new independent agency might be needed to coordinate the
changes. But he was not sure what form this should take, and he speculated. "My own notion of how to go about it is vague, and of no value, except that in trying to find the solution of any problem there has to be some
sort of tentative hypothesis to start with. How, then, would it be to set up
in place of the Federal Reserve Board a new body of men appointed for
long terms, if not for life, which might be called, let us say, the High Court
of Finance? It should, I think, have a good, resounding name, and the governors of the court should be given very high rank in the hierarchy of

Washington officialdom. They should, of course, be men who have retired from active business of every kind. By tradition, if not by law, they should be considered ineligible after they have sat on the court for any elective office" (HT 1/19/34).

The direction of Lippmann's reading and thinking was determined by the policy issues of the day, and economic issues were not the only matters that came before him. But the years in which he lived were filled with economic questions and crises, and his attention gravitated often to economics. There he found a few trusted friends to check some of his facts and his reasoning, but with the discipline of newspaper columns to write every second day or so he seems not to have had the time to ask friends to read drafts. Nor did he tolerate intervention from an editor. His columns were all his own. He came to know, or at least to meet, nearly every important economic thinker of his time. He was personally charming and a good listener, and he captivated nearly everyone he met; and undoubtedly the prospect of having their thoughts conveyed to millions of readers was an important magnet for his interlocutors. If he found a correspondent stimulating and insightful he usually initiated an exchange of letters, a meeting, a conversation, or even an extended friendship, such as those he had with Lewis Douglas, Leo Wolman, Alvin Johnson, Walter Stewart, Abraham Flexner, and J. M. Keynes. If he found someone tiresome or boring, he seldom argued or complained; he simply made excuses and stopped corresponding. Some who were treated like this, such as Felix Frankfurter after several years of intense correspondence, felt deeply aggrieved by the tactic, but it worked with most people.

The economics that Lippmann preached to his American readers during this time of major crises in their history would be found generally sound and reasonable by most economists today. Indeed, his columns were usually congruent with the economics of an introductory textbook of the twenty-first century. He was a firm believer in free markets because of their efficient allocation of resources, their built-in restraints over rent-seeking behavior, and their limited need for government intervention. But he was conscious also of market failures, the case for public goods, and the need to compensate for positive and negative externalities. Although he thought that government had many complex tasks to perform and that the libertarian doctrine of absolute laissez-faire was no more than a pipe dream and a distraction, he did believe that some of the greatest dangers to a well-functioning economy came from ill-advised schemes, like the NRA and the AAA, that originated with foolish policy advisers. When in the 1930s he came to know and to respect the Chicago economists, especially Henry Simons, he made valiant efforts to reconcile with his moderate progressive heritage their demands for "rules" rather than "authorities" in economic policy making.

He chided those progressives who rejected rules and seemed to forget that nations evolved and problems could not be solved once and for all by some legislative gimmick or new governmental program. At the same time he rejected those conservatives who said that all wisdom lay with a narrow conception of the Constitution and that any creative approach to problem solving by the central government was bound to fail. "To look to the Court or to a new amendment for anything like a final definition of the Federal power is to misunderstand the essential nature of a Federal Constitution. It is as unreal an expectation as the attempt to square a circle or the alchemist's dream of transmuting base metal to gold. The Federal system in an evolving economy must be self-evolved, as the Constitution has in fact evolved, by gradual interpretation. The so-called Progressives who wish to settle the question finally by a new amendment or by some grandiose decision are in the same bed with the legal fundamentalists who think the question was settled finally more than a century ago. Both take an impossibly rigid and historically unrealistic view of our long constitutional development" (HT 7/13/35). He applauded those conservative reformers who tried to bring about change by modifying the incentive system rather than by setting up some new agency with hordes of additional bureaucrats. "Broadly speaking, the first test to be applied to a reform, assuming its objectives are desirable, is whether the result can be achieved without creating another regiment of inspectors and administrative officials who have to exercise wide and uncertain discretion. If the reform requires that, the presumption ought to be against it, and reformers ought to go home, reexamine the problem and see whether they cannot find another method of attaining the result—a method which does not call for a great amount of inspection and administration" (HT 1/9/37).

The Case for Reform

Lippmann's greatest residual concerns about the outcomes of free markets lay with the prices for productive factors that determined the income distribution of an economy. He found the marginal productivity theory of factor price determination to be not helpful as a guide to policy because it was based on unrealistic assumptions, and the interpretations were seldom accepted by all parties. As he drifted away from a focus on the economy at the end of World War II the biggest unsolved policy problem that remained, he concluded, was how to achieve a just and widely accepted determination of wages and working conditions. He was deeply troubled by what he took to be resort to sheer force in settlements of disputes by strikes and lockouts. He found some reason for optimism about prospects for labor peace in the 1950s and 1960s, but he remained unhappy with the uncertainty that remained in industrial relations. Somehow a better way had to be found than violence or arbitration, but he himself could not yet see it. He was always conscious that the free market system was fragile and not well understood or fully endorsed by the mass of the people. Therefore radical solutions should be treated with skepticism. However, unsatisfactory industrial relations could be the Achilles heel of the whole system.

Like John Maynard Keynes, Lippmann thought his mission was to save the free market system, not to revolutionize it, to correct flaws before they became serious enough to lead to revolution. In the case of industrial relations as with other unsolved problems he was convinced that thoughtful inquiry and careful experimentation would yield solutions. For those who railed against the engagement of professional economists like Keynes in the policy process Lippmann made it clear early on that professional economists were there to stay, in numbers far greater than the Brain Trust, and by and large for the good. To make the point clearly in 1934 he rattled off with some irony a list of his Washington-based friends among the economists.

There is in the first place no Brains Trust as popularly conceived. There are in Washington somewhere between fifty and seventy-five young and middle-aged academically-trained men who would in England rank as upper civil servants. They have no common philosophy. They are not an organized group.

But they represent something new in American politics, something which is probably permanent, that is to say men who are professionally trained in the field of political economy. We have become accustomed to academically trained men in the scientific bureaus and, of course, in the legal departments. But professional economists are an innovation here, though Theodore Roosevelt used them continually in his Bull Moose days, and they are so common as to pass unnoticed in England, France, Germany or any other country with an established civil service.

During the war, for example, the British Treasury had in highly influential posts Messrs. Keynes, Salter, and Layton, all of them theoretical economists who write and lecture. The Bank of England in recent years has had as economic advisers a whole series of men from academic life. Mr. Walter Stewart, formerly professor of economics at Amherst, Professor Sprague of Harvard, and now Professor Clay. For years the chief adviser to the Bank of France and the French Government on monetary matters has been Professor Charles Rist. The Swedish Government was represented at the London Conference last year by Professor Gustav Cassel, among others. The plans for the Australian recovery from this depression were worked out by a group among whom professional economists, like Mr. Douglas Copland, played a leading part. The Spanish government is represented in almost all international conferences by Salvador de Madariaga, who is not only an ex-professor but what is even more appalling, perhaps, a novelist.

So the presence of professors in government posts is a sight to which we shall probably have to accustom ourselves. (HT 6/13/34)

An important consequence of having professional economists in public life, Lippmann pointed out, was that patently absurd statements would be refuted, like that of the chair of the Republican National Committee, who suggested that the cost of the New Deal during its first two years was seven billion dollars when, by Lippmann's estimate, the cost was somewhere between two and three billion (HT 7/10/34). Lippmann was always glad to have economic data, but he commented often about the need for them to be used carefully and continually improved. "Just because statistics seem so cold and impersonal they tend to tyrannize over reason and common sense and men will often believe on the authority of a statistical curve something which cannot be true according to all the rest of their knowledge" (HT 4/13/35). On one occasion, after straightening out a variety of statistical inferences that he was convinced were faulty and that annoyed him, he remarked: "This does not prove that all is right with the world. But it does prove that unanalyzed figures are not to be generalized from too readily" (HT 4/13/35).

There were other unsettled issues in the free market economy that Lippmann identified and that left him puzzled. Most were related to his sense of the complexity of the human mind. He rejected what he took to be the consensus among many policy makers that the behavior of agents in the economy could, and should, be neatly divided into the two categories of private and public. In the private sector, it was thought, everyone did, and probably should, act in their own self-interest so as to maximize utility in consumption and profit in production. In the public sector, by contrast, it was presumed that everyone acted in "the public interest." In reality in a well-functioning economy, he observed, behavior in both sectors was a mix of public and private interests. Many market failures in the private sector could never be solved if all participants ignored the interests of the community of which they were parts. This was especially true for the modern economy with its large enterprises. Something like a new economic ethic had to be developed that would condition behavior throughout both the public and private sectors of the market economy. He thought he could detect this ethic among some of his friends. He urged his friend, the businessman Owen Young, to stay out of politics so that his judgments of principle could remain credible among those in government and without: "in the present state of popular government the man in office is inevitably hopelessly compromised, and our ultimate salvation must lie in the influence of men who are listened to and are, at the same time, disinterested" (WL to Young, May 18, 1932, WLPIII F2298). If guided by men such as Young, behavior in private enterprise and in government would come to reflect "business morals" that went beyond self-interest and ultimately would become virtually automatic to the participants.

> A great corporation is not a private business, like a farm or a small store or the kind of factory where the owner is the manager. It is in some measure a public institution occupying so large a position in its own labor market, its wage policy is affected with the public interest; occupying so large a part in the commodity market, its price policy is of public concern; since its capital is publicly subscribed, its financial management is a public trust. . . . But in the domain of corporate business, including finance and banking, the moral confusion exists. . . . The reason why public office has come to be considered a public trust, rather than a hereditary private possession, is that as social organization becomes more complex, the impact of government on every one is overwhelming. A primitive society can get along with all manner of corruption at the court of the king. But not a modern society. . . . But what a giant corporation or a depository of other people's money does is like what the government does: it affects so many people that it is intolerable if it is not managed for them. (HT 12/29/33)

When he first addressed the subject of economic ethics Lippmann did not suggest how this could be developed in the public and private sectors of society, but he thought it was important to try. One way would be to bring leaders from one side together with the other as often as possible. Too often each tended mainly to vilify the other. Concerning the Brain Trust he observed that "[w]henever opposition has raised its head, they have beaten it down by charging that sinister financial interests were seeking to thwart the New Deal. So, I suppose, it is merely a case of tit for tat when the attempt is made to show that the New Deal is a communist plot, and the red professors are trotted out to offset the black bankers" (HT 4/3/34). If these extreme positions could just be modified the two groups might arrive at compromises that would be best for the nation.

While his concern for a modified economic ethics was rooted in a sense that unqualified self-interest received too much honor, he worried also that the opposite was true: excessive empathy for the poor and suffering when not well informed and based on more than sentiment could be as damaging to the economy as selfishness. He thought that the understandable concern to protect the weak and afflicted during the Great Depression had simply exacerbated the situation because actions taken had included tariff protection and restrictions on production. Unfortunately, "No nation can become rich by discouraging efficiency and encouraging inefficiency" (HT 1/5/34). Yet he appreciated that a critique of sentimentality did not resonate well with voters, especially when the sentiment was misrepresented by its critics. Lippmann returned to the question of how to find a way of restraining selfish human behavior in a market economy for the public good in his 1955 book, *Essays in the Public Philosophy,* where he explored the possibility of discovering a universal guide based on natural law.

The general intolerance among contending parties during the depression and their apparent willingness to misrepresent the other at every opportunity were deeply annoying to Lippmann. His comment on the situation in 1936 would resonate well in the twenty-first century: "By their respective supporters, and no doubt by themselves, this kind of talk is probably regarded as evidence that they are men of principle, ready to fight for their convictions, that they are bold, forthright, and uncompromising. I should like to raise the question whether the men who take such absolute positions are entitled to claim that they alone are men of principle, and I should like to ask whether in a nation where the interests are complex and diverse, the principle of toleration, which means a refusal to take an absolutist position, which requires a determination to moderate differences and to reconcile opposing interests, is not in itself a high and necessary principle" (HT 1/30/36). The rudeness and ill-temper of modern politicians, he noted, was in contrast to the decorum of the founders of the Republic. "To the New England Federalists Jefferson was a Jacobin, the equivalent in those days of a Bolshevik. To the Jeffersonian Party Hamilton was a monarchist, the equivalent in those days of a Fascist" (HT 2/8/36). Still, President Washington insisted on listening to both sides to keep the peace and avoid conflict. "There was no sense in it, as Washington with his cool judgment knew so well that he kept both Hamilton and Jefferson in his Cabinet and

warned his countrymen against fighting out their differences under European banners" (HT 2/8/36). For a modern democracy to work effectively
there must be moderate men from both parties meeting and working together in the middle of the political spectrum. "The principle, which men
of the Center regard as paramount, rests on the conviction that political
progress is the story of the gradual suppression of lawless and arbitrary violence in human affairs, of the laborious development of the habit of courtesy
and good faith in the transactions of men. Thus to the man of the Center
the partisans to the extreme right and left look very much alike, both being
from his point of view profoundly reactionary. For they do not have that
indispensable courtesy by which, through imputing good faith to others,
good faith is bred" (HT 1/16/37).

From the start of his career as a journalist Lippmann was satisfied that
most social and economic catastrophes arose from misunderstandings, by
which he meant not just failure of communication but failure to apply "reason," one of his favorite words, to the circumstances at hand. Both the
Great Depression and World War II, he thought, were the result of crucial
mistakes by actors who did not comprehend the nature of the crises or what
to do about them. Therefore the best hope for a better future lay with improved education that consisted of disciplined inquiry, civilized discourse,
and communication that most citizens could understand. He had faith that
the study of economics, if well conducted, could contribute to the improvement of human understanding and the making of better economic policy.
His main concern was that with its increasing abstraction and use of obscure
jargon the discipline was cutting itself off from effective communication
with everyone but the initiated. He wrote with some frustration in 1933: "So
much of our current discussion has to do with statistics and graphs and
broad general tendencies and movements and forces and what not, that it
gets to be tiresome and unreal. We are not really at home among these abstractions and impersonal things, and every now and then we cry out with
Leonato in 'Much Ado About Nothing' that you cannot 'Fetter strong madness in a silken thread, Charm ache with air, and agony with words.' We
must have something substantial to chew, something personal and definite
to deal with. Like Leonato, we then exclaim: 'Which is the villain? Let me

see his eyes'" (HT 12/14/33). By the 1960s Lippmann had become more satisfied with progress in economic education. He spoke warmly of both Walter Heller and Paul Samuelson as teachers of college students and of the wider public.

Lippmann called for stronger analytical units throughout government and for university teaching in the social sciences that would be combined with the humanities and the arts. Education must not stop with familiar formal structures. The effective "enlightenment of public opinion" was one of the most important tasks in a democracy. Government had a critical role to play because it alone had access to many of the facts and feasible policy options. One of Lippmann's sharpest critiques of the New Deal was that "the enlightenment of public opinion had not kept step with the evolution of policy." "The education of opinion is an essential part of leadership, and this is most particularly true where a program is being adopted which can be made to work only by the intelligent co-operation of a multitude of men" (HT 5/17/33). During the early years of the New Deal he complained that rather than careful public education the American people were provided with gossip. "Thus the country is being told what it must hope or fear on the basis of sentences extracted from Mr. Tugwell's latest book or some-body's account of what somebody heard Mr. [Raymond] Moley or Mr. [Adolf] Berle say at dinner" (HT 5/17/33). It was possible to do better. Lippmann was intrigued by the potential of the new media to facilitate public education, and he was impressed by the use made of it by President Roosevelt with his fireside chats over radio. Perhaps conscious of the use of radio by the Fascists in Europe, however, he was uneasy that it could be used also by those in authority to dominate the debate. "Though the authors of the American Constitution never knew about the radio, there was no conviction more firmly in their minds than that free government could not be preserved if the direct action of mass opinion was not checked by debate. They had read history and they knew that government in which the ruler directly dominated mass opinion has usually ended in the miseries and confusion of tyranny" (HT 1/4/36). In his later years he was a regular participant in television interviews, which came to rival his columns in popularity.

Will We See His Like Again?

Walter Lippmann may have been unique as a public intellectual, not only for his own contributions but also because his kind of public presence may not be possible anymore. What difference does that make? How much can we say that Walter Lippmann contributed positively to the course of American and world history in the twentieth century? We cannot do more than speculate, of course, but it seems reasonable to suggest "quite a bit." He led and instructed millions of influential readers in a way that few if any journalists have done before or since. In his role as regular informer and interpreter to leaders in the highest places and also to many of those below, he was a strange animal, not political, not ideological, not profit seeking, not disciplinary, not even journalistic in the conventional sense. He was more like a sophisticated, trusted, well-informed, and beloved teacher and adviser. For a great nation moving through apocalyptic change he was deeply comforting. If you had neither the time nor the wit to figure out what was happening around you, here was someone who could do it for you; and his success in doing the job so well gave confidence that he could do it again.

Is it possible to think of training some few to become the Walter Lippmanns of the future? Perhaps, but it would not be easy. They are likely born, not made, and none has come on the scene since his departure. The nearest thing to a recipe for doing so was the advice Lippmann gave to President Conant for setting up the Neiman Fellows Program at Harvard. The most promising young journalists should be given exposure in depth to what the scholarly disciplines had to offer. There are aspects of Lippmann's performance as a public economist that would be difficult for anyone to replicate, such as his sheer brilliance, charm, and self-discipline. And there may be some to avoid. Aspects of Lippmann's style that have been criticized, perhaps with justice, include his impatience with political leaders and his readiness sometimes to become involved with these same leaders to a degree that threatened his objectivity.

His capacity and self-confidence to look across the breadth of a discipline and to determine which parts were useful for understanding the world, and then to translate these findings into simple messages for readers, were rare gifts. He also demonstrated unusual restraint with the scholars who were often his sources. He kept away from academic internecine battles, like that between the Austrians and the Keynesians, and with the possible exception of *Public Opinion*, he did not attempt to make academic contributions of the conventional kind. He saw his role clearly as a commentator and not a contributor in the scholarly world, and he exercised strong self-discipline in this regard. His two books that had the greatest impact on other intellectuals were probably *The Good Society* and *Essays in the Public Philosophy*, and these were easily recognized as polemics more than scholarly works. One particular reason why it is hard to think of a successor to Walter Lippmann in our time is the evolution in communications. Could even another Walter Lippmann today have anything like the impact of his namesake facing the Internet and social media? Could he hold the attention of his readers in the way that was Lippmann's hallmark in competition with Facebook and Twitter? It seems unlikely.

Have there been others who have followed closely in his footsteps, at least to some degree? The columnist James Reston was the nearest person to a protégé and follower. Leonard Silk, editor of *Business Week* and *New York Times* columnist, bears comparison, as does his friend Archibald MacLeish, editor of *Fortune* magazine. In our day, George Will, David Warsh, David Brooks, and Paul Krugman come to mind. Warsh and Krugman, of course, have from the start been more directly rooted in the economics discipline. Lippmann came into the subject in mid-career. But Lippmann's legacy was wider than people. It can be seen also in the op-ed sections of the newspaper, the Sunday morning talk shows, and in National Public Radio, for which he long advocated. As we reflect on the American colloquy over public policy in the twenty-first century, with its sharp ideological and political divides and with media in turmoil over rapidly changing technology and commercial crises, we may think how comforting it would be if we could wake up in the morning as our parents did to coffee and the almost daily ration of Today and Tomorrow.

During his lifetime, and afterward, a flood of encomia were voiced about Walter Lippmann and his accomplishments. He was awarded twenty-two honorary degrees and many medals and other forms of recognition.

His image appears on a six-cent stamp, and T-shirts with his aphorisms are still available on the Internet. This study of Lippmann as public economist concludes with shrewd assessments by two of his good friends with similar commitments to public education and the future of artists and writers in a democracy. The first is from the art historian and public intellectual Kenneth Clark when proposing Lippmann for an honorary degree at the University of York in 1969, the first bestowed on an American at that university:

> Walter Lippmann holds the position which, ever since the time of Socrates, wise men have considered most admirable. He is the philosopher king. He has consistently applied the standards of reason, justice and human sympathy to the confusing episodes of current affairs; and he has done so in such a persuasive manner that he has induced millions of people to read and accept his conclusions. He has made ordinary men and women think reasonably and dispassionately about public affairs; an almost incredible feat. This could not be achieved by philosophic detachment alone. Walter Lippmann has always been at pains to listen at first hand to the other point of view, even if it has meant playing badminton with K[h]rus[h]chev. He is an unrivalled listener. But having heard what everyone has to say, he refers it back to his own philosophic principles, the principles of reason and humanity. What a heartening experience it has been to hear that quiet, sensible voice, year after year, audibly through all the screams and catcalls and sham rhetoric of politics; and I say, one up to the American people that they have listened to it. (WLPIII F2140)

The second assessment is by Alastair Buchan, historian and journalist, for many years correspondent of the London *Observer* in Washington, biographer of the British journalist Walter Bagehot, to whom Lippmann has sometimes been compared, and latterly director of the International Institute for Strategic Studies. Buchan wrote two obituaries, pieces of which are combined here:

> We have witnessed the death not only of perhaps the most famous journalist the world has known since Caxton, but of a man whose public distinction has bridged an enormous arc of time and change. . . . The disci-

pline of his calling and the kind of person for whom he wrote, the open-minded but not necessarily sophisticated American middle-class reader, imparted simplicity both to his style and his arguments, and he had the eye for the graphic touch which has been the hallmark of great modern journalists—Bagehot, Geoffrey Crowther, C. P. Scott, James Reston. He could sometimes be didactic, returning to the same subject every week or fortnight until he was sure that his readers had got the message, for there was nothing tentative about his mind, even though he sometimes changed it. . . . Walter Lippmann belonged, like his fellow countryman Reinhold Niebuhr, to the great tradition of Christian pessimism, the premise that man is inherently sinful and society inherently corrupt, though both may redeem themselves. Certainly little happened in the long bridge of time that Lippmann traversed to undermine this premise, while his realism and historical knowledge formed a counterweight to the buoyancy and optimism of his countrymen. (WLPIII F317)

Draft of Declaration of Principles, 1936 (WLPIII F640)

Since the time is at hand when political parties and their candidates must once again declare their principles and their purposes, we venture to submit to our fellow-citizens a statement of our views. Although the signers of this declaration are normally and traditionally members of the Democratic Party, we are not an organized political faction seeking by force of numbers to impose our views upon either political party. Nor are we seeking to organize such a faction. We are stating our views in the hope that they will find favor and that they will have influence upon the party platforms and the declarations of the candidates.

It is our conviction that in certain fundamental respects the course of national policy in the whole post-war period is jeopardizing the highest interests of the American people, that it has marked a departure from the enduring principles of American society, that it is profoundly reactionary, however much its sponsors may imagine it to be enlightened and progressive. We believe that the time has come to challenge the policies which, under the twelve years of Republican rule, fostered the growth of private monopoly subsidized by exclusive privilege of tariff protection, which then, under three years of Democratic rule, has sought to check, balance, and supplement these private monopolies by state-created monopolies based on more legal privileges and more subsidies. We see perfectly well that if certain favored industrial interests are to enjoy privileges and immunities which enable them to exercise monopolistic or quasi-monopolistic control in the markets for goods and for labor, then as a matter of justice, similar privileges and immunities must be extended to farmers, to wage-earners, and to other groups. But we hold that this course of policy, begun under the Republicans and continued under the Democrats can lead only to the progressive impoverishment of the people and the destruction of their liberties.

It must lead to their impoverishment, we believe, because the whole array of privileges is in the last analysis a system for restricting the production of wealth in order to provide monopolistic profits for favored groups. By means of exclusive tariffs, by means of devices for reducing production and raising prices, a premium is put upon the less efficient use of the nation's capital and labor, a penalty is laid upon the free exchange of the most efficient work. However much particular interests may argue that they have benefited by these privileges, the nation as a whole is injured and its progress towards a higher material standard of life arrested.

This course of policy must lead to the destruction of the liberties of the people because these powerful private monopolies, in business, agriculture, and in labor, can be restrained and regulated only by an excessively powerful government. The evidence is already at hand which demonstrates, we believe, that in order to have a government strong enough to cope with the great privileged interests which it has fostered, it becomes necessary to delegate powers to a bureaucracy, —powers to legislate, to tax, and to spend, —over which neither Congress nor the voters can exercise an effective check. The record shows, too, we are convinced, that this enormous concentration of power in the hands of appointed officials cannot be exercised wisely, that it is beyond the capacities of men to use that much power successfully, that it can lead only to waste, confusion, bureaucratic rigidity, and the loss of personal liberty.

Holding these views, we cannot subscribe to the view that the monopolistic tendencies, which had official sanction from 1920 to 1932, were conducive to material efficiency, and we cannot subscribe to the view of those New

Dealers who claim that their experiments in monopoly, restriction, and centralized political power are in the interests of the abundant life. We believe that the New Era and the New Deal are two streams from the same source. The one fostered private monopoly in the name of national prosperity. The other has fostered state controlled monopolies in the name of national welfare. We believe that both are an aberration from the basic principles upon which this nation has grown great and has remained free.

We believe, therefore, that if a political party is to be worthy of the confidence of the people, it should declare itself in favor of these principles:

1. The withdrawal, step by step, of the immunities and privileges on which monopolistic practices depend with a view to the regulation of the economic order, not by the fiat of government, but by genuinely free bargains in the open market.
2. The withdrawal from appointed officials and the restoration to Congress of the power to make national laws governing the rights and duties of individuals.
3. The withdrawal from the central government and the return to the states and to local communities of responsibility for the regulation and the relief of individuals, the federal government intervening to assist the states only when there is exceptional need.
4. The restoration of responsible government finance in the nation and in the states by substituting for taxes that are now largely indirect and regressive, direct, visible, and progressive income taxes, levied as generally as possible.
5. The unqualified reiteration of the belief that all officials, and the government as a whole, are under and not above the law, and that the lawfulness of any act of government may be tested by individuals before independent tribunals.

We regard these five principles not merely as basic but as indivisible. Thus we suggest to those who may be disposed to agree with our desire to stop the delegation of power, the centralization of power, and the irresponsible spending, that none of these things can in practice or as a matter of justice be stopped, unless accompanied by a withdrawal of the privileges and immunities, the exclusive tariff subsidies and the tolerated monopolies, enjoyed by big business. The evils of bureaucracy, centralization, and extravagant expenditure are a popular reaction to the evils of private privilege. They are defensive and complementary. They are fire used to fight fire, and only those who are prepared to deal with the causes can deal with the consequences.

We believe that these principles are no more than a reaffirmation of the great tradition which comes down to us from the foundation of this Republic and that in them are to be found the guaranties of our security and the promises of our national life.

Columns by Walter Lippmann

Columns by Walter Lippmann cited or quoted from the series Today and Tomorrow, published and syndicated from September 8, 1931, until January 1, 1963, by the *New York Herald Tribune* and from January 1, 1963, until the end on May 25, 1967, by the *Washington Post*.

8/26/43	(five columns)
10/7/43	"Taxes and Dangerous Money"
10/30/43	"The Serious Study of War"
11/9/43	"European Relief and the U.S.A."
11/23/43	"The A.B.C. of Subsidies"
12/4/43	"The Case for the Subsidies"
12/16/43	"Taxes the Best Solution"
12/28/43	"A Double Standard of Morality"
1/11/44	"Lend-Lease: The Accounting"
1/18/44	"Not Debt but Dislocation"
1/29/44	"Why No Labor Policy Exists"
2/24/44	"On the Baruch-Hancock Report"
2/26/44	"Time for Some Resignations"
3/2/44	"To Keep the Score"
5/20/44	"Discovered in Our Time"
7/6/44	"Bretton Woods"
7/13/44	"Bretton Woods and Senator Taft"
8/5/44	"On Preparing Our Minds"
9/7/44	"Paramount at Home"
9/23/44	"Set High the Sights"
9/26/44	"Ruin and Reconstruction in Germany"
12/26/44	"Intelligence Work"
1/25/45	"Mr. Wallace in the Scheme of Things"
1/27/45	"Concerning Henry Wallace"
1/30/45	"Stop, Look and Listen!"
3/17/45	"The Bankers and Bretton Woods"
3/20/45	"Pandora's Box"
3/24/45	"The Economic Treatment of Germany"
3/26/45	"Pandora's Box"
5/28/45	"Very High Stakes"
6/12/45	"The Senate and Mr. Churchill"
9/11/45	"The Rise of the United States"
9/18/45	"Loose Words on Full Employment"
10/4/45	"Trust the People"

References

Auchincloss, Louis. 1991. *The House of the Prophet*. New Brunswick, NJ: Transaction.

Barber, William J. 1996. *Designs within Disorder*. New York: Cambridge University Press.

Berle, Adolf, and Gardiner Means. 1932. The *Modern Corporation and Private Property*. New York: Macmillan.

Blum, John Morton, ed. 1985. *Public Philosopher: Selected Letters of Walter Lippmann*. New York: Ticknor and Fields.

Chase, Stuart. 1930. "Twenty Years After: A Study of an 'Educated' Group," reprinted from the *Journal of Adult Education,* n.d., contained in WLPI F241.

Cooper, John Milton, Jr. 2009. *Woodrow Wilson: A Biography*. New York: Alfred A. Knopf.

Currie, Lauchlin. 1935. *The Supply and Control of Money in the United States*. Cambridge: Harvard University Press.

Dewey, John. 1927. *The Public and Its Problems*. New York: Holt.

Dickinson, Z. Clark. 1922. *Economic Motives: A Study of the Psychological Foundations of Economic Theory*. Cambridge: Harvard University Press.

Dorfman, Joseph. 1934. *Thorstein Veblen and His America*. New York: Viking.

Eulau, Heinz. 1951. "Mover and Shaker: Walter Lippmann as a Young Man." *Antioch Review* 11:291–312.

———. 1952. "Man against Himself: Walter Lippmann's Years of Doubt." *American Quarterly* 4:291–304.

———. 1954. "Wilsonian Idealist: Walter Lippmann Goes to War." *Antioch Review* 14:87–108.

———. 1956. "From Public Opinion to Public Philosophy: Walter Lippmann's Classic Reexamined." *American Journal of Economics and Sociology* 15:439–451.

Galbraith, John Kenneth. 1971. *A Contemporary Guide to Economics, Peace, and Laughter.* Boston: Houghton Mifflin.

Goodwin, Craufurd. 1995. "The Promise of Expertise: Walter Lippmann and the Policy Sciences." *Policy Sciences* 28:317–345.

———. 2008. "Ecologist Meets Economics: Aldo Leopold, 1887–1948." *Journal of the History of Economic Thought* 30:429–452.

———. 2013. "Walter Lippmann: The Making of a Public Economist." In *The Economist as Public Intellectual,* edited by Tiago Mata and Steven G. Medema. *History of Political Economy* 45 (supplement): 92–113.

Goodwin, Doris Kearns. 2013. *The Bully Pulpit.* New York: Simon and Schuster.

Halberstam, David. 1972. *The Best and the Brightest.* New York: Modern Library.

Hartshorn, Peter. 2011. *I Have Seen the Future: A Life of Lincoln Steffens.* Berkeley: Counterpoint.

Hodgson, Godfrey. 2006. *Woodrow Wilson's Right Hand: The Life of Colonel Edward M. House.* New Haven: Yale University Press.

Johnson, Alvin S. 1915. "Causes of Crises." *New Republic* (February 6): 17–19.

Keynes, John Maynard. 1920. *Economic Consequences of the Peace.* New York: Harcourt Brace.

———. 1923. *A Tract on Monetary Reform.* London: Macmillan.

———. 1930. *A Treatise on Money.* London: Macmillan.

———. 1936. *The General Theory of Employment, Interest and Money.* London: Macmillan.

———. 2010. *Keynes on the Wireless.* Edited by Donald Moggridge. New York: Palgrave Macmillan.

Latour, Bruno. 2010. "The Year in Climate Controversy." *Artforum* (December): 1–3.

Lippmann, Walter. (1913) 1962. *A Preface to Politics.* Ann Arbor: University of Michigan Press.

———. (1914a) 1985. *Drift and Mastery.* Madison: University of Wisconsin Press.

——. 1914b. "Life Is Cheap." *New Republic* (December 9): 12–14.

——. 1915a. "The Economists." *New Republic* (January 2): 9–10.

——. 1915b. "The N.A.M. Speaks Out." *New Republic* (July 3): 221–223.

——. 1915c. "The Campaign against Sweating." *New Republic* (November 21): 1–8.

——. 1917. "Freud and the Layman." *New Republic* (April 17): 9–10.

——. 1920a. "Can the Strike Be Abandoned?" *New Republic* (January 21): 224–227.

——. 1920b. "The Crude Barbarian and the Noble Savage." *New Republic* (December 15): 70–71.

——. 1920c. *Liberty and the News*. New York: Harcourt, Brace and Howe.

——. (1922) 2007. *Public Opinion*. New York: Harcourt, Brace and Company.

——. (1925) 2009. *The Phantom Public*. New Brunswick, NJ: Transaction.

——. 1927. *Men of Destiny*. New York: Macmillan.

——. (1929) 2009. *A Preface to Morals*. New York: Macmillan.

——. (1934). *The Method of Freedom*. New York: Macmillan.

——. (1937) 1943. *The Good Society*. New York: Grosset and Dunlap.

——. 1955. *Essays in the Public Philosophy*. Boston: Little, Brown and Company.

——. 1960. "America Must Grow," in consultation with Francis M. Bator. *Saturday Evening Post,* November 5, 1960, 36 and 91–94.

——. 1965. *Conversations with Walter Lippmann*. With an introduction by Edward Weeks. Boston: Little, Brown.

Mitchell, Wesley Clair. 1927. *Business Cycles: The Problem and Its Setting*. New York: National Bureau of Economic Research.

Niebuhr, Reinhold. 1930. "Review of *A Preface to Morals* by Walter Lippmann." *Annals of the American Academy of Political and Social Science* 149:199–200.

Parker, Carleton H. 1918. "Motives in Economic Life." *American Economic Review* 8:212–231.

Parker, Cornelia Stratton. 1919. *An American Idyll: The Life of Carleton H. Parker*. Boston: Atlantic Monthly Press.

Pastore, Nicholas. 1978. "The Army Intelligence Tests and Walter Lippmann." *Journal of the History of the Behavioral Sciences* 14:316–327.

Qualter, Terence H. 1980. *Graham Wallas and the Great Society*. London: Macmillan.

Reed, John. 1919. *Ten Days That Shook the World*. New York: Boni and Liveright.

Riccio, Barry D. 1996. *Walter Lippman: Odyssey of a Liberal*. New York: Transaction.

Ricks, Thomas E. 2013. *The Generals: American Military Command from World War II to Today*. New York: Penguin.

Rovere, Richard H. 2001. "Walter Lippmann." *American Scholar* 44:585–603.

Rutherford, Malcolm. 2011. *The Institutionalist Movement in American Economics, 1918–1947: Science and Social Control*. New York: Cambridge University Press.

Schudson, Michael. 2008. "The 'Lippmann-Dewey Debate' and the Invention of Walter Lippmann as an Anti-Democrat." *International Journal of Communication* 2:1031–1042.

Seligman, Edwin R. A. 1916. "A National Inheritance Tax." *New Republic* (March 25): 212–214.

Stave, Bruce M. 1975. *Socialism and the Cities*. Port Washington, NY: Kennikat Press.

Steel, Ronald. 1980. *Walter Lippmann and the American Century*. Boston: Atlantic Monthly Press.

Steffens, Lincoln. 1910. "It: An Exposition of the Sovereign Political Power of Organized Business." *Everybody's Magazine* 23:291–298.

Tead, Ordway. 1918. *Instincts in Industry*. Boston: Houghton Mifflin.

Wallas, Graham. 1914. *The Great Society: A Psychological Analysis*. London: Macmillan.

"Walter Lippmann Colloquium, Report of the Sessions, August 26–30, 1938." 1997. *Studies of the International Research Center for the Renewal of Liberalism*, vol. 1, no. 1. English translation by Herbert J. Izzo and Olga F. Izzo.

Williams, Dustin. 2007. *Walter Lippmann's Democracy*. Ann Arbor, MI: ProQuest.

Yohe, William P. 1982. "The Mysterious Career of Walter W. Stewart, Especially 1922–1930." *History of Political Economy* 14:583–607.

———. 1990. "The Intellectual Milieu at the Federal Reserve Board in the 1920s." *History of Political Economy* 22:465–488.

Index